MW01165537

A.82
m. Bk. S.

Fundamentals
of
BEHAVIOR

Fundamentals of BEHAVIOR

Richard B. Powers
J. Grayson Osborne
Utah State University

West Publishing Company

St Paul • New York • Boston • Los Angeles • San Francisco

Library of Congress Cataloging in Publication Data

Powers, Richard, 1932 -
Fundamentals of behavior.

Includes index.
1. Operant conditioning. I. Osborne, James Grayson, joint author. II. Title. [DNLM:
1. Conditioning, Operant. 2. Reinforcement (Psychology) BF319.5.06 P88f]
BF319.5.06P68   153.1'5   75-40098

ISBN 0-8299-0073-X

PREFACE

To the Instructor and the Student:

The material in this section may little affect your behavior; likely, you will use this book in a manner that is best for you and that may not be best for someone else. This fact notwithstanding we feel there are several general issues that we should treat that may raise your level of awareness of the book's contents and intent.

The book is a primer of conditioning principles intended for beginning students in psychology. We have attempted to make the principles real by providing an experiment in each unit which shows how the principles have been used to solve a human problem. The student is involved in each unit with a graphics problem which insures his interaction with and understanding of the experiment. The result is that the principle will be more easily remembered, better understood and the student learns a new set of skills — the construction and reading of graphs.

The book is compatible with systems of personalized instruction (i.e., the Keller plan), hence, the units explore a few kernel concepts and are usually short. This can allow frequent examination of unit mastery whether by oral interview, written interview, written examination, or both. A reasonably exhaustive list of the important vocabulary and concepts of each unit can be found in the examination questions at the end of the unit. These questions can be used to structure formal interviews, as material for study guides, or as source material for written examinations. We suggest they be used in all these ways concurrently.

A useful feature of book, we think, is its emphasis on graphic techniques. We have found that graphing skills and the utility of graphs are not understood by undergraduate students in the social sciences. Yet we are convinced of the importance of a graphics repertoire in understanding scientific material. We are hopeful that the student will acquire a skill which goes beyond the boundaries of this text and even psychology in general. To all of us at first, there is no reinforcement for discerning what happened in an experiment by examining the data of the experiment. With experience and added reinforcement, however, eventually there is the thrill of discovery. This cannot occur unless dependencies are arranged to produce this graphic repertoire. We have attempted to arrange some of these conditions but, of course, cannot at this distance arrange them all. Each exam set contains questions, the answers to which will be facilitated by engaging in the graphic exercises provided. It is important that these questions not be omitted.

Although we obtained student feedback in constructing and revising the graphic exercises, there may be instances where we have been too oblique or the step-size from one graph to the next is too large. In these cases you should expect to assist the student.

The book can be divided a large number of ways to fit courses of varying lengths and differences in the interests of particular instructors. The first three units are introductory, the next seventeen cover basic principles, and the remaining five units are applications or extensions of conditioning principles. Thus an instructor could omit the application units if the course were only basic in nature. The converse is probably not true. Much of the material in the application section depends on a thorough understanding of earlier material.

We don't know whether one order of proceeding through the basic units is more important than another. Units 1, 2, and 3 are largely introductory and should remain first. In a short course (e.g., a workshop) Units 1 and 3 might be omitted. The basics presented through Unit 20 probably are best covered in the order they are printed. Unit 11 on complex schedules of reinforcement could be omitted in short or otherwise elementary courses. The three units on stimulus control (Units 13, 14, and 15), the three units on aversive control (Units 18, 19, and 20), and the two units on emotional behavior (Units 16 and 17) are to a large extent independent of each other and reordering across these subsections may be possible. These latter units do demand an understanding of such basics as differential reinforcement, respondent conditioning, operant conditioning, extinction, and schedules of reinforcement and thus should probably always succeed the earlier units.

A book of this scope forces many omissions. Yet we are content with a briefer statement if only to avoid the encyclopedic quality that most introductory psychology texts have. Our experience has shown us these latter texts leave students confused as to what psychology is and what the psychologist does. One class of material we have slighted is a conditioning approach to some traditional areas of psychology (e.g., perception, motivation, concept formation, problem solving). A second class involves very recent material in the experimental analysis of behavior (e.g., auto-shaping). Finally, there are exciting new applications of conditioning principles in the natural environment (e.g., to litter control; to mass transportation; to business and industry) and in the control of body systems (e.g., biofeedback) with which we have not dealt. These omissions notwithstanding, we are hopeful the book will provide a useful treatise on conditioning psychology, a paradigm we feel has been extremely successful in providing us an understanding of the behavior of organisms, including man.

Thanks are due to Tony Edwards and the introductory psychology students who provided instructive comments on earlier drafts of this book.

The fact that we are still happily married attests less to our abilities as operant conditioners and a good deal more to the patience of our wives, Elki and Jan. We thank them for helping in numerous ways: for fixing last-minute lunches to hustling permissions from busy authors, jealous of their privacy.

Finally, we accept responsibility, as poorly defined and understood as that concept is, for any errors and the chance that this book will accomplish some of the purposes we intended.

R.B.P.

J.G.O.

Logan, Utah
February 1975

*

ACKNOWLEDGEMENTS

We thank the authors and publishers listed here for generously allowing us to reproduce the following figures.

The Society for the Experimental Analysis of Behavior, Inc., and the authors below for:

Figures 11-3 and 11-4. Source: Figure 2, p. 183 and Figure 3, p. 185 from H. L. Lane and P. G. Shinkman, Methods and findings in an analysis of a vocal operant. *Journal of the Experimental Analysis of Behavior*, 1963, **7**, 179-188.

Figure 11-6. Source: Figure 7, p. 287 from R. T. Kelleher, Fixed-ratio schedules of conditioned reinforcement with chimpanzees. *Journal of the Experimental Analysis of Behavior*, 1958, **1**, 281-289.

Figure 11-10. Source: Figures 5, p. 169, Figure 7, p. 170 and Figure 9, p. 171 from R. T. Kelleher and W. T. Fry, Stimulus functions in chained fixed-interval schedules. *Journal of the Experimental Analysis of Behavior*, 1962, **5**, 167-173.

Figure 11-14. Source: Figure 5, p. 364 from R. Orlando and S. W. Bijou, Single and multiple schedules of reinforcement in developmentally retarded children. *Journal of the Experimental Analysis of Behavior*, 1960, **3**, 339-348.

Figure 11-15. Source: Figure 3, p. 355 from H. Weiner, Controlling human fixed-interval performance. *Journal of the Experimental Analysis of Behavior*, 1969, **12**, 349-373.

Figures 14-3 and 14-4. Source: Figure 2, p. 115 and Figure 1, p. 115, from W. Waite and Osborne, J. G., Sustained behavioral contrast in children, *Journal of the Experimental Analysis of Behavior*, 1972, **18**, 113-117.

Prentice-Hall and M. Sidman for:

Figure 20-3. Source: Figure 6, p. 456, from M. Sidman, Avoidance Behavior. In W. K. Honig (Ed.) *Operant Behavior: Areas of Research and Application*. Englewood Cliffs, New Jersey: Prentice-Hall, Inc. 1966.

The New York Academy of Science and P. Dews for:

Figures 11-7 and 11-8. Source: Figure 2, p. 270 and Figure 3, p. 271, from P. Dews, Modification by drugs of performance on simple schedules of positive reinforcement. *Annals of the New York Academy of Science*, 1956, **65**, 268-281.

The Psychonomic Society, Inc. and the authors for:

Figure 20-1. Source: Figure 1, p. 294 from J. Khalili, M. F. Daley and C. D. Cheney, A titration procedure for generating escape behavior. *Behavior Research Methods and Instrumentation*, 1969, **1**, 293-294.

N. Davidson for:

Figure 13-3. Source: Figure 2, p. 27 from N. Davidson, Fixed-ratio and fixed-interval matching-to-sample in children. Unpublished Doctoral Dissertation, Utah State University, 1972.

*

CONTENTS

Fundamentals
of
BEHAVIOR

Introduction

1

The Unique Nature of Psychology

Humans are social animals. They live in groups with similar individuals. One consequence of this is that all humans become familiar with the behavior of other humans. This is because much of the behavior we emit is in the presence of other humans; we also see people behaving toward other people and we are always in the presence of at least one behaving individual: ourselves. The behavior that human beings produce is the primary datum of a science of psychology and therein lie difficulties for this science.

An example of a contrasting science is astronomy. Most all of us have some passing acquaintance with some of the findings of astronomy: that the earth travels around the sun; that we live on a planet in a minor galaxy; and so forth. Also we are exposed to some of the subject matter of astronomy. We have all seen the sun, the moon, the stars, and some of us can identify a number of the latter. However, our acquaintance with this subject matter occurs nonsystematically. Very few of us watch the sky each night and systematically graph data such as the brightness of stars and the movements of the planets. If we did, we too might be able to make general statements about the behavior of stars and planets that were accurate. We might be considered expert in the area, and our peers would accept our statements regarding the behavior of the universe.

The subject matter of psychology is much more readily available to all. We are continually exposed to other behaving organisms. We do not need a telescope or other equipment to come in contact with this subject matter; it is always there, exposed to our view. Whether we like it or not, we become very familiar with the subject matter of psychology. However, very few of us systematically examine the subject matter in this field either. We tend to make casual observations — for example, "spanking my child results in his refraining from doing what he was spanked for." We tend to generalize these casual observations — for example, "It worked for my child, therefore it should work for yours." These nonsystematic observations usually are incorrect. They may be likened to statements in astronomy prior to the time of Copernicus, when it was thought that the earth was the center of the universe and that the sun revolved around the earth. The systematic observation of Tycho Brahe and Copernicus, his student, disproved this. Regardless, our familiarity with the behavior of other beings leads us to act as experts regarding behavior. Psychology is probably the only science with this problem to this degree; all sciences' data are available to some extent to the layman, but not to the same extent as that of psychology. The consequence of this is that psychology is loaded with "experts," most of whom have never performed an experiment, but who still maintain that they know why behavior occurs.

The study of behavior from a scientific standpoint is not very old so we must expect that, as in other sciences, many of our most cherished notions about the reasons for behavior may be wrong.

Explanations of the Reasons for Behaving

Scientific explanation. One's acceptance or rejection of an explanation is usually based on criteria constructed before the evaluation is made. The scientific method is characterized by the ways it prescribes for the validity of an explanation. It is a way of acting toward the subject matter of a given area. The method is used today because it alone has told us more about our environment than any alternative method yet tried or devised. It seems reasonable that if the scientific method has been profitable in other areas of science, then it may well be profitable in the area of psychology. The explanations of the reasons for behavior occurring in the remaining units of this book are largely a function of this approach.

Other explanations. There are many explanations of the reasons why people behave that are nonscientific. Upon close scrutiny many of the explanations turn out to be invalid. One major problem is that many of them are engrained in our language. We will look briefly at three related language problems.

One language problem — that of *circularity* — is evidenced in the following statements of the reasons for the behavior of a little girl. She does not walk and she is nine years old:

Q: "Why doesn't Mary walk?"

A: "She is mentally retarded."

Q: "How do you know she is mentally retarded?"

A: "Well you can see for yourself, she doesn't walk." (Adapted from Meyerson, Kerr, & Michael, 1967)

Mental retardation is used to explain why Mary does not walk, and the fact that Mary does not walk is used to explain that she is mentally retarded. Scientifically, the variables that are the reason for Mary not walking must be deduced independently. That is, it should be shown what produces nonwalking in children. As this experiment is ethically nonfeasible and its outcome undesirable, it will never be done with children. Almost as useful, though, would be a demonstration of what it takes to get Mary to walk. If we can get her walking, we may be able to make reasonably strong inferences as to why she did not walk because we will have proved that we can control her walking. (In fact, Meyerson et al., using conditioning methods, did get Mary to walk and other children like her as well, so their statements regarding her former inability to walk and present ability to walk must be considered the best explanation thereof.)

Another language problem is called *reification*. It is closely tied to the foregoing circularity problem and occurs when our repeated use of a word that is an adjective results in use of the word as a noun. When this happens the word often begins to indicate the existence of an entity that did not exist before. This seems to have happened with the adjective *intelligent* when used as a noun; that is, "He has intelligence."

We begin to expect the existence of an entity called "intelligence" when the original use of the adjective *intelligent*, was simply a shorthand *description* of a collection of behaviors.

Another example of reification is the term *unconscious*. Freud originally used the term to describe psychological activity which could not be observed even by the "behaver himself." *Unconscious* began its life as an adjective used as a modifier, as in the phrase, "unconscious activities." However, Freud began the reification process himself by referring to *"the Unconscious."* Today, *Webster's New International Dictionary* (3rd ed.) defines this word as both adjective and noun! In fact, Freud contributed a wealth of terms to psychological use that for uncritical readers became actual entities. The Ego, the Id, and the Super-Ego all have been reified by sloppy language habits. For example, in discussing the Id, Stagner (1948) writes, " . . . the Id is not allowed to express *itself* directly in adult life" (p. 279, italics added). Here we see the actual creation of an entity, giving the Id the animate properties of selfhood. This is a good example because it comes shortly after textual material in which Stagner states precisely that the Id is not an entity, but an abstraction. He says that, "It is convenient to speak of the Id as 'striving,' although, of course, that must not be treated literally" (p. 279). Frankly, this is amazing because the example represents the work of an author who knows of the reification pitfall, says as much to his reader, and then jumps in the pit himself. Later in the same section, after specifically defining the Ego as an abstraction, he qualifies personality forces in the following way: "The Ego is thus essentially selfish, as is the Id, but the Ego is intelligently selfish . . ." (p. 279). Note that the adjective, *selfish*, and the adjective phrase, *intelligently selfish*, are usually descriptors of human or animate behavior, not of abstractions. Is it any wonder that if — the above disclaimers notwithstanding — reification takes place by the author, it should no less happen to the reader?

A simple test is possible to guard against a reified abstraction. Simply ask yourself if it is possible to *see* the thing directly or with an instrument. If it is not, there is a good chance the term is nothing but an abstraction; in the case of reified terms in psychology, most often a description of behavior.

A third language problem involves a *description becoming an explanation*. In the examples above, a label for certain behavior comes to be used as an explanation for the occurrence of some behavior: labelling a child mentally retarded is used to explain why he does not walk and does not emit other behaviors; similarly, labelling a child intelligent is often used to explain why he does well in school and in other endeavors. In the recent history of psychology the practice of labelling behavior either as instinctual, emotional, as a need, or as a drive has led psychologists and others to consider the label as the cause of behavior. Examine, for instance, the sentence, "Birds build nests because they have a nest-building instinct." Note that the word *instinct* has been substituted for the word *behavior*. If the word *behavior* is reinserted in the sentence, we have two halves of the sentence that say precisely the same thing (e.g., Birds build nests. Birds have a nest-building

behavior). Obviously neither of the sentences explains the other.

Perhaps the greatest examples of our third language foible are where "self " is used as a prefix in our psychological language, such as in *self-actualization* or *self-concept*. A teacher may describe a child as having a poor self-concept. What the teacher has seen may be some or all of the following: The child says to the teacher that he doesn't feel capable of performing in some area; he may also make deprecatory statements about general aspects of his behavior ("I'm just no good"; "I'll never be a good student"; "When they passed out the brains, I guess I was out to lunch," and so on). So far what we have is a shorthand description of a collection of behaviors, mostly verbal, that describe how an individual feels about himself, and that shorthand (a negative self-concept) is adequate to the task. The problems arise when the phrase, "negative self-concept," is used to explain instances of the very behavior it is used to describe. For example, when the student emits a self-deprecatory remark, the tendency may be for the teacher to attribute the remark to the child's poor self-concept. The child is thought to say those things *because* of his negative self-concept, and description has become explanation, albeit pseudo-explanation.

This is an especially insidious phenomenon when its occurrence may result in the unplanned worsening of another's behavior. Take the case of a child who has been administered a battery of tests at school. A psychologist noting a certain performance (usually very poorly defined) decides the test performance suggests that the child has "minimal brain dysfunction" (called MBD in the vernacular of educators). This is a descriptive term only. There are several major problems with the term. If a child is labelled with the term, in casual use it appears to explain his classroom behavior, generally a failure to perform at the level of his peers on certain tasks, such as reading. A worse consequence, though, may be that the child will learn to act in a way that will fulfill the teacher's expectations that he has "minimal brain dysfunction."

Lastly, it should be carefully pointed out that as a descriptor the phrase, "minimal brain dysfunction," describes a sample of an individual's behavior taken from a test, that is, is the individual's behavioral response to visual or auditory stimuli. Yet the term is used to infer physiopathology in the nervous system often without a direct look at that system. It can be unequivocally stated that no one has ever directly seen this type of "brain damage"; thus, not only is the term used as an explanation when it is only a descriptor (and is involved in circular cause-effect relationships too), but it is also used to suggest a physical state that no one has ever seen.

The Tasks of a Scientific Psychology

The tasks of a science of psychology are the same as those for any science, namely **PREDICTION** and **CONTROL**. The two concepts have often taken on extra meaning in psychology and it is important to define them clearly, and in addition specify what they do not mean.

The job of the psychologist is to predict behavior. The prediction of behavior will lead to the specification of that behavior in its relations with stimuli both preceding and succeeding it. Hence, it will be necessary for the psychologist to specify the surrounding stimulus conditions in order to predict behavior. When he discusses the prediction of behavior, the psychologist does so according to the laws he already knows about, or he may describe laws as a function of observing orderly sequences of behavior. These laws describe the ideal case just as is frequently true of the laws of physics. Just as it may be very difficult for the physicist to predict the time that a stone rolling down a hillside takes to reach the bottom, it may be difficult for the psychologist to predict the behavior of a rat in a meadow. The physicist, however, may make very accurate predictions where he has control of more variables, say a plane of calculable incline, and a steel ball with highly polished surface. So also may the psychologist make accurate predictions of the turning behavior of a rat in a T-maze.

The physicist is not often expected to make predictions outside his laboratory. The early space program failures showed that the application of the principles of physics outside the lab necessitated a new technology. Later successes simply showed that experience outside the laboratory could be adequately predicted using the principles of physics. Similarly, psychologists have accepted the challenge of predicting and changing behavior outside the laboratory. It cannot be expected immediately that techniques employed outside the laboratory will be as successful as those used within, although initial successes are quite encouraging. Eventually, however, prediction of behavior outside the laboratory of psychology should be as good as that emanating from within.

When a scientist speaks of control, he generally is speaking of control over a narrow bit of his subject matter, and when he demonstrates control over this bit of subject matter he will in every sense of the word have explained it. For example, by inserting carbon rods in a nuclear reactor the physicist may slow down the chain reaction occurring in the reactor. It can be said that he is controlling the reaction. He can state to us certain relations between the speed of the reaction and the carbon rods, and can predict the speed of the reaction based on the rods, their size, number, distance from the reaction, and so on. Note here that the physicist does not explain the reaction in our example; he explains the speed of the reaction by manipulating the carbon rods. Hence, when control takes place in science, prediction can follow, and explanation will have taken place. In this case, the physicist will have explained the speed of the reaction by detailing changes in that speed effected by changes in the parameters of the carbon rods.

The scientific psychologist does no differently. Let us take a specific example. A psychologist deprives a pigeon of food and then uses food to reward the pigeon when it pecks a plastic key that is illuminated by a yellow light. The pigeon learns to peck the key vigorously to produce food. On occasion the psychologist turns off the yellow lamp so the key is unilluminated and at the same time disconnects the food dispenser. Peck responses now do not produce food, and the bird soon learns this fact. After repeated exposure to the light-on (food for pecking), light-off (no food for pecking) conditions, the bird will not peck the unlighted key. As soon as the light is turned on, the bird begins pecking; as soon as the light is turned off, it ceases. Under these specific circumstances the individual who turns the light on and off controls the pigeon's pecking behavior in the sense that he can make it occur or not occur just as the physicist controlled the nuclear reaction in the preceding example. Additionally, the bird's pecking behavior can be clearly predicted. We can predict that the probability of pecking when the light is on is very high (near 1.0) and with the light off is very low (near 0.0).

It is also important to note that this prediction and control of the bird's pecking response serves as explanation for its behavior in this particular instance. From a scientific viewpoint other explanations will be insufficient unless they, too, accurately predict and control the same behavior. If there is more than a single explanation that appears valid, the scientist then asks a number of questions:

Which explanation makes the best predictions?

Which is the simplest?

Which explanation precludes the greatest number of other explanations?

Bugaboos Regarding Behavior Control

Discussions of behavior control sometimes produce visions of Orwell's *1984*, brainwashing, and other extreme measures of control. Most recently the specter of a controlled society and more controlled man has been raised by Skinner in his work, *Beyond Freedom and Dignity*. This is most interesting because, to psychologists, the book is clearly understood as being an attempt to help mankind understand itself, while to laymen, the book has raised the very specters it was supposed to dispose of.

The word *control* most frequently is associated with nondemocratic political systems. We are most ready to associate it with dictatorships such as Nazism, fascism or communism. We are less ready to associate the word with democracy and freedom. Within our own "free" society we associate the word *control* with institutions in which freedom is restricted, such as the penitentiary, the mental hospital, or indeed, the army. Because of all these associations, it is necessary to specify rather precisely what the scientific psychologist means by control, as we did above. It is further necessary to deal with the fallacies that are engendered by the use of the word.

The notion of behavior control is frightening for five reasons: 1) the failure to recognize the fact that all behavior is controlled; 2) the locus of the control; 3) the failure to differentiate between kinds of control; 4) the programmatic aspects of control systems that lead to stereotypic behaviors; and 5) the effectiveness of control systems.

All behavior is controlled. We don't like to accept this fact because we don't like to think of ourselves as being controlled, and because the common meaning of the word implies circumstances that we dislike. First the meaning: as stated above, carbon rods control a nuclear reaction when they change the vigor of the reaction

probabilistically. Man's environment also can be said to control his behavior when a probabilistic relation exists between his behavior and the environment, as it always does. To most people, the worrisome aspect of this is the case where the probability of a given behavior in a given environment is unity (i.e., $p = 1.0$; given some environment A, behavior A *will* occur). This case suggests the lack of freedom of the individual *not* to produce behavior A. We can unequivocally state that there are few behaviors and few environments that produce this state of affairs. Given a red stoplight (the controlling environment), the response of braking to a halt in an automobile will occur nearly 100 percent of the time for all drivers. Yet the reader can easily conceive of slight changes in the environment that may make this response (stopping) less likely to occur. For example, a man is driving his wife who is in the late stages of childbirth to the hospital. They live in a rural area (not many cars to hit) and it is 4:00 A.M. (the few cars there are, are not on the road). Quite likely, the man may just slow down instead of stopping at the red light. Note, however, while we may say that the control of the light has been reduced, we would argue that the control has shifted to other aspects of the environment (e.g., the late hour; his wife in pain, etc.). That is, there is no absence of control, the control is now simply located in different aspects of the environment than formerly.

Most all situations will control behavior somewhere *between* the limiting conditions of repeated nonoccurrence ($p=0.0$) or repeated occurrence ($p=1.0$), and it is these intermediate situations that are most interesting to the experimental psychologist because they allow room for behavior to become either more or less likely in the long run rather than just one or the other. The intermediate probabilities suggest that behavior occurs less than all the time in a specific circumstance. Taking one specific occasion, rather than the long run, a behavior must either occur or not occur. The fact that the given behavior can either occur or not occur on a specific occasion is compatible both with a scientific psychology and our democratic notions of freedom. Behavioral psychologists might define freedom as the fact that a behavior need not occur. This definition implies an alternative. If one behavior doesn't occur, another one does, because organisms behave as long as they are alive. More elaborately, freedom might also be defined as the number of possible alternative behaviors that an individual can emit in a given environment.

The locus of control. When we speak of control, we mean the likelihood of a behavior given a specific environment (e.g., the likelihood of taking a cigarette when a pack is proffered). Control can lie in different parts of the environment, and where we think it primarily centers is related to our acceptance of it. For example, control can lie with other living organisms, that is, the animate environment or the inanimate environment. We worry little about the latter, incorrectly considering our behavior to be not much affected by it. However, note that a bicycle controls considerably different responses than an automobile does, while one could be said to be driving either. While we use both feet to control either one, we only pedal the former. We are much less aware of control in this sense when the

control source is inanimate. This type of control is apparently not obvious to us, perhaps because we erroneously conclude that we can affect the inanimate environment without being reciprocally affected by it. Think of some other situations and try to discover their controlling features. Where these features are inanimate they may be very difficult to detect even in the laboratory. They may be rooted in the individual's history. For example, what controls writing from left to right? It is obviously not an innate behavior when the Chinese and Japanese write from top to bottom of a page and the Jews write from right to left. It must be acquired; in fact, we explicitly teach our children to write in one direction only.

More obvious is where control lies with animate aspects of our environment. There are two major sources of control within the animate sector: where the locus is the individual himself (called *self-control*), or where it is located in others (this might be called *social control*). We are not bothered by social control where we have been taught to accept it. We condone parental control of child behavior. We say as a society that parents have a responsibility for their children. This is even backed up with law. A parent whose offspring commits a misdeed may be punished by the courts for the offspring's misdeed. Ostensibly, the parent is punished for his failure to control his child. We condone general family control over individuals in the family. An older brother may attempt to control the behavior of a younger brother ("for his own good"). We do not, on the other hand, accept that children frequently control parents, especially where this control is blatantly obvious, such as in the whining or tantruming child who gets his way. Our lack of acceptance here is based on the obviousness of the relationship and on whether we have been taught the relationship is a normal one. We generally condone control by society's representatives over our behavior. The policeman directing traffic, the prison officer guarding inmates, the teacher keeping a child in after school, the priest admonishing his parishoners to behave righteously, and an employer asking an employee to get to work on time — all are sources of social control that we accept, largely because we have been taught to accept them. This doesn't make their control any less real.

The last examples were chosen for their obviousness, but there are also social controls that are tacit, yet are no less powerful. Husbands and wives control each other's behavior subtly. Often where the control becomes obvious, marriage counseling or divorce follow. The mores of classes within a culture may not be written in law but may control social behavior. In the writing example above, the control is probably social as social contingencies are sufficient to produce writing by children and children don't learn to write where the educational contingencies don't exist. This historical source is not an obvious one. Obviousness often seems critical to our acceptance of the reality of the controls, and this obviousness is facilitated by the current presence of the individual doing the controlling (e.g., Boss to secretary: "Please bring the file on the ABC company.").

In the case of mores the control is just as social, powerful, and real, but is less obvious because the individuals present may not be the direct source of the control. For example, an adolescent female may refuse to engage in heavy petting with an adolescent male based on the duration of time they have known each other, even though her mother and father who may be the controllers in this example, are not physically present.

Perhaps one of the reasons why Skinner's book, mentioned above, has been so criticized is that it unmasks many of these sources of control and makes them painfully obvious.

Control by self is also an interesting form of this issue which we deal with more completely in other units. It can be considered social because it depends for others on its generation and if one argues that he is in fact self-controlled, then he is being controlled by a human, animate organism. Society fosters this kind of control because it implies that the individual can become independent of *external* environments. Particular human endeavors seem to be more easily explained in terms of self-control: the dedication of the writer, the decathlon champion, and the religious isolate are possible examples. Whether the actual control in these cases is largely self-control or other control is another issue, however. One's behavior is self-controlled when he responds to his own behavior systematically and produces changes in it thereby. He may praise himself for behaving well and curse himself when he behaves badly and these events may change his behavior. In any case, where conditions external to the body don't appear to account for behavior, it is possible that it is still being controlled from within the body, a location this text includes in the concept *environment*.

Kinds of control. This bugaboo will become more easily understood when the reader has progressed through the units on positive reinforcement and aversive control. Given that all behavior is controlled, we ask under which of the various control systems would individuals rather behave? Suffice it to say at this point that all animals dislike aversive control and appear to function happily under systems in which there are many rewards for behaving. Although only a few studies specific to this question have been performed, it can be strongly inferred that systems of reward are to be much preferred to aversive control. Ask youself whether you would rather work for $10.00 per hour, for a steak and lobster dinner, or to avoid being electrically shocked, thrown in jail, or beaten. We think the answer is clear.

We should emphasize that the last conclusion is one based on animal conditioning studies alone. There is little work that unequivocally shows what makes humans happy or sad; thus, we all can have an opinion here. Skinner thinks that a high density of reward is necessary to happiness and wrote *Walden II*, a utopian novel of a community run entirely by positive controls, to reflect this belief. Conversely, he suggests an excess of aversive controls and losses of reward are conditions which produce anger, grief, and depression (Skinner, 1953). Skinner's critics have argued that a reward system alone will be insufficient to produce happy men. Naturalistically, the only data would appear to come from different cultures and political systems. While we have no cross-cultural measure of happiness, it seems that where there is poverty (i.e., few rewards), and military or other totalitarian control (i.e., more aversive than positive control), individuals may

not be happy. However, since no one has ever designed a system run only by positive controls in which men have actually lived for a long period of time, whether this method produces happier men is an empirical question. Most societies contain a mixture of positive and negative controls. The positive controls are generally a function of individual people in the society, while the negative controls are exerted by people collectively through their governments. Few governments are in the business of dispensing rewards. They occasionally disburse money for contributing to the society in some way (" . . . for leading to the arrest and conviction of . . . "), or they provide recognition (e.g., medals, certificates, etc.), but these are rare compared to the frequent use of aversive controls. Entire legal systems are codifications of what the government will do to you if you behave in a punishable fashion. The list is great, starting with the simple fine, progressing through incarceration (prison, army, mental hospital), and continuing to banishment and loss of life. All these conditions are either outright punishing (painful) or deprive the individual of rewards that he once had (e.g., mobility, family rights, money). They certainly serve to control behavior in some cases, while in others (e.g., capital punishment) they may not. We would predict that man will be most happy where the mix between positive and aversive controls is tipped largely in favor of the positive.

Programmatic aspects of control systems. People detest the programmatic aspects of control systems because they feel they want to be treated as humans, not rats; as individuals, not masses; to control themselves rather than being controlled by others, and so forth. There is nothing inherent in a programmatic approach to behavior control which specifies that humans must be treated like rats. Here this statement seems to indicate that all of the rewards for a rat's behavior can be used with humans. While there is some truth to this, the individual's environment itself will specify effective rewards. There are certainly many stimuli which may be rewards for one species that are not rewards for another, and the same goes for individuals within species. Note that this in no way restricts the applicability of behavioral laws to the behavior of one species alone. Whether or not a law works the same way in rats as in people can and should be scientifically subject to test.

Detractors of scientific psychology claim that a programmatic approach to behavior control appears to suggest that individual differences may be done away with; the unique conditions which produce creativity in the arts will be lost, and so on. This is nonsense. If individuals with artistic behaviors are desired, it is simply a matter of programming those conditions which are likely to foster artistic behavior. This is not a throwback to J. B. Watson's pronouncements of one-half century ago; we are not talking about forcibly making a youngster into something he currently is not. What we are saying is that in a society where artistic behavior is strongly rewarded, there will be production of a great many artists. Presently, only a few people attain the levels achieved by a Picasso or a Segovia; many do not. Given that we know the important variables for making a musician a virtuoso, we may strengthen that behavior in an individual. Currently, unique environmental conditions do this infrequently. Because there is no formal programming, because the attempts are poor, and because the attempts are few, the number of fine artists is small. The future may show this need not be.

One way to start would be to encourage (read: *reward*) individuals who are artists to continue to function as artists and to teach others to become artists, or to do this wherever we wanted expertise. This probably occurred on a national level in the sciences with the advent of sputnik in 1957. Thereafter, being a scientist paid off with employment, good wages, notoriety, and other marks of success because the government decided to reward this behavior in individuals. (This analysis is conceptually very loose, but if the reader gets a feel for it, that is sufficient). All sciences flourished. Graduate schools accepted more students, more Ph.D.s were awarded, and the result was substantial technological achievement and the development of a huge array of individuals who today are engaged as scientists rather than in some other occupation. This degree of success was possible with a reasonably unsophisticated positive control system by the government. The sophistication of the control system and thereby its effectiveness leads us to our last bugaboo regarding behavior control.

The effectiveness of control systems. How much we like or accept the notion of behavior control seems to depend on how ineffective the delivery system is. This is likely because ineffective systems may be less obvious, as we have discussed above. We have argued that behavior is not less controlled because the control is less obvious, so that is not an issue. It seems easier to implement punitive control systems than positive ones, so effectiveness may seem correlated with aversiveness just because the systems that have been effective in our own histories have been punitive. To repeat, whether we would feel unhappy about a very effective positive control system remains an empirical question, although we doubt we would. Education is a good example of a poorly delivered behavior control system, because many people fail to acquire a decent education. Those that do are said to do so in spite of the system. When education is made more effective, however, it is called brainwashing and is not condoned.

Effectiveness also seems negatively correlated with freedom and other of our cherished political concepts. Again, we seem to feel that a very good system could make someone do something "against his will." As before, the argument remains that this probably won't occur because the effective conditions are impossible to produce. This is especially the case with an aversive control system. These systems appear to foster *countercontrol* of the controllers. Revolution, escape, aggression, and strikes are all examples of effective measures that have been used by people historically to counter excessive aversive control. It is not clear that countercontrol would occur given a totally positive control system, which may make the latter more effective in the long run. Does it also make it more insidious? We would say that this would not be so with an informed populace.

Illustration

J. B. Rhine and L. E. Rhine, An investigation of a mind-reading horse. *Journal of Abnormal and Social Psychology*, 1929, 23, 449-466.

This article provides a good example of the difficulty of answering the question: Where does the control of the behavior lie? Rhine is best known for his experiments in parapsychology, an area where the question above often needs to be clearly answered. The horse in his article was called "Lady Wonder," and was owned by a Mrs. Claudia Fonda. The horse behaved as many trained animals do. Without apparent signal, Lady could answer questions by nosing lettered or numbered blocks. Rhine noted that Lady could only answer questions correctly when Mrs. Fonda was near. Thus, it seemed that the owner's presence or absence was related to the horse's behavior. Where did the control lie? Rhine reached the incredible conclusion that Lady communicated telepathically with Mrs. Fonda. He argued that this conclusion followed because Mrs. Fonda had no knowledge of the number the horse was to guess on several occasions and the horse still responded correctly. His conclusion would have been more forceful, however, had he examined Lady with Mrs. Fonda, a potential source of control, effectively out of the horse's environment. This would have approached a more reasonable scientific test.

Let's make the problem more difficult. Suppose the horse did perform with Mrs. Fonda out of the room. Have we ruled out *all* other reasonable environmental sources of control? Not likely. In fact, we learn that when Rhine kept Mrs. Fonda "ignorant of the number" he did so by writing it on a pad. Martin Gardner, in his delightful book called *Fads and Fallacies in the Name of Science* (1957), states that there are over fifty ways by which a mentalist can gain information that has been written down (p. 352). A magician friend of Gardner ran an impromptu check that alluded to the source of control over Lady's behavior without being unequivocal. The magician assisted Mrs. Fonda in one performance without stating his profession. His instructions were to write a number on a pad. The magician made the motions to write the number *8* but actually only touched the pencil to the pad's surface enough to write a *3*. The horse signaled the number *8*. Gardner suggested that Mrs. Fonda was "pencil reading," a behavior not uncommon to mediums and mentalists, where the reader discriminates the movements of the pencil to infer what is being written. Rhine's experiment contained no "catch" conditions such as this, and if it had he might have been more reluctant to conclude in favor of telepathy. "Catch" conditions which we will discuss later are important to scientific method.

Exam

1. Why should we utilize the scientific method in psychology?

2. How does the "availability" of the subject matter of psychology affect the acceptance or rejection of ideas about the causes of behavior?

3. An individual states that people want to kill him and reports vivid hallucinations of this. He is diagnosed as being "paranoid schizophrenic." A psychiatrist says that the patient hallucinates *because* he is schizophrenic. State what is wrong with the foregoing sentence.

4. What is meant by prediction in a science of psychology?

5. What is meant by control of behavior in a science of psychology?

6. What are five reasons why the word *control* frightens the layman when it is used by behavioral psychologists?

7. Define and give examples of the terms *reification, circularity,* and *description-as-explanation.*

8. Why can we infer that Mrs. Fonda and Lady Wonder probably did not communicate telepathically? (Consider Mrs. Fonda's location with respect to Lady Wonder.) What evidence suggested one source of control?

References

Gardner, M. *Fads and fallacies in the name of science*. New York: Dover Publications, 1957.

Meyerson, L., Kerr, N., & Michael, J. L. Behavior modification in rehabilitation. In S. W. Bijou & D. M. Baer (Eds.), *Child development: Readings in experimental analysis*. New York: Appleton-Century-Crofts, 1967. Pp. 214-239.

Rhine, J. B., & Rhine, L. E. An investigation of a mind-reading horse. *Journal of Abnormal and Social Psychology*, 1929, 23, 449-466.

Skinner, B. F. *Walden II*. New York: The MacMillan Co., 1948.

Skinner, B. F. *Science and human behavior*. New York: The MacMillan Co., 1953.

Skinner, B. F. *Beyond freedom and dignity*. New York: Alfred Knopf, 1971.

Stagner, R. *Psychology of personality*. New York: McGraw-Hill, 1948.

How to Graph Data

2

Reasons for Graphing Data

The purpose of this unit is to teach you how to take data from tabular form and to graph it so that the results will be more meaningful to you. There are several reasons why graphs and graphing skills are important.

First, you may decide to try some modification of your own behavior or that of your family. One of the first steps in modifying behavior is to record what your current rate of activity is and to graph it. Graphing is important because it will help define the magnitude of the problem. Sometimes a problem is not as serious as we think it is. A teacher might want to transfer Johnny into a special classroom because he is "always fighting with everyone." After recording and graphing Johnny's aggressive behavior for a 2-week period, she might discover that Johnny has been in 2 fights and hit 4 children, including 1 girl. The teacher may be surprised to see the actual frequency with which Johnny engages in aggressive behavior and, on the basis of this information alone, may decide that she was premature in recommending his transfer. Johnny's aggressive behavior seemed frequent because it was obnoxious to the teacher. The only way to know the severity of the problem is to record and graph the obnoxious behavior over a **BASELINE PERIOD**. This is simply a measure of how frequently a given behavior occurs over a period of time (e.g., 2-3 weeks) prior to any manipulation.

A second reason for graphing data is perhaps more obvious. How do we know if a treatment is effective? Is there

15

so much variability in the results that conclusions about treatment effects are unwarranted? The easiest way to answer questions like these is to graph the results. What appear as unsystematic fluctuations can sometimes become meaningful trends when graphed. Like a bikini, a good graph reveals the results in an unequivocal way and can be either quite flattering or painfully embarrassing.

The third reason for asking you to do the graphs in this text has to do with students' reading habits. We have discovered that students, even graduate students, frequently do not examine the graphs in texts. They report, in their more honest moments, that a graph is somewhat like coming across a blank white space in the chapter. You don't have to read it!

Graphic illustrators are very ingenious in using bright colors and good design principles to make graphs pleasing to look at, but by doing so, they defeat the purpose of a graph. As B. F. Skinner (1968) said, attractive designs reinforce students for looking at graphs, but for the wrong reasons. Students should not look at graphs because they are attractive but because they teach. A graph summarizes the results of an experiment in a way that permits the student to understand just where and how fast a manipulation affected a change. It permits a quick evaluation of different treatments that are simply not visible in unorganized data or even tables. We have found that if a student can reproduce a graph in the text, he or she can invariably summarize the complete experiment. The reverse is not true. Experiments are reported in texts in such a way that students focus on unessential procedural details and cannot describe

the results, or else are inaccurate in their summaries of the results. Such inaccuracies are much less likely to occur if the student can reproduce a graph. Throughout this book, we will ask you to construct many of the figures in the text. These graphs will be excellent devices to help you understand and remember the material, but they must be done accurately and consistently.

Steps in Making a Graph

1) Choose a standard graph paper which has ten squares to the inch and has a heavier line for every tenth line.

2) The dependent variable in an experiment, some measurable aspect of behavior such as its frequency or its magnitude, is plotted on the vertical axis or **ORDINATE**. On the horizontal axis, or **ABSCISSA**, time, trials, or sessions are the usual dimensions that are plotted.

3) Select the scales to use. Try to make use of *all* the graph paper. Students sometimes use such a compressed scale that it is hard to see any trends in the data. On the other hand, there is no reason why you should run off your scales either. Before doing any plotting, examine the range of values for both sets of data — the dependent measure and the time period or trials — and check the number of divisions available on your graph against the range for each set of data. It is customary to have the abscissa one and one-half times the length of the ordinate.

4) Now, plot the data points and then connect the data points by lines. If a data point is separated from the others by reason of a change in condition,

change in time scale, or a break in the continuity of the experiment (a previous data point is missing because the subject was sick, for instance), do not connect it to other data points.

5) Label all axes and conditions fully. This is important if you want the graph to help you remember what the experiment was about. It is also important if you want to communicate to others and you are relying on a graph. Complete labels make it possible for another person to read the graph and understand what it summarizes without having to get information somewhere else, that is, from you or a text.

An Example of an ABAB Graph

Let's look at an example of a graph that represents data collected by one of the authors (JGO) at a school for the deaf. The teacher, Ms. RM, was having difficulty controlling her class of 5 students. The students fought, played, and "talked" (with their hands) while the teacher was attempting to teach. Occasionally, a child would throw a tantrum. The student who was observing this class noted that the teacher gave her attention to students who were momentarily causing her a problem. The student-observer inferred that the teacher's attention was a social reinforcer (reward) that maintained the inappropriate behavior. He instructed the teacher to follow a program that consisted of praising the children when they were attending to her or were on task and ignoring them when their behavior was inappropriate.

Figure 2-1 shows the results of the modification along with some control observations. The student-observer decided to measure the number of

1-minute periods during which the children were attending to the teacher or during which no inappropriate behavior occurred. The percentage of 1-minute attending intervals becomes the dependent variable and we label the vertical axis as "Attending Intervals (%)." The horizontal axis is the time period over which the experiment took place and it is labelled "Sessions" (it could just as well be labelled "Class Periods" or "Days").

Observe that during the first baseline condition (the first "A" condition), the percentage of attending intervals hovered around 20 percent. Four days is rather a short period of time for a baseline, but this baseline does appear stable and one sometimes must balance the requirements for good research design with the exigencies of the problem. The teacher was having a difficult time with this class and if we had taken a leisurely 2-week baseline she might have become discouraged with our "do-nothing" student-observer and thrown him out of her class.

In the next phase of the experiment (the first "B" or experimental condition), the teacher attended to appropriate behaviors and ignored inappropriate ones, and there was a dramatic rise in the percentage of attending intervals. The three arrows under the data points for sessions 5, 6, and 7 tell the reader that prompts were given to the teacher by the student-observer. Since she was new at attending to the children when they were attending to her, she had to be reminded during these sessions to attend when a child was behaving appropriately and to ignore a child when the behavior was inappropriate.

The next condition was a return to the baseline condition (back to the "A"

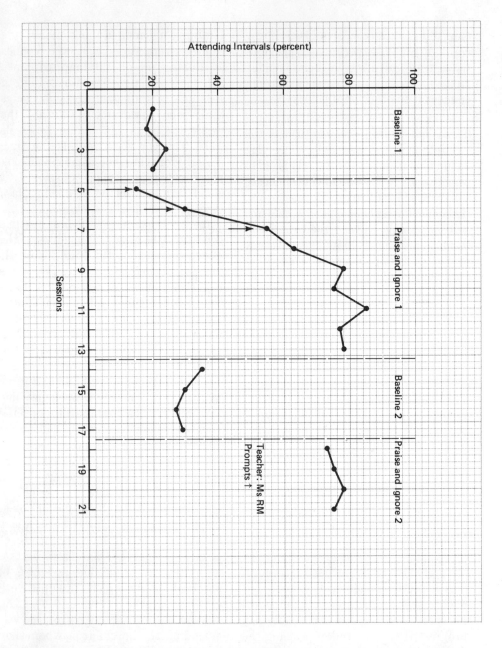

Figure 2-1 The percentage of 1-minute attending intervals across daily sessions for a small class of deaf children. During baseline conditions, the teacher taught class in her usual way. During the "praise and ignore" conditions, she attended to children when they were on task and ignored them when they were behaving inappropriately. The arrows under the data points for sessions 5, 6, and 7 indicate that the student-observer gave the teacher prompts when she was supposed to praise or ignore a given child.

condition). She was instructed to "teach" as she had before in the first baseline condition. This procedure may strike you as a bit odd. Why go back to the old ways when things have improved? The purpose of this manipulation was to demonstrate to the teacher and to anyone reading this graph that what was changed was, in fact, critical in controlling the behavior. There is no better way of showing this than by turning the behavior "on" and "off" like a light by introducing and then removing the independent variable (in this case, teacher-attention for good behavior and inattention for bad behavior).

In Session 14, the percentage of attending intervals dropped to about 35 percent, indicating that a return to the old conditions reinstated the children's inattentive ways. During the next 4 sessions, teacher attention was again made dependent upon the children's attention, and the curve jumped up to 75 percent and stayed there (return to "B" or experimental condition). Thus, the percentage of attending intervals returned to the level it reached during the last part of the first manipulation. If you examine this graph carefully and are able to reproduce it, you should have no trouble summarizing the entire experiment. Now, let's try constructing a graph from data organized in tables.

Application

Joan's Swearing Problem

Joan, a college freshman, has been aware for some time now that she swears a lot and has been called a "foulmouth" by one of her former girlfriends. She has learned a few ways of modifying behavior and has decided to try them out herself to see if she can eliminate her habit of swearing. She starts by recording the frequency of her swear words over a 12-day period. She has a wristcounter and every time she swears, she pushes the counter. She has asked her friends to remind her to count if she forgets. For the first few days of the project, Joan finds that she has to be reminded quite often by her friends that she has sworn, not uncommon for a strong habit. Her baseline record looks like this:

Table 2-1

Frequency of Joan's swearing during a 12-day baseline period.

Day	Swear Words	Comments
1	120	
2	93	
3	89	
4	—	Misplaced wrist counter: No data today
5	81	
6	61	
7	76	
8	84	
9	80	
10	67	
11	73	
12	79	

Joan was surprised at how frequently she actually used swear words, and was somewhat puzzled that the frequency of swearing decreased over the first 3 days. She talked to a psychology major and found that it is sometimes the case for the mere act of recording a behavior to change the frequency of that behavior. After all, he pointed out, the act of counting swear words would make one aware of them. There would probably be some embarrassment at this awareness which, in turn, might decrease the rate of swearing.

After the first 3 days, Joan's rate settled down to between 60 and 80 swear words a day, and she believed that this was stable enough to evaluate any treatment effects. She decided on a five cent fine every time she swore, since she had learned that punishment (a fine) was effective in eliminating undesirable behavior. She tried this program for 8 days and found that it was not working and that it probably would not. She discovered that she would rob her "fine bank" whenever she needed money and had taken to writing IOU's and putting them into her bank instead of money. Furthermore, when she went home on the weekend and explained the program to her family, her little brother made it difficult for her. He would pester and tease her until she lost her temper and swore at him, after which he would gleefully bring the fine bank to her. Joan's data for this first treatment are presented in Table 2-2.

On the basis of Joan's experience with her little brother and her failure to decrease her frequency of swearing, she decided to try another consequence for swearing. She had a long talk with her three roommates and told them about her lack of success with fines. One of her roommates suggested that each time Joan swore, whomever she was talking to should ignore her by simply walking away. All four girls thought this might be a good plan because Joan talked more than any of them, liked attention, and spent more time talking to them than to anyone else. Joan promised that if they were consistent in their treatment of her, she would take them out to dinner

Table 2-2

Frequency of Joan's swearing during a treatment plan using fines. Every time Joan swore, she imposed a 5¢ fine on herself.

Day	Swear Words	Comments
13	64	
14	58	
15	56	
16	71	Needed money, so left IOU in fine bank
17	68	Wrote IOU's
18	69	Wrote IOU's
19	87	Little brother teased and pestered me — I was really mad at him
20	73	Decided fine system was not working

at the end of the quarter. Joan also decided, after further discussion with her roommates, that to eliminate her swearing completely would be extremely difficult. All the girls reported that they swore once in a while, and a more reasonable target for Joan was established at 5 or fewer swear words a day. The "walk away" program was in effect for 31 days, and the data are presented in Table 2-3.

Joan was very pleased with these results but wondered if her treatment plan had "really taken" or if she would start swearing again after the consequence was removed. After 6 months, she dug out the wrist counter and started counting swear words again. She told no one else what she was counting and since she now had new roommates, nobody knew what she was up to.

Table 2-4 shows the results during the follow-up period when there were no programmed consequences for swearing.

At the end of this follow-up period, Joan concluded that her treatment plan had been successful. **Now that we have the results of Joan's project, let's graph them.**

The dependent variable is the "number of swear words," and we plot this on the Y axis (vertical axis or ordinate). Let's turn the graph paper so that the short side (usually 7 or 8 divisions of 10 squares each) represents the vertical axis. We must record numbers that go from 0 to 120 (minimum to maximum number of swear words). If we used a scale of 1 swear word for each square, we would run off the scale, but a ratio of 2 swear words to 1 square will easily fit and will not compress the data so much that trends will be missed. The total

Table 2-3

Frequency of Joan's swearing during the "walk away" treatment. Every time Joan swore when she was talking to one of her roommates, that person would walk away from her.

Day	Swear Words	Comments
21	74	
22	53	
23	31	
24	29	
25	27	
26	16	
27	19	
28	17	
29	11	
30	14	
31	17	
32	15	
33	10	
34	—	Sick; didn't go out
35	9	
36	9	
37	12	
38	7	
39	47	Had big fight with boyfriend
40	37	Broke up with boyfriend
41	21	
42	16	
43	8	
44	4	
45	5	
46	3	
47	2	
48	4	
49	0	
50	3	
51	1	

Table 2-4

Frequency of Joan's swearing during a 10-day follow-up. The follow-up occurred 6 months after the last treatment day, and no consequences were programmed for swearing.

Day	Swear Words	Comments
1	13	
2	11	
3	9	
4	4	
5	10	
6	6	
7	5	
8	1	
9	2	
10	2	Hurray! Swearing is no longer a problem

range of 120 swear words will cover 60 squares, which is most of the space available on the vertical axis and is in keeping with the maxim of using all the graph paper.

Time is plotted on the horizontal axis, and since we have 61 days to plot (this includes the 10-day follow-up) and 10 divisions of 10 squares each, we can use a scale of 1:1 — 1 square equals 1 day. Now, since both the vertical and horizontal squares will fit on the graph paper with space left over, we can give ourselves some room to label the axes. Start by drawing coordinates, 10 squares in and 10 squares up from the outermost lines on the graph. Next, write in the numbers on the vertical coordinate with every 10th division being labelled: 0, 20, 40, and so on. Mark the days off by making a small line for each day and labelling every 5th day (this is arbitrary; every 10th would do as well). The reason we don't label every day is that it is difficult to write numbers so close together, it is not necessary, and the chances of misreading the graph are greater.

Before we can label all of the horizontal coordinate, we must decide what to do with the follow-up data. There were 51 consecutive days in the program prior to the follow-up period, but there was a 6 month gap between the last experimental day and the first follow-up day. It would be misleading to label the first follow-up day "52" because that would imply that no time interval had separated the two conditions. It is customary to make a break in the continuity of the graph to inform the reader that there was a break in the continuity of the program; so leave a break in the graph and label the follow-up days separately from the rest of the days, that is, 0, 1, 2, and so on. The space between the follow-up period and the last experiment can also be used to label this time interval.

After labelling the two axes, proceed to plot the data points. In the baseline condition, the datum for Day 4 is missing, so leave that space blank; because we have no way of knowing what that point would have been, we are not justified in connecting the point for Day 3 to that for Day 5. We simply leave a gap in our graph. Likewise, whenever we start plotting data points for a new condition, we leave a gap to inform the reader of this change. Continue to plot data points for the next two conditions. On Day 34, Joan was sick and no data were collected, so leave a gap as you did earlier. On Day 39, Joan had a fight with her boyfriend which probably accounts for her increase in swearing that day. Place an asterisk above that point to alert the reader that something out of the ordinary happened that day which might explain the sudden increase in swearing. The asterisk is then explained in the figure caption. At the end of the "walk away" condition, we have left a space; label it "6 months." (Incidently, if at all possible the labelling of each condition should be done on the same horizontal line. This practice makes it easier and quicker for the reader to discover what the various conditions were.) After plotting all the data points and connecting those that should be connected, label each of the conditions. We have drawn vertical lines separating the conditions which provide a customary emphasis to changes in the experiment. We have also drawn a horizontal line through all conditions at a frequency of 5 swear words, which was Joan's final goal. This is optional but it does allow the reader to see quite rapidly when and on how many days she reached her goal. The finished graph you have drawn (Figure 2-2) provides a fast and easy-to-grasp summary of Joan's entire project.

Exam

1. Define:
   a. ordinate
   b. abscissa
   c. baseline period
   d. X axis
   e. Y axis
2. What are the steps in constructing a graph?
3. What is the rationale for constructing and studying a graph? (You should be able to identify and discuss three reasons.)
4. Examine the results for the second baseline condition in Ms. RM's class (Figure 2-1). Would you say that the original baseline had been recovered? If not, why not? (Hint: If you had been the teacher, how would you have felt about going back to the old condition?)
5. If you thought that the original baseline was not recovered in Figure 2-1, do you see this as a major problem with the project? Why or why not?
6. After examining Joan's graph (Figure 2-2), at what point would you say that she had solved her swearing problem? (This question is not an easy one to answer, but choose some time period and justify your choice.)

References

Skinner, B. F. *The technology of teaching*. New York: Appleton-Century-Crofts, 1968.

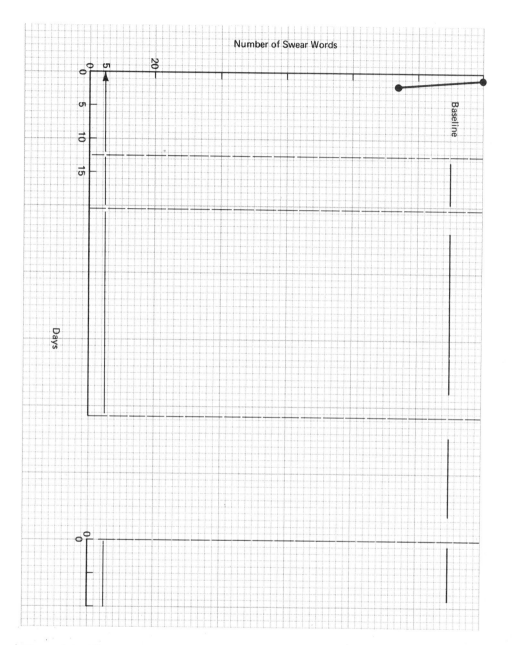

Figure 2-2   The number of swear words made in several conditions by a college coed. *Baseline*: Frequency of swear words were counted with the aid of a wrist counter. There were no consequences for swearing during the baseline. *Fines*: A 5¢ fine was levied every time the subject swore. *"Walk away technique"*: Every time the subject swore in the presence of one of her roommates, the roommate would walk away from the subject. *Follow-up*: A 10-day follow-up occurred after a 6-month period. During the follow-up, there were no consequences for swearing. The asterisk denotes the day on which the girl had a fight with her boyfriend.

*

Psychology as a Science

UNIT

3

The Definition of Psychology

Psychology is the scientific study of the behavior of living animals. This statement may appear simplistic upon first reading, but a thorough analysis of it will show what a "scientific study" is, what "behavior" is, and what "living animals" are. In this unit we will attempt to delineate these concepts, and some concepts related to them.

Defining psychology as the scientific study of the behavior of living animals largely determines the methods the psychologist will use to study his animal and what he defines as the behavior of that animal.

Scientific methods. Scientific methods are sets of procedures that scientists employ systematically to provide increased knowledge of nature. The utilization of these procedures may also produce a particular set of attitudes regarding nature in those who use them. These attitudes are nothing more than inferences about nature that have been verified by specific findings across sciences. The strongest of these inferences is that events occurring in nature do not occur haphazardly but are related to other events in nature in very particular ways. It is the job of the scientist to discover these relations and then to describe them as precisely as possible. In psychology, this is the discovery of relations between behavior and the environment in which the behavior takes place. The inference specific to psychology is that behavior does not occur haphazardly in time but is lawfully related to events that are proximate to it. Behavior may *look* haphazard simply because we are unaware of the events related to it.

Typically, when engaging in scientific behavior the scientist does the following: He isolates the phenomenon he wishes to study as best he can. This may mean designing special equipment to record a response, or simply finding a quiet room. In any case, an environment is chosen that is as free from unwanted influence as possible. (The unwanted influence extends to the scientist's own behavior as well; he will wish to keep this out of the study as much as possible.) Next, he manipulates a variable (an event) that he considers may produce a change in the phenomenon he is studying. Initial discovery may simply be a relation between the successive presentation and withdrawal of a given event and the appearance of a repeatable effect on the phenomenon observed.

When sufficient controls are employed so that our scientist considers the observed effect to be a real one, he will submit his findings to his peers (other scientists) for their criticism. Note that we are using the word *control* in a different sense here. Control, as used here, means the employment of a suitable number of "catch" conditions — conditions which rule out alternative explanations of the reason for a phenomenon's occurrence. As an example of a catch or control condition, Gardner suggested that Rhine might have run a series of tests on Lady Wonder with Mrs. Fonda out of the room (see Unit 1).

In many psychology experiments, an acceptable control condition is to expose subjects to all of the experiment except the feature thought to be critical to the result. An alternative is to expose subjects to the critical feature and to the remaining features of the experiment, but at different times. Thus, we may reward a child for doing his homework during one portion of an experiment, and continue the same conditions but not reward him during a subsequent period — while still recording whether he does his homework. Or we could have one group of boys who are rewarded for doing their homework and compare their outputs with another group of boys who are not rewarded for doing their homework. The nonreward control condition may be sufficient for us to conclude something about the effect of rewards on homework.

In any case, the scientific community then passes judgment on the validity of the phenomenon by acquiescing to its printed or oral publication. In either case the scientist will have written his experimentation and his findings, and discussed them logically.

As a first example of how experimentation and discovery can take place in psychology, we document a field experiment. It is a powerful demonstration of the effect of the environment on human behavior, and it was produced by Haughton and Ayllon in the Saskatchewan Hospital at Weyburn, Saskatchewan, Canada. Ayllon did pioneering work in behavior modification at this institution (Ayllon, 1963; Ayllon & Haughton, 1962; Ayllon & Michael, 1959), and Haughton both assisted and did work on his own. A primary interest of these scientist-therapists was to show that ordinary environmental circumstances were related to the abnormal behaviors exhibited by mental patients, specifically the schizophrenic women on their own ward. However, this kind of proof is difficult when the person being studied already exhibits the (abnormal) behavior.

In this case, Haughton chose a behavior that neither he nor Ayllon had seen one woman exhibit — holding a broom. This behavior certainly isn't weird, especially if the person holding the broom is also sweeping or otherwise occasionally using it. Just standing holding a broom, though, may look silly and abnormal because it appears purposeless. It is the kind of behavior that could lead to an unfavorable clinical diagnosis. For over a year the two investigators had carefully examined and recorded how this woman usually spent her time and found that it was largely unproductive. She had been hospitalized for 23 years, refused to do anything — choosing to sit idly, lie in bed, and, significantly, smoke cigarettes. They deprived her of cigarettes except for one each meal. She was then presented with a broom, and while holding it was given a cigarette. After repeating this procedure, the woman was given a cigarette only when holding the broom and standing upright. Haughton and Ayllon report that quickly, " . . . the patient developed a stereotyped behavior of pacing while holding the broom" (p. 96). Here we have the beginning of the discovery of a relation between an abnormal behavior (stereotyped broom holding) and an environmental event associated with that behavior (i.e., being given a cigarette). Haughton and Ayllon thereafter waited for the broom to be held a longer period of time before presenting cigarettes, and the patient soon came to hold the broom most of her waking hours.

Because the study was an experiment and had no (direct) therapeutic value, Haughton and Ayllon eventually stopped giving cigarettes for broom holding. As might be expected, the woman gradually stopped holding the broom under this last circumstance. The last condition, a "catch" or control condition, shows that it was the relation of the cigarette to the broom holding that was important to the woman's behavior. Thus, witholding a cigarette was also a necessary condition in establishing proof of the authors' interpretation. Note that the variable that is related to broom holding is first added to the woman's environment and then is withdrawn. Had this cycle been repeated and the woman's broom holding changed each time with the change in our variable, we would have been even more confident of the relation between the behavior and our manipulated event.

Of great importance to one of our points in Unit 1 is an aspect of the above study that documents the extreme difficulty of knowing what controls behavior in a specific set of circumstances.

Having been presented with the critical relation (i.e., broom holding leads to cigarettes), we know why the woman held the broom. But what of someone who knew nothing of what Haughton and Ayllon had done? Further, what if the individual was an "expert" in psychology or psychiatry? Should he not know? The answer is at once disappointing and illustrative. Haughton and Ayllon asked two psychiatrists to view the woman and offer their opinions about why she held the broom. One suggested that the broom " . . . represent(ed) . . . some essential perceptual element in her field of consciousness . . . a habit which has become essential to her peace of mind." The other suggested that the broom and the pacing were " . . . a ritualistic procedure, a magical action . . . " by which she controlled others. Thus, the broom could function as " . . . a phallic symbol; (or) the scepter of an omnipotent queen" (pp. 97-98). We can see that even "experts" can be incorrect and this is disappointing; however, this example illustrates the necessity of doing a scientific analysis such as that of Haughton and Ayllon. It also illustrates that "experts" can be caught up by their own theories.

In our second example, we look at how a psychologist might study the effects of temperature changes on behavior in the laboratory. The psychologist has some reason to suspect that temperature can be related to bar pressing by rats.[1] This reason may be a function of someone else's theory of behavior, the scientist's own theory of behavior, or it may simply be something noticed about behavior. If the latter, the psychologist goes to the literature to see if others have seen or documented anything similar; if they have, he may avoid wasting his time doing an experiment over unknowingly. If no work has been done, the literature may still provide him with hints as to how good his guess is about the particular relation he wishes to isolate. He already has sound-attenuating chambers for his animal with electromechanical switches therein. He simply adds an infrared lamp to the top of the cage — which is close to the animal. To facilitate penetration of the heat to the animal he shaves the animal prior to insertion in the cage. He then can turn the light on and let the animal's bar press turn it off for a while or he can let the animal's bar press turn the light on for a while. In any case, he will record the rate of bar pressing as it is related to light onset or termination. He finds that when the light is turned on the animal will respond to turn it off. Presumably, this is related to the in-cage temperature. If the animal's cage is placed in a deep freeze and the cage temperature considerably lowered, the animal responds frequently to keep the lamp on. After the discovery of the initial relations, the psychologist in this case may be interested in a number of parameters of his variables. For instance, the temperature inside the cage might be varied in one experiment; in another the amount of time the light is turned on per response might be examined. In a third, the fat content of the animal's diet might be manipulated. In any case, a whole new set of problems to be studied will have arisen as a function of the initial findings of the relation between temperature and behavior.

The Scope of Psychology

Responses. In our initial definition of psychology, it was stated that psychologists study behavior. A large and necessary part of the subject matter of psychology, therefore, is the behavior of animals.[2] By behavior we mean anything the animal does as it

---

[1]The reason for doing an experiment is called a *hypothesis*, especially when the reason is formally stated. However, even if it is not formally stated the scientist probably has an informal hypothesis. Bachrach (1962) called the latter *hypothesitos* (p. 64).

[2]We use "animals" in the biological classification sense, and most certainly include humans as a part of this classification.

interacts with its environment. Some typical behaviors have been bar pressing by the rat and monkey, key pecking by the pigeon, and salivation by the dog. More recently, complex behaviors such as problem solving, the formation of concepts, and creativity have been examined. With children, classroom behaviors have been studied as well as their crying, crawling, climbing, smiling, thumbsucking, and use of adjectives. The current list of responses under study in man alone is a large one.

A behavior to be studied is generally chosen for a number of reasons. It may be easy for the organism to emit, easy to measure, or it can vary through a wide range of values (e.g., pressing a bar takes little energy and can be emitted at high rates as well as low rates). A behavior may also be studied because it is of theoretical or social importance, as is the case with thumbsucking, tantruming, or aggressive behavior.

Within a science of behavior, responses to be studied must meet the criterion of either being observable or being potentially observable. It is not possible for a science to deal with events that are inherently nonobservable and unmeasurable. By potentially observable, we mean that the *effects* of an event may be observed and the event itself inferred even if the event itself cannot be directly measured. An example of this is a toothache. This is certainly a real event to the person experiencing it. However, it cannot be directly observed by others. Related events may be used to infer its existence, such as swelling of the jaw, verbal behavior describing the pain, and so on.

Stimuli. Behavior does not take place in a vacuum. It is always preceded and followed in time by environmental events. The events comprise energy changes in the environment and may be specified in the language of physics. For example, when a light is turned on or off, the change in illumination can be specified physically (in foot-lamberts). This constitutes a **PHYSICAL DEFINITION OF A STIMULUS.** Turning a light on or off may also be related to specific behaviors which precede or follow the illumination change. If a relation exists between the stimulus and a response, the stimulus not only has physical dimensions but is also **FUNCTIONAL WITH RESPECT TO BEHAVIOR.** We may note that humans are very likely to turn on the lights in a room when the room has less than a certain amount of illumination. However, at other levels of illumination, a person may make no response. In each case we have a physically specified stimulus (the illumination level), but only in the former do we have a functional stimulus (i.e., only there is it related to behavior).

Psychologists are interested for the most part in stimuli that are functionally related to behavior. In fact, the basic task of a science of psychology is to discover functional relations between stimuli and responses. Hence, the scientific psychologist is in the business of manipulating stimuli and observing responses or changes in responses that occur as a function of the manipulated stimuli.

Finally, the behavioral scientist will attempt to derive general statements from the specific stimulus-response relations he locates. If these general statements stand the test of further experimentation, they may attain the status of principles or laws of behavior.

Psychology's Subjects

Experimental psychologists have examined the behaviors of a myriad of creatures — from arthropods to humans. At the present time much of the work in psychology utilizes humans, rats, nonhuman primates (monkeys and chimpanzees) and many other mammals. In addition, research is being conducted with pigeons, fishes, and octopi. The psychologist often studies organisms other than humans for good reason. First, the manipulations that he may wish to make may have unknown effects or be potentially harmful to the organism and therefore ethically unfeasible for study using human beings. The effects of drugs on behavior offer a case in point. Secondly, the organism may have a particular quality (i.e., physiology, anatomy, or behavior) that is of interest. For example, dolphins have a highly sophisticated communication system. In addition, their brains are comparable to man's using the ratio of brain weight per body weight and cortical development as indices. There is a wealth of anecdotal lore regarding the intelligence of the dolphin. The visual behavior of the octupus is studied because he has a unique eye. Monkeys and other primates are studied because they presumably are closest to humans on the evolutionary scale.

Some animals end up being studied more than others for interesting reasons. First, some of their attributes may make them easy to study. Rats may be studied more than elephants because of their size, and children more than adults because of their availability. Second, earlier work on a species may

result in the easy availability of equipment for use with species and easier availability of the species itself. Third, earlier work means the scientist has some data to which he can relate his work on the same species. Fourth, the species may be studied because its life cycle allows the gathering of a "lifetime" of information in a fraction of the lifetime of humans. Rats or mice, for example, live just a few years. Fifth, the species may be studied because of its similarity to man in some respect (e.g., dolphins). Some or all of these reasons account for the use of particular organisms by psychologists. In any case, the reason for studying the organism is twofold: first, to find and describe principles of behavior, and second, to see if these principles hold for other species, especially man.

In general, the species studied by the psychologist will be observed in confined settings that reduce the chance of contaminating factors disguising the effects of the variables manipulated. Other sciences do likewise. The physicist interested in studying rates at which bodies fall does not do so utilizing a feather in an unpredictable breeze. He may begin instead in a vacuum jar with items of specified mass, where the results will be uncontaminated by winds. So too, the principles of behavior have been derived in the constrained setting of the laboratory. However, just as it is the task of the engineer to study the behavior of structures in high winds, it is the task of the psychologist to study the application of his principles in the world outside the laboratory. The latter endeavor can also be pursued in a scientific fashion, as the following study shows.

Illustration

B. M. Hart, K. E. Allen, J. S. Buell, F. R. Harris, and M. M. Wolf, Effects of social reinforcement on operant crying. *Journal of Experimental Child Psychology*, 1964, 1, 145-153.

These authors were associated with a nursery school attached to a major university. They wished to show that the attention of the teachers in the school was the critical feature maintaining the crying episodes a boy had each day at school (average/day = 8). That is, the response they were studying was crying and the physical stimulus they thought might be functionally related to the crying was the teachers' solicitous attention to the boy whenever he cried. Before they began the analysis, they already had a reasonable idea that this relation might exist because it was known that adults could control child behavior and they could see the teachers attend to the child when he cried. The idea was to prove that adult attention was a functional stimulus for this child; specifically, that it was functionally related to his crying behavior. Therapeutically, of course, these scientists wished to stop the boy's crying because it probably would have affected the child's social development had it been allowed to continue.

The procedure they executed was simple to talk about, but difficult to carry out. If attention seems to be maintaining crying, cut off all attention for crying. They did this for 10 successive days after first measuring crying for 10 days without making any changes (i.e., the teachers still attended to crying). After 10 days of not attending to crying, the teachers again attended to it for 10 more days, followed by a final 10 days in which crying was again ignored.

In the first 10 days, during which the teachers attended to the boy when he cried, crying continued at its usual rate; however, when attention for crying was withheld during the next 10 days, the rate of crying decreased to near zero. Re-attending to crying during the third 10 days reinstated the earlier rate, and, in the final 10 days, ignoring crying again decreased it almost to zero. Thus, the authors were able to show that teacher attention was a functional stimulus with respect to the crying behavior of this boy. In effect they demonstrated the existence of a functional relation between attention for crying and crying. This illustration is important because it contains several features of this and the earlier units: 1) a physical stimulus, that is, teacher attention; 2) a response, that is, crying; 3) a functional relation demonstrated between the stimulus and response, that is, if teacher attends to crying, crying increases, while if teacher does not attend to crying, crying decreases; 4) proof that the physical stimulus is a functional stimulus because of (3); and, 5) a demonstration of the control of behavior.

In order to provide further experience with this study and to facilitate your graphic skills, graph the data of the above experiment before going further. The graph you are to construct is labelled for you at the end of this unit. It is a special kind of graph called a CUMULATIVE RECORD. In a cumulative record

each successive point added is added above and to the right of the last point graphed when graphing from left to right. In other words, a cumulative record always moves parallel to or away from (but not toward) the horizontal coordinate of the graph (i.e., the abscissa). As you can see, the days (1-40) are on the abscissa while cumulative crying episodes are on the vertical axis (i.e., the ordinate). The data of the experiment follow in tabular form (Table 3-1), and the first three points as well as one point beginning each of the four 10-day periods of the study are drawn for you. Use filled circles for days 1-10 and 21-30, and unfilled circles for days 11-20 and 31-40. You will need to cumulate the crying episodes of

Table 3-1

The number of crying episodes of a 4-year-old boy during 40 days of nursery school. Extrapolated from: Harris, B. M., Allen, K. E., Buell, J. S., Harris, F. R., & Wolf, M. M.   Effects of social reinforcement on operant crying. *Journal of Experimental Child Psychology*, 1964, 1, 145-153.

Day	Crying Episodes	Cumulative Crying Episodes*	Day	Crying Episodes	Cumulative Crying Episodes*
1	10	10	21	2	108
2	8	18	22	2	
3	7	25	23	4	
4	12		24	6	
5	7		25	8	
6	9		26	6	
7	6		27	4	
8	7		28	6	
9	6		29	8	
10	8		30	4	
11	7	87	31	4	160
12	7		32	2	
13	4		33	4	
14	3		34	0	
15	0		35	1	
16	3		36	0	
17	0		37	0	
18	0		38	1	
19	2		39	0	
20	0		40	0	

* Cumulate the remainder yourself and use the cumulated numbers on the graph.

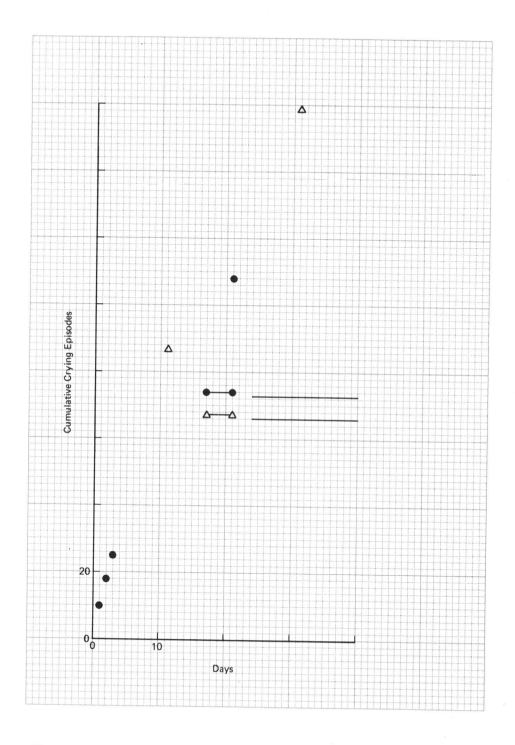

Figure 3-1   The number of crying episodes of a four-year-old boy during 40 days of nursery school.

Column 2 in Column 3 of the table. Do this by adding the previous day's episodes to the cumulative total in Column 3. (It will help to look at how the first three numbers were produced.) That way you get a cumulated total for each of the 40 days. Do an accurate job — your answers to exam questions at each chapter's end throughout the book depend on it.

Exam

1. What does psychology study?
2. What organisms does psychology study and why?
3. What is the task of a science of psychology?
4. What is a major assumption that scientists make about events occurring in nature?
5. What behaviors does a scientist emit?
6. Why does a particular behavior become the subject of study?
7. Distinguish between a physical and a functional definition of a stimulus. Give an example of each.
8. In the study by Hart et al., what is the general shape of the curve of cumulative crying episodes? Answer this by describing the slope of the curve during attention-to-crying periods and nonattention-to-crying periods. Contrast these slopes in your answer.
9. Summarize the Haughton and Ayllon experiment. What did this experiment demonstrate?
10. What is a cumulative record?

References

Ayllon, T. Intensive treatment of psychotic behavior by stimulus satiation and food reinforcement. *Behavior Research and Therapy*, 1963, **1**, 53-61.

Ayllon, T., & Haughton, E. Control of the behavior of schizophrenic patients by food. *Journal of the Experimental Analysis of Behavior*, 1962, **5**, 343-352.

Ayllon, T., & Michael, J. The psychiatric nurse as a behavioral engineer. *Journal of the Experimental Analysis of Behavior*, 1959, **2**, 323-334.

Bachrach, A. J. *Psychological research: An introduction.* New York: Random House, 1962.

Haughton, E., & Ayllon, T. Production and elimination of symptomatic behavior. In L. Ullmann & L. Krasner (Eds.), *Case studies in behavior modification.* New York: Holt, Rinehart and Winston, 1965. Pp. 94-98.

*

Respondent Conditioning

4

One way that psychologists have classified behavior is into either operant or respondent categories. **OPERANT** behavior utilizes the "voluntary" musculature and is modifiable by its consequences. **RESPONDENT** behavior is "reflexive" behavior and is not modified by its consequences. In recent years, researchers have shown that this rigid distinction between operant and respondent behavior is not completely accurate; however, for didactic purposes the distinction is useful.

Reflexes

A reflex is composed of a stimulus component and a response component. It is *not* a response only. The stimulus and response composing the reflex are related in such a way that changes in the stimulus produce or are related to changes in the response (i.e., they are functionally related).

Some examples of reflexes in humans are:

1) Pupillary reflex: Change in the size (by contraction or dilation) of the pupil of the eye *in response to* a change in the intensity of light.

2) Patellar reflex: Jerk of the lower leg *in response to* a blow delivered just under the kneecap.

3) Tearing reflex: Tearing of the eye *in response to* a foreign object in the eye (dust particle) or *in response to* the aroma of a freshly peeled onion.

4) Salivary reflex: Flow of saliva into the mouth *in response to* food in the mouth, or *in response to* a weak acid solution in the mouth.

5) Piloerection reflex: Erection of hair *in response to* cold or to extreme fright.

Notice that in all of the reflexes mentioned above, the stimulus for the reflex is identifiable. The specification of the stimulus is one of the ways by which you can tell whether the behavior in question is operant or respondent. With operant behavior, it is not always easy, and it is sometimes impossible, to specify the stimulus that controls the response. For instance, if we see a person get up from his chair and open the door, we have no way of knowing, without more information, what controlled his action. It could have been the ring of the doorbell, the sound of footsteps on the porch, it may have been time to go on some errand, or it may have been in order to get some fresh air. Without further investigation we could not specify what controlled the person's leaving his chair and opening the door. To emphasize the difference between operant and respondent behavior, we say that respondent behavior is **ELICITED;** the stimulus "calls forth" the response. Operant behavior, on the other hand, is **EMITTED;** the organism makes a response which may or may not be preceded by an easily observable stimulus.

Conditional and Unconditional Reflexes

The reflexes that were mentioned in the previous section were all examples of **UNCONDITIONAL** reflexes, reflexes that are not dependent upon special training or learning procedures. The

stimulus which is the appropriate stimulus for the reflex is called the **UNCONDITIONAL STIMULUS (UCS).** By appropriate, we mean any stimulus which regularly, without training, elicits the response. A response to an appropriate stimulus is called the **UNCONDITIONAL RESPONSE (UCR).** Thus, increase in the intensity of light is the appropriate stimulus (UCS) for the contraction of the pupil (UCR). Together, the UCS (light intensity) and UCR (size of the pupil) make up the pupillary reflex.

When, through the process of conditioning, a different stimulus elicits the UCR, the new stimulus is called a **CONDITIONAL STIMULUS (CS)** and the response to this stimulus is called a **CONDITIONAL RESPONSE (CR).**

The words *conditional* and *unconditional* were used by I. P. Pavlov, the great Russian physiologist, to emphasize the nature of the relation between the stimulus and the response in both cases.[1] In the conditional reflex,

---

[1]Due to an error in translation made during one of Pavlov's presentations, the words *conditioned* and *unconditioned* were substituted for *conditional* and *unconditional*, respectively. As others have shown, Pavlov himself certainly used the word *conditional* when referring to a conditional reflex because he emphasized its impermanence. A thorough discussion of this point can be found in Diamond, S., Balvin, R. S., and Diamond, F. R., 1963.

To be consistent with Pavlov's usage, we will use the terms *conditional* and *unconditional* in this chapter and throughout the text when we refer to respondent conditioning. Since the words *conditioned* and *unconditioned* are so prevalent in American usage, especially in operant conditioning terminology, we have elected to continue using these terms when discussing operant conditioning and phenomena related to it. By attending to the ending of the terms *conditioned* and *conditional*, the student will have an additional set of cues to distinguish the kind of conditioning being discussed.

a stimulus elicits the response, but it is subject to certain conditions: A special conditioning procedure must be used to establish the connection. The connection is only transitory. If the UCS is not occasionally paired with the CS, the CS will lose its power to elicit the CR. These special conditioning procedures are not necessary for the UCS to maintain its power to elicit the UCR. Hence, the term *unconditional*, or "not subject to conditions." The relation exists from birth. Membership in a particular species provides the individual with a set of built-in behaviors related to specific stimuli which may help that individual survive (e.g., coughing in response to an object caught in the throat).

Respondent Conditioning

The basic operation in respondent conditioning is very simple: It consists of pairing the UCS with the stimulus you would like to establish as the CS. In practice, however, the establishment of a reliable conditional reflex requires good instruments, a thorough understanding of both the organism and the unconditional reflex in question, and a considerable skill on the part of the experimenter.

Assume that we wish to condition the sound of a buzzer to produce the pupillary UCR. First, as a check on the conditioning procedure, we should establish that the buzzer does not already elicit the UCR (change in the size of the pupil). This part of the procedure would be diagrammed like this:

NS(Buzzer) ───/──→ UCR (Change in the size of the pupil)

The diagram simply states that the neutral stimulus (NS) *does not* (the arrow with the slash through it) elicit the unconditional response prior to conditioning. (It will, however, elicit other unconditional responses, which in Figure 4-1 are indicated by a small r. These responses are not of interest to us.)

The so-called neutral stimulus may have already been conditioned to this unconditional response or it may be another appropriate stimulus for that unconditional response.[2] If so, then it cannot be used to demonstrate the efficacy of our conditioning procedures because we would have no way of knowing whether or not the procedure was effective.

After we have determined that the stimulus we would like to condition is indeed neutral, that stimulus and the UCS are presented simultaneously. Actually, the best conditioning occurs if the NS is presented about 0.5 sec before the UCS and overlaps it.

The pairing operation is repeated a number of times, usually between 30 to 50. In the final step, the NS is presented by itself. Now, if the buzzer elicits pupil contraction, a new conditional reflex has been established and the buzzer is a CS. Note that we must always check to see whether, in fact, the response occurs to the NS before we can claim that a conditional reflex has been established. The complete paradigm can be diagrammed in three stages as in Figure 4-1.

---

[2] An unconditional reflex may have more than one appropriate stimulus (UCS). For example, both food in the mouth and a weak acid solution elicit salivation, so both are UCSs for salivation. Can you think of another UCS for the tearing reflex?

Figure 4-1

Phases in the establishment of a conditional reflex. The left column shows the procedure while the right column gives the reason for the procedure.

Phase I: Testing the Neutral Stimulus   Purpose

 NS$_{(Buzzer)}$ ⇸ UCR$_{(Pupil\ contraction\ or\ dilation)}$

The supposed neutral stimulus is presented several times by itself to test whether it is *indeed* neutral. If it is already a functional stimulus with respect to the UCR in question, it cannot be used to demonstrate conditioning.

Phase II: Pairing Stimuli

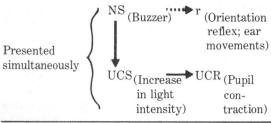
Presented simultaneously {
NS$_{(Buzzer)}$ ⋯▶ r (Orientation reflex; ear movements)
UCS$_{(Increase\ in\ light\ intensity)}$ ▶ UCR$_{(Pupil\ con-traction)}$
}

The pairing of the NS with the UCS is the key operation which establishes the NS as a CS. Usually, between 30 to 50 pairings are required for the CS to reach its maximal strength.

Phase III: Testing for a Conditional Reflex

If the NS ⟶ UCR,

Then the NS has become a CS:

CS$_{(Buzzer)}$ ⟶ CR$_{(Pupil\ contraction)}$

The NS must be presented *without the UCS* to determine whether it has become functional. If it has, then a conditional reflex has been formed.

Note that the small r elicited by the NS, the sound of the buzzer, is included in Figure 4-1, Phase II. This is to remind you that, initially at least, there is a response to the buzzer — a response which is part of an orienting reflex. The newly established CR may contain components of this other response as well as components of the UCR. Thus, the CR and UCR, although similar, *are not* identical. For example, the salivary glands typically do not produce as much saliva to a CS as they do to the UCS.

Measuring Respondent Behavior

There are three commonly used measures of the strength of reflexive behavior. They are: 1) the **LATENCY** between the UCS and UCR. Latency is the time between the onset of a stimulus and the onset of a subsequent response. In a well-established conditional reflex, the latency of the CR is short. 2) The **AMPLITUDE** of the response. Amplitude refers to the size of the response, for example, the distance the leg travels given a blow of specific force to the patellar tendon. 3) **FATIGABILITY** of a UCR. Fatigability refers to the number of times a UCR can be elicited by a UCS before the UCS will no longer produce the UCR.

An example of how these measures might be used follows: If a small rubber hammer were repeatedly struck just below your kneecap with a constant force, the amplitude of the response would gradually decrease, the latency would increase, and eventually the UCS would not elicit the UCR. In order to produce a response at this point, the intensity of the UCS would have to be increased. This points to another measure of a reflex, the **THRESHOLD** of the response. The threshold of a reflex is that intensity at which a UCS will elicit a UCR 50 percent of the time. In the illustration above, the UCR might occur 50 percent of the time when the hammer was struck with x force prior to the fatiguing of the reflex. After some fatigue, the force needed to obtain a response to the UCS 50 percent of the time would have to be increased.

Illustration

K. M. Bykov, *The cerebral cortex and the internal organs.* New York: Chemical Publishing, 1957.

K. M. Bykov was one of Pavlov's students, and he and his colleagues have been conducting experiments in respondent conditioning for some forty years. He is interested in various organs of the body, such as the kidneys, and how their functioning is regulated by the cerebral cortex. Bykov, like Pavlov, uses healthy dogs as subjects in what are called "chronic" experiments. In a chronic experiment, the animal is examined over a long period of time under a variety of experimental conditions and is returned to a baseline or "normal" condition between experimental manipulations. Typically, some organ such as a kidney is surgically prepared so that its functioning can be more closely scrutinized than it ordinarily could be. With this approach, the experimenter hopes to learn something not only about a given variable in a particular experiment, but also about the process by which an organ recovers its normal functioning. In short, some of the complexity of an organ's functioning can be seen in the chronic experiment that would probably be hidden in the "acute" or one-shot experiment.

In an experiment with the dog "Norka," Bykov first determined the amount of urine secreted over a period of several weeks. The dog's bladder had been extirpated and the ureter externalized. At this time, Bykov was interested in the kidneys, not the bladder, and this operation made sure that only kidney functions would be studied. When urine production had stabilized, he administered the UCS, an injection of 100 cc of warm water into the rectum, and recorded the increased urine production over several hours. After repeated administrations of the UCS in the experimental stand, the dog was placed in a different room, in a stand unlike the experimental one and in the presence of a different handler. In the new experimental stand, Stand B, the dog was never given the UCS. In the old stand, Stand A, the injections were continued as before.

For a number of weeks, the dog was alternated between rooms and the amount of urine secreted in each stand measured. **The data from this experiment are presented in Table 4-1. Plot these data on Figure 4-2 using a different code for the trials conducted in each room. Connect the data points within each condition. The results show the gradual formation of a discrimination between experimental stands.**

Application

J. P. Foreyt, and W. A. Kennedy, Treatment of overweight by aversion therapy. *Behavior Research and Therapy*, 1971, **9**, 29-34.

Aversion therapy is based upon respondent conditioning and involves the pairing of some noxious stimulus with the conditional stimuli that control the "maladaptive behavior." Alcoholism, smoking, and homosexuality are problems in which aversion therapy has been used with some success. It should be emphasized that aversion therapy is used in conjunction with other techniques as part of an overall treatment plan. It would not do, for instance, to eliminate a male homosexual's desire for men without also teaching him to desire women. The latter half of such a program would require the use of rewards and has nothing to do with aversion therapy.

In this experiment, the authors used seven noxious-smelling substances (UCSs) in an attempt to help overweight women lose weight. There

Table 4-1

Amount of urine secreted per 2-hour period by the dog, Norka, under two conditions. Data taken from Bykov, K. M. *The cerebral cortex and the internal organs.* **New York: Chemical Publishing Co., 1957.**

	Urine Secreted (cubic centimeters)	
Trial	Old Room (Stand A)	New Room (Stand B)
1	11.0	
2		13.0
3		4.7
4		5.5
5		9.0
6		5.4
7		7.4
8	12.7	
9		6.2
10		5.7
11		5.6
12		6.4
13		6.3
14		1.5
15		1.3
16	14.7	
17	13.4	
18		3.6
19		3.1
20	14.2	
21	8.7	
22		1.8
23		1.7
24	16.6	
25	19.0	

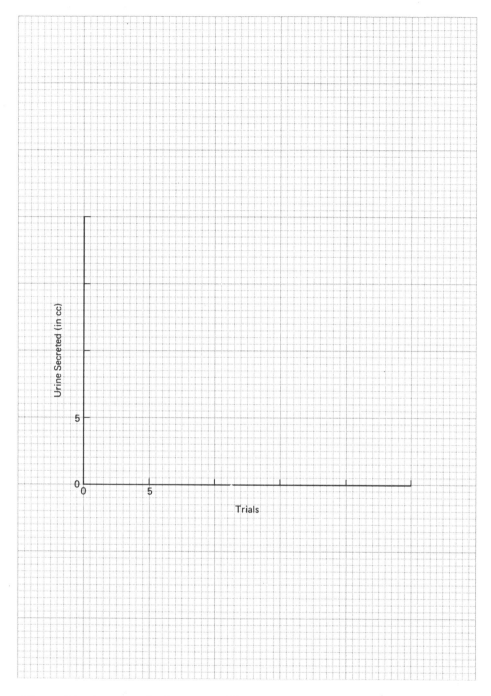

Figure 4-2 Amount of urine secreted by the dog, "Norka," in two conditions. On Stand A the dog continued to receive the UCS. On Stand B the UCS was never presented to the dog.

*

were six women in the experimental and six in the control group. The average initial weight of the experimental group was 191 pounds (range: 152 to 233 lbs.) while the weight for the control group was 172 pounds (range: 152 to 237 lbs.). Three of the women in the experimental group were volunteers from the local TOPS club (Take Off Pounds Sensibly), while all of the women in the control group were from TOPS. The authors used women from this club because they wanted to make sure the women in the control group were trying to lose weight and would receive rewards for any attempts to lose weight. Such a group would control for the rewards the experimenters might deliver (inadvertently or otherwise) through their interactions with the experimental subjects.

A list of favorite foods was obtained from the experimental subjects, and those foods high in calories (cakes, pies, candy, doughnuts, and fried foods) were selected as the foods to be eliminated from the subjects' diets. When the subject was brought into the experimental situation, one of her favorite foods was heated in front of her and she was instructed to smell it, handle it, imagine taking a bite, and so on. When the subject indicated to the experimenter that she was smelling and thinking about eating that food, he immediately asked her to place an oxygen mask on her face and sniff. When the subject had the mask in place, a noxious odor, such as pure skunk oil, was blown into the mask.

The CS-UCS pairings (smell of favorite food paired with a noxious odor) were repeated about 12 times a session and there were about 21 sessions in all spread over a 9-week period. After this conditioning period, a 40-week follow-up was initiated in which the subjects were weighed every 4 weeks.

Plot the data in Table 4-2 using a different code for the control and experimental groups. This table shows the cumulative weight change for both groups over the course of the study. The zero point for the ordinate is placed two main divisions above where it would normally be placed. Thus, the first main division reads +20, the next +10, the next 0, and so on. This was done because in some weeks the control group had a net gain in "poundage" from the previous week and this was recorded as a + score.

The treatment was effective during the conditioning period and the effects did last over the 40-week follow-up period. At Week 9, the experimental group had lost an average of 13 pounds while the control group had an average loss of 1 pound. After 48 weeks, the experimental group had gained some weight but still showed an average loss of 9 pounds while the control group had an average gain of 1 pound.

When the experiment ended, the experimental subjects were questioned about the experiment, and five of the six subjects said that the conditioning was effective. These five felt feelings of uneasiness when exposed to their favorite foods as well as lessened desire for these foods. One subject reported that on one occasion when she was at a drive-in, one of her friends ordered some french fries and she reported that she had to open a window or she would have vomited. She was puzzled by her reaction because french fries had never been one of the stimuli paired with the UCS in her program. Other fried and

Table 4-2

Cumulative weight change for experimental and control groups of overweight women during a period of 48 weeks. Plus (+) indicates pounds gained; minus (−) indicates pounds lost. During the first 9 weeks, the experimental group underwent treatment by aversion therapy. Data were taken from Foreyt, J. P., & Kennedy, W. A.   Treatment of overweight by aversion therapy. *Behavior Research and Therapy*, 1971, 9, 29-34.

Conditioning Weeks

Week	Control Group	Experimental Group
0	0	0
1	0	− 3
2	+2	−18
3	No weight recorded	−34
4	+7	−46
5	No weight recorded	−55
6	+2	−63
7	−4	−73
8	−5	−74
9	−6	−80

After Conditioning

Week	Control Group	Experimental Group
12	− 6	−70
16	− 7	−72
20	+ 5	−70
24	No weight recorded	−73
28	+10	−70
32	+15	−52
36	+ 9	−61
40	+ 8	−52
44	+ 9	−55
48	+ 9	−54

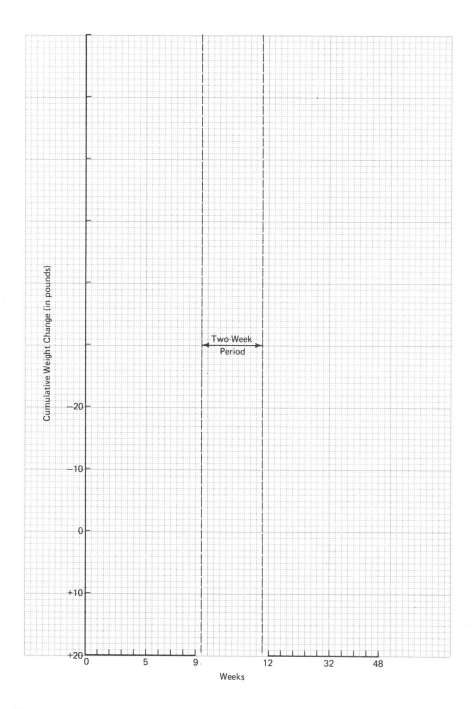

Figure 4-3 Cumulative weight change for two groups of overweight women. The experimental group received presentation of a noxious-smelling substance along with the odors of preferred foods for a 9-week period. The control group belonged to TOPS and attempted to lose weight in whatever manner they could.

*

greasy foods had been paired with the UCS, though.

This experiment demonstrated how aversion therapy might be used to help people keep away from certain foods. But this treatment, by itself, does not form a complete program. The authors point this out and say that they had formed a positive relation with the experimental subjects and the knowledge that the experimenters "cared" about them and wanted them to lose weight probably contributed to the success of the experimental group as well. Part of a more comprehensive program might include rewards dependent upon restricting overall caloric intake (counting "bites" of food is an effective way to do this) and for engaging in some regular exercise.

Exam

1. Define the following terms:
   a. UCS
   b. UCR
   c. CS
   d. CR
   e. respondent behavior
   f. elicit
   g. emit
   h. NS
   i. latency
   j. threshold
   k. amplitude
   l. fatigability

2. Define a reflex and give an example of one that is not mentioned in the text. How is a reflex measured? (You should be able to list and discuss four measures.)

3. Select any reflex and diagram the steps in respondent conditioning.

4. Cite an example of respondent conditioning in your own history, for example, fear of bugs or spiders. How was it (or might it have been) conditioned?

5. With respect to Bykov's experiment, what evidence of learning was demonstrated in your graph? (Hint: Look at the change in the amount of urine secreted in both experimental rooms.) What do these data tell you?

6. What was the CS in Bykov's experiment?

7. What are the steps in aversion therapy?

8. How do you explain the feeling of nausea experienced by the subject in the aversion therapy experiment who smelled french fries at a drive-in?

9. Examine Figure 4-3, and observe what happened to the experimental group's curve after conditioning. How do you account for this change? What would you predict if the follow-up period had continued for another 48 weeks? Why?

References

Bykov, K. M. *The cerebral cortex and the internal organs.* New York: Chemical Publishing, 1957.

Diamond, S., Balvin, R. S., & Diamond, F. R. *Inhibition and choice.* New York: Harper & Row, 1963.

Foreyt, J.P., & Kennedy, W. A. Treatment of overweight by aversion therapy. *Behavior Research and Therapy,* 1971, **9,** 29-34.

Dependencies,
Contingencies, and Bribery

UNIT

5

Dependencies

One of the most important ideas discovered and developed by psychologists, especially B. F. Skinner, is the dependent relation between behavior and its *immediately* ensuing consequences. Operant behavior is simply behavior that operates on the environment and makes up a large portion of the everyday behavior we engage in each day. It has been known for several thousand years that rewards and punishments can control people's behavior. But the degree of control made possible by specifying the exact nature of the relation between behavior and the stimulus that follows it has only been achieved since about 1930.

How should a stimulus be programmed so that the frequency of the response that produced it will change? You should make sure that the stimulus (a shock or piece of food) is produced by a given response and that one only. When the environment is arranged in this way, the stimulus (food or shock) is said to be **DEPENDENT** upon the response. *If* the animal scratches his ear (response), *then* he will receive a cookie (stimulus). The relation between the stimulus and response is causal; the response "causes" the stimulus to occur. After Reynolds (1968), we will say that a **DEPENDENCY** obtains if the organism must engage in the behavior *first*, in order to produce the consequence. This term applies regardless of whether the consequence is an "artificial" one, such as exists in an experimental cage where the animal must press a lever to regulate his temperature, or

53

a natural one, such as opening a door in order to walk through the doorway.

If we desire to increase the rate at which some response occurs, we would deprive the animal of food for a specified time and then make food dependent upon the desired response. When we arrange the environment in this way, we frequently see a quick and dramatic increase in the rate at which the response occurs.

Contingencies

Suppose that an organism engages in some behavior and a positive stimulus (something good) follows that behavior immediately, but that the correspondence between the stimulus and the response is only accidental; that is, the response does not cause the stimulus to occur. Will that behavior increase in strength? Yes. Accidental correlations between a response and a stimulus can come to control our behavior quite strongly. If a crap shooter yells, "Come, seven" just before his dice show a seven, his behavior of yelling, "Come, seven" will increase in strength. It does not matter that his yelling did not cause the dice to behave the way he wanted them to. *The effect of the stimulus consequence is automatic*: It strengthens the behavior that precedes it, whether the behavior caused the stimulus to occur or not.

Behavior, like the crap shooter's peculiar language, which is maintained by the occasional chance pairing of a reinforcing stimulus with a response is called **SUPERSTITIOUS BEHAVIOR.** Superstitious behavior is most likely to develop in situations where the outcome of a person's behavior is very important and where the probability of a favorable outcome is less than certainty, as in gambling, competitive sports, and war. Malinowski (1948), a renowned anthropologist, noted that magic in primitive cultures was only connected to dangerous activities where the outcome was uncertain. In his observations of the Trobriand Islanders, he found that fishing in the inner lagoons, which was done by poison and was easy, had no magic associated with it. However, the open-sea fishing after shark or other dangerous fish was laden with all kinds of taboos and magical incantations because, in spite of all the native's knowledge and preparation, open-sea fishing was only sometimes rewarded.

So far then, we have mentioned two important terms you need to know in order to understand how behavior is controlled by its consequences. The first term is called a **DEPENDENCY** and we use this term to talk about the situation where a response causes the stimulus to occur. The term **CONTINGENCY** is used when referring to an accidental relation between the response and the stimulus that follows it, as the example above portrayed. Remember, though, that the effects of a stimulus consequence will be the same whether the relation is a causal one or not. The effects of the dependency relation will be consistent simply because the relation is consistent; the stimulus will always follow the response. We would expect behavior controlled by contingencies to undergo slight changes or even to drop out competely after a while, simply because a contingency is not usually a consistent relationship. After a prolonged batting slump, a baseball player who is once again hitting the ball may show a whole new ritual of responses before taking his place in the batter's box. This new repertoire will probably persist until the next slump.

Bribery and Dependencies

The beginning student frequently misuses the term *bribery* and believes it wrong to reinforce (read: reward) pets or children to do what they "should" do. There are some important differences between the concept of a dependency as we define it and a bribe as it is used in everyday discourse. There are three general areas where the two terms should be distinguished. Let's take the two easiest cases first:

1) There are many dependencies between much of the physical world and our actions which, because there are no social connotations, do not engender confusion with respect to the terms *bribe* and *dependency*. For example, when we turn a door handle and push (response), the door opens (a positive consequence). This is a dependent relation but no one would use the term *bribe* here. The door is not bribing us by opening when we make the appropriate response. Because the door is inanimate there is no social aspect to this dependency. Without this social aspect, there can be no bribery since the only one who profits from the dependency is the person making the response.

2) When a lobbyist offers money or some special favor in order to induce a politician to vote in support of the lobbyist's position, the lobbyist is offering a bribe. *Webster's New International Dictionary* (2nd ed.) defines a bribe as "A price, reward, gift, or favor bestowed or promised with a view to *pervert* the judgment or *corrupt*

the conduct of a person in a position of trust, as an official or voter" (p. 333; italics added). The lobbyist is stating a dependency between the politician's actions and the consequence (money or favor) and this type of dependency we will label a bribe. The behavior in question is illegal, immoral, or unethical and the word *bribe* is appropriate here. There is no disagreement between everyday usage and professional usage.

3) The grey area and the one that causes the most problems involves unusual reinforcers, large amounts of reinforcement, or behavior that is typically not deliberately reinforced in our culture. For example, there is a program in one of the midwestern states which pays inner-city children for going to school and doing their lessons. Many people, when they learn of such a program, say that the practice is no different than bribery and should not be condoned. They argue that children should not be paid for doing something that most children in our culture do without pay. It does not matter that these ghetto children are not learning anything under the present system or that they might get in trouble if they were not in school; going to school as a child is prescribed by law. Our culture expects children to go to school and learn for learning's sake. Therefore, many people believe it is wrong to pay children to go to school.

Cultural norms also dictate that certain reinforcers cannot be used in a dependent relation no matter how desirable the final behavior. Sex and drugs (with the exception of tobacco) are two examples of powerful positive reinforcers which are proscribed by society. "Girlie" magazines make very effective reinforcers for teenage boys in institutions but programs which permit such magazines as reinforcers in their programs get into trouble when visitors or representatives from outside agencies come by. The observer thinks it wrong to use sexual material in such a deliberate way. Hence, they call such reinforcers *bribes* because our culture forbids using these stimuli as consequences.

Finally, if we give more payment than is customary for some behavior, the word *bribe* is likely to be used. In teaching retarded children effective job skills, we occasionally have to give large amounts of reinforcement for some small, but necessary, component of the task the person is being trained to do. For instance, a teenage retarded boy might be training to operate a drill press and he may be having trouble learning the chain of responses necessary to begin the work correctly. Some steps in this chain are to: 1) select appropriate size drill; 2) insert drill bit into clamping jaws and center before tightening with wrench; 3) adjust platform height so that drill will go through work to desired level; 4) center drill platform hole under work so that if drill goes completely through work, the drill will not go into the drilling platform; 5) clamp work securely. Such a perliminary chain would be learned in a few hours of instruction by a person of average intelligence, but for a retarded person, classified as "trainable," the acquisition of such a chain would be time-consuming and difficult. Thus, in order to encourage the boy to persist, we might pay him most of the tokens he earns for the day just for learning parts of the overall chain. An observer, viewing this training program and comparing it to one in which another boy takes a whole day to earn an equal number of tokens, might conclude that the boy learning to run the drill press was overpaid, and the temptation to use the word *bribe* would be strong.

Some Further Considerations on Atypical Dependencies

We would like to restrict the meaning and usage of the word *bribe* to that described in the second instance above. There may be both advantages and disadvantages to programs which overpay, use proscribed reinforcers, or use reinforcers other than the customary ones for a given behavior. We think it important that any program be evaluated by both its ends and its means. Simply because a dependency violates our expectations is no reason to label it bribery and to close our eyes to the possible benefits of the program. The authors have personal knowledge of a case in which shock was used to punish a severely autistic child for her autistic behavior and in which the researchers were having considerable success in eliminating the undesirable behavior. On one occasion, an important visitor saw this child receiving shock for an autistic response and reacted in horror. No account of what the child was like before treatment or of the credentials or good intentions of the research team could persuade this person that the program was benefitting the child, so the program was terminated. This girl now lies in a state institution under restraints night and day, has lost weight, has numerous bruises, has pulled most of her hair out again (it had regrown during treatment), and faces a custodial routine where the only sure contact with another human will be when she is fed and when her sheets and clothes are changed. In short, she has returned to her original state. Which course of conduct do you think was more ethical?

Although the concept of bribery was not at issue in this example, the broader issue of using a consequence (shock) in a way that violates our culture's norms is; that is, "one does not punish a sick person." Behavior is controlled by its consequences and there are occasions when the most effective and fastest means of changing behavior involve the use of a consequence or a dependency which goes against our society's norms.

When such an instance occurs, it is all too easy to label the practice with a pejorative term like *bribery* and to attempt to forbid such practices. It is much better, we believe, to examine the means in the context of the possible benefits to the person who is the recipient of the treatment program.

Admittedly, there will be difficult cases which present no clear answer to the question of whether a treatment program should be undertaken. Should a new and relatively untried but promising treatment program be undertaken with a person who has a "minor" problem such as a facial tic? If the program involves the use of an aversive stimulus such as shock, we run the risk of alienating the person if the treatment fails. Even if the program is faster, less expensive, and more permanent, the severity of the treatment may make the client less likely to come for help in the future. In this example, we would argue that an alternative program using rewards, even if slower, would be more ethical. Other professional psychologists might disagree with this conclusion, but at least the judgment of which program to use would be examined on the merits of

that individual's case. We believe this is a more desirable practice than to come to our client with a priori notions about a plan of treatment.

Schedules

Experimental psychologists study dependencies under controlled conditions so that they can determine the long-term effects of a single dependency. This kind of investigation cannot be done as easily in real-life situations because each one of us is exposed to a variety of contingencies and dependencies each day, and these conditions change frequently. When the psychologist designs an experimental environment, he may arrange it so that the animal must make 100 responses in order to receive one small pellet of food. Such an experimentally established dependency is called a **SCHEDULE**. The schedule of 100 responses mentioned above is technically called a **FIXED-RATIO** 100 schedule of positive reinforcement. As you might guess, there are also schedules of punishment. If a rat received a shock every 10th time he pressed a lever, he would be operating under a **FIXED-RATIO** 10 schedule of punishment. A more detailed discussion of schedules is presented later in Units 10 and 11.

More Complex Dependency Relations

Behavior usually occurs in situations where more than one dependency is in effect, and psychologists frequently examine schedules that contain several dependencies which are ordered in some way. For example, the behavior of a pigeon might be examined in an experiment that required him to peck the left response key 20 times if a red light were on and to peck the right key 20 times if a green light were on. A complete description of the schedule is rather long, but part of it would go something like this: *If* the red light is on and *if* the pigeon pecks the left key 20 times, *then* he will receive food (a food-deprived pigeon is typically given several seconds access to grain as a consequence). When "green" and "right" key are included in the statement above, we would have a more complete description of the dependencies under which the bird is working.

In thinking about the example just described, you might wonder what happens when the bird makes a mistake; that is, he pecks the right key in the red light or vice versa. To eliminate mistakes, the experimenter might insert another set of dependencies such that when the bird made an error, all the lights in the cage were turned out for 10 seconds and when the lights were out, no food was given.

So you can see that even "simple" experiments can have a number of dependencies controlling the animal's behavior. If the experimenter has so many dependencies in operation and takes so much trouble in making them consistent in order to understand a pigeon's behavior, you can imagine how much more difficult it might be to understand a human's behavior in everyday situations where a great many dependencies are in operation. To get some feeling for the problems of trying to examine human behavior in a natural situation, you might try listing the dependencies that governed your behavior today.

Illustration

C. K. Rovee and D. T. Rovee, Conjugate reinforcement of infant exploratory behavior. *Journal of Experimental Child Psychology*, 1969, 8, 33-39.

Rovee and Rovee were interested in the exploratory behavior of human infants, specifically, to see how susceptible newborns are to the learning of an operant response. This study is particularly suitable to our purposes because it demonstrates the difference in effects between a dependency and the mere presentation of a reinforcing stimulus.

The researchers used 18 healthy, normal infants ranging in age from 9 to 12 weeks, and tested them during the infants' normal high-activity time. A brightly colored mobile with several wooden figures was suspended directly above each infant's head. A soft, silk cord was tied to the baby's left ankle and connected to the mobile so that when the baby moved its leg or ankle, the mobile moved and the wooden figures jangled. Large and fast leg movements made the mobile jump and clank, so that a greater magnitude of responding produced more visual and auditory stimulation than smaller movements did.

Both the experimental and control groups were first observed for a 3 minute baseline period during which the **OPERANT LEVEL** was determined. The operant level is the rate of a response prior to any manipulation and is useful in determining if the experimental variable has any effect; that is, does the treatment increase (or decrease) the rate of responding over that found in the operant level? If it does, we can conclude that the variable of interest had an effect.

After a 2-minute break, a 15-minute acquisition period was begun. For the experimental group, any movement of the left leg or ankle caused the mobile to move. For the control group, the experimenter moved the mobile while the cord was attached to the baby's ankle. This group, then, received visual and auditory feedback (movements of mobile) as well as somesthetic feedback (the leg was pulled by the cord when the experimenter pulled the mobile), but the infants had no opportunity to move the mobile by themselves. There was another control group which received visual feedback only, but the results obtained with this group did not differ from the other control group so there is no need to mention it further.

The findings were that the experimental group increased its rate of leg movements by three times over its operant level, while the control group responded at the same rate as it did during its baseline period. After this acquisition phase and following a 2-minute break, a 5-minute extinction period was initiated. The mobile was present for the baby to see but the cord was not attached, so leg movements did not produce movements of the mobile. The rate of leg movements for the experimental group declined to its operant level and to the rate at which the control group was responding.

These results are presented in Table 5-1. Plot them allowing 2 squares for 1 response on the vertical axis and 2 squares for 1 minute on the horizontal axis. Use different codes for the experimental and control groups and show the 2-minute breaks between conditions.

Table 5-1

Mean response rates for two groups of six infants, 9-12 weeks old. During the acquisition phase, each of the experimental infants had a silk cord tied from the ankle to a mobile. Movements of the infant's left foot made the mobile move. In the control group, the experimenters moved the mobile during the acquisition period. Data estimated from Rovee, C. K., & Rovee, D. T. Conjugate reinforcement of infant exploratory behavior. *Journal of Experimental Child Psychology*, 1969, 8, 33-39.

Minutes	Experimental Group (N=6)	Control Group (N=6)	Condition
1	9.0	5.5	
2	9.0	7.0	Operant Level
3	9.0	8.0	
4	—	—	Pause
5	—	—	
6	13.0	9.0	
7	11.5	5.0	
8	17.0	3.5	
9	21.5	7.0	
10	24.5	6.0	*Acquisition Phase*
11	28.5	5.5	
12	23.0	6.0	*Experimental:* Infant's
13	25.0	7.0	left foot caused mobile
14	26.5	6.5	to move
15	23.5	6.0	
16	19.0	8.0	*Control:* Experimenters
17	20.0	6.0	moved the mobile
18	24.5	6.5	
19	25.0	5.0	
20	27.0	5.0	
21	—	—	Pause
22	—	—	
23	16.0	8.0	
24	17.5	6.5	
25	14.0	7.0	Extinction
26	13.0	5.0	
27	6.5	6.5	

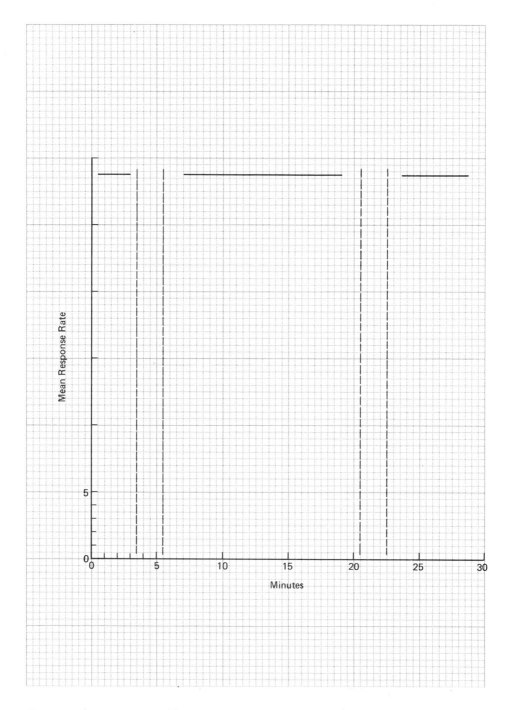

Figure 5-1 Mean rates of leg movements for two groups of infants. In the
experimental group, each of the infants moved a mobile by moving his left leg. In
the control group, the experimenters moved the mobiles for the infants.

*

Exam

1. Define the following terms:
   a. operant behavior
   b. dependency
   c. contingency
   d. schedule
   e. superstitious behavior
   f. operant level
2. Under what conditions is superstitious behavior likely to develop?
3. Give three examples of dependency relations in your everyday activities. Put them into "if — then" statements.
4. What are three conditions under which the layman is likely to use the term *bribe* inappropriately?
5. What are the differences and similarities between bribery and dependency?
6. How would you answer a person who stated, "It is no use trying to reinforce that retarded child. He won't understand what you are trying to do." (Hint: Review automatic nature of a stimulus consequence.)
7. In the Rovee and Rovee experiment, how long would you say it took the infants to learn to move their feet consistently? Use your graph to make a decision and try to defend your criterion for learning.

References

Malinowski, B. *Magic, science, and religion.* New York: Doubleday, 1948.

Reynolds, G. S. *A primer of operant conditioning.* Glenview, Illinois: Scott, Foresman, 1968.

Rovee, C. K., & Rovee, D. T. Conjugate reinforcement of infant exploratory behavior. *Journal of Experimental Child Psychology,* 1969, 8, *33-39.*

*

Operant Conditioning

6

Operants

The term **OPERANT** was coined from the word *operate* and refers to any behavior that operates upon the enviornment. Walking, running, speaking, and drumming one's fingers on the table are all examples of operants. These behaviors can change the external environment. Turning on a switch provides a room with light; making a request of another typically brings about compliance with the request; and so forth. In these examples the behavior controls the environment: Turning on a switch produces light.

However, the control works both ways. Our behavior changes as a consequence of the environmental change we produce. Much of our adult behavior has been shaped by the environment into efficient units which deal very effectively with the environment, so that the circular relation between behavior and its consequences is not always obvious. Opening a door to get outside or opening a jar to get at its contents does not alter the form of your response. It is well-practiced and is under the control of antecedent conditions; that is, it is time to take your medicine so you go to the cabinet, open the bottle, and take a pill. For a young child, however, the opening of a jar of jam strengthens the behavior that resulted in getting the jar open. He may have struggled, twisted, and pounded for some time before the lid yielded. On subsequent occasions, the time it takes for the lid to come off shortens, and the form of his behavior changes. His behavior becomes more efficient, with irrelevant behavior such as shaking the jar dropping out. In short, the requirements for getting the lid off actually shape the behavior that is effective in opening the jar.

Strengthening an Operant Already in the Repertoire

When we find it desirable to increase the frequency with which some operant occurs, we can reinforce that operant and record the change in rate as a function of our manipulation. Let's say that we are concerned about a preschool child who is excessively shy and rarely touches any of his peers in nursery school. We would like to increase the frequency of his touching others. The first step is to record this frequency. This rate will serve as our baseline, and it is called the **OPERANT LEVEL**, or the rate of a response prior to any manipulation. The next step is to present a potential reinforcer dependent upon him touching one of his peers. Praise from the teacher is a likely possibility for a reinforcer, so we try it. After several presentations of praise when the child responds appropriately, we examine the rate of touching. If the rate has increased, it suggests that praise was a positive reinforcer. A **POSITIVE REINFORCER** is any stimulus which, when presented dependent upon a response, increases the rate of that response. Notice that we were careful to say that we presented a *potential* reinforcer, since we cannot be sure that a social stimulus such as praise will be a reinforcer for this child. If he had a history of being punished by adults, praise probably would not produce an increment in his rate of touching.

In order to check on our procedure, a third step is usually employed. The dependency is broken. A reinforcer is

no longer given for the emission of the operant; that is, touching is ignored by the teacher. This is called placing the behavior on **EXTINCTION.** Another way to test whether our stimulus is a reinforcer is to present it for behavior incompatible with our first operant. **DIFFERENTIAL REINFORCE-MENT OF OTHER BEHAVIOR (DRO)** is a schedule which reinforces any behavior *but* the one specified. Thus, in our example, the child would receive praise as long as he did *not* touch another child for a given period of time, say 20 or 30 seconds. In either case, if praise were the only reinforcer involved, the rate of touching should decline to its former level.

In summary, for controlling an operant already in a person's repertoire, there is a three-step procedure: 1) Measure the operant level; 2) present a potential reinforcer; 3) break the dependency to make sure that the reinforcer actually controls the response in question (i.e., use extinction or DRO).

Not incidentally, breaking the dependency in the above ways constitutes an important "catch" condition necessary for proof that the reinforcer and not some other unknown event (e.g., the subject's health) controls the behavior in question. Note the use of this kind of "catch" condition in the illustrations and applications employed throughout this text.

Constructing an Operant Not in the Repertoire

Suppose that we are interested in getting a child to engage in a behavior that he has never emitted. As far as we can tell, the child has never exhibited the behavior, or the behavior may be too complex for him to emit on his own. If we were to wait for the behavior to occur, we might have a long wait. Consider a child who never touched anybody and never approached other children. We can deal with this problem by the procedure of shaping. **SHAPING** requires the experimenter to reinforce those instances of an operant that are approximations to the final response and to extinguish instances that are not. As the operants more closely resemble the final, desired response, the criteria for reinforcement and extinction progressively change.

In our example, the final response is touching other children. In order to touch, the child must be close to others. Therefore, the first step might be to place him in a room with another child. The floor could be marked off in grids so that we would have an estimate of how close he was to the other child while in the room. Suppose we find that he never approaches closer than 10 feet from where the other child is playing. Once we know this, we have a criterion for reinforcing a first approximation. Thus, we can say that whenever he is within 15 feet of the child, he is reinforced. Once he is receiving reinforcement consistently for this response, we can demand that he be a bit closer, say 12 feet.

Notice that we start our approximations at distances that the child is already attaining. This is very important for it insures that the child will receive reinforcement and it strengthens an existing class of behavior. A single instance of behavior is always reinforced, and a particular instance of reinforced behavior will differ from other reinforced instances in that it has a topography (form,

intensity, and duration) that is unique. However, it is similar to other instances because it forms a class of behavior which produces reinforcement. When a member of a response class is reinforced, there is always some "spillover" or spread-of-effect to other similar responses. This spillover is what permits us to shift the elements in the class gradually, and this in turn eventually allows us to obtain the final response. When the boy is reinforced for being within the region of 15 feet from the target child, the frequency of being 12, 10, and 8 feet away increases, too. Once the child is often in the 15-foot region, we can demand shorter distances because he sometimes *is* closer than 15 feet.

At this stage, we should point out to the student that we have described only half the shaping process. It is sometimes not so obvious that responses which are not approximations to the final response must be extinguished. Therefore, distances greater than 15 feet are never reinforced, and as we narrow the response class that is reinforced, we simultaneously broaden the response class that is extinguished. Initially, being 15 feet away from the target is reinforced. As the child is at this distance frequently, we can change our criterion by lowering the maximal reinforced distance to 12 feet or less and the distance being extinguished to more than 12 feet.

One of the effects of extinction is to produce variability in the behaviors emitted. In our example, this would mean that distances other than 15 feet away (the previously reinforced distance) would start occurring. Shorter distances, say 5 or 6 feet, which may never have occurred prior to shaping, now appear occasionally and are reinforced. As the subject's behavior shifts to closer distances, we continue to shift the boundaries of the reinforced and nonreinforced behavior closer to our final response.

So there are two processes at work in shaping: *Positive reinforcement*, which strengthens the class of responses that are approximations of the final response; and *extinction*, which weakens the class of responses that are remote from the final response. The procedure of gradually changing the boundaries of the reinforced and extinguished response classes toward the final response is also called **DIFFERENTIAL REINFORCE-MENT OF SUCCESSIVE APPROX-IMATIONS**, which is a more descriptive term than *shaping*, but the two terms have the same meaning.

Returning to our example, once the child is within touching range, the response of touching will have to be shaped. Approximations could include: following the target child with the eyes; reaching movements in the direction of the target child; and finally, a brief touch. Eventually, if we were interested in generating a "warm" friendship between these two children, we would extend our shaping program to include cooperative play and sharing.

Measuring Operant Behavior

The most commonly used measure of operant behavior is its rate of occurrence. If a girl swears 100 times in a 10-hour period, her rate of swearing is 10 per hour. Rate is a convenient measure because it provides an index of change over time that can be easily followed when we introduce a manipulation. Thus, if the subject were using a punishing stimulus to reduce the frequent swearing in the example above, she could follow the changes in rate and make decisions about when to increase or decrease the severity of punishment. Thus, she might see a drop to 8 per hour when she self-administered a 60-volt shock for each curse. She might then observe no further reduction in the rate for several days, at which point she could decide to increase the shock intensity. Without the continuous recording of the rate in a free-operant situation, she would have little indication of the waning effectiveness of the 60-volt shock.

In addition to being a convenient dependent variable, rate can vary over a wide range of values from zero to several responses a second. This means that rate can provide a broad scale upon which to measure the effects of our independent variables. A host of independent variables have been shown to be functionally related to rate: Immediacy of reinforcement, magnitude of reinforcement, schedule of reinforcement, and density of reinforcement (the number of reinforcers delivered per unit of time) are just a few of the variables which have been systematically related to rate.

In conclusion, the rate of responding is a reliable, easy-to-use measure applicable in a wide range of situations from relatively uncontrolled field settings to highly controlled laboratory environments where the behavior of the organism is free to vary. An example of the former would be the girl in the case above who is keeping track of her rate of swearing so that she knows when her program is working. An example of the latter would be a pigeon responding in a choice situation where the rate of pecking on each of two keys is continually monitored.

Rate is not an appropriate measure for respondent behavior because such behavior is controlled by the presentation of the eliciting stimulus. Thus, if the UCS is only presented two times a day, the UCR can only occur twice a day.

Illustration

R. M. Herrick, The successive differentiation of a lever displacement response. *Journal of the Experimental Analysis of Behavior*, 1964, 7, 211-215.

This experiment illustrates how characteristics of a response are shaped through selective reinforcement. The operant in this case was a lever-press response. Herrick defined 8 reinforcement zones (each 5° in width), and the criterion for reinforcement was whether the lever was displaced from the horizontal into the appropriate zone. In the first condition, if the lever was displaced from the "home" position anywhere from 3° to 44° (a loose and easily reached criterion), the rat received a reinforcer. In the final condition, the rat had to displace the lever into a narrow band, between 24° and 29°, to receive reinforcement.

The data in Table 6-1 are taken from one of his subjects and show the percent of responses falling into each of the 8 zones when the criterion for reinforcement was gradually shifted to fewer zones. For 2 days the rats were reinforced for all responses falling into any of the zones (1-8); the next 2 days only zones 2-8 were reinforced; then zones 2-7, and so on. Eventually, only lever presses falling into Zone 5 were reinforced. Extended training (20 days)

was given at Zone 5, and the last column in the table shows the distribution of responses over all lever positions for the last 5 days.

We have plotted the data for the first distribution of responses, lever positions 1 through 8, in Figure 6-1. Plot the remaining seven distributions, making sure to label each histogram.[1] Figure 6-1 is laid out so that the successive histograms are directly under one another, which required that we plot the first four on one piece of graph paper and the second four on another graph. With the histograms stacked like this, it should be easy for you to see what happens to the distribution of responses as the reinforced zone grows smaller. Note that Figure 6-1 starts with the widest reinforced zone, lever positions 1-8, and ends with the narrowest reinforced zone, lever position 5. Shade the zones in each histogram that were reinforced.

[1]The height of the bar in a histogram, or bar graph, depicts the frequency of an event. Histograms, rather than line graphs, are best used for data which occur in separate categories, such as "Men and Women," "Dogs and Cats," or "Republicans, Democrats, and Independents." A line graph, on the other hand, is based on the sampling of a genuine continuum, such as temperature, time, or the rate of responding. Thus, in a line graph, the data points define a curve relating the independent variable to the dependent variable in such a way that any point on the abscissa has a corresponding point on the ordinate. Such a relation does *not* exist for graphs involving discrete categories; one cannot infer anything about the unsampled values of the independent variable therein.

An example may help. If we were interested in the relation between the deprivation level for food (independent variable) and the rate of responding (dependent variable), we could examine the subject's rate when he was responding under 12,

Table 6-1

The percent of responses made to each of eight positions as a function of the size of the reinforcement zone. Data taken from Herrick, R. M. The successive differentiation of a lever displacement response. *Journal of the Experimental Analysis of Behavior*, **1964, 7, 211-215.**

	Reinforcement Zones							
Lever Positions	1-8	2-8	2-7	3-7	3-6	4-6	4-5	5
1	2	2	4	1	3	1	1	0
2	4	1	14	5	6	2	3	0
3	3	5	19	17	23	7	11	2
4	7	8	25	38	42	33	47	18
5	10	18	16	20	15	43	30	71
6	20	28	11	10	7	10	5	8
7	22	24	8	3	2	2	1	0
8	32	22	0	3	2	2	2	0

Application

W. Isaacs, J. Thomas, and I. Goldiamond, Application of operant conditioning to reinstate verbal behavior in psychotics. *Journal of Speech and Hearing Disorders*, 1960, 25, 8-12.

These authors worked with two mute schizophrenics and, through shaping, were able to get them to speak, at least to some degree, within a relatively short time. We will examine the process for one of the patients who at the time of the study was 40 years old and had been mute for 19 years — ever since he had been hospitalized. He was placed in a group therapy program along with some other patients who were not mute. In the therapy group these other patients attempted to engage him in conversation and offered him cigarettes, but he was unresponsive to these overtures.

Now it happened on one occasion that

24, 36, 48, and 60 hours of deprivation. If the data for this subject were consistent, we would be justified in connecting the data points and making an inference about an unmeasured value, say 18 hours of deprivation, because we would be sampling a continuous variable (deprivational level). In contrast, assume we are interested in the percentage of voters of different political persuasions who voted for a given candidate. Suppose we have determined that 68 percent of the Republicans and 34 percent of the Democrats voted for the candidate. We would not be justified in connecting the two points by a line because there is no underlying continuum that we are measuring. What, for example, would be the percentage of "Independents" who voted for the candidate? The data provided by this graph do not help us because there is no logical basis for placing the category, "Independents" between "Republicans" and "Democrats."

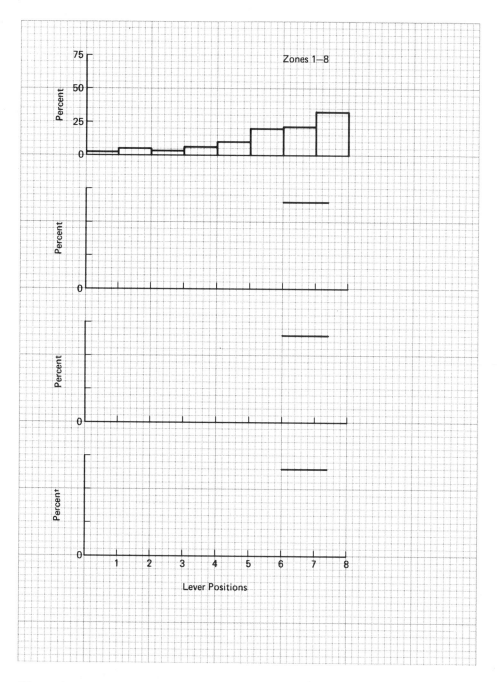

Figure 6-1 The percent of responses made to each of 8 lever positions by 1 rat. In the first panel, responses made to any of the 8 positions received reinforcement. In the following panels, the zones reinforced were made gradually narrower until, in the last panel, only responses in Zone 5 were reinforced. The shaded bars in each histogram indicate the zones which were reinforced.

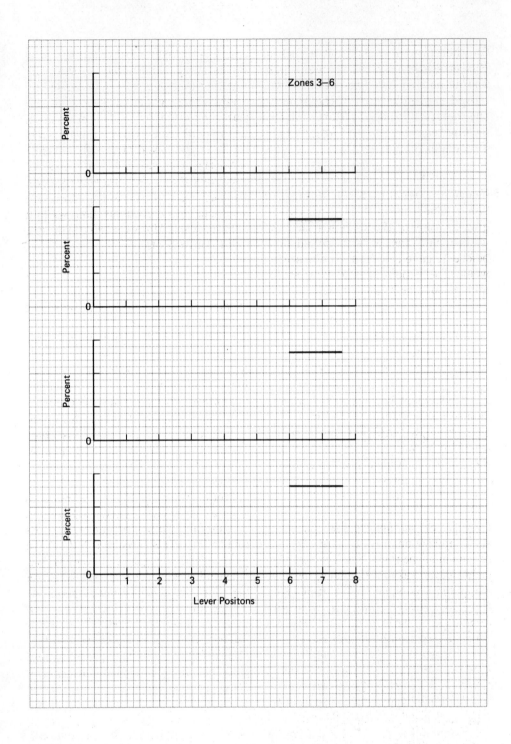

Figure 6-1 *(Continued)*

the therapist, in pulling out a pack of cigarettes, dropped a package of gum and he noticed that the patient's eyes moved in the direction of the gum. So the therapist decided to start with this looking response, suspecting gum to be a potential reinforcer.

Phase 1: Strengthening looking at gum. The therapist held a piece of gum in front of the patient's face and waited until the patient looked at it before he gave it to him. By the second week, the patient was looking at the gum as soon as it was shown.

Phase 2: Strengthening lip movements. The therapist held the gum and waited until the patient moved his lips, no matter how slight. In the third week a lip movement occurred, and this response was reinforced. Within a short time both lip and eye movements occurred when the gum was shown. Note that simply looking at the gum was no longer reinforced.

Phase 3: Strengthening sounds. Now, since lip movements (a necessary response in speech) were occurring regularly, it was easier to demand another component of speech — sound. Any sound, no matter how faint, was reinforced, and soon the patient was making a sound something like a croak.

Phase 4: Production of a word. The therapist held the gum and said, "Say gum." He asked the patient to say these words every time he showed the gum. The therapist gave the gum dependent upon sounds which were closer and closer to the word *gum*. On one occasion the patient said, "Gum, please" when the therapist asked him to say, "Gum." After this, the patient began to answer questions about his name and age. He also began to respond to the therapist's questions in the group sessions as well as in the ward. However, he still did not talk to anyone else.

Phase 5: Generalization to others. The patient was now speaking, but he had formed a discrimination in talking only to the therapist. His speech obviously was still not completely adaptive. So a nurse was brought in and, in the presence of the therapist, she asked the patient questions. Within a month or so, he was answering her questions, also. Speaking was still under the control of too few people, though. For instance, on one occasion the patient made a nonverbal request by bringing one of the aides his coat and waiting until she took him outside for a walk. Thereafter, she was told to follow his directions *only* when he vocalized his requests, and from then on he did vocalize his requests to her. In fact, he now initiated verbal requests whenever his nonverbal antics produced no consequence. However, other patients and visitors continued to "interpret" his nonverbal requests and thus continued to reinforce him for not speaking. At this point, the program was terminated.

Exam

1. Define the following terms:
   a. operant
   b. DRO
   c. shaping
   d. rate
   e. differential reinforcement of successive approximations

2. What are two reasons for using rate of responding as a dependent variable? Is rate an appropriate measure for respondent behavior? Explain.

3. Describe the procedure you would use to determine if your praise was a positive reinforcer for the response of smiling in a 1-year-old child. What are two "catch" conditions, either of which should be used in demonstrating that a stimulus is a reinforcer?

4. Describe some of the approximations you would reinforce to get your pet dog to push open a stiff door.

5. In the Herrick experiment, what happened as the reinforcement zone was made smaller and smaller?

6. What two procedures are at work in the shaping process in the Herrick experiment? (Hint: One procedure strengthens some behavior and the other weakens some behavior.)

7. Summarize the Isaacs et al. experiment. Was the treatment completely successful? Explain.

8. What sets of data (use your own examples) are appropriate only for a histogram? Why?

References

Herrick, R. M.   The successive differentiation of a lever displacement response. *Journal of the Experimental Analysis of Behavior*, 1964, **7**, 211-215.

Isaacs, W., Thomas, J., & Goldiamond, I.   Application of operant conditioning to reinstate verbal behavior in psychotics. *Journal of Speech and Hearing Disorders*, 1960, **25**, 8-12.

Extinction

7

After a response has been conditioned, it can be "de-conditioned" by simply no longer reinforcing it. In operant conditioning, the dependency between the response and the reinforcer is broken, and in respondent conditioning, the UCS is no longer presented along with the CS. In this unit, the procedure and process of operant extinction will be emphasized because many of you will need to understand operant extinction in order to modify your own behavior.

Extinction of an Operant

When a reinforcer is no longer presented for a conditioned response, the strength of the response decreases and, eventually, returns to its operant level. This procedure is called **EXTINCTION** and the response is said to be extinguished when it reaches its operant level. Obviously, one way of getting rid of undesirable behavior is to place that behavior on extinction, and thus the procedure of extinction is used, in combination with other procedures, for many problem behaviors.

But extinction has other effects. One of the first things that an observer will notice is that the organism's behavior becomes more variable when placed on extinction. Instead of the smooth bar-press response that occurred while reinforcement was in effect, the rat may press and hold the bar or he may press with his nonpreferred paw. The force with which the rat presses the bar may also increase. You may have noted your behavior when trying to remove a stubborn bottle cap. You first try your preferred hand and twist with a certain degree of force. If that doesn't work, you may twist harder, use your other hand, place the bottle between your knees for a better hold, and so on. All these responses on your part are not irrelevant; in the past, you have found that twisting harder has been occasionally reinforced. You may have also encountered one of the new caps that some drug companies are putting on pill bottles. You probably struggled with it for some time before discovering that you must first press and then twist. Thus, you can see why a variable topography in extinction may have been reinforced in the organism's past.

Now, if you struggled with that pill cap very long, you may have found yourself getting angry at those "stupid manufacturers." Aggression is another effect of extinction. The rat bites the lever, the pigeon flaps his wings, and humans curse. Anyone who has watched another supposedly intelligent person fume and rage at a vending machine which has just failed to deliver its promised item will testify to the phenomenon of extinction-produced aggression. The punching and kicking of these machines is probably as much a function of the extinction-produced aggression as it is a function of the occasional reinforcement that results from a successful kick.

In summary, extinction leads initially to an increase in the variability of the response — its form and intensity change; aggression frequently accompanies extinction, especially in the first exposure to extinction; and the rate of responding gradually declines until it reaches some arbitrary criterion such as the operant rate of the response.

Resistance to Extinction

One way the strength of behavior can be measured is by its **RESISTANCE TO EXTINCTION.** When psychologists talk about how strong a behavior is, they are generally referring to the persistence of the response. There are two questions that we can ask: 1) How much *time* occurs before the rate of responding returns to its operant level? or 2) How many *responses* are made before the behavior is no longer emitted or returns to its operant level? Both these measures are useful. For example, extinction after a history of exposure to some interval (timed-based) schedules of reinforcement takes quite a while. The organism may not make many responses, but he continues to make at least some for a long time. Extinction after ratio (number-based) schedules of reinforcement can produce many responses. However, the time it takes the rate to reach the operant level may be shorter for ratio than for interval schedules. To answer the question of which schedule produces the greatest resistance to extinction one must specify how resistance to extinction is being measured.

A word of caution is in order here. It is sometimes confusing to refer to the "strength" of a response without specifying the context within which one is measuring that response. Thus, "strength" may be measured in a choice situation (two responses possible) by comparing how frequently an organism emits each of the responses. Strength may also be measured by recording the time or number of responses occurring in extinction before the response returns to its operant level.

To illustrate the point that different measures may lead to different conclusions about the strength of a response, let us consider a choice situation as our first example. Suppose you could play a game in which Button A pays you 10¢ for every press while Button B pays you only 1¢ for every 10 presses. Every rational person would opt to play Button A, and an observer would conclude that responding on Button A was of "greater strength" than Button B.

Now let's consider a situation where the individual is not given a choice and let's measure his "response strength" by noting his behavior in extinction. We allow him to press Button A 100 times and he earns $10.00 for his effort. We then place his button pressing on extinction and count how many responses he makes (or how much time elapses before his rate returns to the operant rate). Let us say that he makes x number of responses in extinction.

Now that we have this information, let's place our subject in the less favorable situation — Button B, where he earns 1¢ for every 10 presses — and allow him to receive the same number of payoffs as on Button A. These 100 reinforcers total $1.00, and he must make 1,000 responses to earn the dollar. When his responses in extinction (on B) are counted, we will find that he makes more here than he did on Button A during extinction. Typically, as many as two or three times more responses will be made on Button B than on Button A.[1]

[1]One of the most consistent findings about schedules of intermittent reinforcement is that they generate more behavior in extinction than do schedules of continuous reinforcement.

Our observer now concludes that the response strength of Button B is much greater than Button A.

Thus, when the resistance to extinction in these separate situations is compared, we find that the intermittent schedule of reinforcement (10 responses required for 1¢) produces the greatest resistance to extinction, and the inference is that the greater response strength was shown on Button B. However, when these two responses are examined in a choice situation, the preference for Button A suggests *it* has the greater response strength. The point of all this is to indicate to you that when you refer to a "strong" response you need to say *how* you assessed this strength, because different measures of response strength may not agree.

Spontaneous Recovery

SPONTANEOUS RECOVERY is the increment in the rate of a conditioned response after a brief recess from the procedure of extinction. The period of time (recess) that the organism is removed need not be long for some recovery to show. A 15-minute removal from the environment will produce the effect, and the amount of recovery increases up to a maximum at about 3 hours. The reasons for spontaneous recovery are not yet well understood but the phenomenon occurs reliably.

It is important for you to be aware of spontaneous recovery because it can cause trouble if you plan to eliminate one of your bad habits with the procedure of extinction. For example, you might be trying to stop smoking and have succeeded for a period of 2 weeks. You might then go on vacation and when you returned to your daily routine, you probably experienced a strong urge to smoke. You might even have found yourself smoking again without realizing it. If you know that any conditioned response will show spontaneous recovery, you can prepare yourself and not be discouraged by the apparent lack of progress you are making. Each time the response undergoes re-exposure to the extinction procedure, the amount of recovery diminishes. For all practical purposes, after two or three periods of spontaneous recovery, the conditioned response will be completely extinguished.

Is Extinction Permanent?

After hearing about spontaneous recovery, students sometimes get the impression that the elimination of a response by extinction is not permanent and that extinction is not as effective as other techniques of changing behavior. This is not true. The question of the permanence of extinction usually arises in the context of the elimination of a strong habit such as smoking. The observer looks at a two-pack-a-day smoker who announces his intention to quit, quits for a week or two, and then resumes smoking — a typical pattern. This pattern confirms the observer's suspicions about the temporary results to be expected with the procedure of extinction. This suspicion seems to hold even when a smoker quits for a year or longer. However, all techniques of modifying behavior are impermanent if the conditions maintaining the behavior in question change. It is always the *current* dependencies interacting with the organism's history which are responsible for the behavior we see.

Smoking: A Habit Controlled by Many Situations

To illustrate how one's history can make it difficult to eliminate a strong habit, let's pursue the smoker and his addiction for a moment. One reason why smoking is such a difficult habit to eliminate is that it is paired with so many other reinforcing activities. The true addict smokes about 40 cigarettes a waking day. This means that he or she smokes after eating; with a cup of coffee; when taking a work break; when meeting and talking to a friend; when visiting over the phone; while reading; while watching TV; while having a B.M.; when "anxious," and so on, ad nauseam. There is hardly any human activity that a confirmed smoker has not smoked before, during, or after! Hence, smoking is part of a chain of behavior that is linked to many non-smoking activities that are reinforcing. Smoking has to be extinguished in the presence of all of the stimuli that serve as "elicitors" (see Unit 13) of smoking, and this is why the urge to smoke seems continual to the heavy smoker. It is also why smoking is a tricky behavior to extinguish. A smoker may have gone for 3 days without a desire to smoke, and then, just after eating an apple, an almost overwhelming urge to smoke may be experienced right "out of the blue." This is extremely disheartening to the smoker who is trying to quit because it appears to him or her that the desire for a smoke will never subside. It also engenders feelings of failure and incompetence because the individual sees himself as lacking in ordinary "will power," whatever that is.

The reason for experiencing the urge to smoke after eating the apple was that this was probably the first opportunity.

for the person not-to-smoke (for the response to undergo extinction) after eating an apple. The smoker must weaken the ties between eating-an-apple and smoking, as well as the ties between other activities and smoking. Of course, there are some weakening effects due to the **GENERALIZATION OF EXTINCTION**. Extinction of a response in one situation weakens the tendency to make that response in similar situations. Like the generalization arising from positive reinforcement, the amount of the effect is related to the similarity between stimulus situations. Extinction of smoking while watching TV also weakens the urge to smoke while reading (similar activities). The urge to smoke after a swim may be almost unaffected, however, by the extinction of smoking while watching TV (dissimilar activities).

Illustration

Table 7-1 shows the extinction of the urge to smoke for one of the authors (RBP) and his wife (E), and provides the reader with some idea of the frequency of the smoking urge and how long an urge can be expected to "live" by a smoker. This couple decided to try to quit smoking at the same time, and as a technique to help them assess how they were doing, they recorded every urge or thought about smoking, cigarettes, pipes, and tobacco during waking hours. Each had a hand counter which was carried throughout the day, and every time an urge or smoking thought was experienced, the person punched the counter. Before retiring each evening, the couple recorded the daily total on a large graph which was displayed in a prominent place in their home.

Plot the data on Table 7-1 in Figure 7-1 in a cumulative graph using a different code for each person. The first two data points are provided for you in the column labelled "Cumulative Count" for E's results. Continue adding the daily count to the cumulative count and use these cumulative counts as your data points. The total number of urges experienced is provided at the bottom of the table for both persons as a means for you to check your addition.

Although the urge to smoke was strong in both persons initially, almost complete extinction of the urge occurred within 25 days. It should be added, however, that both experienced sudden, albeit short-lived, desires to smoke at least a year after they had stopped counting urges. A particularly strong urge was experienced when they were preparing to take a trip and were packing luggage in their car. Both felt uncomfortable and experienced a strong sensation that something was missing. After a while one of them guessed that neither had packed the usual quota of cigarettes and pipe tobacco, and this omission was responsible for their uneasiness. This was the first trip the couple had taken since they quit smoking, and the incident illustrates the specificity of stimulus control that can develop in the case of a long-standing habit.

Application

M. Wolf, J. Birnbrauer, J. Lawler, and T. Williams, The operant extinction, reinstatement, and re-extinction of vomiting behavior in a retarded child. In R. Ulrich, T. Stachnik, and J. Mabry (Eds.), *Control of human behavior*, Vol. II. Glenview, Ill.: Scott, Foresman, 1970, pp. 146-149.

Table 7-1

Extinction of the urge to smoke for a husband and wife. Each time an urge to smoke or a smoking thought occurred, the person recorded it on a hand counter.

"Urges" to Smoke

Days	E	Cumulative Count	R	Cumulative Count
1	150*	150	383*	
2	472	622	299	
3	435		301	
4	267		199	
5	181		147	
6	77		75	
7	91		76	
8	35		66	
9	64		41	
10	21		35	
11	34		46	
12	30		22	
13	10		23	
14	11		11	
15	8		12	
16	5		7	
17	3		1	
18	5		0	
19	2		8	
20	2		1	
21	0		2	
22	0		0	
23	0		0	
24	0		0	
25	0		0	
		1903		1755

*Data are for only part of Day 1.

Laura was a 9-year-old mentally retarded girl who had a history of vomiting. She vomited often when she was first admitted to the institution, but shortly thereafter her vomiting became infrequent. She was then enrolled in a trainable class in her institution, and within a short period of time she started vomiting in class almost every day. Along with vomiting, which as you can

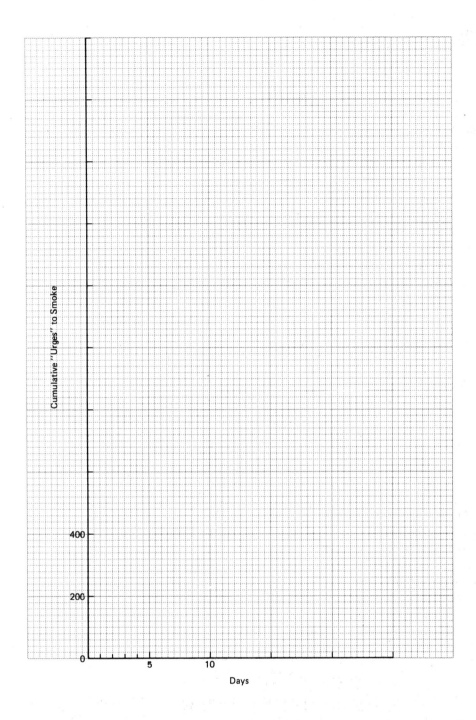

Figure 7-1 Extinction of the urge to smoke for a couple during the first 25 days after they had decided to stop smoking.

*

imagine was disturbing to the teacher, Laura screamed, tore her clothes, and destroyed property. Now it may seem to you that vomiting is respondent behavior, but in Laura's case, the close association of other operants which were unpleasant to the teacher, that is, temper tantrums, suggested that the vomiting was an operant. At least, this is the assumption that the authors made in treating her. It should be remarked that she was given an examination by the staff physician and he concluded that the vomiting was not due to any medical problem.

But if the vomiting was an operant and was increasing in frequency, what could have been the reinforcer that was strengthening it? It turned out that every time Laura vomited and threw a tantrum, the teacher returned her to her dormitory room. There were several possible candidates for reinforcers. The teacher's attention could have been a positive reinforcer which Laura obtained by misbehaving; or the classroom environment could have been aversive, in which case she was escaping from that situation.

The authors decided to remove the dependency between vomiting and Laura's being returned to her dorm. There were three conditions to their study. First, they placed her on extinction; that is, she was not returned to her dorm when she vomited. In the next condition, as soon as she vomited she was immediately returned to her dorm. Finally, she was placed back on extinction again. (You will recall that this is a standard procedure for identifying a reinforcer.) Even though the vomiting behavior declined in the first extinction period, we have no way of really knowing what reinforcer was maintaining Laura's behavior. If the behavior recovered when she was again returned to her dorm, then we have a better idea of what the reinforcer was. A re-extinction period that is successful pinpoints the reinforcer: We demonstrate that we can control the behavior at will, and, therefore, we know exactly what the controlling conditions were in the situation. We are now in a position to recommend changes in the environment which will prevent the misbehavior from re-occurring.

The data in Table 7-2 are from the three conditions the authors used in studying Laura's vomiting. **Plot only the first and second extinction periods on Figure 7-2, and indicate by a break in the graph the beginning of the second extinction period. Be sure to label both extinction conditions.**

Table 7-2

Number of vomiting episodes for a retarded girl in three conditions.
Data adapted from Wolf, M., Birnbrauer, J., Lawler, J., & Williams,
T. The operant extinction, reinstatement, and re-extinction of
vomiting behavior in a retarded child. In R. Ulrich, T. Stachnik, &
J. Mabry (Eds.), *Control of human behavior*, Vol. II. Glenview, Ill.:
Scott, Foresman, 1970. Pp. 146-149.

	1st Extinction	Reinforcement	2nd Extinction
1	0	0	1
2	5	1	1
3	1	1	0
4	21	0	0
5	6	1	1
6	0	0	1
7	0	0	1
8	11	0	0
9	10	1	21
10	1	1	0
11	0	1	0
12	0	0	25
13	5	0	18
14	0	1	2
15	0	0	29
16	0	1	25
17	0	0	2
18	0	0	1
19	0	0	1
20	8	0	0
21	0	0	1
22	0	1	0
23	3	0	14
24	1	1	3
25	0	0	0
26	0	1	0
27	0	1	0
28	6	0	1
29	0	0	0
30	0	1	0
31	0		
32	0		
33	0		

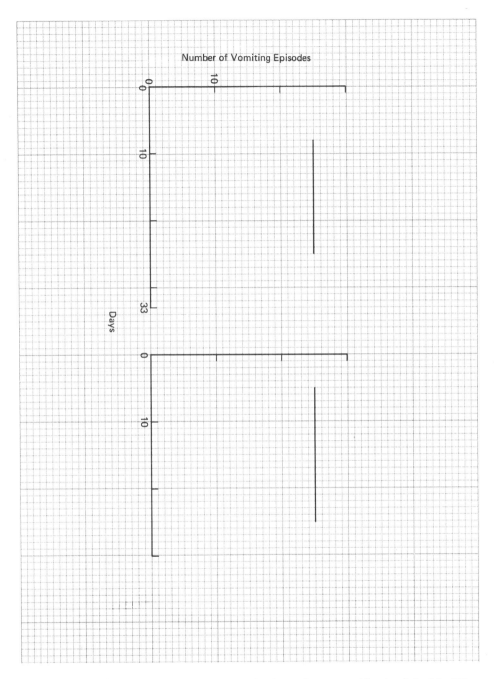

Figure 7-2 Extinction of vomiting episodes in a nine-year-old retarded girl. After the first extinction period, the original classroom conditions were reinstated and the girl received reinforcement (being returned to her dorm) after vomiting on 13 separate days over a 30-day reinstatement period. Thirty days of extinction followed the reinstatement period.

*

Exam

1. Define the following terms:
    a. operant extinction
    b. respondent extinction
    c. resistance to extinction (both definitions)
    d. spontaneous recovery
    e. generalization of extinction

2. How would you answer a person who claimed, "People who kick vending machines because the machine doesn't deliver are dumb?"

3. What do you expect would happen if you did not respond to any of the greetings ("Hellos" or "Hi's") you received during the day. Why? (You might find it helpful to summarize the effects of extinction and then apply them to this example.) You might try this experiment; however, you probably would not want to conduct it for longer than a day or two.

4. What is one difficulty in determining the strength of a response?

5. Is extinction permanent? Explain.

6. What are some reasons why a long-established habit is difficult to extinguish? Provide examples for the reasons you give.

7. The asymptote of a curve is the limiting value it reaches. After the asymptote is reached there is little further increase in the value of the curve. Examine the two extinction curves in Figure 7-1 and determine the asymptote for each. How many days were required before the curves reached an asymptote? At what point was "half-the-battle won?" (Hint: Considering the asymptote as the end point, the question resolves to finding the day on which 50% of the urges had been emitted.)

8. How would you argue with a smoker who states that he has tried many times to quit smoking but he never seems to get rid of the urge to smoke? The longest he has gone without smoking has been 7 days. (Hint: With Figure 7-1 in front of you, what might you tell him about the urge to smoke? What advice might you offer about an anti-smoking program?)

9. In the experiment with Laura, the authors first extinguished her vomiting and then reinstated it. They did not use any drug to induce vomiting, so how were they able to reinforce it in the second condition if it had already been "eliminated" in the first extinction period?

10. In the experiment with Laura, what was the rate of vomiting in the condition where vomiting was reinforced? What was it during the last extinction period? Why was there such a difference between the two rates? (Hint: What happened after vomiting during reinforcement?)

11. During the first extinction period with Laura, the authors found that the total number of vomiting episodes was distributed as follows:
    Monday — 35
    Tuesday — 26

Wednesday — 12
Thursday — 5
Friday — 1

How do you account for this distribution? (Hint: Recall that the experiment was not run Saturday and Sunday; hence, a recess occurred from the extinction period.)

References

Wolf, M., Birnbrauer, J., Lawler, J., & Williams, T. The operant extinction, reinstatement, and re-extinction of vomiting behavior in a retarded child. In R. Ulrich, T. Stachnik, & J. Mabry (Eds.), *Control of human behavior*, Vol. II. Glenview, Ill.: Scott, Foresman, 1970. Pp. 146-149.

Positive and Negative Reinforcement; Punishment; Extinction

UNIT

8

Positive Reinforcement

A stimulus which is in a dependency relation with a response may change the probability of that response, but the direction of the change depends upon what is done when the response is made. For example, if we want to increase the rate at which a dog barks, we can give him a piece of meat after every time he barks. If his rate of barking increases (as it probably would unless he were sick or had just eaten), then we can conclude that the meat is a positive reinforcer. So, a **POSITIVE REINFORCER** is any stimulus which, when presented immediately following a response, increases the rate of that response. The operation of presenting a positive reinforcer is called **POSITIVE REINFORCEMENT.**

Negative Reinforcement

The term *negative reinforcement* causes some confusion among students, probably because the term *negative* is associated with words like *down*, *decrease*, and *minus*. Students tend to think of negative reinforcement as having effects opposite to those of positive reinforcement. Because of your past associations, you may have to practice using this term correctly in a variety of contexts before you feel comfortable with it. In any case, the effects of negative reinforcement are in the same direction as those of positive reinforcement. How can this make sense? Suppose we use

89

the same dog as before and that we still wish to increase his rate of barking, but he has just eaten, so food will not be a reinforcer now. Instead, we place him in a room and turn on a loud noise (a noise the dog would avoid if he could) and leave it on. Now when he barks, as he is sure to do sooner or later, we turn off the noise for several seconds. If his rate of barking increases, then we conclude that noise is a negative reinforcer. A **NEGATIVE REINFORCER** is any stimulus which, when *terminated* following a response, increases the rate of that response. The operation of removing a negative reinforcer is called **NEGATIVE REINFORCEMENT.**

Although these definitions are simple enough, there are several things about them you should notice. First, and most important, a reinforcer, either positive or negative, is defined by its effects. If a stimulus, say ice cream, is presented after a child's response several times and the rate of the response does not increase, the stimulus is not a reinforcer. There may be any number of reasons why ice cream on a certain day at a certain time does not reinforce a behavior. The child might have just gorged himself on ice cream at his friend's house; he might be sick; he could also be thinking about an upcoming football game he is going to play that evening and has so much "anxiety" that food is not appealing.

In the same way, a stimulus which usually acts as a negative reinforcer may not always do so. An electric shock is annoying and usually painful, so it is difficult to conceive of shock as ever having no effect. But it has been shown that animals will deliver intense and frequent shocks to themselves, if those shocks have been paired with food and the animal has been deprived of food. So

even painful stimuli can sometimes fail to effect a change in the rate of a response. If this happens, that is, if an animal is exposed to a painful stimulus and the rate of the response that removes the painful stimulus does not change, then that stimulus is *not* a reinforcer for *that* animal at *that* time. The point to remember about the preceding discussion is that a stimulus, in and of itself, is not a reinforcer. Candy, cigarettes, shock, drugs, food, noise, even money are reinforcers only under certain conditions, and we must always test to see if, in fact, the rate of responding changes when we make any of these stimuli dependent upon a response.

A second point to remember is that if the term *reinforcement* is used, it must, by definition, be referring to an increase in the rate of the response in question.[1] The term *negative reinforcement* is sometimes misused by students (and some psychologists) when they refer to situations in which a response is eliminated from an organism's repertoire by the administration of shock. They say things such as, "We negatively reinforced the patient and thereby eliminated his temper tantrums." That statement is incorrect because the rate of behavior decreased rather than increased as the word *reinforcement*, requires. The term they should have used is *punished*.

[1]More accurately, an increase in the rate of a response is only one way of inferring that a stimulus is a reinforcer. Evidence of control by a schedule of reinforcement is also used as evidence that a stimulus is a reinforcer. One schedule, the **DIFFERENTIAL REINFORCEMENT OF LOW RATE (DRL)** schedule, is specifically designed to produce a low rate of responding. On a

Punishment

Punishment is defined as having effects opposite to those of reinforcement. Actually, the effects of punishing behavior are quite complex (see Units 18 and 19 on Punishment). At this stage, it is only important that you learn that punishment involves a decrease in rate, and reinforcement an increase in rate.

It should be easy for you to arrive at a definition of punishment once you recall the definition of positive reinforcement. If your dog is barking too frequently and you would like to decrease the rate at which it barks, you might present a loud noise every time it barks. Notice that the same stimulus now used to weaken the dog's behavior — the loud noise — was used to strengthen its behavior earlier. The *presentation* of a negative reinforcer following a response is **PUNISHMENT, TYPE I.**

Having made the statement above, we must now hasten to add that there is another way to punish behavior. It is easier to illustrate this type of punishment with humans, but the procedure can be applied to situations involving animals as well. If a driver parks in a no-parking zone and gets caught, he is given a ticket which results, among other things, in a fine. Formally, a positive reinforcer was taken away from him dependent upon his response (parking illegally), and this procedure is called **PUNISHMENT, TYPE II.**

Notice that we can strengthen behavior with a positive and a negative reinforcer and that we can weaken behavior with a positive and a negative reinforcer. The operation (whether reinforcement or punishment) is jointly defined by: 1) the type of reinforcer, and 2) what we do with it. The following fourfold table may make it easy for you to remember the four possibilities.

It should be pointed out that new behavior is not created by punishment. A child can learn *not* to make some response, but if that is all we have taught him, we have taught very little. Frequently, a desirable substitute behavior needs to be acquired in place of the misbehavior. For example, Aversion Therapy (see Aversive Counterconditioning, Unit 21) is used in an attempt to eliminate sexual deviations such as exhibitionism. Concurrently, a program of positive reinforcement is used to shape more acceptable sexual behavior. The combination of punishment for an

---

DRL-20 sec schedule, for instance, a subject must not make a response for at least 20 seconds after the last response or the previous reinforcer. After waiting 20 seconds, his next response will deliver a reinforcer. If the subject responds too early after a previous response, the timer recording the interval will reset to zero and the next reinforcer will not be available for another 20 seconds. Animals with considerable experience on this schedule usually pause about 20 seconds after reinforcement and then emit a short burst of responses. Thus, although a subject's overall rate is low (it *has* to be to earn reinforcers!), the fact that a subject displays the typical DRL pattern of responding is taken as evidence that the stimulus is a reinforcer.

Occasionally, too, the operant level of the response will be high and the imposition of a schedule will lower the overall rate. Skinner and Morse (1958) found that imposing a fixed-interval schedule on rats' ad lib running in an activity wheel lowered the overall rate of running. Nevertheless, when the fixed-interval schedule was in effect, the behavior was orderly and resembled typical fixed-interval behavior. In summary, evidence for a reinforcing effect is sometimes obtained from the pattern of responding characteristic of a schedule.

Table 8-1

Fourfold dependency table. Given that an organism has made a response, there are two operations that are possible with each class of reinforcer, resulting in four possible dependencies.

	Positive Reinforcer	Negative Reinforcer
Present	Positive Reinforcement	Punishment (Type I)
Remove	Punishment (Type II)	Negative Reinforcement

undesirable response and positive reinforcement for a desirable alternative has proved very effective in changing behavior (see the Alternative Response procedure, Unit 19).

Forgetting, Extinction, and Punishment, Type II

The procedure of extinction results in a loss of behavior, as does forgetting. What is the difference? **FORGETTING** is a decrement in performance due merely to the passage of time. Ebbinghaus (in Garrett, 1956) found, for example, that after learning a list of nonsense syllables to a 100 percent criterion, he forgot about 56 percent of the material after 1 hour. He did not practice the syllables during the 1-hour period between the perfect recitation and the test trial, so the loss was occasioned by some process occurring during that hour that was not related to whether the responses were reinforced

or not. In extinction, however, the decrement in performance is attributable to the nonreinforcement of prevously reinforced behavior. For a procedure to be called *extinction*, the conditioned response must be emitted, and must not receive reinforcement. In forgetting, the behavior in question is not emitted.

Distinguishing between extinction and punishment, Type II (a response leads to the removal of a positive reinforcer), is sometimes difficult because there does not seem to be much difference between the two procedures. Both procedures result in a decrement in the rate of responding. However, there is an important difference. Consider a child who has been reinforced by earning 5¢ for taking out the garbage cans once a week. If, for some unusual reason, we wished to eliminate this response from his repertoire, we could place the behavior on extinction. He would no longer receive 5¢ whenever he took the garbage cans out. If he had earned $2.00 by doing this chore, and saved it, he would still have $2.00 after his behavior had been extinguished. If, on the other hand, we had chosen to use punishment, Type II to eliminate his behavior, we could have fined him 5¢ every time he took out the cans. He would have lost 5¢ every time he made the response, and, if he made 20 responses during this procedure, he would have ended up with only a $1.00 in his savings. So you can see how the procedure of punishment, Type II might cause the boy to quit responding much faster than the procedure of extinction.

One last point with respect to the use of the term *extinction*: A behavior can be extinguished or it can be eliminated from a subject's repertoire, but it does not become "extinct." The term *extinct* is used to refer to an animal or species of animals that no longer inhabits the earth.

Application

C. D. Williams, The elimination of tantrum behavior by extinction procedures. *Journal of Abnormal and Social Psychology*, 1959, 59, 269.

The following case study illustrates how positive and negative reinforcers operate to produce and maintain temper tantrums and also the effectiveness of extinction as a treatment for modifying an undesirable behavior.

The subject was a 21-month-old boy who threw temper tantrums when he was put to bed. The child had been sick for an extended time; his parents had given him special care and, necessarily, more attention than they normally would have. Now that he had recovered, the extra care and attention were no longer necessary. However, the child continued to demand attention and was able to manipulate his parents by crying or throwing a tantrum if attention were not forthcoming at bedtime. When Professor Williams was called in, one or the other of the parents was sitting with the child until he fell asleep. This sometimes took two hours! This behavior on the part of the parents seems odd; and it is difficult for us to see how they could have permitted a 21-month-old to control them like this. Their behavior will become more understandable however, when we trace the development of the *tantrum cycle*.

When the child recovered, the parents had no reason to make special trips to the child's room, so the amount of attention at bedtime was reduced considerably. As you will remember from Unit 7, no longer presenting a customary positive reinforcer defines the procedure of extinction, and one of the side effects of extinction is emotional behavior (in this case, crying). Now, if a parent enters the room when the child is crying, the child's crying is reinforced. It does not matter why the parent entered the room; the parent's presence is a conditioned positive reinforcer and will strengthen the behavior that produced it. Of course, what happens when Mommy enters the room is that the baby stops crying and this reinforces Mommy. The response, entering the room, terminates the aversive stimulus, crying, and so is negatively reinforced. Note that in this parent-child interaction, all parties receive reinforcement.

The dependencies in this interaction also favor the development of extreme behavior. That is, the parents may tire of continually going into the child's room, and may resolve to "be strong" and not enter. Again, the child is placed on extinction and more forceful behavior (another temporary side effect of extinction) is emitted by the child. The boy's crying gets louder, he may kick and thrash around, and he may punctuate his performance with those hair-raising screams that children can develop. Eventually, of course, one or the other parent cannot stand it any longer and goes into the room. Again, the child's crying is reinforced. But this time the crying is more vigorous, and is accompanied by thrashing of the arms and legs. At this point, you can probably see how a full-blown tantrum is shaped by parents. Parents may try waiting longer and longer, but the child's crying goes on longer and louder, too. Technically, what the parents are doing is placing the crying on an intermittent schedule of reinforcement (i.e., reinforcements given on an intermittent basis according to either a time or response criterion). One effect of intermittent reinforcement is that the behavior so reinforced is much more difficult to extinguish than behavior that receives continuous reinforcement (i.e., every response reinforced).

Once the child's crying has reached the tantrum level, it is easier for the parents to prevent the tantrum from starting than it is to put up with it once it begins. Hence, a parent stays with the child until he falls asleep. This is an example of **AVOIDANCE CONDITIONING**. The parent engages in a response (staying with the child) to avoid the aversive stimulus (tantrum).

Returning to the case study, Williams decided to use the procedure of extinction to eliminate the tantrums. He simply instructed the parents to put the child to bed, say goodnight, then stay out of the room.

Table 8-2 shows the length of crying for each of the successive times the child was put to bed. Notice that there are two extinction periods. An aunt,

Table 8-2

Duration of crying time for a 21 one-month old "tyrant" during 19 extinction sessions. During Bedtime 10 and 11 one week intervened, and during this period an aunt inadvertently reinforced the child's crying. Data taken from Williams, C. D. The elimination of tantrum behavior by extinction procedures. *Journal of Abnormal and Social Psychology*, 1959, 59, 269.

Times Child Put to Bed	Duration of Crying (minutes)
1	45
2	0
3	10
4	6
5	3
6	2
7	1
8	0
9	0
10	0
11	53
12	12
13	3
14	20
15	10
16	4
17	1
18	1
19	0

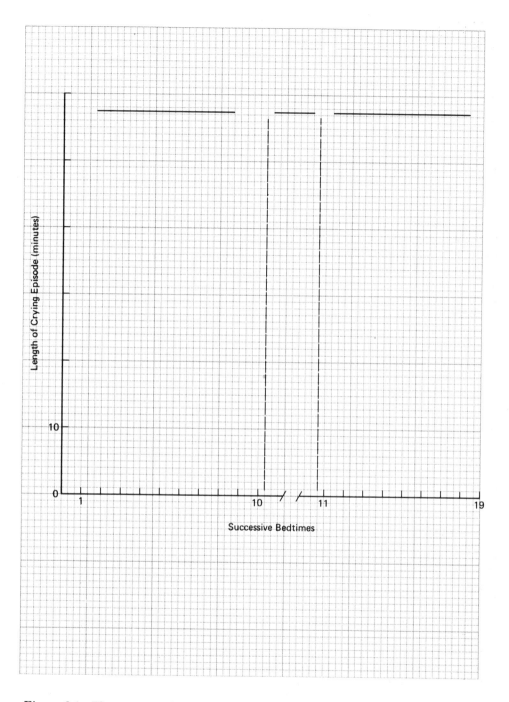

Figure 8-1 The amount of time spent crying by a twenty-one-month-old "tyrant" over the course of two extinction periods. The second extinction period was necessary because the boy was "accidentally" reinforced for crying by an aunt after Bedtime 10.

*

who sometimes took care of the child, went in to the boy's room when he fussed a bit and reinstated his crying after ten extinction trials. Plot the data from this table, but indicate by a break in the chart from Bedtime 10 to Bedtime 11 that one week intervened. After the second extinction period, there were no more bedtime problems, and when the author last saw the child, about two years later, he appeared friendly and outgoing.

Exam

1. Define the following terms:
   a. positive reinforcer
   b. negative reinforcer
   c. negative reinforcement
   d. punishment, Type I
   e. punishment, Type II
   f. extinction
   g. forgetting
   h. operant level
   i. avoidance conditioning

2. What is the difference between the procedure of punishment, Type II and extinction?

3. Is chocolate ice cream a reinforcer? Explain your answer.

4. A boy in a classroom frequently disrupts the class by jumping out of his seat and talking out of turn. You are called in by the teacher to help control this child's misbehavior. You observe that the teacher's attention is the reinforcer which appears to be maintaining the misbehavior. How would you eliminate this misbehavior using extinction? Punishment, Type II?

5. What kinds of reinforcers are involved in the tantrum cycle?

6. Describe the tantrum cycle. In your summary, be sure to mention who receives reinforcement and what kind of reinforcement is operating in this situation.

7. How exactly does the tantrum cycle contain shaping procedures? Point out the dimensions along which the reinforcement criterion is shifted.

References

Garrett, H. E. *Great experiments in psychology*. 3rd ed. New York: Appleton-Century-Crofts, 1957.

Skinner, B. F., & Morse, W. H. Fixed-interval reinforcement of running in a wheel. *Journal of the Experimental Analysis of Behavior*, 1958, **1**, 371-379.

Williams, C. D. The elimination of tantrum behavior by extinction procedures. *Journal of Abnormal and Social Psychology*, 1959, **59**, 269.

*

UNIT
Conditioned Reinforcement and Response Chaining

9

UNCONDITIONED REINFORCERS are those stimuli which have the power to reinforce without any training. Food, water, sexual activity, and air for breathing are examples. The unconditioned reinforcers mentioned above are either necessary to, or important for, life, but not all unconditioned reinforcers fall into this category. Saccharin is a sweet substance which has no nutritional value, but it is an unconditioned reinforcer for many species, including man. Drugs, such as opium and its derivatives, may be other stimuli which are unconditioned reinforcers.

A CONDITIONED REINFORCER is a stimulus which has acquired its reinforcing properties by being paired with some unconditioned reinforcer or another conditioned reinforcer. Review the steps in respondent conditioning (Unit 4). Once you understand these steps, you will know how to make any neutral stimulus a conditioned reinforcer. The essential operation is that of *pairing* one stimulus with another. And if a conditioned reinforcer is to retain its effectiveness, it must be paired, at least occasionally, with an unconditioned reinforcer.

You might wonder at this point why we should try to establish conditioned reinforcers. After all, in the case of almost any human or animal, we can find objects which will act as positive unconditioned reinforcers. Why bother building "artificial" reinforcers? One reason has to do with the dependence of many unconditioned reinforcers upon a state of deprivation. Thus, food will reinforce a child's behavior only if he is hungry. If we were trying to teach a child some new behavior, and were using M & M's as reinforcers, we would soon discover that after a bagful of candy, the child would be satiated and would balk at any further attempts to teach him. So, the length of our lessons in this case would be subject to the conditions of the child's stomach.

Another problem with using certain unconditioned reinforcers is that they must be consumed. Eating can interfere with the behaviors we are trying to establish. A candy bar might make a powerful reinforcer, but once the child has received it, he will spend the next 5 or 10 minutes eating the candy bar. Not much else can go on until he is finished. A group of students in a beginning learning class once got around this problem by cutting each M & M into parts (a sticky procedure at best in spite of the ad man's claim) and reinforcing the child with one-fourth of an M & M each time she made the desired response. There is a better solution, though. We can establish a conditioned reinforcer and present it instead of the unconditioned reinforcer every time the subject is to be reinforced. For example, we take a poker chip and pair it with candy. We might start by giving the child a stack of chips. When she gives us a chip, we give her a piece of candy. After the token has become a conditioned reinforcer, we can reinforce desired behavior with tokens. She can then cash in the tokens at the end of the sessions, or save some for next time.

There are limits, however, even with the procedure described above. Suppose the child has just eaten candy and is temporarily surfeited on sweets. The tokens may cease to reinforce her behavior. We can get around this problem by pairing the token with a variety of unconditioned and conditioned reinforcers such as other foods, soft drinks, pennies, or opportunities to engage in pleasurable activities. Multiple pairings increase the power of the token immensely because it is not tied to any particular deprivational state or particular type of reinforcer. Such a conditioned reinforcer is called a **GENERALIZED REINFORCER**. Money, tokens, and the spoken words, "Good!" and "Right!" are examples of generalized reinforcers for most people.

The Dual Function of Conditioned Reinforcers

A conditioned reinforcer is usually a discriminative stimulus, and this combined function is sometimes not easily seen by beginning students. When a child earns a token (e.g., a penny) by hanging up his coat, the behavior of hanging up his coat is made stronger because the penny has been paired with some unconditioned reinforcer, such as gum. But the penny is also a discriminative stimulus for obtaining gum. Thus, the penny reinforces the behavior that preceded it (hanging up the coat), and is discriminative for the behavior that comes after receiving it (searching out a gum machine and obtaining gum). A more detailed account of stimulus functions is provided in the units on stimulus control. The present account is simplified but should help you understand how conditioned reinforcers control behavior. The entire sequence of events in our example may be diagrammed as in Figure 9-1.

This sequence of responses and stimuli is called a **STIMULUS-RESPONSE CHAIN**. Note that for

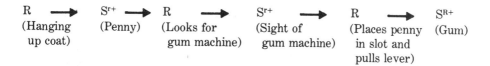

R → S^{r+} → R → S^{r+} → R → S^{R+}
(Hanging   (Penny)   (Looks for   (Sight of   (Places penny   (Gum)
up coat)   gum machine) gum machine) in slot and
                                                  pulls lever)

Figure 9-1

An example of a stimulus-response chain. The symbol, S^{r+}, is an abbreviation for conditioned reinforcer.

any response there is a stimulus (penny) that sets the occasion for the response (looks for gum machine). This same stimulus (penny) follows and reinforces an earlier response in the chain (i.e., hanging up coat). Up to now, we have discussed behavior as if it consisted only of single responses separated by a vacuum. But as you can readily discover, much of our behavior is composed of long sequences or chains of responses. Typing, starting and driving a car, playing a musical instrument, walking to the corner store, and saying the lines in a play are all examples of chains. Recall your activities from the time you arise and you should be able to specify several long response chains that you go through each morning.

The Role of Conditioned Reinforcers in Establishing and Maintaining Response Chains

When we wish to train a child to perform some complex chain such as making his bed or tying his shoes, we rely on conditioned reinforcers in the initial shaping procedure. Without the use of conditioned reinforcers, the shaping of a complex task would be much more difficult. As an illustration, let's consider teaching a child to tie his shoes. The mother's praise, saying, "Good," will be the conditioned reinforcer, and a piece of candy will constitute the unconditioned reinforcer. As you recall, one of the first things to do when teaching a complex task is to break the task down into steps that can easily be performed by the subject. There are about a dozen steps in tying one's shoes. Once the task is broken down, we are ready to start teaching. But where do we start? At the beginning of the chain? No. Pulling up the laces, the first step in the chain, is a long way from the final step, making the bow snug, which means that pulling up laces is a long way from the unconditioned reinforcer, the candy. Components of the chain which are closest to reinforcement are learned faster and exert more control over behavior, so we teach the chain backwards. The very last component, making the bow snug, is taught first. When this response is well-established, we start teaching the next to the last step, and so forth.

Eventually, of course, the mother will give praise only when the entire chain has been completed. A partially tied shoe does not evoke praise from most mothers. This means that components in the middle and early parts of the chain are temporally removed from reinforcement and are, therefore, not as strong as the last components. When reinforcement is delayed, even for one second, the desired behavior is much weaker than when there is no delay. So when you observe a child dawdling in the midst of performing some task, it is probably because the chain has not been well-established; that is, the conditioned reinforcers have been removed too soon in training.

Establishing Strong Behaviors with Conditioned Reinforcers

An experiment performed by Findley and Brady (1965) illustrates the strong effects that conditioned reinforcement can have. The experimenters worked with chimpanzees and trained the animals, after many sessions, to push a button 4,000 times for food. Technically, this is a fixed-ratio schedule, and when the chimp finished the FR 4,000, a feeder light came on briefly and he received 20 banana pellets.

After this training, the experimenters inserted two stimulus conditions. In the presence of a red light, the conditions were as they had been before: FR 4,000 for 20 pellets. In the presence of a green light, every 400 responses produced the feeder light (conditioned reinforcer), and when the chimp completed 10 such FR 400s, he received his banana pellets as well. In short, nine conditioned reinforcers were added to the green stimulus condition. The chimp was given this training for about a month.

Table 9-1 gives the frequency distributions of "dawdling" (pausing before starting to work) for the last day of training in each stimulus condition. Observe that the frequencies are grouped into clusters (called class intervals) 1.3 minutes in length. Thus, in the presence of the green light, there were 9 pauses, 0.0 to 1.3 minutes long; 13 pauses were 1.3 to 2.6 minutes long; and so forth. For this type of data, a histogram or bar graph is useful, and we have drawn the frequencies for the first two class intervals for both conditions. **Complete Figure 9-2 by drawing the remaining bars for each histogram, making sure to label them so that the correct histogram is associated with the appropriate condition.**

One finding was that once the animal started working in the green condition, he worked at a faster rate than he did in the red. Furthermore, in the beginning stages of training, long pauses of 12 to 18 hours occurred in both the red and green conditions. The animal was sleeping during these intervals. Later, however, these very long pauses dropped out completely in the green condition, indicating that the conditioned reinforcers were controlling when the animal would sleep. With a second chimp, the experimenters were able to sustain an FR 120,000 by providing a conditioned reinforcer for every 4,000 responses.

You might try a simple experiment to demonstrate for yourself the effectiveness of procedures which use conditioned reinforcement. Instead of giving a child 10¢ for cleaning up his room, give him 1¢ every time he completes part of the chain involved in cleaning his room. You should observe a rapid increase in the time it takes him to clean up his room as well as a lot less "fooling around" in the midst of the job.

Application

J. D. Burchard, Systematic socialization: A programmed environment for the habilitation of anti-social retardates. *The Psychological Record*, 1967, 17, 461-476.

In recent years, tokens have been used in a systematic way to motivate mental patients, delinquents, children with educational problems, and retardates. Token economies, as these systems are called, have been very successful and are moving from experimental to standard programs in progressive institutions. The following article describes the workings of such an economy for a group of mildly retarded delinquent boys at the Murdoch Center, an institution for the retarded. The boys in this study had a history of fighting, stealing, committing arson, being expelled from schools, and going AWOL from the institution. In sum,

Table 9-1

Frequency of pauses of different lengths in a stimulus condition with and without conditioned reinforcers. Data taken from Findley, J. D., & Brady, J. V. Facilitation of large ratio performance by use of conditioned reinforcement. *Journal of the Experimental Analysis of Behavior*, **1965, 8, 125-129.**

Time (min)	Red (without S^{r+})	Green (with S^{r+})
0.0-1.3	0	9
1.3-2.6	3	13
2.6-3.9	0	6
3.9-5.2	1	2
5.2-6.5	1	1
6.5-7.8	1	0
7.8-9.1	0	1
9.1-10.4	0	0
10.4-11.7	0	0
11.7-13.0	0	0
13.0-14.3	2	0
14.3-15.6	1	0
15.6-16.9	0	0
16.9-18.2	1	0
18.2-19.5	1	0
19.5-20.8	2	0
20.8-22.1	3	0
22.1-∞	15	0

these boys would have more than likely ended up in prison within a short time if they had not been in this institution.

The token economy charged for the necessities as well as the niceties of life. Meals cost 5 tokens; cigarettes and other smoking items cost from 2 to 100 tokens; clothing cost anywhere from 25 to 1,000 tokens; recreational activities, such as going to the movies, ball games, and swimming were 10 to 190 tokens. Residents could also go into town or visit home, and these activities cost 90 to 1,500 tokens.

The boys could earn tokens for going to a morning workshop where they assembled electrical equipment, and for attending a school in the afternoon. In the experiment the author simply wanted to demonstrate that the dependent administration of tokens for the desired response could control the strength of that response. The response the author selected to strengthen was sitting at a desk during workshop and school periods. This was a response which these boys did not make for any length of time and one that is necessary in school or many job situations. Each boy was given one token for every 15 minutes he sat at his desk. The workshop and school sessions were each 2 hours long, so this meant that a boy could earn a maximum of eight tokens a day for these two activities. There were also other activities for which the boys could earn tokens.

During the experimental phase, tokens were dependent upon sitting at a desk. In the control phase, tokens were given nondependently; that is, the boys were met at the beginning of the morning workshop and given a fixed number of tokens. The number of tokens given a boy was based upon the average number of tokens he had earned in the first experimental phase. For instance, if he had earned an average of five tokens per day during the experimental phase, he was given five tokens each day before attending the school or workshop. The third and last phase was a return to the experimental conditions. Each condition lasted five days. **The data in Table 9-2 show what happened in the three conditions. Plot these data with days on the abscissa and time spent at the desk on the ordinate. Remember to label the three conditions.**

The experimenter stated that at the beginning of Phase 2, the nondependent phase, the boys expressed their liking for free tokens. During the last part of this phase, though, several boys expressed a desire to go back to earning their tokens because they felt that they could get more that way. The token program at Murdoch is expanding to teach these boys skills that they will need to function in society such as reading, writing, telling time, using a telephone and public transportation.

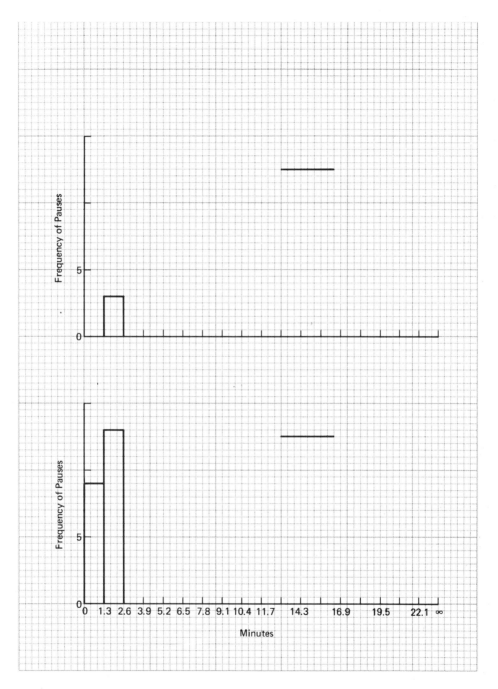

Figure 9-2 Frequency of pauses of various lengths for a chimpanzee responding
on an FR 4000 for 20 banana pellets. In the presence of a green light, every 400
responses produced a conditioned reinforcer (a brief illumination of the feeder
light). In the red light, no conditioned reinforcers were used.

*

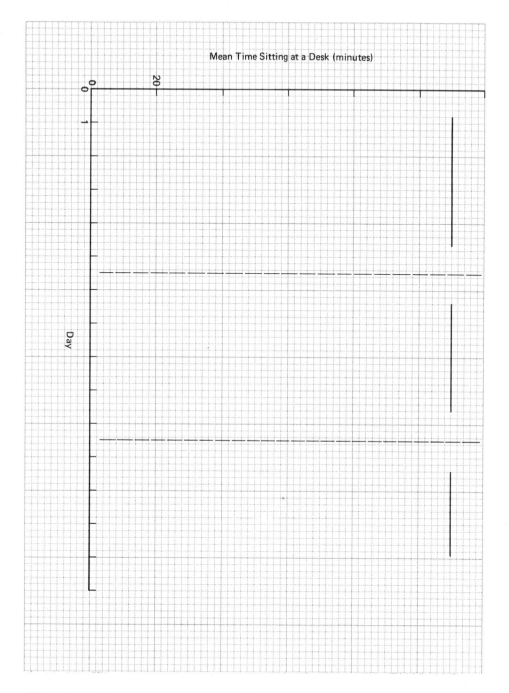

Figure 9-3 Mean amount of time spent sitting at a school desk for nine retarded boys. During the experimental conditions, tokens (generalized reinforcers) were dependent upon sitting at their desks. During the control condition, tokens were given nondependently at the beginning of the school session.

*

Table 9-2

Mean amount of time spent sitting at a desk in a school classroom for nine anti-social boys in three conditions. Data taken from Burchard, J. D. Systematic socialization: A programmed environment for the habilitation of anti-social retardates. *The Psychological Record*, 1967, 17, 461-476.

Day	Experimental (min)	Day	Control (min)	Day	Experimental (min)
1	82	6	30	11	68
2	96	7	15	12	60
3	73	8	12	13	90
4	100	9	2	14	110
5	93	10	5	15	85

Exam

1. Define the following terms:
   a. unconditioned reinforcers
   b. conditioned reinforcers
   c. generalized reinforcer
   d. stimulus-response chain
   e. positive reinforcement
   f. negative reinforcer
   g. operant level

2. Diagram and describe the response chain you go through in starting your car.

3. What are the advantages in using a generalized reinforcer (token) over an unconditioned reinforcer such as popcorn to shape some new behavior?

4. What are the two functions of a conditioned reinforcer? Give an example of each.

5. If a teacher has a 50-page assignment for students to learn and he can give several reinforcers for completing the assignment, how should he set up the study plan? Why?

6. In the Findley and Brady experiment, approximately what percentage of the pauses were equal to or shorter than 2.6 minutes in the condition without the conditioned reinforcers? In the condition with the conditioned reinforcers?

7. In the Burchard study, how do you explain the effects of the control condition? State what happened in the control condition first.

References

Burchard, J. D.   Systematic socialization: A programmed environment for the habilitation of anti-social retardates. *The Psychological Record*, 1967, **17**, 461-476.

Findley, J. D., & Brady, J. V.   Facilitation of large ratio performance by use of conditioned reinforcement. *Journal of the Experimental Analysis of Behavior*, 1965, 8, 125-129.

*

Schedules of
Positive Reinforcement

UNIT

10

A **SCHEDULE OF REINFORCEMENT** is an experimentally arranged dependency, and there are four basic schedules of reinforcement which have been studied extensively. Most often, researchers have used pigeons and rats to study schedules (Ferster & Skinner, 1957), but there has been a growing number of studies using humans, both normal and institutionalized, to test the generality of the findings from animal studies (DeCasper & Zeiler, 1972; Long, Hammack, May, & Campbell, 1958; Orlando & Bijou, 1960; Weiner, 1969; Zeiler & Kelley, 1969). This work will be discussed in the next unit.

Fixed-Ratio Schedules

Ratio schedules require a number of responses for reinforcement. If the number requirement is fixed, the schedule is a **FIXED RATIO** (abbreviated FR). Thus, an FR 100 requires 100 responses for each reinforcer. The smallest fixed-ratio schedule (FR 1) is also called a **CONTINUOUS REINFORCEMENT SCHEDULE** (abbreviated CRF) because the subject receives a reinforcer for every response.

Examples of fixed-ratio dependencies in everyday life are common. Climbing a flight of stairs to get to one's apartment; reading 20 pages in a text, or doing 10 multiplication problems as an assignment for a grade; exercising (doing 20 situps, pushups, etc.) to keep fit are all fixed ratios.

Behavior generated by fixed-ratio schedules is typically bi-valued. Immediately after the subject finishes the ratio

111

and receives a reinforcer, there is a pause in responding. Once the subject starts responding again, though, he works at a steady, high rate. As the size of the fixed ratio is increased, the length of the pause tends to increase. At first, it may appear to you that the subject who is working on a fixed-ratio schedule is simply "resting" from working so hard. After all, there is some effort in, say, mowing the lawn, and it is reasonable to expect that a person would rest after completing a definable section of the lawn. In this example, it is easy for an observer to infer that fatigue may be part of the reason the individual pauses. However, this "reasonable" hypothesis does not hold up under close scrutiny. As you well know, a student will pause after completing an assignment for one course before starting another assignment. How can we attribute his pause to muscular effort or fatigue? There is very little energy expended in studying (although you may find this difficult to accept), and so there is little physiological need for rest. If you argued that studying 50 pages of difficult material produces "psychological" fatigue, you would be guilty of adding a completely different meaning to the concept of fatigue and of making this term relatively useless as an explanatory concept.

Evidence against the "fatigue-pause" hypothesis was provided by an experiment on small and large fixed ratios done by Crossman (1968). The subjects, pigeons, were trained to respond on an alternating FR 10 FR 100, which means that the subject first makes an FR 10, then FR 100, then back to an FR 10, and so on. After an extended history of this schedule, the subjects paused very briefly before the small fixed-ratio schedule and for a long time before the large fixed-ratio schedule. In time, the birds learned that after completing the large ratio, the small ratio was in effect. What is interesting here is that the birds paused only a very brief time before starting to work on the small ratio. Conversely, before starting to work on the large ratio, the pigeons paused a long time. In other words, after making 100 responses they went right back to work, but after making only 10 responses they paused a long time before starting. One would think that the results would have been just the opposite if the pause were due to the need to rest after working. But it would seem that its "what's coming up" that counts, not "what's been done." This finding by no means implies that doing hard work or making a series of effortful responses does not produce fatigue. It is just that fatigue, by itself, is not complete as an explanation of the pausing that occurs on fixed-ratio schedules.

Variable-Ratio Schedules

When the number of responses required from reinforcer to reinforcer varies, the schedule is called a **VARIABLE RATIO** (abbreviated VR). For example, on a VR 100 sometimes the subject must make only 80 responses, while at other times he may have to emit as many as 130. On the average, though, the subject will have to make 100 responses for reinforcement.

Ferster and Skinner (1957) compared the performances of two pigeons, one of which was placed on a variable-ratio schedule while the other was operating under a comparable variable-interval schedule. The bird on the variable-ratio schedule responded about three times as fast overall as the one on the variable-interval schedule even though both were getting paid off at the same rate. This finding points to the importance of the *differential reinforcement of high rates* that can occur on the variable-ratio schedule. That is, the pigeon will sometimes emit a burst of very fast responses and since the faster he works the quicker he receives reinforcement, these bursts will occasionally be followed by reinforcement which strengthens the rapid responding. This sequence of events is much less likely on the variable-interval schedule because it is the passage of time that brings the reinforcer closer, rather than the emission of responses as in the variable-ratio schedule. Hence, on the variable-interval schedule, a reinforcer is likely to follow a response preceded by a pause rather than by a burst of responses.

Behavior under the variable-ratio schedule is characterized by a very high rate of responding, and there is usually little or no pausing after reinforcement. Pausing does not develop because occasionally the subject receives a reinforcer shortly after he has just received one. Hence, the delivery of a reinforcer does not become a signal (discriminative stimulus) for pausing as it may on fixed-interval and fixed-ratio schedules.

The slot machines in Las Vegas are arranged to pay off the customers on a variable-ratio schedule. The power of this schedule to exert strong control over behavior is attested to by the fact that while many people will admit that they can't beat the "slots," they continue to try.

Fixed-Interval Schedules

An interval schedule provides reinforcement according to a time rule. A **FIXED-INTERVAL** schedule (abbreviated FI) provides reinforcement for the *first response* made after a fixed interval of time. Figure 10-1 shows which response receives reinforcement for a hypothetical case on a fixed interval of 1 minute (FI 1).

Note that although the subject made 10 responses within the interval, they had no effect on when he received reinforcement. Responses emitted within the interval don't count. Only the first response made after the 1-minute period produces the reinforcer. Note also that the response that is reinforced does not necessarily have to occur right after a reinforcer becomes available. The subject could wait a long time, an hour or more theoretically, and still get the reinforcer whenever he makes that first response. Usually, however, pigeons and people don't miss many opportunities to pick up a reinforcer,

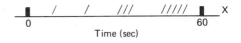

0   60

Time (sec)

Figure 10-1

Schematic record showing how responses might occur on a fixed-interval schedule of 1 minute. Ten responses were made within the interval (slash marks), but do not affect reinforcement. The X marks the 11th response and since it occurred after the 1-minute interval, it was reinforced.

and on fixed-interval schedules subjects are responding at fairly rapid rates close to the end of the interval, so they get the reinforcer within a few seconds after it becomes available.

The looking behavior of a person waiting for a train or bus or the morning mail would be on a fixed-interval schedule. The next time you are waiting for a train or bus, you might observe the change in rate of looking for the on-coming vehicle, or looking at a wrist watch as time to the scheduled arrival approaches.

The performance of many organisms on a fixed-interval schedule is characterized by a long pause following reinforcement and then a gradual shift to a high rate of responding. After a subject has been on a fixed-interval schedule for some time, he learns that shortly after a reinforcer has been delivered he *never* receives another one. With experience, the delivery of a reinforcer comes to control not-responding, that is, pausing. As time in the interval elapses, the probability that a reinforcer has become available increases and the subject starts to respond, slowly at first, and then faster and faster. This pattern of responding is called *positively accelerated*. At the moment of reinforcement, the subject is usually responding at a high rate.

One interesting finding, illustrating the complex nature of the controlling variables in this schedule, is reported by Dews (1966). He showed that if you interrupt the subject's responding in the interval by inserting a blackout (pigeons do not respond very much in the dark), it does not disrupt the rate of responding in the following period without the blackout. It is as if the pigeon has a "clock" that tells it to respond at an increasing rate as time passes in the interval. Forcing the pigeon to stop responding (by blackout) for a short period of time does not cause it to forget where it is in the interval.

Variable-Interval Schedules

When the time requirement between the availability of reinforcers is variable, the schedule is called a **VARIABLE INTERVAL** (abbreviated VI). As in the variable-ratio schedule, lower and upper limits are established and then a number of values within these limits are selected, with the average equal to the value of the variable interval. In a VI 60-sec, the lower limits might be 30 seconds and the upper limits 90 seconds. When discussing time requirements in interval schedules it is easy to forget that the subject must respond in order to receive a reinforcer. In VI 60-sec, the subject will be reinforced for the first response made after an *average* of 60 seconds has elapsed.

Variable-interval schedules have been used extensively as baselines in many research projects because the rate of responding is relatively constant and the pattern of responding is free from long or irregular pausing. This schedule has been used to examine the effects of various drugs and has yielded information about the nature of the drug (stimulant or depressant effects), dosage effects (how much of the drug produces a given effect), and the time course of drug action (the length of time it takes for the baseline performance to fully recover).

One example of variable-interval controlled behavior involves dialing the telephone, the reinforcer being connection with your party. Receiving a busy signal when dialing someone's number places dialing on a variable-interval schedule. Sometimes when you call right back the phone is clear; at other times, 5 or 10 minutes must elapse before you can reach your party. This example illustrates again an important difference between ratio and interval schedules; the number of times you dial does not causally effect your party's hanging up the phone. In ratio schedules the number of times dialed would be related to when your party hangs up.

The Importance of Schedules

It is sometimes not clear why schedules of reinforcement are important. Indeed, what have schedules of reinforcement to do with things in the real world, such as the development of one's "personality"? This is a fair question and deserves an answer.

Let us consider two children of the same age and intellect, who both come from homes where parents care about them. The teacher notes that Susan will work on an assignment, even a difficult one, for a long time and usually completes the work given her. Jimmy, on the other hand, will give up on a problem if he doesn't solve it almost immediately and, if asked to continue trying, will display emotional behavior such as pouting and whining. It is tempting to conclude that the reason for the difference in behavior is due to their different "personalities." One must respect individual differences, and many people would advise the teacher to accommodate her behavior to that of the children. Another possible

explanation, especially if the difference in the behavior is consistent between sexes, is that the different behavior is due to the genetic differences between boys and girls. In this case, one would explain Susan's greater persistence by saying that "girls are more persistent than boys" (see Unit 24 regarding "genetic" explanations).

Another way to account for the discrepancy in persistence is to examine the histories of these two children. In Susan's case, we might find that she was praised for working at puzzles for long periods of time, and that her parents gradually weaned her from working easy puzzles and other tasks to more difficult ones. Both of her parents probably enjoyed working with her on these puzzles and made sure that she received praise for sustained attempts, even if she were not completely successful. In Jimmy's case, his parents, while pleased with his success at solving problems, may have made no effort to reinforce approximations, or were not interested in partially completed tasks. Jimmy learned to try a task for a few minutes, and then, if he did not complete it or solve it within that time, to stop and play with another toy or to go back to an old task that he could solve — one that his parents reinforced him for performing.

In short, persistence in solving a problem or in staying with a task is capable of being shaped. Once the desired behavior is obtained, it can be made stronger by *gradually* raising the requirements for reinforcement; the child must either work at a task a bit longer or emit more responses each time before he is praised. A mother who constantly steps in and helps her child when he encounters a difficulty, and who provides reinforcement for minimal behavior, is denying the child the opportunity to learn to be persistent, as well as the opportunity to build a repertoire of problem-solving behaviors.

Schedules of reinforcement, then, are pervasive. All of our adult behavior has felt the effects of schedules. It is difficult to "see" schedules and their effects because one must observe a given bit of behavior over an extended period of time before one can specify the rule by which the behavior is reinforced. Also, the same behavior is reinforced on different schedules by different people in our lives. For example, a boss who uses positive reinforcement may have praised his secretary only once last year for some efficient service. If this is a daily behavior on her part, we would probably look around to see who else reinforced this woman for her behavior, or look for someone in her past who was less stingy with reinforcers for good secretarial behavior. Like the effects of gravity, the effects of schedules of reinforcement are easily noticed only under special conditions such as exist in the lab when the complexities of the real world are simplified.

Application

B. L. Hopkins, Effects of candy and social reinforcement, instructions, and reinforcement schedule learning on the modification and maintenance of smiling. *Journal of Applied Behavior Analysis*, 1968, 1, 121-129.

The subject in this experiment was a retarded boy who was a "poker face" — he rarely smiled when he encountered anyone at his school. The author had two problems. First, he had to achieve control of smiling through the manipulation of consequences. Second, he had to shift control from a contrived reinforcer (he used candy in this experiment) to the social stimuli and reinforcers that usually control expressions of friendliness.

The procedure involved taking the child on a series of walks around the school where he would be sure to encounter other people. He was walked each day until he had an opportunity to smile in response to at least 10 other people, and there was a total of 130 walks during the course of the experiment. The proportion of occasions on which he smiled was measured during several experimental conditions. For the first 5 walks, a baseline measurement was obtained in which the experimenter gave the subject no instructions when he met anyone and the child received no reinforcement for smiling.

In the next experimental condition, a dependency was established between candy and smiling. If the child smiled at anybody, the experimenter gave him a piece of candy. In addition, the experimenter said nothing to the subject for 15 seconds if he did not smile. This condition was followed by one in which the experimenter gave the child instructions. On meeting a person, the experimenter would say to the subject, "Smile." There were no consequences for smiling during this phase.

In the next few experimental phases, candy reinforcement alternated with control (extinction) conditions. This series of manipulations was done to determine whether the candy reinforcement by itself controlled smiling.

At this point, the experimenter wanted to insure that smiling would not undergo extinction when the candy reinforcement program was discontinued. After all, children do not normally receive candy when they smile and greet people. The abrupt cessation of the candy reinforcers might have led to the extinction of the smiling response before it could come under the control of meeting other people. Hopkins decided to use an intermittent schedule of reinforcement to strengthen the smiling response. He started with a variable-ratio schedule which was initially very "rich" (a favorable payoff ratio approximates a 1:1 ratio of responses to reinforcers). Over successive walks, he gradually made the schedule "leaner" (more behavior required per reinforcer). Beginning with Walk 56, the schedule of reinforcement was changed from an FR 1 (or CRF) to a VR of 1.25 (5 responses for 4 reinforcers), and by Walk 88 the schedule was a VR 7.5.

Beginning with Walk 103 and for the remainder of the experiment, all candy reinforcement was discontinued. During a portion of the walks in the last phase of the experiment, the subject wore a sign which instructed the people he encountered to talk to him only if he did *not* smile. This condition was followed by one in which people he met were instructed to interact with him only if he *did* smile. These conditions were inserted to determine whether the smiling response of the boy was under the control of social reinforcement, that is, the smiles and greetings of other people. During the last 8 walks of the study, the signs were not used.

The data given in Table 10-1 show the number of times the subject smiled during the several conditions of the experiment. Plot the data with the "Proportion of Smiles" on the ordinate and "Walks" on the abscissa. Since there were 10 walks taken per day, the number of smiles listed in the table is easily converted to a proportion. Connect all the data points within each treatment condition and leave space between them so that you may compare treatment effects more easily.

In conclusion, this experiment was successful in establishing appropriate smiling behavior in the subject, and it illustrates how an intermittent reinforcement schedule can be used to guarantee lasting results. The use of a gradually increasing variable-ratio schedule was of value for two reasons: (1) It helped bring smiling under the control of social reinforcers. If candy were given every time, the change to "real life" conditions (only occasionally are candy and goodies paired with meetings and greetings) would be easily discriminable and the child could quickly learn not to respond to others when candy was not given. (2) It also strengthened the smiling response so that it would not easily be extinguished.

Table 10-1

The number of times an 18-year-old retarded boy smiled at people he met on daily walks under several experimental conditions. Note that the sessions are not numbered consecutively because some of the conditions in the original experiment have been deleted. Data taken from Hopkins, B. L. Effects of candy and social reinforcement, instructions, and reinforcement schedule learning on the modification and maintenance of smiling. *Journal of Applied Behavior Analysis*, 1968, 1, 121-129.

1		2		3		4		5		6		7		8		9	
Baseline		Candy Reinf.		Instruction to Smile		Candy Reinf.		VR Schedule Introduced		No Candy Reinf.		Sign: "If he smiles — ignore him"		Sign: "If he smiles — talk to him"		No Signs No candy Reinf.	
Walk	Smile	Walk	Smile	Walk	Smile	Walk	Smile	Walk	Smile	Walk	Smile	Walk	Smile	Walk	Smile	Walk	Smile
1	0	6	0	11	0	20	2	56	10	103	10	112	10	117	4	122	10
2	0	7	0	12	8	21	3	57	10	104	10	113	9	118	5	123	9
3	0	8	0	13	6	22	6	58	10	105	10	114	8	119	9	124	9
4	0	9	0	14	9	23	5	59	10	106	9	115	5	120	8	125	10
5	0	10	0	15	6	24	6	60	8	107	9	116	6	121	10	126	10
				16	6	25	8	61	9	108	10					127	8
				17	5	26	10	62	10	109	10					128	10
				18	6	27	9	63	9	110	10					129	10
				19	4	28	9	64	10	111	9					130	10
						29	10	65	10								
						30	10										
						31	8										
						32	10										
						33	10										
						34	9										
						35	10										
						36	10										
						37	10										

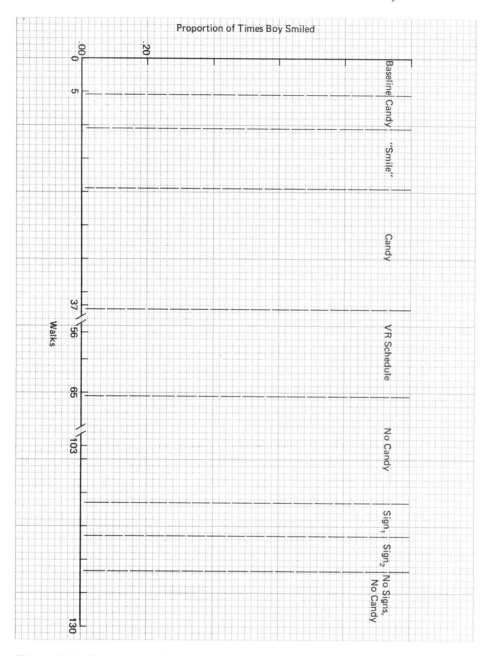

Figure 10-2 Proportion of time a retarded boy smiled at others he met in the course of 130 daily walks under a variety of conditions. In the condition labelled "Smile," the boy was instructed to smile by the person taking him on his walks. In the condition labelled "Sign₁," the boy wore a sign which read, "If he smiles, ignore him." In the condition labelled, "Sign₂," he wore a sign which read, "If he smiles, talk to him." Note that data from walks 38 through 55 and 66 through 102 are omitted.

*

Exam

1. Define the following terms:
   a. schedule of reinforcement
   b. fixed ratio
   c. variable ratio
   d. fixed interval
   e. variable interval
   f. continuous reinforcement schedule
   g. "leaning" the schedule of reinforcement
   h. "fatigue-pause" hypothesis

2. Draw a positively accelerated curve.

3. Which of the variable schedules, variable interval or variable ratio, generates the highest rate of responding? Why?

4. Describe the pattern of behavior that occurs under a fixed-interval schedule. How does it differ from the pattern found under a fixed-ratio schedule?

5. Give an example of each of the basic schedules in everyday life.

6. The data in Table 10-2 show the days on which two students took their written exams in a self-paced class. **Plot these data in cumulative form with two squares equal to one exam on the ordinate and one square equal to one day on the abscissa. Separate the curves for each student but plot both on the same piece of graph paper so that you may readily compare them** .
   a. Which schedule of reinforcement does the behavior of Student A typify? What about Student B?
   b. Which pattern of responding do you think represents the study behavior of most students?
   c. How could you change Student B's behavior so that it more nearly resembled Student A's? (Hint: Think in terms of manipulating some schedule of reinforcement.)

7. Refer to your graph of the data in Table 10-1 to answer the following questions:
   a. Compare the results obtained in the first candy reinforcement condition to the second. How do you account for this difference?
   b. What do you think would have happened if the experimenter had left the "instructions to smile" (Phase 3) condition in effect for another 10 sessions? Why?

8. What was Hopkins's purpose in using an intermittent schedule of reinforcement?

9. Why do you think he used a variable-ratio schedule?

10. Give a plausible account for the "dedication" of a writer using the concept of intermittent reinforcement. New writers report that only an occasional article or story is purchased by a publisher. Most often, the beginning writer is faced with a preponderance of rejection slips. (Hint: Review section on the importance of schedules.)

References

Crossman, E. K. Pause relationships in multiple and chained fixed-ratio schedules. *Journal of the Experimental Analysis of Behavior*, 1968, 11, 117-126.

Dews, P. B. The effect of multiple $S^\triangle$ periods on responding on a fixed-interval schedule: IV. Effect of continuous $S^\triangle$ with only short S^D probes. *Journal of the Experimental Analysis of Behavior*, 1966, 9, 147-151.

Ferster, C. B., & Skinner, B. F. *Schedules of reinforcement.* New York: Appleton-Century-Crofts, 1957.

Hopkins, B. L. Effects of candy and social reinforcement, instructions, and reinforcement schedule learning on the modification and maintenance of smiling. *Journal of Applied Behavior Analysis*, 1968, 1, 121-129.

Table 10-2

Class days on which a written exam was taken at Utah State University by two students in an introductory psychology class. Day 43 was the last regularly scheduled day of the class. Ten exams were required in all, but students could work at their own pace.

Day	Student A	Student B	Day	Student A	Student B
1	—	—	23		—
2	—	—	24		—
3	1	—	25		—
4	2	1	26		—
5	3	—	27		—
6	—	—	28		—
7	4	—	29		—
8	—	—	30		—
9	5	—	31		—
10	—	—	32		—
11	6	—	33		3
12	7	—	34		—
13	8	—	35		—
14	9	—	36		4
15	10 (finished)	—	37		5
16		—	38		6
17		—	39		—
18		2	40		7
19		—	41		8
20		—	42		9
21		—	43		10 (finished)
22		—			

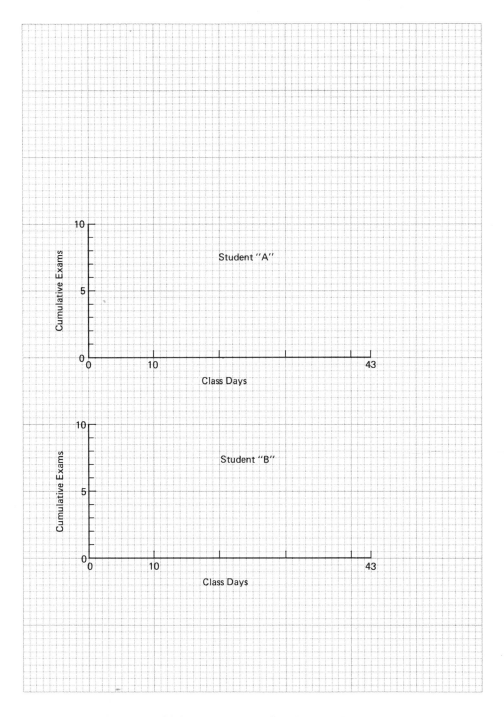

Figure 10-3 Days on which exams were taken by 2 students in an introductory psychology class. The course was arranged so that students could take exams at any pace they desired.

*

Complex Schedules of Reinforcement

In the last unit we presented a few facts about each of the four basic intermittent schedules of reinforcement. In order for you to understand the effects of schedules more completely, it is necessary to show how the raw data are generated and, for this, there must be some understanding of a cumulative recorder. Once one can describe graphically the effects of a simple schedule, cumulative records of complex schedules will be much easier to follow. In addition, with an understanding of the effects complex schedules are expected to produce, one may evaluate schedule research with humans, and compare schedule effects obtained from humans with those obtained from other, nonhuman subjects.

The Cumulative Recorder and Its Records

A **CUMULATIVE RECORDER** is an apparatus which records the responses a subject emits per unit of time (in other words, the **RATE** of responding). It also depicts the pattern of responding within the intervals between reinforcements as well as the pattern across a complete session. The recorder has a roll of 6-inch paper mounted on a cylinder which unrolls at a constant speed (30 cm/hour or 60 cm/hour, for instance). A response pen draws a *horizontal* line (indicating the passage of time) across the bottom of the paper *if* no responses are made. Every time a response is made, the response pen moves *vertically* one small increment (2 or 4 responses/mm, for instance). Thus, the

125

subject actually "draws" the cumulative record by his/her responding or lack of responding. An event pen mounted just below the response pen is used to record the beginning and ending of a session, changes in the stimulus conditions of the experiment, or other events of importance.

Figure 11-1 shows a cumulative record of one complete session for Jimmy, a 7-year-old retarded boy. This is his first session on an FR 10 schedule after he had several days exposure to fixed ratios of smaller values. Jimmy earned 50 tokens (which he deposited in exchange for a variety of goodies) and made more than 500 responses in a little more than 9 minutes. The slope of his response curve yields his overall rate of responding, which was consistent and relatively rapid at 58 responses/minute (533 responses/9.2 min) or almost 1 response/second.

Some idea of Jimmy's consistency may be gained by comparing his rate in the first part of the session to that in the last half. Note the distance between the start of the session (the first "pip" on the event line) and the first reset line (the response pen resets very quickly when it reaches its maximum excursion which, in this case, was about 250

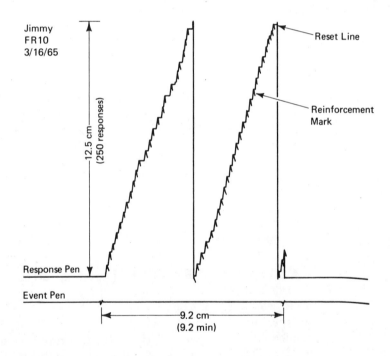

Figure 11-1

Cumulative record of an FR 10 performance made by Jimmy, a retarded boy, after a brief history with fixed-ratio schedules. Note the regularity of his performance, which is very similar to that produced by non-humans (Powers, R., & Powers, E., unpublished data).

responses). Compare this distance to the distance between the two reset lines. They are almost identical. This indicates that the time required to make the first 250 responses was nearly equivalent to that required to make the second 250 responses — typical of the fixed-ratio performance of many organisms, including normal humans. A second type of consistency found in fixed-ratio records is the pattern of responding between reinforcements. Jimmy works at a high rate until he receives a reinforcer, pauses a few seconds (the **POST-REINFORCEMENT PAUSE**), and then goes back to work at the same high rate.

Figure 11-2 shows three sessions of Jimmy's FR 15 performance after being exposed to several social conditions (cooperating with another boy and responding at the same time as the other boy) and after considerable experience with small fixed-ratio schedules (more than 50 sessions). In order to show the stability of Jimmy's performance, it was desirable to show several successive cumulative records and, to do this, it was necessary to collapse the cumulative records for each session. (Each run of 250 responses has been shifted closer to the preceding run by removing the paper between the runs.) Note that the collapsed records do *not* distort the rate — the slope of the response curve still defines the overall rate of responding. It is customary to insert a miniature scale to help the

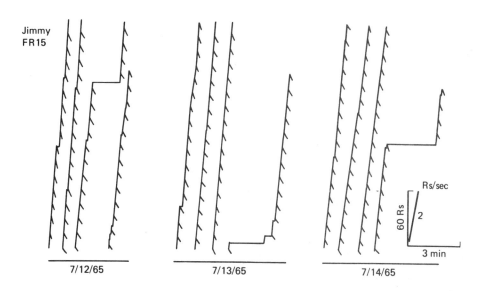

7/12/65   7/13/65   7/14/65

Figure 11-2

Cumulative records of three successive sessions of Jimmy's responding on an FR 15 schedule. This performance was after a history of 50 sessions on low-valued, fixed-ratio schedules. The records for each session have been collapsed (Powers, R., & Powers, E., unpublished data).

reader determine the rate of responding when the records have been collapsed. The scale on the lower right hand side of Figure 11-2 shows that Jimmy was responding faster than 2 responses a second.

There are several things that can be seen about Jimmy's performance here that did not appear in his earlier fixed-ratio performance. First, the post-reinforcement pauses have disappeared after most of the ratio runs. Second, there is one, long pause (between 1 and 3 minutes) in the latter part of each session. Incidentally, if we had only shown you one session, you would have had no way of knowing whether this long pause was an anomaly or a systematic occurrence. As the pause appears in all three records, it seems systematic. These pauses are explained by Jimmy's saving of the tokens he earned. He saved until he had 40 or more tokens and then turned them in at one time and was given a large number of "back-up" reinforcers (candy, soft drinks, and trinkets), hence, the long pauses. Third, the long pauses in Figure 11-2 shift progressively toward the end of the session and, by the last session, almost the entire session occurred before he exchanged the tokens. If the experiment had continued, it looks as if he might have redeemed his tokens after the session was over.[1]

Although Jimmy's later fixed-ratio performance (Figure 11-2) was different in many respects from his earlier performance (Figure 11-1), they are similar in their consistency and lawfulness. This lawfulness is difficult to see without the help of cumulative records.

VI and CRF Schedules

Now that you have some idea what response patterns look like on fixed-ratio schedules, we can examine schedules which generate response patterns contrasting strongly with those produced by the fixed-ratio schedule. The top two records in Figure 11-3 show the performance of two women college students on a VI 100-sec schedule after they had received 15 minutes of continuous reinforcement (CRF). In this experiment (Lane & Shinkman, 1963), the operant was a vocal response — the vowel sound U. This sound was used as a signal that the subjects were ready to perform a simple copying task. On the CRF schedule, the U sound was always followed by the presentation of the task, while on the VI schedule, only the first vocal response after an average of 100 seconds led to the presentation of the task. After receiving 40 reinforcements on the VI

[1] Although this experiment was not designed to study self-control, perhaps the student can see how some interesting questions arise about the development of self-control from Jimmy's performance. How far could we have extended Jimmy's saving of tokens? What would happen if we increased the size of the fixed ratio for each token? Would Jimmy have saved as many tokens if we had used a different schedule, such as a fixed interval, which fixes the rate at which tokens are delivered? Does the saving of tokens exhibited in this laboratory situation generalize to a field situation; for example, would Jimmy save 40 or more tokens in a classroom where he was reinforced for reading or other academic tasks, and where he must wait until the class is recessed before exchanging his tokens?

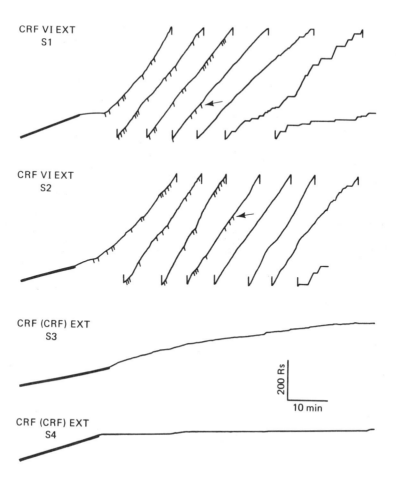

CRF VI EXT
S1

CRF VI EXT
S2

CRF (CRF) EXT
S3

200 Rs

10 min

CRF (CRF) EXT
S4

Figure 11-3

Cumulative records of 4 female college students responding on
several schedules. Top: S_1 and S_2 were given 15 minutes of
continuous reinforcement (CRF), followed by 40 reinforcements
on VI 100-sec, followed by a 73-minute extinction period. The
last reinforcements given on the variable-interval schedule are
marked by the arrows. Bottom: S_3 and S_4 were given an
additional 40 reinforcements on CRF instead of being placed on
the VI schedule, and were then placed on extinction (from Lane
& Shinkman, 1963).

100-sec schedule, the subjects were
placed on extinction for 73 minutes. The
arrows mark the last reinforcements
given on the variable-interval schedule.

The performance of two subjects who
received 15 minutes of CRF followed by
an additional 40 reinforcers on CRF is
shown in the bottom two cumulative

records. Even though these latter two women earned as many reinforcers as those in the CRF-VI condition, they made many fewer responses in extinction. This comparison vividly demonstrates the power of intermittent schedules to produce much greater resistance to extinction than the CRF schedule. Notice also the regularity of the rate of responding when the variable-interval schedule was in effect. This regularity and the ease with which the experimenter can "dial" the rate he desires, make variable-interval schedules ideal as baselines for investigating other independent variables such as drugs, deprivation level for a reinforcer, or phenomena such as conditioned suppression (Unit 17) and behavioral contrast (Unit 14).

Figure 11-4 provides an even more striking example of resistance to extinction after a variable-interval history than that shown in the previous figure. This subject, a male college student, had been given 117 reinforcers on a CRF schedule and 60 on a VI 100-sec schedule. The arrow marks the last reinforcement he received on the VI 100-sec schedule. Even though the

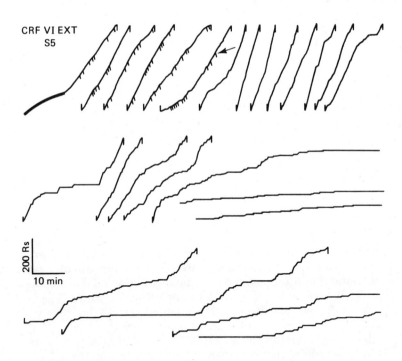

Figure 11-4

Cumulative record of a male college student given essentially the same history as S_1 and S_2 in Figure 11-3. With this subject, the extinction period was allowed to run 11 hours (from Lane & Shinkman, 1963).

instructions to the subjects had suggested that the experiment would last no more than 3 hours (at most), this subject made over 8,000 responses during the extinction period which lasted 11 hours. A very persistent fellow! His performance is not abnormal, however. Resistance to extinction after a variable-interval history is very strong for other animals, too (Ferster & Skinner, 1957, Chapter 6).

Complex Schedules

There are several complex schedules of reinforcement which have been studied. As we will occasionally refer to them in later units, it is important that you become familiar with the more common of these schedules and their effects. When a simple schedule such as an FR 10 is studied, the subject is typically exposed to a succession of FR 10s until the session is over — the length of a session generally being defined by a fixed number of reinforcers or by a fixed period of time. In the previous illustration with Jimmy, later sessions lasted until he had received 60 tokens. As you might imagine, we could insert an occasional fixed-interval schedule (or any other schedule, including a period of extinction) into the series of fixed-ratio components to see how it affects performance. Instead of an FR 10 followed by an FR 10, we might program an alternating series of FR 10/FI 30-sec schedules. Will the performance reflect the dependencies in each schedule or will some altogether different performance develop? Suppose a different stimulus occurs with each schedule; will that help maintain the performance characteristic of

each schedule? Questions like these have been examined in schedules which have had programmed stimuli associated with each component, and results from these schedules have been compared to similar schedules without programmed stimuli. In some complex schedules, the delivery of an unconditioned reinforcer has been given after each component, and, in others, it has been withheld. The combination of correlated stimuli *present* or *absent* with each component and unconditioned reinforcement *given* or *withheld* after each component generates the four schedules, **MULTIPLE, CHAIN, MIXED,** and **TANDEM**, shown in Figure 11-5.

In the *mult* FR 10 FI 30-sec, the red light is illuminated when the FR 10 is in effect, the green light is illuminated when the FI 30-sec is in effect, and food is dispensed as the subject completes each schedule component. The red and green lights accompany each of the components in the *chain* VI 30-sec VI 90-sec, but food, the unconditioned reinforcer, is presented only after completion of the VI 90-sec component. The only thing that happens when the subject completes the VI 30-sec component is that the red light changes to green. Since the red light is never directly paired with food, the rule for establishing a neutral stimulus as a conditioned reinforcer is not satisfied. Do you think that the red light would become a conditioned reinforcer under these conditions? Later, we will present some research that bears directly on this question.

On the right side of Figure 11-5 there are the two schedules that have no stimuli correlated with the schedule components. In the *mix* VR 100 VI 120-sec, food is given after the

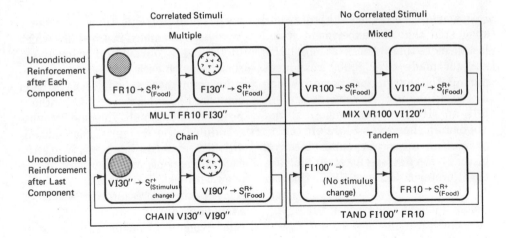

Figure 11-5

A 2 x 2 table showing the four basic complex schedules of reinforcement.

requirement of each schedule is satisfied, and this schedule is often used as a control for studying the effects of the added stimuli in the multiple schedule. For the same reason, the tandem schedule is used as a control in studying the chain schedule. The tandem schedule is unique because it is the only one of the four complex schedules which gives the subject no clue that a component has been completed. It may seem to you that such a schedule could not tell us very much about behavior because the subject doesn't "know" that there are two different schedule requirements. This objection may be made only if one over looks the fact that the behavior of organisms is subject to the dependencies specified by a schedule regardless of the subject's state of awareness about those dependencies. Ferster and Skinner (1957) have shown that tacking on even a small fixed-ratio requirement (FR 10) to a large fixed-interval schedule (FI 45-min) dramatically changes the

subject's pattern of responding (pp. 416-429).

Some Representative Research with Complex Schedules

Token reinforcement schedules. Another way of conceptualizing the fixed-ratio schedule under which Jimmy was responding is in terms of what Kelleher (1966) has called an **EXTENDED CHAIN**. In the ordinary chain schedule, a stimulus change occurs when the component, remote from reinforcement, is completed.[2] With a token reinforcement system, tokens are delivered at the end of each component, which is a stimulus change. As Kelleher has

[2]It is customary to label the component directly associated with unconditioned reinforcement as the first component, the next component as the second, and so forth.

suggested, though, schedules of token reinforcement are more complex than ordinary chain schedules because the gradual accumulation of tokens by the subject is *itself* a stimulus change which may affect responding. Jimmy had to earn 2 tokens before he could deposit them for his back-up reinforcers (this is called the **EXCHANGE RATIO**), but he saved 30 or 40 tokens before depositing them. We found that Jimmy played with his tokens and stacked them in piles as he accumulated them, and periodically looked at the stacks as he worked. All of Jimmy's behavior with respect to tokens may have been important in controlling when he would pause in the session.

In an ingenious experiment, Kelleher (1958) examined the effect of a lump-sum advance payment of tokens on the pausing of chimpanzees who were responding on a token reinforcment schedule. The chimps were trained on an FR 125 schedule of token reinforcement and had to accumulate 50 tokens before exchanging them (exchange ratio of 50). When they had earned 50 tokens, a red light came on and in the presence of this light they could deposit their tokens and receive unconditioned reinforcement. The top half of Figure 11-6 shows the pattern of responding under the extended chain of 50, FR 125s. This schedule is also called a **SECOND-ORDER** schedule and is written, FR 50 (FR 125). The gaps in the cumulative record indicate pauses in the chimp's responding, and the numbers above each gap give the amount of time deleted. In this session, Chimp 119 paused a little over 3 hours before acquiring 50 tokens, and most of the pausing occurred before he

completed a single FR 125. Kelleher observed that the chimps, even after they started responding, responded irregularly until they had a few tokens. With some tokens in hand, they generally responded at a steady, high rate throughout the remainder of the session. Kelleher wondered what would happen if he gave the chimps 50 tokens at the start of the session. Of course, he

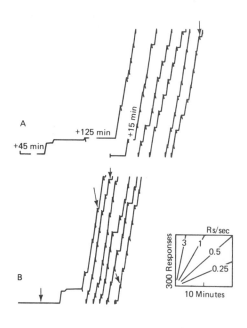

Figure 11-6

Cumulative records of a chimpanzee responding on a token reinforcement schedule. After every 125 responses (FR 125), the chimp received a token, and after 50 tokens, the animal could exchange the tokens for food. A: Typical pattern, with long pauses in the early part of the session. B: At the beginning of this session, the chimp was given 50 tokens. Arrows mark the premature insertions of poker chips (from Kelleher, 1958).

did not let the chimps exchange any of the tokens until they had earned 50 more tokens in the usual way. The bottom part of Figure 11-6 shows that the long pausing was almost eliminated by this procedure and suggests that the number of tokens in the chimp's possession was a strong stimulus governing the animal's motivation. Kelleher found that the chimps were not very active at the beginning of a session, but "They became extremely active when they had numerous poker chips, and continually manipulated several poker chips with one hand. Often, they held several poker chips in their mouths and rattled these against their teeth by vigorous head movements. All this activity was accompanied by high rates of responding as well as the screaming and barking which usually occurred during daily feedings" (p. 288).

All of these observations strengthen the hypothesis that the token reinforcement schedule is a chain schedule. Each token is a conditioned reinforcer for the completion of the previous component and adds a small amount to the subject's cache of tokens. As the pile of tokens grows larger, the unconditioned reinforcer grows closer, and, as Kelleher argues, the size of the pile becomes a discriminative stimulus for food-related behavior, for example, depositing of tokens. The arrow in the top cumulative record of Figure 11-6 indicates that the chimp inserted a token at this point. This deposit was premature and occurred after the chimp had 47 tokens in his possession — very close to the required 50. In the bottom record, the chimp inserted a token on four different occasions (arrows), and 3 were inserted early in the session. Recall that, in this session, the animal

started with 50 tokens, the amount which usually led to reinforcement when he started depositing, and these premature deposits become understandable. This evidence suggests that the number of tokens the subject has can be a powerful discriminative stimulus controlling not only the amount of pausing that occurs in the beginning of a session but also where in the session tokens will be deposited.

Complex schedules as baselines: Drug effects. It was early recognized that the stable responding maintained by schedules of reinforcement could be used to advantage in studying other independent variables. Some clever yardsticks were created when investigators utilized intricate baselines, such as those controlled by complex schedules, to study drugs. In fact, one entire symposium sponsored by the New York Academy of Sciences was given over to the behavioral effects of drugs prior to the publication of Ferster and Skinner's classic study of schedules of reinforcement in 1957.

Peter Dews's experiments (1956) are illustrative of the early recognition by psychologists of the promise held in schedule research for analyzing other variables of interest. A baseline that can be maintained and recovered over an extended period, (months and years, in some cases) eliminates many research problems. Such questions as, "How long does the effect of a drug last?" or, "What dosage level produces the maximum change in behavior (suppression or facilitation of the rate of responding, for instance)?" can be asked of a subject repeatedly, given that the baseline performance can be recovered. This ability to repeat a question to the same subject and compare the "answers" we receive over several repetitions gives us confidence that the effect seen is indeed due to the drug in question and not to individual differences in subjects, or to the subject's acquisition of new skills, or to the fact that the animal was sick on the test day and so forth.

Figure 11-7 shows a cumulative record of a multiple-schedule performance by a pigeon. In the presence of a red light, the pigeon was reinforced on an FR 60 schedule. When the light changed to blue, the schedule was an FI 15-min. Dews programmed this multiple schedule in a series called a "standard run" and the component sequence was: FR, FI, FR, 3 FI, 10 FR, 2 FI, and 3 FR.[3] One of the typical fixed-interval performances is marked by the vertical dotted lines, and the horizontal dotted lines indicate the FR 60s. The difference in the pattern of responding generated by the ratio and interval schedules is easy to see. The fixed ratios were emitted at a high rate by the bird, and there was no discernible pausing after reinforcement. In contrast, the bird paused 5 or more minutes before making the first response in the

fixed-interval schedule, and then the rate started to accelerate until, at the moment of reinforcement, the bird was responding at the same rate (about 3 responses/sec) as he did during the ratio runs.

Figure 11-8 shows what happened to the same pigeon's responding after he had been given a dose of phenobarbital sodium (approximately 70 milligrams of the drug per kilogram of body weight).

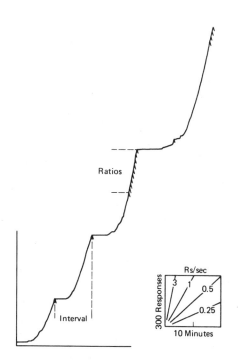

---

[3]It is now customary to program a complex schedule in either of two ways: randomly (within certain limits) or with the components alternating. Experimenters have discovered that even such creatures as rats and pigeons can learn a given sequence such as Dews's "standard run," and if the experimenter wishes to make sure that the programmed stimuli (e.g., colored lights) are the controlling stimuli, he had better program his components randomly. Otherwise, the experimenter may find that the subject has learned that, for example, the third component is a fixed-ratio, and emits FR-like behavior while ignoring the stimulus associated with that component.

Figure 11-7

Cumulative record of clearly differentiated responding by a pigeon on a *mult* FR 60 FI 15-min schedule. The dotted vertical lines indicate one FI 15-min record, and the dotted horizontal lines show 10 successive FR 60 records (from Dews, 1956).

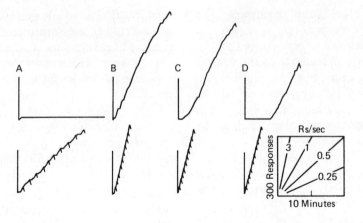

Figure 11-8

Using the same bird as in Figure 11-7, cumulative records
of the *mult* FR 60 FI 15-min performance at different
times after the injection of a drug. The records have been
separated for ease of comparison, with the interval
performances at the top and the ratio performances on the
bottom. Times after injection of the drug were, A: 18
hours, B: 24 hours, C: 36 hours, and D: 48 hours (from
Dews, 1956).

For clarity, the multiple-schedule performances have been separated, with the fixed-interval responding on the top and the fixed-ratio responding on the bottom of each of the four panels in Figure 11-8. The fixed interval Dews selected to present was the one just preceding the 10 fixed ratios. He presented the data in this way so that the time period sampled would be almost identical for both performances. The panel labelled "A" shows both performances 18 hours after the administration of the drug, and successive panels show performances at 24, 36, and 48 hours after drug injection.

Observe that the drug completely destroyed the fixed-interval performance while only increasing the post-reinforcement pause and lowering the **RUNNING RATE** (the rate once the subject has started to respond, also referred to as the **LOCAL RATE**) in the fixed-ratio component. By 24 hours after injection, the pigeon had resumed pecking in the fixed-interval component, but there was no post-reinforcement pause. The fixed-ratio performance had completely recovered by this time. Fixed-interval responding was still atypical even 36 hours (Panel "C") after injection. The pigeon did pause slightly after reinforcement, but the pause was much shorter than in the normal performance. In "D," the fixed-interval performance had fully recovered.

One very important conclusion can be reached by examining Figure 11-8. The use of a multiple schedule as a baseline to study the time course of drug action was fortunate. Suppose Dews had used only the fixed-ratio schedule as a baseline? He would have concluded that the effects of the drug had dissipated by the end of 24 hours (Panel "B"). What if he had used only the fixed-interval schedule as the baseline? He would probably have concluded that the dosage level he had given "knocked out" all behavior even after 18 hours (Panel "A"). As you can see, both of these conclusions would be wrong! The more robust and insensitive fixed-ratio behavior tells us that the animal could still respond on the key — that the bird was not lying unconscious on the floor of the cage (Panel "A," bottom). The more sensitive fixed-interval performance tells us how long the drug effect lasted (Panel "C," top). Since the *same* animal generated *both* performances at the *same* time, there was little danger of the confounding influences that are encountered when different groups of animals are compared (e.g., drug group vs. no-drug group), or when the same subject is used at different times (the subject is always learning, hence there is the possibility of learning accounting for a given effect instead of the drug). We can conclude that the double-scaled

"behavioral barometer" established by Dews's multiple schedule was sensitive and extremely informative.

The use of chain and tandem schedules to study conditioned reinforcement. Consider a three-component chain schedule like the one in Figure 11-9. In the third component, when the subject completes the fixed-interval requirement, the white light changes to green; similarly, when the fixed-interval requirement is satisfied here, the green light changes to red. Finally, in the first component, and in the presence of the red light, the satisfaction of the fixed-interval schedule provides food. Since only the red light is paired with the unconditioned reinforcer, food, this stimulus is the only one for which the rule establishing a neutral stimulus as a conditioned reinforcer is satisfied. What about the white and green lights, though? Will they maintain behavior? Will they become conditioned reinforcers?

Kelleher and Fry (1962) attempted to answer questions like these using three-component chain and tandem

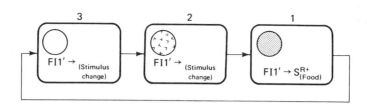

Figure 11-9

A three-component FI 1-min chain schedule. When the subject completes the schedule requirements in the third and second components, a stimulus change occurs. Only in the first component is a stimulus (red light) paired with an unconditioned reinforcer, food.

fixed-interval schedules. They used pigeons as subjects and allowed the birds' behavior to stabilize over 120 sessions on a three-component fixed-interval chain with the stimuli as shown in Figure 11-9. (Kelleher and Fry shorten the designation of this schedule to a "fixed chain.") The fixed-interval value was 60 seconds for 40 sessions and 90 seconds for 80 sessions. The cumulative records for one bird's (P-11) performance on this fixed chain are shown at the top of Figure 11-10. The large letters, A, B, C, refer to sessions 80, 90, and 100, respectively. The small letters, a, b, c, indicate instances of positively accelerated responding occurring in the middle component of the fixed-chain schedule. In some records there is a gap which indicates that a portion of the record has been deleted. In these places, pauses were so long that they could not be shown, but the amount of time missing is given just above the break in the record. Note that all of these very long pauses occurred in the interval most remote from unconditioned reinforcement.

Compare the pigeon's performance on the three-component fixed chain with that on a three-component tandem schedule (middle set of records, Figure 11-10). The tandem schedule had the same time requirement — that is, FI-90 sec, FI-90 sec, FI-90 sec — as the chain schedule. In A, the white light

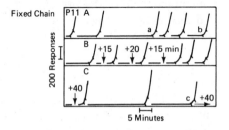

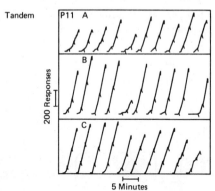

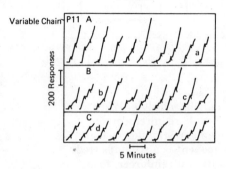

Figure 11-10

Responding of a pigeon on a three-component FI 90-sec fixed chain with stimuli and schedules as in Figure 11-9. Top: Panels A, B, and C show sessions 80, 90, and 100, respectively. Points marked a, b, and c show instances of positive acceleration. The break in some of the records with a time designation above it refers to the pause time deleted from that record. Middle: A three-component FI 90-sec tandem schedule. In Panel A, the white light was on in all three components. In panels B and C, the red light was on. Bottom: A three-component FI 90-sec variable chain. The three stimuli were presented in random order so that each stimulus was paired with the unconditioned reinforcer about one-third of the time (from Kelleher & Fry, 1962).

was illuminated in all three components. Recall that this was the stimulus most remote from unconditioned reinforcement in the fixed chain. Even so, the bird made many more responses in the second and third components than he did in the fixed-chain schedule, and the long pauses disappeared. The next two records, B and C, show the tandem schedule with the red light (the stimulus that was most closely associated with unconditioned reinforcement) as the stimulus present in each component. The rate in each interval was very high, and there was even less pausing than in the tandem schedule with the white light, which is what you would expect.

These findings suggest that the stimuli associated with the components not directly paired with unconditioned reinforcement were very weak conditioned reinforcers, especially the stimulus associated with the third component. The white light maintained very little behavior and was not discriminative for the pattern of responding characteristic of fixed-interval schedules. The tandem schedule is an excellent "catch" condition because it tells the experimenter that there was nothing about the schedule per se (too difficult for the pigeon, or too long between reinforcements, for example) which would produce long pausing. Therefore, it must have been the addition of the different colored stimulus lights which produced the pigeons' desultory reponding in the first two components of the chain schedule.

To confirm the importance of directly pairing a neutral stimulus with an unconditioned reinforcer in order for that neutral stimulus to become a conditioned reinforcer, Kelleher and

Fry exposed these same birds to a variable-chain schedule. In this chain, each of the stimuli was occasionally made the terminal one in the sequence and, hence, was paired with food about a third of the time. On one trial, the stimulus sequence was red, green, white. On the next, it was white, red, green, so the bird had no way of "predicting" what the sequence would be on each trial. The last panel in Figure 11-10 shows P-11's responding on this variable chain. The main point to note in this figure is that responding was maintained in all components and that there were only short post-reinforcement pauses in each of the three components. This provides strong evidence that *each* of the three lights was a conditioned reinforcer and suggests that the maintenance of good control in an extended chain requires that the stimuli associated with the different components in the chain be directly paired, at least some of the time, with the unconditioned reinforcer.

Complex schedules and observing behavior. In a now classic study, Wyckoff (1969) found that the opportunity to observe a discriminative stimulus was itself a conditioned reinforcer. That is, organisms will respond to find out whether a reinforcing condition is in effect or not. Such a response has been called an **OBSERVING RESPONSE**. Since Wyckoff's original experiment, many studies on observing behavior have been done and one of the questions raised by this work is: Is information a reinforcer? On the surface, this seems an easy question to answer. Obviously, if a subject works to learn what the world is like, he or she is working for information, and the fact that the subject works to observe would seem prima facie evidence that information, per se, is reinforcing.

An alternative explanation is available, however, which accounts for observing behavior and which does not invoke a new concept, *information*, to explain the findings. Suppose that the subject only works to find out about a good state of affairs? To make an analogy to everyday human events, suppose you had learned that a rich, old relative of yours had just died and that the terms of his will would be made known sometime soon. You, as an heir, might be quite active in trying to find out whether you had inherited anything. Letters, phone calls, and even visits to the lawyer handling the estate would be made by you and other interested parties. As you might imagine, information about when the contents of the will would be made explicit would be information that would be welcomed by you. This ancedotal evidence would be taken as supporting the "information-as-

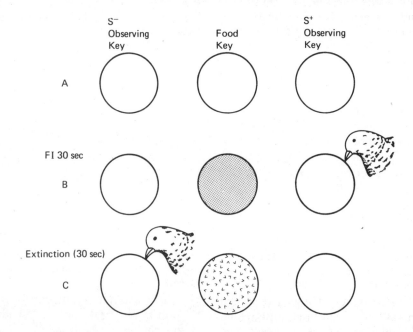

Figure 11-11

A 3-key observing response paradigm. A: All 3 keys are illuminated white at the start of a trial. B: If an FI 30-sec schedule is in effect and the bird pecks the S+ observing key, the food key turns red. Pecks on the food key are then reinforced according to an FI 30-sec schedule. C: If an extinction schedule is in effect and the bird pecks the S− key, the food key turns green, indicating a 30-second extinction period. Pecks at the wrong observing key have no effect.

a-reinforcer" hypothesis discussed above.

Suppose, on the other hand, that your recently deceased relative had been destitute — had, in fact, a number of zealous creditors at his door when he died. You are notified, as one of his surviving relatives, that you might be held accountable for some of his debts and that you would soon be notified of the extent of your responsibilities. Under these conditions, you might not attempt to find out when the final disposition of the will would be made. Not only would you *not* call the lawyer handling the case, but you might not answer the phone, you might hide from strangers who knocked at the door, you might move, and so on. In this example, information about your relative's financial condition is not sought — it is actively avoided, in fact — and it would be hard to argue that information is a reinforcer here. The alternative explanation is that organisms work to observe a reinforcing state of affairs, that observing behavior is maintained by positive conditioned reinforcement only. Thus, organisms would not work to observe a conditioned aversive stimulus as the information interpretation would maintain.

Bruce Wald, a graduate student at Utah State University, has been working with pigeons in an attempt to resolve the question, "What maintains observing behavior?" Figure 11-11 shows a diagram of his procedure. The pigeon has three keys which it can peck. Pecks on the center key produce food according to an FI 30-sec schedule. Sometimes, however, a 30-second extinction period is in effect, and the FI 30-sec schedule is intermixed with the 30-second extinction period on a random basis so that the bird cannot learn what

schedule is forthcoming. There is a color associated with each of these schedules: Red is associated with the FI 30-sec component, and green with the extinction period. However, the bird has to respond on either of the two side keys in order to see the color on the food key. A trial starts as in Panel A, Figure 11-11, with all three keys white. Let's suppose that the FI 30-sec schedule is in effect. If the bird pecks the S^+ observing key once (Panel B), the food key changes from white to red and stays red for the remainder of the 30-second interval. In the presence of this red light, the first response after 30 seconds gives the bird a few seconds' access to grain, and the food key turns white again.

Now, suppose extinction is in effect; if the bird pecks the S^- key, the food key turns green (Panel C) and stays green for 30 seconds. Pecks on the wrong key do not change the food key (e.g., a peck on the S^+ key when extinction is in effect).[4] So by responding on the

[4]The observant student will see a problem with this procedure. Suppose the bird happens to peck the S^+ observing key just at the end of an extinction period and that the next interval happens to be the FI 30-sec component. The bird's peck would be followed by the onset of the red light and pecking the S^+ key in extinction would be adventitiously reinforced. This is a common problem in the training of a discrimination, and a customary solution is to insert a **PROTECTION DEPENDENCY** at the end of the extinction component which prevents the close association of a response with the onset of a discriminative stimulus. In Wald's experiment, a 3-second protection dependency was used, which meant that in the extinction component, at least 3 seconds had to occur *without* a response before the next component went into effect. If the bird continued to respond in extinction, as PB-5 did in Figure 11-13, the onset of the next component was delayed.

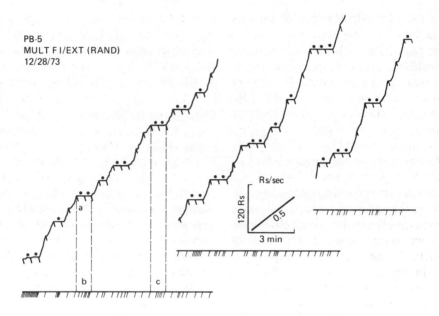

PB-5
MULT F I/EXT (RAND)
12/28/73

Figure 11-12

Responding of a pigeon after 60 sessions in an observing response situation as depicted in Figure 11-11. Extinction periods are marked by a dot. Observing responses on the S⁺ key are shown on the event pen. This bird did not make any S⁻ observing responses at this stage of training. Point "a" shows an instance of positive acceleration in an FI 30-sec component. Points 'b" and "c" show places where two successive extinction periods occurred. Records have been collapsed and offset upward (unpublished data generously supplied by Bruce Wald).

observing keys, the pigeon can provide cues as to what schedule is in effect and can change a mixed schedule to a multiple schedule.[5] What does the pigeon do?

Figure 11-12 shows a very clear discriminative performance by one of Wald's birds after about sixty sessions.

The cumulative records for one session have been compressed slightly and offset upward to fit on one page. Reinforcement marks indicate the delivery of a reinforcer in the FI 30-sec components and the end of an extinction component when that schedule

[5]Extinction has been treated as a schedule, and usage has permitted such designations as multiple FR EXT, which, according to the classification scheme presented in Figure 11-5, is not possible

because no food is given in the extinction component. This usage is so widespread that it would be difficult to change now, and we simply inform the student of this exception to the general rules for classifying complex schedules.

occurred. To help the reader identify extinction components, a small dot has been placed above them. The event pen recorded observing responses to the S⁺ key *only*. There were initially very few observing responses to the S⁻ key, and eventually there were no observing responses to this key. The bird's performance resembles that of a well-differentiated, multiple fixed-interval extinction performance. This pigeon made only six responses on the food key in all of the extinction components over the session; the responding in the fixed-interval components is typical with positively accelerated responding within the interval as at the spot marked "a." The dashed lines are extended down from two successive extinction periods, at "b" and "c," to help you identify where the observing responses occurred. This figure shows that many observing responses were made on the S⁺ key during extinction! The pigeon did *not* respond on the S⁻ key and thereby change the food key to green. In effect, the bird used only one key, S⁺, to discover the schedule in effect. When he pecked this key, the food key either turned red, indicating that an FI 30-sec schedule was in effect, or the key color did not change, indicating a period of extinction.

One could argue that the bird gets as much information from one key as he does from two. If he pecks the S⁺ key and it changes to red, the schedule is a food schedule; if the food key does not change color, the schedule is extinction. The bird's fine differential responding in the randomly presented components certainly suggests that the S⁻ key was superfluous. Indeed, this is quite true: Wald inserted a "catch" condition to see if the pigeon would use the information provided by the S⁻ key if it were the

only information available. Suppose we no longer provided the subject with a red light when the FI 30-sec schedule was in effect; only the S⁻ light was available. The bird could still discover what schedule was operating by responding on an observing key; in this case, it must respond on the S⁻ key. For example, if the schedule were extinction, and the bird pecked the S⁻ observing key, the food key would turn green. If the bird pecked the S⁻ key, and the food key light did not change, the schedule would be FI 30-sec. As before, the bird could have relied on one key for information about the schedule in effect. Figure 11-13 shows what happened in the first session when the S⁺ observing key was made ineffective. As you can see, the bird did *not* use the S⁻ key. All the responses on the event line are S⁺ responses, so the food key remained white throughout the entire session (a mixed schedule), and the well-differentiated performance between the fixed-interval and extinction components was lost. The last run of 500 responses shown in Figure 11-13 is characteristic of a mixed schedule (i.e., a randomly presented *mix* FI 30-sec EXT 30-sec).

These results are not consistent with the information hypothesis. Instead, they support a conditioned reinforcement hypothesis of observing behavior. The red light, paired with positive reinforcement, became a conditioned reinforcer and maintained observing responses. The green light, paired with extinction, would not maintain observing responses. It seems that pigeons, at least, will respond to find out the state of the world only when the observing response provides "good news." Pigeons, like people, stop watching the news when it's only bad!

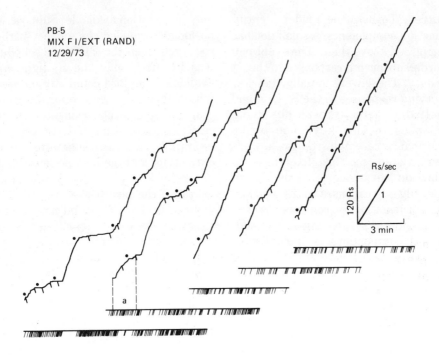

PB-5
MIX F I/EXT (RAND)
12/29/73

Figure 11-13

Responding of Bird PB-5 in the first session after observing responses to the
S⁺ key were placed on extinction. The event pen shows S⁺ observing
responses. Since the pigeon still did not utilize the S⁻ observing key, the
schedule changed from a multiple to a mixed schedule, and the bird's
responding in the last run of 500 responses closely resembles what a
randomly presented *mix* FI 30-sec EXT 30-sec schedule would generate. The
dashed interval labelled "a" shows S⁺ observing responses during a
fixed-interval period and a subsequent extinction period (unpublished data
generously supplied by Bruce Wald).

Schedule Research with Humans

One of the problems of doing schedule research with humans has been obtaining **STEADY-STATE BEHAVIOR,** that is, behavior over several sessions which does not show significant trends. Jimmy's cumulative records (Figure 11-2) are a good example of steady-state behavior with respect to fixed-ratio performance. However, it appeared that the long pause he made in each session when depositing his tokens was shifting toward the end of the session. With respect to the long pause, his records would not exemplify steady-state behavior.

Some of the effects of a schedule take time to become manifest. The place where Jimmy paused in the session is one example. Another, more common one is the pause after reinforcement on a fixed-interval schedule. The post-reinforcement pause grows gradually longer across as many as 50 sessions until it stabilizes around a value that is about one-half the length of the fixed interval. Thus, in lower organisms such as pigeons and rats, the majority of the post-reinforcement pauses would be around 30 seconds on an FI 1-min. As you can imagine, it is difficult to get normal human subjects to spend five, 1-hour sessions on an experiment, let alone 50.

One of the early studies (Long, Hammack, May, & Campbell, 1958), attempting to extend schedule research to humans, used 4 to 8-year-old children and found that maintaining motivation was difficult. The reinforcers were pennies, trinkets, and slides projected on a wall. The schedules examined were fixed ratio (from FR 5 to FR 150), fixed interval (from FI 30-sec to FI 3-min), and variable interval (VI 30-sec and VI 1-min). Responding on fixed-ratio schedules resembled that obtained from other organisms, but the performances of most of the children deteriorated as they collected a large supply of trinkets. Pausing increased after reinforcement, and the local rate fell off as it does with animals responding for food who have become satiated. The authors inferred that the children had become satiated with the trinkets. The addition of new trinkets and doubling the number given, returned the behavior to its original pattern.

Fixed-interval patterns did not resemble those typically found with other organisms. With other subjects, as you recall, there is a pause after reinforcement which lasts about one-half the interval, and then the rate accelerates as reinforcement approaches (see the fixed-interval cumulative records in Figure 11-7, for example). Several of the children developed a pattern of spacing their responses and making only a few responses within an interval; others responded at a high rate with no pausing after reinforcement. Both these patterns are not commonly found in nonhuman subjects. On the short variable-interval schedules examined, however, the children had patterns of responding that were similar to other organisms.

Orlando and Bijou (1960) examined 46 retarded children over a longer time period than Long et al. and reported no problem with motivation (they used candies as reinforcers). The four basic schedules — fixed ratio, fixed interval, variable interval, and variable ratio — were studied, and again only the fixed-interval schedule produced records that were at odds with those generated by animals such as rats and pigeons. As before, some of the children developed a low-rate, pacing performance on the fixed-interval schedules. Except for this discrepancy, the authors concluded that the effects of the schedules studied were similar to those found with nonhuman and normal human subjects.

Figure 11-14 shows cumulative records of five subjects who were responding on different multiple schedules. The top three records illustrate a clear discrimination that each of the subjects had formed between the stimulus associated with a ratio schedule and a stimulus associated with a period of extinction. The bottom two records show accurate performance of two subjects who were responding on an interval schedule which had a programmed cue informing them when to respond. After a fixed period of time,

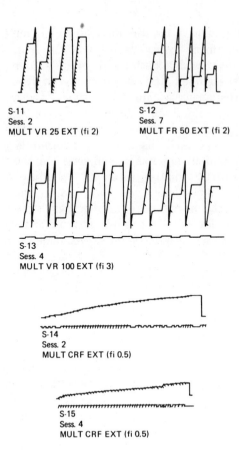

S-11
Sess. 2
MULT VR 25 EXT (fi 2)

S-12
Sess. 7
MULT FR 50 EXT (fi 2)

S-13
Sess. 4
MULT VR 100 EXT (fi 3)

S-14
Sess. 2
MULT CRF EXT (fi 0.5)

S-15
Sess. 4
MULT CRF EXT (fi 0.5)

Figure 11-14

Cumulative records of 5
multiple-schedule performances
obtained from retarded children. The
top three records show multiple ratio
extinction schedules. The event pen in
these three sets of records shows which
discriminative stimulus was in effect.
The bottom two sets of records show a
cued performance. After a fixed time, a
cue was presented and the child was
reinforced for responding in the
presence of the cue. The event pens
were depressed when the cue was
presented and moved up when the child
responded. The number inside the
parentheses indicates the duration in
minutes that a component was in effect
(adapted from Orlando & Bijou, 1960).

a light would come on and if the subject
responded in the presence of the light,
he/she was reinforced. So, in effect, this
is a multiple CRF EXT schedule. The
event pen dropped down when the cue
was presented and stayed down until
the subject made a response. Thus, the
length of the event pen line in the
depressed position represents the
latency of the subject's responses. This
schedule is useful because it shows the
extent to which the child can refrain
from responding when the cue is off and
how fast he/she responds when the cue
is presented. Both these performances
exemplify good discriminative control.

Zeiler and Kelley (1969), using
normal children and 30 seconds of a
cartoon as a reinforcer, also found more
variability on the fixed-interval
schedules than on other schedules they
studied. On fixed-interval schedules,
the children's patterns were either a
low-rate pacing (described earlier) or a
steady, high rate throughout the
interval.

Long (1962) developed special
techniques to produce good multiple
fixed-ratio, fixed-interval control in
normal children. Others (Bijou &
Orlando, 1961) also found it necessary to
develop special training procedures to
obtain discriminative control in multiple
schedules. Without special training,
both normal and retarded children tend
to respond similarly in both
components. Rats and pigeons usually
develop fixed-interval and fixed-ratio
patterns in the multiple schedule
without any difficulty.

Because of the problem of obtaining
long-term data with humans, DeCasper
and Zeiler (1972) developed a special
procedure to see if the variability and
peculiarity of the fixed-interval
behavior obtained with children to date

was due to an insufficient number of sessions or to a genuine species difference. They rigged a child's school locker with 10 lights and with controlling equipment so that when the child completed one schedule component, one of the lights would light. This is a 10-component chain schedule. When all 10 lights were lit, the locker opened and was available for the child to use the rest of the day. The use of this natural reinforcer was clever because each morning the child came to school, he would produce information about the schedule being studied, and also the experiment could run the entire school term. This technique very nicely avoided the problem of satiation encountered by many of the early schedule studies with humans.

DeCasper and Zeiler found that even after extended exposure to the multiple fixed-ratio, fixed-interval schedules, the children did not respond differentially. However, when the schedule was changed to multiple FR DRL (Differential Reinforcement of Low Rate), the low rates that developed in the DRL 10-sec component persisted when the schedule was returned to a multiple FR FI. Their findings suggest that it is not the length of the experimental history that was responsible for the lack of a differential performance in the multiple FI FR schedule, but rather, the kind of history the subject was given that determined the multiple performance.

Finally, Weiner (1964, 1969) found that the performance of normal, human adults on fixed-interval schedules is different than nonhuman performance. Some of his subjects responded at a steady rate throughout the interval, while others paused almost the complete interval before making a response, similar to the patterns found in both normal and retarded children. Like DeCasper and Zeiler, he found that the behavioral history of the subject was important in determining fixed-interval patterns. Subjects who had been given a history of fixed-ratio responding (high rates of responding are differentially reinforced) before being placed on the fixed-interval schedule responded at a high rate throughout the interval. Other subjects, who had been given a history with a DRL schedule, would pause a long time and make only one or two responses per interval when placed on the fixed-interval schedule. Thus one's behavioral history can interact strongly with the current schedule of reinforcement to determine the rate and pattern of responding.

Figure 11-15 shows some of Weiner's (1969) data with subjects given either an FR 40 or a DRL 20-sec history.

The subjects were male and female psychiatric nursing assistants from 18 to 50 years old. They were paid by the hour and were told to try to earn as many points as possible by pressing a button on a console. A reinforcer consisted of 100 points added to the counter. Sessions lasted an hour, and each subject had at least 10 sessions on a given schedule. The top four rows of cumulative records show various fixed-interval schedule performances *after* a conditioning history of FR 40. These subjects continued the high-rate responding developed in the FR 40 schedule when placed on the fixed-interval schedules. Subject 161 is a partial exception, as his ratio performance breaks down under the FI 60-sec and FI 300-sec schedules.

Subjects given the DRL history continued to respond in a similar fashion

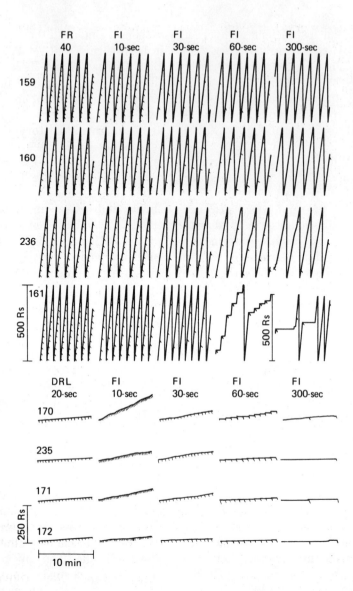

Figure 11-15

The effect of a differential history upon fixed-interval responding for 8 adult humans. After being exposed to an FR 40 schedule, the top 4 subjects responded almost uniformly at the same high rate on fixed-interval schedules of different lengths. The bottom 4 subjects were given a DRL 20-sec history and continued the pattern of responding developed on that schedule when exposed to the fixed-interval schedules (from Weiner, 1969).

on the fixed-interval schedules (the bottom four records). For these subjects, the post-reinforcement pause lengthened as the fixed interval grew longer, and most of the responses in the interval were made just prior to reinforcement. These subjects, in contrast to those given an FR 40 history, developed an accurate temporal discrimination.

In conclusion, most of the evidence with respect to schedule effects on humans is consistent. With the exception of the fixed-interval schedule, patterns of responding on the various schedules reveal a remarkable similarity across species. It should be added, however, that a multiple-schedule performance (e.g., multiple FR FI) may require special training procedures (see Bijou & Orlando, 1961; DeCasper & Zeiler, 1972; Long, 1962) to develop a well-differentiated performance.

Exam

1. Define:
   a. post-reinforcement pause
   b. extended chain schedule
   c. token reinforcement schedule
   d. fixed-chain schedule
   e. variable-chain schedule
   f. exchange ratio
   g. local rate or running rate
   h. observing response
   i. protection dependency
   j. steady-state behavior

2. Describe a cumulative recorder. What data does it provide?

3. Construct a 2 x 2 table which defines the four complex schedules of reinforcement. How does a multiple schedule differ from a tandem schedule? How would a performance on a *mult* FR 50 FR 50 differ from one on a *tand* FR 50 FR 50? (Draw a rough cumulative record of each performance to help you make comparisons.)

4. Draw a cumulative record of an alternating *mult* FR 25 FI 1-min on Figure 11-16. Use a scale of 5 responses for each square on the response axis (vertical axis), and 12 seconds for each square on the time axis (horizontal axis). Assume that the response pen resets after 250 responses, and construct a record of 500 responses. Since time in the fixed-ratio schedule and the number of responses within an interval in the fixed-interval schedule are free to vary, you have some freedom in constructing the curves. However, try to use the information you have learned about these schedules to draw representative performances.

5. How does a well-established fixed-ratio performance differ from a comparable variable-interval performance? (Contrast the performances in Figure 11-1 with those in Figures 11-3 and 11-4).

6. Compare and contrast extinction after a variable-interval schedule with extinction after continuous reinforcement.

7. How does a token reinforcement schedule differ from a simple chain schedule?

8. What was the purpose of Kelleher's (1958) experiment in which he paid the chimp 50 tokens at the beginning of the session? What did this experiment demonstrate?

9. Summarize the Kelleher and Fry (1962) experiment. How did the tandem schedule serve as a "catch" condition? Can a stimulus not associated with an unconditioned reinforcer, as in a chain schedule, become a conditioned reinforcer? Explain.

10. Describe Dews's experiment with drugs. What happened to the ratio and interval performances after the drug was injected? What advantages were there in using a multiple schedule instead of a simple schedule in assessing the effects of the drug?

11. Why did the bird's performance in the observing response experiment deteriorate (Figure 11-13)?

12. Is information a reinforcer? Explain and summarize the evidence that is germane to this question.

13. What is the conditioned reinforcement hypothesis of observing behavior?

14. What did DeCasper and Zeiler (1972) do, and what was the purpose of their study?

15. What do the cumulative records in Figure 11-15 show? What do these results mean?

16. Summarize the research with respect to the performance of humans on schedules of reinforcement and compare the findings to those for nonhumans. How would you answer a critic who maintains that " . . . research findings on schedules with rats and pigeons are of little value in understanding human behavior; that is data from animal studies are not generalizable to humans"?

References

Bijou, S. W., & Orlando, R. Rapid development of multiple-schedule performances with retarded children. *Journal of the Experimental Analysis of Behavior*, 1961, 4, 7-16.

DeCasper, A. J., & Zeiler, M. D. Steady-state behavior in children: A method and some data. *Journal of Experimental Child Psychology*, 1972, **13**, 231-239.

Dews, P. B. Modification by drugs of performance in simple schedules of positive reinforcement. *Annals of the New York Academy of Sciences*, 1956, **65**, 268-281.

Ferster, C. B., & Skinner, B. F. *Schedules of reinforcement*. New York: Appleton-Century-Crofts, 1957.

Kelleher, R. T. Chaining and conditioned reinforcement. In W. K. Honig (Ed.), *Operant behavior: Areas of research and application*. New York: Appleton-Century-Crofts, 1966. Pp. 160-212.

Kelleher, R. T.   Fixed-ratio schedules of conditioned reinforcement with chimpanzees. *Journal of the Experimental Analysis of Behavior*, 1958, **1**, 281-289.

Kelleher, R. T., & Fry, W. T.   Stimulus functions in chained fixed-interval schedules. *Journal of the Experimental Analysis of Behavior*, 1962, **5**, 167-173.

Lane, H. L., & Shinkman, P. G.   Methods and findings in an analysis of a vocal operant. *Journal of the Experimental Analysis of Behavior*, 1963, **6**, 179-188.

Long, E. R.   Additional techniques for producing multiple-schedule control in children. *Journal of the Experimental Analysis of Behavior*, 1962, **5**, 443-445.

Long, E. R., Hammack, J. T., May, F., & Campbell, B. J.   Intermittent reinforcement of operant behavior in children. *Journal of the Experimental Analysis of Behavior*, 1958, **1**, 315-339.

Orlando, R., & Bijou, S. W.   Single and multiple schedules of reinforcement in developmentally retarded children. *Journal of the Experimental Analysis of Behavior*, 1960, **3**, 339-348.

Weiner, H.   Conditioning history and human fixed-interval performance. *Journal of the Experimental Analysis of Behavior*, 1964, **7**, 383-385.

Weiner, H.   Controlling human fixed-interval performance. *Journal of the Experimental Analysis of Behavior*, 1969, **12**, 349-373.

Wyckoff, L. B.   The role of observing responses in discrimination learning. In D. P. Hendry (Ed.), *Conditioned reinforcement*. Homewood, Ill.: The Dorsey Press, 1969. Pp. 237-260.

Zeiler, M. D., & Kelley, C. A.   Fixed-ratio and fixed-interval schedules of cartoon presentation. *Journal of Experimental Child Psychology*, 1969, **8**, 306-313.

*

Figure 11-16 Cumulative record from a hypothetical session showing a
well-differentiated, *mult* FR 25 FI 1-min performance.

The Nature of
UNIT
Reinforcement

12

Within the last few years a psychologist, David Premack, has demonstrated that our conceptions about the nature of reinforcement have been much too narrow (Premack, 1965). As you recall, a reinforcer is any stimulus that increases the rate of the response which produced the stimulus. When asked to give an example of the reinforcing operation, a psychologist or student may say something like the following: "If you present food to a food-deprived animal dependent upon the animal's exercising (running in an activity wheel), the frequency of exercising will increase." There is nothing wrong with this example. Observe, however, that food is used as the reinforcer and exercise is used as the activity to be strengthened. Psychologists have tended to use such stimuli as food, water, and sucrose solutions so frequently as positive reinforcers that they tend to view them only as reinforcers. Premack has forced us to re-examine these preconceptions by showing us that the activities of eating and drinking themselves are reinforceable.

Premack's Rule

Consider any two activities, Behavior A and Behavior B, and let us observe how an organism spends its time in those activities when it is free to engage in either. Suppose that over a given time period, say 24 hours, we note that Behavior A is engaged in more frequently (or the organism spends

155

more time doing A) than Behavior B. We conclude that Behavior A is more probable than Behavior B. Premack has discovered that the more probable behavior can serve as a reinforcer for the less probable behavior, regardless of the kinds of behaviors involved. His principle states: *Of any hierarchy of behaviors, the more probable will reinforce any of the less probable behaviors.* This powerful generalization says that if we want to increase the frequency of a low-probability behavior, all we have to do is make the opportunity to engage in the high-probability behavior (HPB) dependent upon engaging in the low-probability behavior (LPB). A dependency statement would read, "If you do an LPB, then you may do an HPB." As an example, let's consider a fairly common low-frequency behavior such as writing letters to your friends or your congressman. (Letter writing is reinforced by an answer only after a long delay, which is one reason why writing letters is not a strong response in many people's repertoire.) Suppose further that you would like to increase the number of letters you write. Knowing about positive reinforcement and the importance of establishing a dependency between the behavior and a reinforcer, you might state to yourself that if you write a letter, you may have an ice cream sundae.

If you have to watch your calories, though, you would want to use a high-probability behavior other than eating. You might observe that you usually call at least one of your friends or acquaintances on the phone each day, and in comparing phone calls to letter writing, you might find that while the rate of phone calls is about 30 per

month, the rate of letter writing is less than 1 per month. According to Premack's rule, the opportunity to make a phone call, if made dependent upon writing a letter, will increase letter writing. The point is that one does not have to always rely on such stimuli as food, candy, and money to increase low-probability behavior.

The Relativity Principle of Reinforcement

An experiment conducted by Premack (1962) with rats illustrates the power of his rule. He placed a rat in a specially constructed cage so that the amount of drinking and exercising could be controlled. In the first condition, the rat had free access to a water bottle, and the rate at which he licked the drinking tube was recorded. During this same period, the exercise wheel was locked except for 1 hour, during which the number of turns of the wheel was measured. In this situation, the rate of running in the wheel was higher than the rate of licking. He arranged the apparatus so that the animal had to drink in order to free the activity wheel for a short while. With this dependency, the rate of drinking increased over normal rates, indicating that the opportunity to exercise was a reinforcer.

Next, he reversed the relation: The activity wheel was unlocked for 24 hours and the drinking tube was made available for only 1 hour. In this condition, he found that drinking was more frequent than running. When he established a dependency between running and drinking — the rat had to run to drink — he found that the rate of running increased over its baseline rate. Thus, he showed that the relation between the two activities was reversible. Which activity, running or drinking, reinforced the other was dependent upon which one was more probable at a given time.

This might be called the *relativity principle of reinforcement*. Instead of thinking "food is a reinforcer," which many of us tend to do, we should think that food is a stimulus which provides the organism with the opportunity to eat; at times, eating will be more probable than playing, and, at times, the reverse will be true. The activity that is momentarily more probable can be used as a reinforcer for the momentarily less probable.

Illustration

A. J. Bachrach, W. J. Erwin, and J. P. Mohr, The control of eating behavior in an anorexic by operant conditioning techniques. In L. P. Ullmann and L. Krasner (Eds.), *Case studies in behavior modification*. New York: Holt, Rinehart & Winston, 1965. Pp. 153-163.

A dramatic case illustrating that food is simply another stimulus which may or may not control eating is reported by Bachrach, Erwin, and Mohr (1965). A woman patient had a condition referred to as *anorexia nervosa*, in which the person simply does not eat or eats very sparingly. At the time they took the case, the therapists found that the woman weighed only 47 pounds. She was 5'4", so she was a veritable skeleton and close to death. Although she did not eat much, she did enjoy radio, television, and visitors, and she lived in an attractive hospital room. Preliminary treatment consisted of placing her in a bare room and not permitting any visitors. The hospital nurses were told not to talk to her, other than to say hello, and not to give her sympathy, which they had previously done.

As a part of the treatment, one of the authors was present when a meal was served. If the patient engaged in the low-frequency behavior, that is, picked up a utensil, took a bite of food, or chewed food, then he talked to her. She could engage in socializing (a high-probability behavior) only when she emitted some low-probability behavior. At first, the therapists required only that she pick up the fork or make a motion toward her food. Later she had to take a bite and swallow before they would talk to her. This dependency caused her to increase her intake of food. As she began to put on weight, other desired behaviors were permitted, such as having visitors, television, and dining with other patients. All of these activities were dependent upon eating and, later on, weight gain. This woman gradually gained weight until, at the time she was discharged, she weighed 88 pounds. Five years after this therapy she had maintained her weight and was employed in a job.

The Response-Deprivation Hypothesis

In a recent review article, Timberlake and Allison (1974) took a close look at Premack's rule and after considering some new research findings concluded that the rule should be modified. The problem arose because of an experiment Premack did (1965) to see whether a dependency between a pair of responses with differing probabilities

$$(LPB \longrightarrow HPB)[1]$$

always resulted in an increase in the response with the lower probability. He required a rat to emit only a small amount of the LPB (wheel running) to obtain a large amount of the HPB (licking for water). In other words, the rat could get all the water it normally drank without doing any more wheel running than it normally did. Under these conditions, there was *no* increase ᵢn wheel running! Even though ·emack's rule

$$(LPB \longrightarrow HPB)$$

was satisfied, there was no increase in the LPB, which meant that something else was necessary to produce a reinforcing effect.

Timberlake and Allison suggested that if an organism is deprived of making its normal, baseline rate of a given response (let's call this the **DEPENDENT RESPONSE**), it attempts to resolve the discrepancy between what it normally gets and what it is not getting by increasing the rate of an **INSTRUMENTAL RESPONSE** (the response that allows access to the deprived response). Let's suppose that a base rate for pressing a lever by a rat is 10 responses a day, and that the base rate for licking is 500 responses a day. When the experimenter places constraints upon access to one of these responses (the dependent response), he guarantees that in order for the rat to maintain the baseline rate for the dependent response (licking), the rat *must* necessarily increase the rate of

the instrumental response (lever-pressing). He does this by imposing a schedule of some type; that is, 100 lever presses (the instrumental response) provides the rat with 1 lick of water. The organism must be *deprived* of the opportunity to emit his normal, baseline rate of the dependent response (hence the term *Response Deprivation*), and a dependency must be established between the instrumental response and the dependent response for an increase to occur in the rate of the instrumental response.

We are now in a position to revise Premack's rule as follows: **FOR ANY PAIR OF RESPONSES, THE RATE OF THE INSTRUMENTAL RESPONSE CAN BE INCREASED IF ACCESS TO THE DEPENDENT RESPONSE IS RESTRICTED AND A DEPENDENCY IN THE FORM, INSTRUMENTAL RESPONSE LEADS TO DEPENDENT RESPONSE, IS ESTABLISHED.** Notice that this rule says nothing about which member of a response pair is more probable initially, so it is a much more general and powerful rule than Premack's. The following diagram, Figure 12-1, illustrates the possibilities for a pair of responses with different baseline rates. In the top panel, the baseline rates of responding have been determined for two responses in a free-responding situation, and R_1 occurs at one-half the rate of R_2. In Panel B, a dependency has been established between R_1 and R_2 such that $R_1 \longrightarrow R_2$, ($25R_1$ permits $10R_2$, for instance). Since the opportunity to make R_2 has been limited (by controlling how much access the organism has to that behavior, e.g., eating or drinking), the subject increases the rate of R_1 in an attempt to increase the rate of R_2.

[1]This statement should be read as follows: The opportunity to engage in a high-probability behavior is dependent upon first engaging in a low-probability behavior.

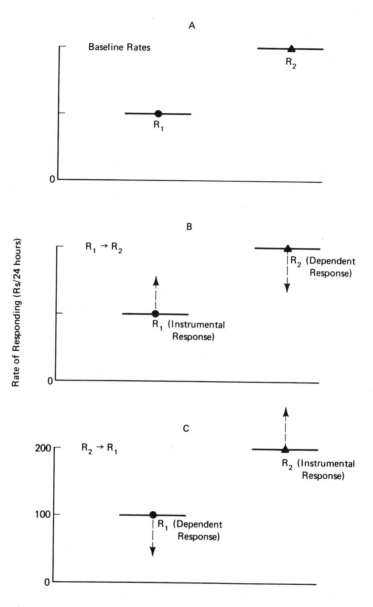

Figure 12-1

A schematic graph which illustrates the arrangements possible for a pair of responses under the response-deprivation hypothesis. Panel A: Baseline rates for the two responses. Panel B: When the subject is deprived of the opportunity to make the base rate of R_2, and a dependency is established so that R_1 allows access to R_2 ($R_1 \longrightarrow R_2$), the rate of R_1 increases over its base rate. Panel C: When the subject is deprived of the opportunity to make the base rate of R_1, and a dependency is established so that R_2 allows access to R_1 ($R_2 \longrightarrow R_1$), the rate of R_2 increases over its base rate.

Panel B thus represents Premack's rule for establishing a reinforcing relation: An HPB is made dependent upon an LPB.

The last panel, C, shows the reverse of Premack's rule. When access to R_1 is restricted (the organism cannot make his base rate of R_1), the rate of R_2 can be

Table 12-1

The mean number of wheel turns and licks for seven rats under a free-responding situation and two dependencies. In the first dependency, subjects were deprived of the opportunity to make their base rate of licks. In the second, they were deprived of the opportunity to make their base rate of wheel turns. Data estimated from Timberlake, W., & Allison, J. Response deprivation: An empirical approach to instrumental performance. *Psychological Review*, 1974, 81, 146-164.

Trial Blocks	N. of Wheel Turns	N. of Licks	Condition
	375	1215	Baseline
1	270	105	
2	375	135	
3	410	150	Dependency:
4	435	165	30 Turns ⟶ 10 licks
5	475	190	(Response deprivation of licking)
6	480	200	
1	480	1200	
2	510	1085	
3	415	1215	Baseline
4	310	975	
5	315	885	
1	75	840	Dependency:
2	120	1560	60 licks ⟶ 5 turns
3	145	1700	(Response deprivation of running)
4	135	1575	
1	345	1395	
2	355	1155	
3	445	645	Baseline
4	395	950	
5	380	960	

increased by establishing a dependency of the form: $R_2 \longrightarrow R_1$ (100 $R_2 \longrightarrow 5 R_1$, for instance). The HPB, R_2, must be engaged in for an opportunity to make the LPB, R_1. It seems backward according to Premack's rule, but it works and provides strong evidence for the Response-Deprivation Hypothesis postulated by Timberlake and Allison.

Table 12-1 gives the results of an experiment with rats which shows outcomes similar to those schematized in Figure 12-1. The pair of responses used was running in an activity wheel and licking a water bottle containing a saccharin solution, which rats like. The experimenters first measured the baseline number of running responses and drinking responses over a 4-day period and found that the average number for drinking was about 400 responses a day and for wheel turns was 1,200 responses a day. They then established a dependency between running and drinking such that 30 wheel turns gave 10 licks of the saccharin solution and after 10 licks were made, the wheel was unlocked so that the cycle could be repeated.[2] This schedule deprived the rat of drinking and, under these conditions, wheel running increased. After a return to baseline conditions, the dependency was changed so that 60 licks gave the rat an opportunity to make 5 wheel turns, and 5 wheel turns were required before the rat could gain access to the saccharin solution again. This schedule deprived the rat of running.

Plot the data in Table 12-1 on Figure 12-2 and note what happened to the rate of the instrumental response (licking) in the second dependency. Note that a double ordinate is used — the left is for wheel turns and the right is for licks. It is standard graphing procedure to plot data points from left to right so remember to start plotting lick frequency on the lefthand side of the figure. The baseline rates of each response for the first four days are already plotted for you. Observe that the scales for wheel turns and licking are different!

Application

L. E. Homme, P. C. deBaca, J. V. Devine, R. Steinhorst, and E. J. Rickert, Use of the Premack principle in controlling the behavior of nursery school children. *Journal of the Experimental Analysis of Behavior*, 1963, **6**, 544.

In a nursery school or kindergarten, children are often required to attend to

---

[2]This schedule has been termed a **RECIPROCAL SCHEDULE** by Allison (1971). It specifies the number of responses the subject has to perform for each response in the dependency. It is useful because it controls *exactly* how many responses will be made on each side of the dependent relation. The ordinary schedule only specifies the number on the instrumental side of the dependency; that is, an FR 10 schedule provides the rat with a 45-mg pellet of food (or the pigeon with a few seconds' access to grain) when the 10 responses have been made. The behavior of the subject with respect to the food is left unspecified. Pigeons prefer certain kinds of grain and eat those first when available. The food pellet frequently crumbles in the paws of the rat, with a large portion of the pellet falling through the floor of the experimental space. These conditions permit variability to occur with respect to food responses and will obscure the relation found in the response-deprivation formulation. (For a more thorough discussion of this problem, see Timberlake & Allison, 1974, p. 158).

the teacher or blackboard for a considerable stretch of time. The authors of this experiment were involved in helping teachers establish control over the children so that they would pay attention for a few minutes. When the experimenters first started, they noticed that each of the teachers had very little control over the children. When the teacher told them to sit in their seats and to pay attention, the children continued to run around and talk noisily. The authors decided to try Premack's rule. It was clear to everybody that the low-probability behavior was sitting in the seats and attending to the teacher's instructions. The high-probability behaviors were running around and yelling. The authors made the opportunity to run and scream dependent upon sitting still and attending to the teacher (response deprivation of running and screaming).

They started the experiment without requiring much of the low-probability behavior and gradually increased the length of time the children had to sit quietly (instrumental response). When the children had met the requirement of sitting in their seats for 3 minutes, a bell was rung. The bell was the signal for the children to get up, run, and scream. After a short period of the dependent behavior, another signal was given and the children were required to return to their seats. When the children returned to their seats, they were required to be attentive and quiet for another 3 minutes. Sometimes, however, as soon as they sat down, the bell was rung immediately and they could get up and run and scream again. This practice was very clever because it reinforced the children immediately for returning on command and for sitting down quickly.

Gradually, the requirements were lengthened. Later on in the experiment the children were given tokens for their desired behavior, and the various reinforcing activities could be purchased by the tokens at the end of the class. Meeting the requirements now produced a conditioned reinforcer, the token, and the opportunity to engage in the dependent activity, running and screaming, was purchased by a number of tokens. The use of tokens is convenient for several reasons: The reinforcing activity can be given at one time; the children can buy any number of activities, which increases the power of the token; and the number of tokens required to purchase a particular reinforcing activity can be increased as the target behavior grows stronger, which is economical.

Some of the activities nursery school children engage in are behaviors that adults often find aversive. Children run around, scream, yell, and throw erasers. All these are behaviors which adults usually control through punishment. Notice that the authors used the very behaviors that adults dislike and children enjoy to bring about good classroom control. This experiment points out that a highly reinforcing activity for one person may be seen as aversive by another. If the latter person desires to control the behavior of the former, he must disregard his feelings about the behavior of the learner. After all, it is always the learner, whether animal or child, who determines what will be reinforcing, *not* the teacher.

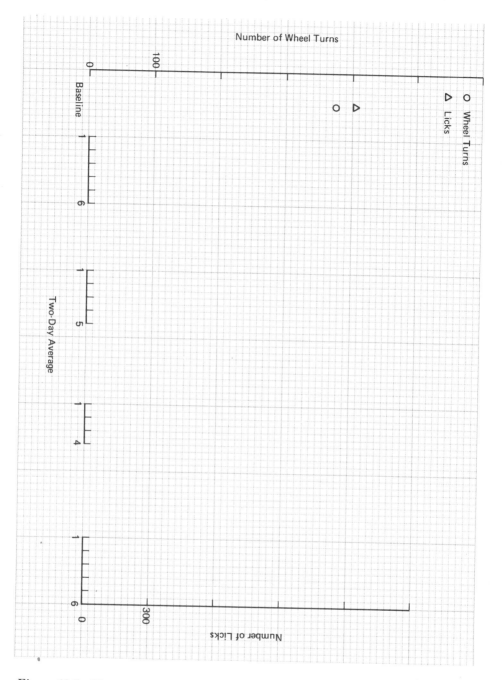

Figure 12-2 The mean number of wheel turns (left ordinate) and licks (right ordinate) under baseline and 2 response-deprivation conditions for 7 rats. In the first dependency, response deprivation was in effect for licking. In the second, response deprivation was in effect for running. After the first baseline condition, each data point is an average over 2 days.

*

Exam

1. State Premack's rule. List and describe the steps in applying Premack's rule.

2. What is the response-deprivation hypothesis? How does it extend Premack's rule?

3. A teacher remarks to you that she uses ice cream to reinforce good behavior in her classroom, but that there are two or three children who continue to be troublemakers in spite of her efforts to change their behavior. She suggests that some children are just stubborn and nothing can be done for this type. With respect to Premack's rule, or the response-deprivation hypothesis, how would you answer her?

4. A mother complains to you that her son "forgets" to practice his piano lessons even though she reminds him about it every day. She reports that if she would let him, he would spend all his time playing games with his gang. She also says that she rewards him with praise when he does practice, and that she has promised him a bicycle at the end of the year (!) if he will practice one hour regularly. In spite of her efforts, he rarely practices, and when he does he usually quits long before the hour time limit is up.
   a. What is wrong with this mother's approach?
   b. Using the response-deprivation rule, set up a program which would increase the amount of practice the boy does. (HINT: Utilize all the principles that seem relevant to the solution of this problem; i.e., where does some strengthening of his behavior with respect to practice time seem to be indicated?)

5. Describe the instrumental and dependent behaviors in the case of the woman who would not eat.

6. Summarize the steps that Homme et al. used to control the misbehavior of the nursery school children.

7. Summarize the experiment conducted by Timberlake and Allison. What evidence is there to support their hypothesis? What portion of the results graphed in Figure 12-2 are most detrimental to Premack's rule? Why?

References

Allison, J. Microbehavioral features of nutritive and nonnutritive drinking in rats. *Journal of Comparative and Physiological Psychology*, 1971, 76, 408-417.

Bachrach, A. J., Erwin, W. J., & Mohr, J. P. The control of eating behavior in an anorexic by operant conditioning techniques. In L. P. Ullmann & L. Krasner (Eds.), *Case studies in behavior modification*. New York: Holt, Rinehart & Winston, 1965. Pp. 153-163.

Homme, L. E., deBaca, P. C. Devine, J. V., Steinhorst, R., & Rickert, E. J. Use of the Premack principle in controlling the behavior of nursery school children. *Journal of the Experimental Analysis of Behavior*, 1963, 6, 544.

Premack, D.   Reversibility of the reinforcement relation. *Science*, 1962, **136**, 255-257.

Premack, D.   Reinforcement theory. In D. Levine (Ed.), *Nebraska symposium on motivation*. Lincoln: University of Nebraska Press, 1965. Pp. 123-180.

Timberlake, W., & Allison, J.   Response deprivation: An empirical approach to instrumental performance. *Psychological Review* 1974, 81, 146-164.

Stimulus Control: Introduction

13

In everyday life, behavior is largely controlled by changes in the environment that precede and accompany responding. There are many examples of this phenomenon that are so commonplace we take them for granted. When we approach an intersection with a red light while driving an automobile, under nearly all circumstances we apply the brakes and come to a stop. We may say that the red light controls the response of applying the brakes in this situation. When the light turns green, we release the brake and depress the accelerator. Here the green light controls the response of depressing the accelerator. The entire topography of the response is more complex than this might imply; that is, the complete response might well consist of removing the right foot from the brake, moving it over the accelerator, and subsequently extending the leg, resulting in acceleration.

There are more subtle examples, however, that are familiar to most. A cigarette smoker "feels the urge" for a cigarette when having a cup of coffee. The cup of coffee may in this case be said to control the smoking response. A smile from a woman may produce a return smile and perhaps a greeting from a passing man. Here the presence of the man controls the woman's smile, and her smile in turn controls the man's responses of smiling and saying hello. Telling ourselves a funny story may evoke overt laughter, just as recalling a time of embarrassment may produce blushing. In these cases, stimuli produced by oneself control some subsequent response.

Definitions of a Stimulus

Recall that a stimulus is any physical energy change that produces a change in behavior (Unit 3). If no change occurs in behavior, then there is a physical stimulus but no functional stimulus. That is, there is a stimulus that can be measured in physical units, but it is not related to behavior.

Two points need to be made emphatically regarding the definition of stimuli in physical terms: 1) We need to measure them in the manner just mentioned in order to communicate our findings to other scientists (common units of measurement have served other sciences very well); and 2) a definition of a stimulus in physical terms says nothing about, and carries no implication that, the stimulus is behaviorally functional. The latter point cannot be stressed heavily enough, so let's continue with another example. Many stimuli can be physically defined and have nothing to do with behavior. For example, high frequency sounds are physical stimuli but not functional for humans because we cannot hear them. A sound of 30,000 Hz. may be within the hearing range of a bat and can be directly functional for that animal. A 30,000 Hz. tone does become functional for humans when we use an instrument that detects sounds of that frequency and we respond discriminatively to the scales on the instrument.

It should be mentioned that just because a physical stimulus is not presently functional does not mean the results of its effects on the body might not become a stimulus at a later time. Ultraviolet rays on the Sunday bather may not produce behavior on Sunday. On Monday, however, the resulting sunburn pain may control going to the doctor. In ordinary language, physical and functional stimuli are confused often by our usage. Generally, when most people talk about a stimulus, they are referring to a physical stimulus. Stimuli dealt with in this book and by many psychologists are events functionally related to behavior.

Control by Antecedent Stimuli

Unconditional stimuli. A number of responses are directly controlled by preceding stimuli with no history of conditioning. We might say that this type of stimulus control is innate. It is exhibited in unconditional reflexes of the kind Sherrington and Pavlov dealt with; that is, responses of smooth muscles and glands. The stimulus of lemon juice in the mouth controls a salivation response. In the case of respondents, it is said that the stimulus elicits the response. Stimulus control of this kind has typically been of interest to the physiologist. He has been able to show that the magnitude of the stimulus (within limits) controls the magnitude of the response. For example, a light tap on the patellar tendon will elicit a smaller knee jerk than will a heavier tap.

Conditional stimuli. We said in Unit 4 that respondent conditioning takes place when a neutral stimulus — that is, a physical but nonfunctional stimulus — is paired with an already functional, unconditional stimulus. After numerous pairings, our formerly neutral stimulus now is functional because it elicits respondent behavior similar to that elicited by the unconditional stimulus.

This relation can also be thought of as

one kind of stimulus control. Here a specific neutral stimulus may become functional for the elicitation of a respondent via the procedures of respondent conditioning. If the unconditional stimulus elicits a number of respondents (which it may do), the conditional stimulus can become functional for all of these. To differentiate this type of stimulus control clearly from that existing over operants, we can call it **RESPONDENT STIMULUS CONTROL**.

Both of the above kinds of stimulus control are restricted to respondents. Respondent stimulus control is extremely important because respondent behavior comprises a crucial aspect of emotional behavior (see Units 16 and 17).

Control by Consequent Stimuli

We may also consider that the control over behavior by consequent stimuli is a form of stimulus control. That is, if a consequent stimulus produces an increased rate of responding — as food does when delivered dependent on a rat's bar-pressing responses — we may say that the consequent stimulus controls the rate of that responding. For example, food pellets delivered after every 10th bar press will control a different rate of responding in the rat than will food pellets delivered only if the animal responds *less* than once every 10 seconds. Additionally, the pattern of responding produced by these two schedules will be different. These rates and patterns are due to the schedule dependency itself — that is, when, in relation to behavior, the reinforcing stimulus occurs. As the reinforcing stimulus controls behavior

when it is variously scheduled, we consider this kind of stimulus control as **SCHEDULE CONTROL**.

When other stimuli are added to a reinforcement schedule, but are not the primary reinforcing stimulus, they may still come to control responding because of their association with the reinforcing stimulus and the responding the latter generates. For example, one could turn on a blue light when a child was responding on a fixed-ratio schedule and a red light when he was responding on a fixed-interval schedule. Eventually, these lights would control responding appropriate to each of the above schedules. This can be demonstrated by interchanging the lights and the reinforcement schedules: Blue is now associated with fixed-interval reinforcement and red with fixed-ratio reinforcement. For some time our subject will continue to produce behavior appropriate to a fixed-ratio schedule in the presence of the blue light and fixed-interval behavior in the presence of the red light, suggesting the control of these lights over his behavior. Eventually, however, his behavior will again correspond to the schedule on which it is currently reinforced. The type of stimulus control produced by the lights in the above example we will call **DISCRIMINATIVE CONTROL**. Note that it is a form of antecedent stimulus control, that is, control by a stimulus over a response where the stimulus occurs prior to the response. The stimulus *sets the occasion for*, or *cues* the response. This control doesn't just happen; its existence depends on what happens after the response — on the existence of a response-reinforcing stimulus relation such as exists in schedules of reinforcement. In general, the phrase, "stimulus control", as used by psychologists today, refers to this type of control by antecedent stimuli over operants. We will deal with this aspect of stimulus control more completely in Unit 14.

We can note at this point that there are only three functions of a stimulus. The stimulus may serve to 1) **ELICIT** responding as we have discussed above; 2) reinforce or otherwise **CONSEQUATE** responding; or 3) be **DISCRIMINATIVE**, that is, set the occasion for responding. In real-life situations, it is unlikely that these functions are separate and much more likely that they occur together. In other words, a stimulus that functions as an elicitor for some respondent behavior, simultaneously is discriminative for some operant behavior, and concurrently consequates some other operant behavior. In the laboratory, these functions are most often studied separately. A real-life example involves an infant being fed by his father. The infant's seeing the food is the stimulus to be examined. It may function to produce salivation in the child's mouth. If it does, the sight of the food functions as an eliciting stimulus. If the vocalization following the sight of the food is likely to be consequated by father placing the food in the infant's mouth, then the sight of the food is likely to be discriminative for the babbling which follows. Finally, the sight of the food may be a reinforcer strengthening behavior that produces it. If this is the case, any behavior which results in the sight of food on a spoon may be strengthened. For example, looking at the spoon may be consequated by seeing the food.

The entire sequence is diagrammed in Figure 13-1. Although the stimulus in

the example has several functions, we know little about the mutual exclusiveness of these functions. For example, we do not yet have much information regarding whether: 1) a stimulus can be discriminative but not reinforcing; 2) a stimulus can be reinforcing, but not discriminative; and 3) a stimulus can be a reinforcer, but not an elicitor.

Let us look at an example of the problem of determining whether a stimulus is always an elicitor when it is a reinforcer. A boy may cut lawns for $2 each and evince no emotion when paid for his work. One of his clients, playing psychologist, could on one occasion give him $50 for the same work. The responses produced by the $50 now might be described as surprise, joy, confusion, or, in short mixed emotions. A reinforcer, which appeared to have no eliciting functions, has gained one as a result of increasing its intensity. This is only a hypothetical example, and we simply do not know much about these relations yet. More to come.

Illustration

N. A. Davidson, and J. G. Osborne, Fixed-ratio and fixed-interval schedule control of matching-to-sample errors by children. *Journal of the Experimental Analysis of Behavior*, 1974, 21, 27-36.

As the title in this suggests, this illustration will deal primarily with schedule control of children's behavior. The technique the authors employed in their study is called **MATCHING TO SAMPLE**, which is a variety of **CONDITIONAL DISCRIMINATION**. A conditional discrimination is a

Figure 13-1

A plausible stimulus-response sequence involving the interaction of an infant and his father. The sequence illustrates the three functions a stimulus can have.

1) Consequating function: R (Looks at spoon and food) $\longrightarrow$ S^{r+} (Sight of food)

2) Eliciting function: CS (Sight of Food) $\longrightarrow$ CR (Increased saliva flow)

3) Discriminative function: S^D (Sight of food) $\longrightarrow$ R (Babbling)

4) Consequating function: R (Babbling) $\longrightarrow$ S^{R+} (Father places food in mouth)

task in which the subject's reinforcement for responding is dependent on at least two stimulus properties of the environment. In a simple discrimination, a subject may only have to learn that pressing a red key is reinforced while pressing a green key is not reinforced. In this example the correctness of the response is based on a single environmental property — the wavelength of light that produces the red on the response key. In a conditional discrimination, the red key might be correct only if a white vertical line is superimposed on it. When a horizontal white line is superimposed on the key, responding is not reinforced. Now let us add another color. When green is the background color and the horizontal line is superimposed, responding is also reinforced. Finally, when the vertical line is superimposed on the green background, responding is not reinforced. These four stimulus combinations are depicted in Figure 13-2. If you think carefully about them, you will note that in order to be correct (i.e., to respond only to the two stimuli correlated with reinforcement), our experimental subject must look at both properties of the key — color *and* line orientation. One

stimulus property will not allow the subject to discriminate reinforcement from nonreinforcement because red alone is sometimes correct and sometimes incorrect. Similarly, the vertical line is sometimes correct and sometimes incorrect. Hence, the foregoing is a *conditional* discrimination.

Matching to sample is a conditional discrimination and an important one. Variants of this task appear on diagnostic and intelligence tests. The task is also widely used in education. In a typical matching paradigm there are at least three responses that can be made. Initially a single stimulus is presented (let's say the color red), then several more stimuli are presented in a group. The color red is within the group; perhaps the remaining colors are blue, green, yellow, and orange. If the subject chooses the red stimulus from the group, he has matched the original stimulus. The initial stimulus to be matched is called the *standard* or the *sample*. The stimuli from which the subject indicates a match are called the *comparisons* or *choices*. Important to this technique is that on a trial following the above example, a different stimulus (color) will be the standard; hence, a

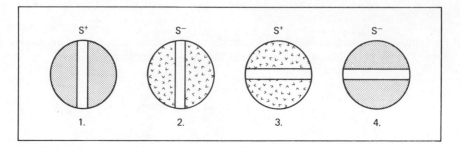

Figure 13-2

Four different states of a response key in which correct responding is conditional upon two environmental properties. The key is illuminated by either a horizontal or vertical white line and at the same time the background color is either green (lines) or red (dots). Responding is reinforced only when it occurs during stimulus combinations labelled S⁺ and not in those labelled S⁻.

different comparison will be correct. If red were the standard every time, the subject could ignore the standard and simply choose red each time from the comparison stimuli. In this example there is no conditional relation.

Where the standard changes irregularly from trial to trial, the correctness of the subject's choice from among the comparisons is *conditional*, dependent on which stimulus is the standard on that trial. Not only must the subject discriminate one stimulus from all the others in the comparison group, but he must also know what the standard to be matched is. Thus, correct responding is conditional in the above example on two environmental properties and the discrimination is a conditional one. Three typical matching-to-sample procedures are portrayed in Figure 13-3.

Davidson and Osborne reinforced children on a line orientation matching-to-sample task. Correct matches were reinforced in one

experiment on fixed-ratio schedules for token reinforcers. That is, the child could make 10 correct matches (an FR 10) and the 10th match would produce a token, exchangeable after each session for toys, candy, and the like. In another experiment the first correct matching response after the elapse of a fixed period of time was reinforced (e.g., FI 12-sec). Subjects were also reinforced on variable-ratio and variable-interval schedules of reinforcement at other times during the experiment. These latter schedules were the control ("catch") conditions of the study.

The behavior of greatest interest to Davidson and Osborne was mismatching, or failing to match, which did not lead to reinforcement and was considered an error. Errors did not advance the subjects through a ratio and never produced a token. Psychologists are interested in why errors occur because errors may be considered maladaptive behavior. It is interesting to find that certain

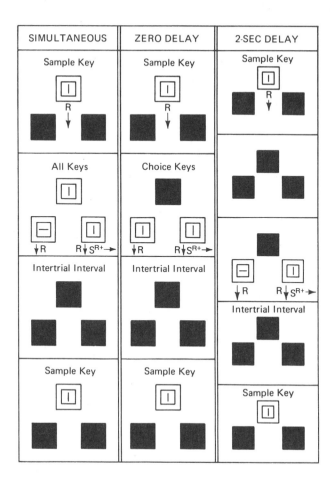

Figure 13-3

Three typical matching-to-sample procedures. Each
panel should be read from top to bottom. Note that
in simultaneous matching to sample, the sample
remains illuminated while the choice stimuli are
illuminated. This is not the case for the two types of
delayed matching. The top panels represent the start
of a trial; the second panels represent the condition
occurring after a response to the sample (panels two
and three for the 2-sec delay); the third panels
represent the state after a choice response is made
(the fourth panel for the 2-sec delay condition).
(Drawing courtesy of N. A. Davidson.)

schedules of reinforcement produce reliable patterns of errors on discrimination tasks. Investigators working with pigeons had already shown that the following pattern of errors occurred when their subjects were reinforced on fixed ratio: The greatest likelihood of an error was during initial responding in the ratio after reinforcement, and the farther the pigeon went in the ratio, the fewer errors it produced (Nevin, Cumming, & Berryman, 1963). Does this pattern of decreasing errors depend on reinforcement being on a fixed-ratio schedule? One way to determine this is to use a variable-ratio reinforcement schedule that reinforces the same number of matching responses on the average as the fixed-ratio schedule; that is keep the average number of responses per reinforcement the same, but deliver the reinforcers after different numbers of matches have been emitted. This constitutes a "catch" condition. Davidson and Osborne were able to show that children, too, produced the same error pattern on fixed-ratio schedules of reinforcement. Similar patterns did not occur on variable-ratio schedules for matching. Their study suggests that schedule control of responding, a kind of stimulus control by the reinforcing stimulus, can have an effect on human as well as animal behavior.

In Table 13-1 we have included the results of one child from the Davidson and Osborne study who showed evidence of the response patterns on simultaneous matching to sample. Most of the remaining children produced error patterns on zero-delay rather than simultaneous matching to sample.

Ratios of incorrect to correct matching responses are presented in the table for the last 3 days of responding on FR 3, FR 4, FR 5, and VR 3. Sum the ratios at each ordinal position of the FR and VR across the 3 days; divide by 3 for each ordinal position of each ratio value and write these sums and means in the indicated locations of Table 13-1. Then graph the means in your figure. Use a different symbol for each FR value. Make VR values filled symbols and FR values nonfilled symbols.

Ordinal position in the ratio will constitute the abscissa; you will need six locations to accommodate VR 3. The ordinate will be the ratio of incorrect to correct matching responses. Your figure will contain four different sets of symbols. In a corner of the figure indicate which symbols correspond to which ratios.

Table 13-1

The ratio of incorrect to correct responses for one subject (LO) on simultaneous matching to sample as a function of the ordinal position in the schedule. Data taken from Davidson, N. A., & Osborne, J. G.   Fixed-ratio and fixed-interval schedule control of matching-to-sample errors by children. *Journal of the Experimental Analysis of Behavior*, 1974, 21, 27-36.

	Day	Ordinal Position in the Fixed-Ratio Schedule		
		1	2	3
FR3	1	.13	.03	.03
	2	.10	.07	.03
	3	.13	.07	.03
	Sum			
	Mean			

	Day	1	2	3	4
FR4	1	.30	.17	.17	.13
	2	.17	.07	.10	.07
	3	.13	.07	.03	.10
	Sum				
	Mean				

	Day	1	2	3	4	5
FR5	1	.47	.27	.20	.33	.03
	2	.40	.27	.37	.27	.30
	3	.33	.43	.27	.07	.07
	Sum					
	Mean					

	Day	1	2	3	4	5	6
VR3	1	.07	.20	.06	.15	.08	.00
	2	.13	.05	.00	.17	.10	.33
	3	.21	.05	.29	.00	.00	.33
	Sum						
	Mean						

Exam

1. Present an example (that is not contained in the text) of human behavior under the control of antecedent stimuli.
2. Differentiate between the physical and functional aspects of stimuli.
3. What are the three functions of a stimulus? Give an example of each.
4. Describe an instance, not in the text, in which a stimulus has three functions for one individual's behavior.
5. Produce an example from your own experience in which a reinforcer has taken on an additional function.
6. Define the following terms:
   a. matching to sample
   b. conditional discrimination
   c. standard stimulus
   d. comparison stimulus
7. Describe Subject LO's pattern of errors on FR 3, FR 4, and FR 5 in your figure. Contrast the shape of these patterns with the error pattern produced on VR 3. How are these data evidence for schedule control of behavior?

References

Davidson, N. A., & Osborne, J. G. Fixed-ratio and fixed-interval schedule control of matching-to-sample errors by children. *Journal of the Experimental Analysis of Behavior*, 1974, **21**, 27-36.

Nevin, J. A., Cumming, W. W., & Berryman, R. Ratio reinforcement of matching behavior. *Journal of the Experimental Analysis of Behavior*, 1963, **6**, 149-154.

Figure 13-4 The ratio of incorrect to correct responses for one subject (LO) on simultaneous matching to sample as a function of the ordinal position in the schedule.

*

Stimulus Control:
Operant Behavior

14

Producing Stimulus Control

Traditional operations for producing stimulus control have been the reinforcement of a response in the presence of one stimulus and the extinction of the same response in the presence of another stimulus. Here is a simple example: A rat, deprived of food for 24 hours, presses a bar in the presence of a white light and receives a pellet of food for each bar press. After a number of reinforcements, the food dispenser is disconnected at the same time as the light is changed from white to blue. Bar presses no longer produce food reinforcement (extinction). The experimenter now waits until the rate of responding in the presence of the blue light is near zero. He then turns on the white light and at the same time reconnects the food dispenser; responding in the presence of the white light is again reinforced. This same sequence of events is repeated until the following pattern of behavior is exhibited by the rat: When the blue light is on, the animal does not respond on the bar, but when the white light comes on the animal immediately approaches the bar and responds for the duration of the white light. The white light sets the occasion on which bar pressing, if it occurs, will be reinforced. As the white light is discriminative for reinforcement, it is called a **DISCRIMINATIVE STIMULUS**. In fact, any stimulus which sets the occasion for a response to produce a consequence (either reinforcing or aversive) is a discriminative stimulus. General usage calls the stimulus present when reinforcement occurs an S^D (pronounced *ess-dee*), and the stimulus present during extinction an S^Δ (pronounced *ess-delta*). However, it should be stated that S^Ds and S^Δs are both discriminative stimuli.

Evidence of a Discrimination

Evidence that a discrimination has been formed comes from the differential response rate in the presence of the two lights. In the presence of the white light, the animal responds frequently, while in the presence of the blue light he does not respond very much at all.

There are other bases for determining that a discrimination exists. If the response rates do not differ in the presence of two different stimuli, the investigator can determine whether the response pattern, the distribution of responses in time, is different in the presence of the two stimuli. A discrimination exists when the response patterns emitted in the presence of two or more stimuli are unique to each individual stimulus. For example, if the schedule of reinforcement in the presence of one light is fixed ratio and the schedule of reinforcement in the presence of another is fixed interval, response rates could be the same on both schedules. Thus, the response rates, by themselves, would provide no evidence of a discrimination. However, if the investigator examines the pattern of responses in these examples, he should easily be able to find evidence of a discrimination. We know that repeated exposure to a schedule of reinforcement eventually produces behavior characteristic of that schedule. Experts in the field can look at a cumulative record and identify the schedule of reinforcement that produced it. A standard case is depicted in Figure 14-1 where we show in stylized form how FR and FI schedules may produce similar overall response rates, but have their own characteristic patterns.

Another way to examine possible differences in the patterning of responses is to examine the frequencies of **INTERRESPONSE TIMES (IRTs)** produced by a given schedule. An **IRT** is the time measured from one response to the next response, hence interresponse time. Distributions of IRTs differ for different schedules.

Further evidence of a discrimination exists when a stimulus controls one response and a different stimulus controls a different response. In the presence of a blue light, bar pressing might be reinforced, while in the presence of a red light, pulling a chain might be reinforced. If each response occurs only when its stimulus is present, stimulus control exists over these responses.

In Table 14-1, the responding of an elementary school child on a bar in order to produce tokens is recorded. In the presence of the red light (S^D), the token schedule of reinforcement was VI 20-sec. Tokens could be exchanged after each session for toys, candies, soda-pop, and the like. In the presence of the blue light, an extinction schedule was in effect; that is, responding was never reinforced in the presence of the blue light (S^Δ). **On your graph paper, plot separate curves for responding in the presence of the blue and red lights.**

Observe that there is an extra column provided in the table labelled "S^D/S^Δ Ratio." This ratio is another way a psychologist can determine the

Table 14-1

The initial development of a discrimination in an elementary school child. Data taken from Waite, W., & Osborne, J. G. Sustained behavioral contrast in children. *Journal of the Experimental Analysis of Behavior*, 1972, 18, 113-117.

	Number of Responses		
Sessions	Blue Light (S$^\Delta$)	Red Light (S^D)	S^D/S$^\Delta$
1	228	190	0.83:1
2	238	252	
3	242	334	
4	99	284	
5	190	325	
6	82	282	
7	57	227	
8	23	230	
9	10	334	
10	10	415	
11	10	356	
12	7	364	
13	10	382	38.2:1

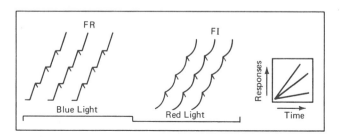

Figure 14-1

Stylized FR and FI performances in which the general response rate is the same on each schedule as determined by viewing the overall slope of the curves, while the distribution of responses is unique to each schedule. Note the pause after reinforcement and the abrupt higher rate characteristic of the FR, and the pause after reinforcement and the gradual acceleration to a high rate on the FI.

quality of the discrimination his subject is forming. A good discrimination is considered to be one in which the subject emits at least 10 responses in the presence of S^D for every response emitted in the presence of S$^\triangle$ — or, an S^D/S$^\triangle$ ratio of 10:1. Calculate this ratio by dividing the number of responses occurring for each session in the presence of S$^\triangle$ *into* the number of responses occurring for each session in the presence of S^D. The first and last ratios are already calculated to provide discriminative stimuli for the reader. Note that the ratio is of responses in S^D to responses in S$^\triangle$; therefore, the S^D figure comes first in the ratio.

Errorless Discrimination Formation

The operations of differential reinforcement, that is, reinforcement and extinction, were for many years considered to be the only ones capable of producing a discrimination. However, recently another set of operations called either **STIMULUS SHAPING** or, after their progenitor, H. S. Terrace, *the Terrace technique*, have been shown to produce stimulus control. A primary difference is that stimulus shaping avoids the responding that usually takes place in extinction.

Stimulus shaping capitalizes on prior discriminations, either conditioned or innate, that the organism makes. For example, pigeons have a higher probability of pecking a lighted key than a dark one prior to any training. Given this discrimination, a pigeon can be taught to discriminate two hues without ever responding to the stimulus the

psychologist chooses to remain unreinforced.

A critical aspect of the technique is to make the stimuli to be discriminated initially unlike each other in order to facilitate the likelihood of the stimuli controlling differential responding. As the discrimination forms, the S$^\triangle$ is made more like the S^D until they differ only on the dimension on which the discrimination is to be based. This operation is called **FADING**, and is synonymous with stimulus shaping.

In his original experiment Terrace began with reinforcements in the presence of S$^+$. S$^+$ and S$^-$ are used here instead of S^D and S$^\triangle$ to connote that the stimuli became functional via stimulus shaping rather than via traditional reinforcement and extinction procedures. To begin with, few reinforcements are given in S$^+$ rather than many, so the likelihood of responding to other stimuli will be minimized. The S$^+$ was a red light, while S$^-$ was a green light. However, when first presented, S$^-$ was no light at all. The light remained off for a few seconds only, further restricting the likelihood that responding would occur. Alternating with times in which the light was red, the time it was dark was gradually increased until it was equal in duration to the red light. Under these conditions, most pigeons responded infrequently — if at all — when the light was off, and continued responding when the light was red. Then, in S$^-$, a dim green light was introduced. The time this color was present was set back to the short time that S$^-$ was present initially. Interspersed by presentations of the red light, the intensity of the green light was gradually increased until it was equal in intensity to the red. Thereafter, the time the green light was on was progressively lengthened until it

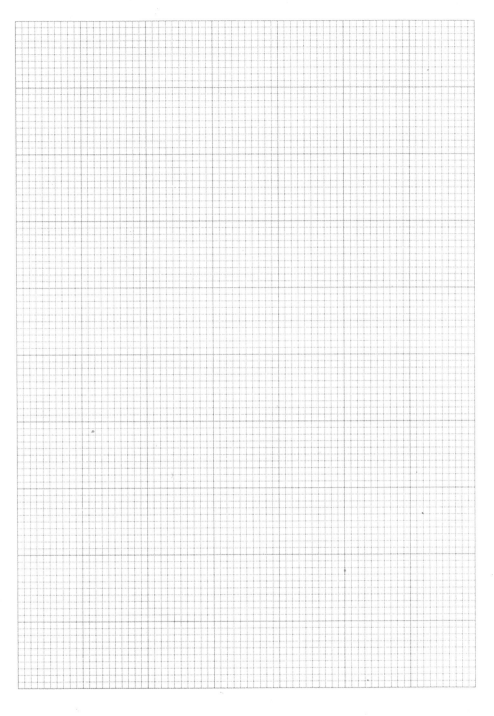

Figure 14-3 The development of a discrimination by an elementary school child as measured by a discrimination index ($S^D/S^\triangle$).

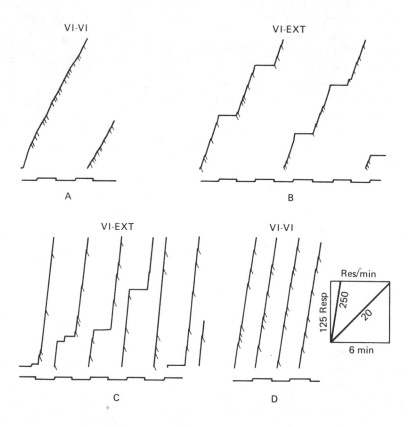

Figure 14-4

Cumulative record of the responding of an elementary school
child on *mult* VI 20-sec VI 20-sec (Panel A), *mult* VI 20-sec EXT
(Panels B and C), and *mult* VI 20-sec VI 20-sec (Panel D). Note
increased response rate during *mult* VI EXT. (Panel B is an early
session on *mult* VI EXT and Panel C is 6 sessions later.) The
event line across the bottom of each panel indicates which
component is in effect (from Waite & Osborne, 1972).

was present as long as the red light. Throughout the final fading operations, little or no responding occurred to the green light (S⁻), while responding continued when the red light was present. Because few or no responses occur to S⁻ using this technique, and responses to S⁻ might signify that the organism is responding incorrectly, discriminations formed by this technique have been called *errorless discriminations*.

There are some intriguing differences between discriminations formed *with* and *without* responding in extinction. First, a discrimination formed errorlessly appears to be a better discrimination than one formed with errors. In the latter, the animal may always continue to make a few responses to the S^Δ. Further, errorless discriminations appear to be formed with no emotional responding. While it must be emphasized that no punishment is used to produce a discrimination with errors, presentation of the S^Δ-extinction phase often elicits emotional behavior. Little emotional behavior is seen during the S⁻ of an errorless discrimination.

There are a number of other differences in animal discriminative behavior when the discrimination is errorlessly formed, and these are described below along with phenomena that are known to be associated.

Some Phenomena That Occur with Regular Discrimination Formation

Behavioral contrast. When an animal or child is responding on a multiple schedule of reinforcement, let's say

mult VI 20-sec VI 20-sec, the response rate is about the same in each component. (See Figure 14-4, Panel A, for an example of this rate equality.) If we change one component to extinction so that the schedule is now *mult* VI 20-sec EXT, we have begun a procedure which may eventually produce discriminative responding by our subject. We may note that the response rate decreases during the extinction component. Often, however, the response rate in the VI 20-sec component increases over what it was during the original schedule. (This occurrence can be seen in panels B and C of Figure 14-4). At first glance there seems to be no reason for this. Responding faster in the VI components does not produce more reinforcement, as beyond a certain minimum response rate for a given VI schedule the reinforcements per unit time are constant. When response rate in the unchanged component increases and response rate in the changed component decreases as a function of a manipulation in the changed component, the change is called **BE-HAVIORAL CONTRAST.**[1]

Contrast is an example of a schedule *interaction* where a change in one schedule of reinforcement produces a behavior change in another schedule

[1]Where the rate in the unchanged component increases concomitantly with a decrease in the changed component, the effect is called *positive* behavioral contrast. The converse is *negative* behavioral contrast and is seen where the response rate in the unchanged component decreases concomitantly with an increase in response rate in the changed component. Critical to the definition of an interaction as contrast is that the rates in the separate components change in opposite directions.

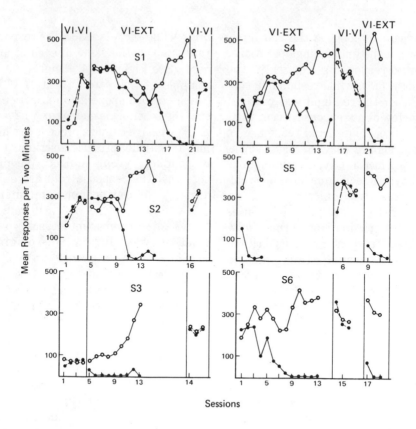

Figure 14-5

The number of responses emitted in each component of a *mult* VI 20-sec VI 20-sec and a *mult* VI 20-sec EXT schedule by 6 elementary school children (from Waite & Osborne, 1972).

that is not directly manipulated.[2] By now this is a routine finding with animals (Amsel, 1962; Reynolds, 1961) and children (Nicholson & Gray, 1971; O'Brien, 1968; Waite & Osborne, 1972) during traditional discrimination formation. Figure 14-5 depicts the occurrence of both positive and negative behavioral contrast by children who were switched from *mult* VI 20-sec VI 20-sec to *mult* VI 20-sec EXT and back again. See if you can

[2]A second kind of interaction among schedules is called *induction*. Response rates in separate components of a complex schedule must change in similar directions (both increase or both decrease) as a function of a change in only one component of the schedule.

point to the evidence for contrast in each subject, and prepare to answer questions regarding this figure on the exam at the end of this unit.

With regard to contrast, errorlessly formed discriminations differ from those formed where many errors occur. Subjects behaving discriminatively, without having made errors, do not produce behavioral contrast (Terrace, 1966).

Illustration

R. B., Powers, C. D., Cheney, & N. Agostino, Errorless training of a visual discrimination in preschool children. *The Psychological Record*, 1970, **20**, 45-50.

Shortly after Terrace's original work with pigeons (Terrace, 1963a, 1963b) Robert Moore and Israel Goldiamond, (Moore & Goldiamond, 1964) demonstrated that errorless discriminations

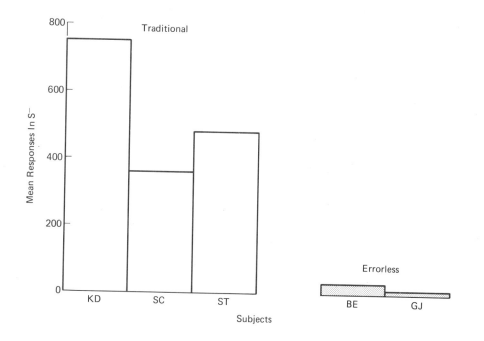

Figure 14-6

The mean number of responses made in the presence of the S⁻ (errors) for 5 children, 3 of whom were trained under traditional discrimination procedures and 2 of whom were trained under errorless discrimination procedures (data estimated from Powers, Cheney, & Agostino, 1970).

could also be formed by nursery school children. They employed a matching-to-sample task using the orientation of triangles in space as the solution to the matching problem. That is, the children had to match a comparison triangle to a standard triangle based on the fact that the apex of the comparison pointed in a similar direction to the apex of the standard. This is not an easy discrimination for young children. Moore and Goldiamond made the brightness of the standard and the correct comparison stimuli equal, and lowered the brightness of the incorrect comparisons. Across trials the incorrect comparisons were made incrementally brighter until eventually there were no brightness differences among correct and incorrect comparisons. In most cases the children, who were initially under the control of brightness alone, transferred to the orientation dimension and continued to respond correctly. When children were not given the brightness difference to rely on initially, they made many errors. This was the first demonstration of errorless discrimination by children.

Important application and extension of this work next took place by Sidman and his associates at Massachusetts General Hospital in Boston (Sidman & Stoddard, 1967; Stoddard & Sidman, 1967; Touchette, 1968). They showed that this same technique could be used to help severely retarded youngsters make discriminations among form stimuli (circles and ellipses). Importantly, their work showed that their most severely retarded subjects could discriminate among a circle and a set of ellipses (that were very circle-like) about as well as normal children did. This allowed the inference,

at least for the children in their sample (who had a wide variety of diagnoses), that the visual perception of the retarded children was little different than that of normal children. We might loosely say they "see" the same things. Educators have long suggested the opposite of retarded children, based on very weak evidence.

Powers et al. extended the above work by suggesting that the addition of a stimulus from a dimension not included in the final discrimination may facilitate errorless discrimination. A suggestion of their results is that this additional stimulus helps make the S⁻ "look" more different to the subject than it would if the additional stimulus were not present. They used five preschool children, training three traditionally, for comparison purposes, and having two use Terrace's procedures. First, the children received marbles on FR 10 for presses on a lever below a plastic window lit with a red light (S⁺). For the traditionally trained subject, the red light (S^D) alternated every minute with a red-orange light (S$^\Delta$) during which responses were not reinforced. For the errorless subjects, the S⁻ was originally a white light presented for no more than 5 seconds and accompanied by a loud noise. Across sessions the length of time that S⁻ was present for the errorless subjects was increased to 60 seconds in 5-second increments. Simultaneously, the experimenters decreased the intensity of the accompanying noise. After a number of sessions the noise disappeared and S⁻ (white light) was present as long as the S⁺ (60 seconds each occasion). Finally, a sequence of colors, which grew closer to red-orange with each step, was presented in lieu of the white light. Each time a new color step in the S⁻ series was introduced, it was accompanied by re-introduction of the noise at a moderate intensity. Remember that throughout these sessions S⁺ presentations went on as usual.

One set of results from the experiment is shown in Figure 14-6. This figure shows the mean number of errors made by children in the traditional and errorless groups. While this figure is drawn for you, it should still be scrutinized carefully so that you are able to answer questions concerning it on the unit exam. For instance, you will want to note the differences in the number of errors produced by children from each of the treatments.

Exam

1. How does differential reinforcement result in stimulus control?
2. What is fading?
3. What is the stimulus shaping technique for producing stimulus control?
4. How is an errorless discrimination different than one formed via traditional reinforcement and extinction?
5. What are three ways in which responding provides evidence of stimulus control?
6. Plot a graph from Table 14-1 having sessions on the abscissa and your calculated $S^D/S^\triangle$ ratios on the ordinate. Then answer the following questions based on your graph:
   a. How does the ratio change as the discrimination develops?
   b. What factor contributes most to the change in this ratio?
   c. By what session has a "good" discrimination formed?
7. Define behavioral contrast. Give an example of negative behavioral contrast. (Hint: Draw a freehand graph with response rates depicted over time.)
8. Examine Figure 14-4. Point to evidence to positive behavioral contrast in the figure.
9. Point to evidence of positive and negative behavioral contrast in Figure 14-5.
10. Present a number that approximately describes the mean number of errors produced by the three children in Powers et al. who were trained to discriminate colors in the traditional way. Present a similar number describing the two subjects in the errorless group.
11. What can we conclude about the effect of the noise added to the S⁻ in the Powers et al. study? (Be careful. Hint: Are there "catch" [control] conditions in which some subjects are run through the experiment without the noise at all? Consider the design of the study in formulating your answer.)
12. What is it about the S⁻ that may help make errorless discrimination operations work?

Fundamentals of Behavior

References

Amsel, A. Frustrative nonreward in partial reinforcement and discrimination learning: Some recent history and a theoretical extension. *Psychological Review*, 1962, **69**, 306-328.

Moore, R., & Goldiamond, I. Errorless establishment of visual discrimination using fading procedures. *Journal of the Experimental Analysis of Behavior*, 1964, **7**, 269-272.

Nicholson, J. N., & Gray, J. A. Behavioral contrast and peak shift in children. *British Journal of Psychology*, 1971, **62**, 367-373.

O'Brien, F. Sequential contrast effects with human subjects. *Journal of the Experimental Analysis of Behavior*, 1968, **11**, 537-542.

Powers, R. B., Cheney, C. D., & Agostino, N. R. Errorless training of a visual discrimination in preschool children. *The Psychological Record*, 1970, **20**, 45-50.

Reynolds, G. Behavioral contrast. *Journal of the Experimental Analysis of Behavior*, 1961, **4**, 57-71.

Sidman, M., & Stoddard, L. T. The effectiveness of fading in programming a simultaneous form discrimination for retarded children. *Journal of the Experimental Analysis of Behavior*, 1967, **10**, 3-15.

Stoddard, L. T., & Sidman, M. The effects of errors on children's performance on a circle-ellipse discrimination. *Journal of the Experimental Analysis of Behavior*, 1967, **10**, 261-270.

Terrace, H. S. Discrimination learning with and without "errors." *Journal of the Experimental Analysis of Behavior*, 1963, **6**, 1-27. (a)

Terrace, H. S. Errorless transfer of a discrimination across two continua. *Journal of the Experimental Analysis of Behavior*, 1963, **6**, 223-232. (b)

Terrace, H. S. Stimulus control. In W. K. Honig (Ed.), *Operant behavior: Areas of research and application*. N.Y.: Appleton-Century-Crofts, 1966. Pp. 271-344.

Touchette, P. E. The effects of graduated stimulus change on the acquisition of a simple discrimination in severely retarded boys. *Journal of the Experimental Analysis of Behavior*, 1968, **11**, 39-48.

Waite, W. W., & Osborne, J. G. Sustained behavioral contrast in children. *Journal of the Experimental Analysis of Behavior*, 1972, **18**, 113-117.

*

Stimulus Control: Stimulus Generalization

UNIT

15

The Definition of Stimulus Generalization

When a response is conditioned in the presence of a stimulus, other stimuli that are similar to the training stimulus (S^D) will also control the response. This is called **STIMULUS GENERALIZATION.** A corollary of this statement is that the greater the similarity between the training stimulus and the test stimulus, the more likely the test stimulus will be responded to. The less like the training stimulus our test stimulus is, the less likely our subject will respond to it. These relations obtain for both respondent and operant conditioning.

We will present some examples to clarify this relation and then talk about its significance in terms of conditioning principles and the adaptability of the organism. Let us arrange a laboratory situation in which a young child makes a response in the presence of a yellow light. Responses are consequated on a CRF schedule by tokens which the child may exchange for toys or candy at the end of each session. After one session the schedule of reinforcement is changed to VI 30-sec, and a fairly rapid, stable rate of responding quickly develops. Now we disconnect the token dispenser and change the light color to blue. Responding (unreinforced) continues. This is an example of stimulus generalization. We may say that responding has generalized to a stimulus in the presence of which our hypothetical

Powers & Osborne—Fund. Of Behavior—13

193

subject has received no conditioning. We may further present many different colors and find that our subject continues to respond to all of them, although to different extents, depending on the similarity of training (S^D) and testing ($S^\triangle$) stimuli.

Similar examples may be observed in the natural environment, and the child developing language provides well-known instances. In the presence of his own father (S^D), a child will be reinforced for saying, "Daddy." Once this response is strong in the presence of his real father, however, the child will respond to other men ($S^\triangle$s) by calling them "Daddy" as well (much to the embarrassment of Mommy). However, these latter responses are usually not reinforced either by parents or the recipients of the salutation. Again, this is the phenomenon of stimulus generalization where a response conditioned in the presence of one stimulus (saying "Daddy" when Daddy is present) occurs in the presence of stimuli similar to the original one (other men), but, in the presence of which, there has been no conditioning history. The developing child's language provides other examples as well — all fluids may be initially called milk, all post-pubescent females, "Mommy," and so on.

The Relativity of Generalization

If, in fact, each conditioning experience with a stimulus led the individual to respond equally to all other stimuli of a given type, we would respond to red lights as we do to green and vice versa, and the result would be disaster. This does not frequently happen. Most often, our subject will respond primarily to stimuli that are physically like the original conditioning stimulus along one or more dimensions — for example, color, size, texture, or form. The more dimensions that are like the training stimulus, the more likely our subject will respond to the test stimulus. Thus, a child may be frightened by a large dog and then will be frightened by all fur-bearing, four-legged animals of similar size, even though he has never had an encounter with the latter. However, in this case we may be able to change enough of the stimulus characteristics from the training stimulus to find an animal, perhaps even a dog, that does not frighten the child. For instance, a Chihuahua may not produce crying if the child were originally frightened by a German Shepherd. In that case, there are enough differences that the child discriminates, even though the two animals have many similar characteristics.

When a generalized response occurs, its relation to the environment is changed from what it was prior to the response occurring. This is because the response is either reinforced, punished, or extinguished. In order for the organism to continue to respond to the test and training stimuli in the same way, the environment would have to treat responses to them in precisely the same way each time. In fact, this rarely occurs. For instance, we may begin our experience by responding similarly to red and green lights. However, this generalization will soon be changed to a discrimination because of the punishment dependent on stopping at green lights or running through red lights when driving our automobiles. Similarly, a child in the laboratory will soon stop responding to all other colors of lights but red, if those other lights are always paired with extinction.

Generalization as Description

Generalization is not a failure to discriminate, nor is it a process. By process, we allude to any speculation that the physiological functioning of the organism somehow accounts for generalization; that is, the organism is built to respond this way. Generalization is simply a description of some specific relations between stimuli and responses. The organism responds to stimuli other than the ones he has been conditioned to. The definition is based on *procedure*, not process, and the results are those of that procedure.

Note the case of the child who can point to a red light when asked and to a blue one when asked. We can say that he discriminates them. The same child may still respond in the presence of red and blue lights equally when in an experimental setting; that is, generalization may be total. Verbal discrimination of colors should not necessarily lead us to believe that a motor discrimination (pointing to the correct color and no others) will occur. To reiterate, the word *generalization* simply describes a class of phenomena in which responding takes place to a stimulus to which the organism has not been conditioned. Conditioning may have occurred to other stimuli in the organism's past that are similar to the stimulus of interest.

The Generalization Gradient

The numbers in Table 15-1 constitute responses made by pigeons to 11 different hues (represented in terms of their wavelengths). These birds were given food reinforcement on a VI 1-min schedule dependent on key pecking in the presence of a training stimulus (550 nm).[1] The effects of this procedure are to make responding frequent in the presence of the training stimulus and less frequent in the presence of the test stimuli. After a certain number of reinforcements have been earned, or the response rate in the presence of the training stimulus is stable, the subject is placed on extinction. During extinction, testing for generalization is carried out by randomly presenting a representative number of stimuli along some physical dimension of the training stimulus. In this case, the dimension was hue, so a number of different wavelengths were presented randomly to preclude order effects. The number of presentations of each stimulus was carefully controlled so the bird was exposed to each of them an equal amount of time.

Table 15-1 presents the hues in order along with the mean number of responses made to these hues by six pigeons. Construct a graph using the wavelength values from low to high on the abscissa and number of responses as the ordinate. Plot the number of responses occurring at each wavelength and join these points. The resulting curve is called a GENERALIZATION GRADIENT.

The Shape of the Generalization Gradient

The shape of the generalization gradient is used to infer the amount of stimulus control a given set of stimuli

[1] nm = nanometer or 1×10^{-9} meter. Wavelength of light, you can see, truly implies a length measure, albeit very small — in this case 550 billionths of a meter.

Table 15-1

Mean generalization gradient for six pigeons. Data estimated from Guttman, N., & Kalish, H. I. Discriminability and stimulus generalization. *Journal of Experimental Psychology*, 1956, 51, 79-88.

Wavelength of Light (nm)	Number of Responses
490	0
510	10
520	20
530	50
540	100
550	170
560	90
570	55
580	20
590	5
610	2

referred to as *dimensional control* (Hearst, Besley, & Farthing, 1970).

It is very important to repeat that there is never a time when an organism is not controlled by some stimulus. When we say that a flat gradient denotes absence of control by the stimuli presented, it means the behavior of the organism is under the control of other stimuli which we have not identified. In a very simple case, we may find that an animal taught to respond to a red circle may produce a flat generalization gradient when we present hues, but a sharply peaked gradient when form stimuli are presented. Hence, the organism's response would be controlled in this case by form, not hue.

More Phenomena That Occur with Discrimination Formation

has over a response. Differential responding in the presence of various stimuli, you will recall from Unit 14, is what we use as evidence of stimulus discrimination, or stimulus control, and the generalization gradient provides a graphic description of this control.

If the gradient is sharply peaked at one stimulus location as it is in Figure 15-1, it is indicative of control by that stimulus dimension. If the gradient is flat, that is, the organism responds equally to all the stimuli presented, there is no evidence of stimulus control by the stimuli and the dimension on which the stimuli lie. Where a group of stimuli that can be physically ordered along a dimension differentially control behavior, as in Figure 15-1, this is

Peak shift. Note that the peak of the generalization gradient that you drew from Table 15-1 is at the training stimulus; maximum responding occurs to this stimulus. This occurs with nondifferential training, training in which there is simply reinforcement for responding in the presence of a single stimulus. The traditional operations which produce discriminated responding, however, are reinforcement for responding in the presence of a specific stimulus (S^D), *and* extinction for responding in the presence of another stimulus (S^Δ). You will recall (Unit 14) that usually a large number of responses occur to S^Δ when it is first presented (we have called them errors) and that, eventually, these responses decrease to near zero. Concomitant with this decrease in responding in the

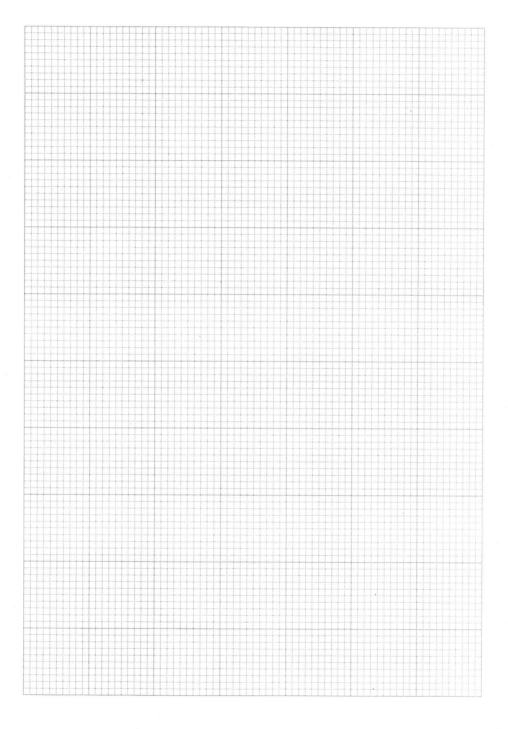

Figure 15-1   The mean number of responses for 6 pigeons to various wavelengths of light after reinforcement for responding to one of the wavelengths.

*

presence of $S^\triangle$, there is often increased responding in the presence of S^D (behavioral contrast). If, after the discrimination is well established, we try for another generalization gradient, an interesting phenomenon — called **PEAK SHIFT** — occurs. As in the Guttman and Kalish example, we could use a 550 nm light as S^D, but for our discrimination we will also require an $S^\triangle$ of 560 nm. After responding is greater than 10:1 (S^D to $S^\wedge$ responses), we present in extinction, all the hues of Table 15-1. Because the gradient is obtained after discrimination training, it is called a **POST-DISCRIMINATION GRADIENT (PDG)**, to differentiate it from a generalization gradient where there have been no discrimination operations performed. We are now likely to see that the peak of the PDG has shifted from the S^D in a direction on the continuum *away from* the $S^\triangle$. In our example, maximum responding would probably be at 540 nm. This is called *peak shift*. It is often accompanied by a shift in areas of the curve as well (called *area shift*), so that the amount of the area residing over various locations on the continuum may have changed. Where the generalization gradient is usually symmetrical, as in Figure 15-1, a PDG is often skewed away from the region of the $S^\triangle$.

Note particularly that peak shift is seen only in PDGs obtained after traditional (error-producing) discrimination procedures. Terrace (1964) noted the absence of a peak shift in the PDGs he obtained in pigeons after errorless discrimination training, and this is another difference between discriminations produced by the two techniques.

To further your understanding of the post-discrimination gradient, plot the data in Table 15-2 on the following

Table 15-2

Mean post-discrimination gradient for five pigeons given discrimination training on a line-tilt continuum. Data taken from Bloomfield, T. M. A peak shift on a line-tilt continuum. *Journal of the Experimental Analysis of Behavior,* **1967, 10, 361-366.**

Degrees of Line Tilt	Total Responses
−90	40
−75	57
−60	78
−45	145
−30	265
−15	325
0 (S^D)	238
+15	100
+30	45
+45 ($S^\triangle$)	45
+60	35
+75	32
+90	40

graph and prepare to answer exam questions about your figure. Use arrows to indicate the locations of the S^D and $S^\triangle$. Start your abscissa with −90° and place each additional line tilt (in the order of Table 15-2) farther to the right. Responses will be on the ordinate.

In the experiment, the data of which you are plotting, Bloomfield (1967) reinforced a group of homing pigeons for responding to a 0° (vertical) dark line on an illuminated key and extinguished responding to the dark line when it was oriented at +45°. After the discrimination between the two line tilts was well established, generalization testing took place in extinction. Each of 12 stimuli were presented (0°, ±15°, ±30°, ±45°, ±60°, ±75° and 90°). Pay particular attention to the location of the peak in your graphed PDG.

Inhibitory stimulus control. The evidence of peak shift, behavioral contrast, and emotional behavior in the presence of $S^\triangle$ contrasted with the evidence of no peak shift, contrast, or emotional behavior in the presence of the S^- of errorless-discrimination procedures, has led to the suggestion that the two stimuli ($S^\triangle$ and S^-) function differently. Terrace (1966) concluded from his data that S^- could be considered neutral with respect to behavior while $S^\triangle$ was inhibitory. The concept of inhibition has always been a thorn in the side of psychologists because the referrents of the word have been unclear. Early tendencies were to neurophysiologize, and it was thought difficult to separate a state of inhibition from a state of lowered excitation. A clear set of defining operations and a set of results corresponding to the operations were needed. These were provided by Hearst et al. (1970), who defined an inhibitory stimulus as one "that develops during conditioning the capacity to decrease response strength below the level occurring when that stimulus is absent" (p. 376).

For the most part this area is beyond the scope of the present text. It is discussed here briefly because it is now a major area of stimulus-control research and because inhibition may be a standard phenomenon of some types of discrimination formation.

A standard experiment to demonstrate inhibitory dimensional control follows. Pigeons are exposed to an S^D, which is a color (e.g., 550 nm), and an $S^\triangle$, which is a black vertical line (0°) superimposed on a white background. Reinforcement occurs for responding in the presence of the former and not in the presence of the latter. These stimuli can be seen in Figure 15-3. Note that the $S^\triangle$ is on a different continuum than the S^D. After discrimination training, we vary the orientation of the black vertical line (e.g., 0°, ±15°, ±30°, ±60°), counting responses at each orientation. There is no confounding of the results because the inhibitory gradient obtained is on a dimension orthogonal to the S^D dimension (i.e., orientation and hue are not physically relatable), thus the curve we get is a curve of inhibition, not one of lack of excitation, or a mix of excitation and inhibition.

Under these procedures, the usual inhibition gradient is a U-shaped curve with minimum responding at $S^\triangle$. The curves are usually not the inverted mirror image of the post-discrimination gradient, but shallower, one reason for this being that there is less overall responding.

To continue with our errorless-traditional discrimination differences, we note that Terrace (1966) failed to find an inhibitory gradient after errorless-discrimination training, and it was this evidence that led him to suggest that the S^- of the errorless procedure was not an inhibitory stimulus. However, Deutsch (1967) and Hearst et al. (1970) have pointed out that Terrace's results may not reflect the absence of inhibition. The flat (inhibitory) gradients obtained after errorless training may simply be due to the relatively greater absence of responding produced on the S^- dimension after errorless training. This, it can be argued, may

Figure 15-2 The mean number of responses to 12 line tilts for 5 pigeons produced in extinction after discrimination training in which a 0° line was S^D and a $^+$45° line was S$^\triangle$.

*

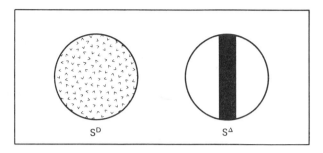

Figure 15-3

Two states of an illuminated response key which may be used to determine the presence of inhibitory stimulus control. Because the line tilt is colorless (i.e., black), it is unrelated to the stimulus continuum (color) on which the S^D lies.

reflect even stronger inhibition. Consider the necessity of some responding occurring at the "ends" of the U-shaped curve, if in fact, the curve is to exist. Most recently, some studies (Biederman & Colotla, 1971; Rilling, Richards, & Kramer, 1973) have shown, in fact, that the S$^-$ of errorless procedures may have inhibitory features, so this controversy is far from settled.

The Evolutionary Significance of Stimulus Generalization

Historically, theories of behavior have always encountered difficulty when they have discussed man's relation to his environment, because it has been necessary to postulate that each response made is a response to a stimulus. The environment has been pictured as controlling man in robot, machine-like fashion. What has been the principal cause of the difficulty is the notion that each response has to be conditioned to a specific stimulus. Given this view, the explanatory task of psychology became insurmountable.

However, we now know from the data in the area of stimulus generalization that a conditioning experience with a single stimulus makes many other similar stimuli functional with respect to a given response. The necessity of pinpointing a conditioning experience to explain the functionality of any stimulus is considerably reduced thereby, although certainly not done away with. One conditioning experience may now account for many functional stimulus-response relations.

As it turns out, conditioning experiences are not necessary to make specific stimuli in the environment functional for behavior; thus, the robot-like analogy of the environment's control over man's behavior is diminished. Given current findings, we do not need to posit that the environment is so systematic and thorough in producing and changing stimulus control over behavior as was once supposed. The results of generalization research lead us to believe that control of behavior is a simpler process than that pictured by earlier theories.

It is conceivable that stimulus generalization makes the organism more adaptable to its environment by allowing that environment a surer means of control. If every response a species made to any stimulus needed a conditioning experience to make the stimulus functional, the species would soon perish; it might be speculated that **the species which have survived did so because they generalized to some extent.** We may encounter an extremely painful (sometimes killing) stimulus, and that single encounter may serve to make similar lethal stimuli avoidable. However, extreme generalization, i.e. equal control (or lack of) by many stimuli, would seem just as dangerous as no generalization. Generalizing between a gopher snake (harmless) and its neighbor, the diamondback rattler (not so harmless), could be fatal if handling were the response. Organisms likely to survive are ones that generalize but also can be taught quickly by their environment to discriminate. Not incidentally, generalization and discrimination are at the root of a functional analysis of concept formation, an important set of procedures for educators.

Application

D. M. Baer, & M. M. Wolf. The entry into natural communities of reinforcement. In R. Ulrich, T. Stachnik, & J. Mabry (Eds.), *Control of human behavior*, Vol. II, Glenview, Ill.: Scott, Foresman, 1970. Pp. 319-324.

There are many types of generalization that may be used as examples for this unit. Most representative here would be an example in which, after some original conditioning, the environment was changed somewhat and the conditioned behavior continued to occur. However, remember from our generalization-gradient examples that changing the environment, while permitting conditioned behavior to occur, usually results in less of that behavior than if the conditioning environment had been maintained exactly. Note also that generalization may take place in the same stimulus environment as that of the original conditioning, but if reinforcement is no longer programmed, then the environment has changed even if all else is constant, and it has changed in an important fashion.

In one sense we must consider generalization to be temporary. If a response is no longer reinforced, it may continue to occur for some time — an example of generalization — but we should not expect it to occur forever. *Without further reinforcement, invariably a response will extinguish.* Hence, all behavior change is relative to its supporting (or nonsupporting) environments. The child whose tantrums are extinguished may no longer tantrum only as long as there are no further reinforcements for tantrums. The child who has learned to speak may no longer speak if all reinforcement for speaking is discontinued. Fortunately, in the latter case, it is quite likely that reinforcements for speaking will be continuingly programmed by the natural environment — for speakers, there are usually listeners, and often the speaker can function as his own listener (Skinner, 1957).

One type of generalization, therefore, might be a demonstration of some conditioning followed by the ever-increasing support for that behavior reinforced by the natural environment. Baer and Wolf, through a student, programmed exactly this type of environment. First, they remembered a general rule suggested by the shape of the generalization gradient: When behavior is no longer reinforced *and* the environment is changed thereby, it is likely the behavior will no longer occur. This rule argues strongly for special generalization-producing operations in every behavior modification project — operations still seen too infrequently in behavior modification studies. Baer and Wolf established conditions they hoped would, after their original operations were concluded, make it likely the conditioned behavior would thereafter be reinforced. Here is how they did it.

The subject was a 4-year-old boy who attended a nursery school. Most of the children at the school spent their time playing with one another; just 10 percent of a school session was spent gazing at others while about 30 percent of the time was spent in social activities such as playing games, sharing toys, and so on. The child in question spent only 3 percent of his time playing and 30 percent staring at the teachers and children while the latter played. Thus, a good reason existed for attempting, as the authors did, to reverse these percentages. The boy's social activities took much less of his time than might be expected of the average 4-year-old. Baer and Wolf employed two basic techniques. The first is called **PRIMING**. Priming means that a behavior is directly instigated either by verbally describing it or by physically guiding it. In this example, the teachers approached the other children and suggested an idea to them which involved the boy; that is, they primed the other children. As you can see from Table 15-3 this had a small but durable effect, increasing the child's social play to 7 percent (Condition 2). Next, the teachers suggested ideas to the boy for play with the other children; that is, they primed him. Examine Table 15-3 to see the effect of this manipulation. Next (Condition 4), to see whether generalization would occur, the teachers discontinued priming the boy. His social interactions decreased to 4 percent. The teachers then decided on a massive assault since priming alone had been insufficient. They began (Condition 5) priming both the boy and the other children concurrently, as well as socially reinforcing the boy once he had begun an interaction. However, they did not continue their reinforcement throughout the interaction. Next, to see the effects of this procedure, they discontinued it (Condition 6) after several days. In Condition 7, they resumed double priming and intensively reinforced any social interaction that ensued. That is, as long as an interaction occurred, they would express happiness that it was still ongoing. Once again, to check for generalization and to see whether the natural environment was maintaining this behavior, they discontinued this priming and massive social reinforcement (Condition 8). These procedures were each repeated once again as you can see from Table 15-3. Baer and Wolf reported that by Condition 7, the "quality" of the boy's interaction with the other children was much improved. He cooperated more with the other children, talked more with them, and followed their lead more often.

Table 15-3

The effect of generalization-producing procedures on the social play of a 4-year-old boy. Data taken from Baer, D. M., & Wolf, M. M.   The entry into natural communities of reinforcement. In R. Ulrich, T. Stachnik, & J. Mabry (Eds.), *Control of human behavior*. Glenview, Ill.: Scott, Foresman, 1970. Pp. 319-324.

Conditions	Percent of Nursery School Session in Social Play	Note Generalization Conditions
1. Baseline	3	
2. Priming others	7	
3. Priming subject	7	
4. No priming	4	Generalization
5. Double priming and social reinforcement	17	
6. Neither priming nor social reinforcement	10	
7. Double priming and social reinforcement	24	
8. Neither priming nor social reinforcement	19	
9. Double priming and social reinforcement	23	
10. Neither priming nor social reinforcement	22	

Starting with baseline as the first generalization condition (no programmed reinforcement), draw a graph noting first in Table 15-3 which are generalization conditions. (One of these conditions is noted for you to "prime" your behavior of noting the remaining generalization conditions.) Put all conditions on the abscissa of your graph. The data in this experiment are noncontinuous, so you should use bars rather than joined points. Use one type of bar to represent conditioning procedures (e.g., black) and another to represent generalization conditions (e.g., white). The ordinate will be the same as the heading for Column 2 in Table 15-3; label the abscissa "Conditions." As usual, prepare for exam questions regarding the figure.

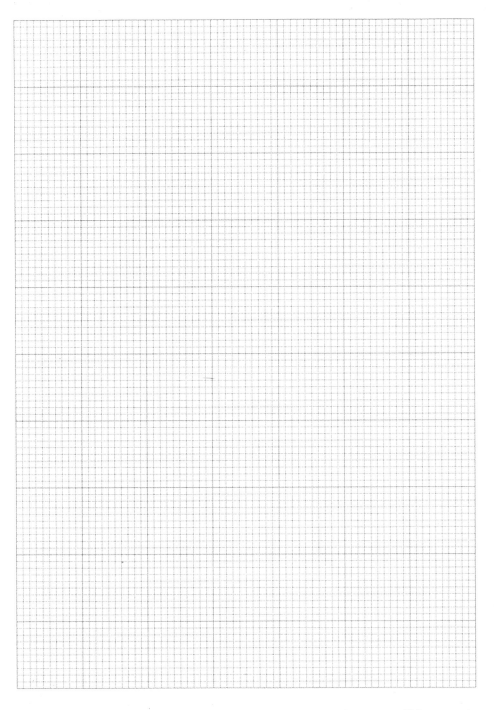

Figure 15-4   The percentage of nursery school sessions a four-year-old boy spent in social play with his nursery school peers.

*

Exam

1. Define the following:
   a. stimulus generalization
   b. training stimulus
   c. test stimulus
   d. inhibitory stimulus control
   e. peak shift
   f. priming
   g. S^D; $S^\triangle$; S^+; S^-

2. From Figure 15-1, determine the wavelength of the stimulus in the presence of which the birds in this group were reinforced.

3. What is the shape of the generalization gradient in Figure 15-1?

4. In terms of the shape of the generalization gradient in Figure 15-1, what can be said about stimulus control over the behavior of the birds in this group?

5. From an evolutionary point of view, why may it be important that organisms generalize among stimuli?

6. What is a generalization gradient?

7. Does the term *generalization* explain anything? Describe a process?

8. Give an example of stimulus generalization from your own life.

9. Give an example of priming not from the text.

10. Which conditions of Column 3 of Table 15-3 did you mark as generalization conditions?

11. What is the general trend across generalization conditions in Figure 15-4 from the beginning to the final generalization conditions?

12. Why is it likely that Baer and Wolf stopped their study when they did? (Hint: Consider the difference between the final conditioning and generalization percentages.)

13. What is a post-discrimination gradient?

14. In Figure 15-2, where does the peak of the PDG lie? Over which line tilts (negative or positive) is most of the area of the curve located?

15. Given your knowledge of discrimination formation under traditional and errorless procedures, discuss at least four phenomena which distinguish these two types of discriminations.

References

Biederman, G. B., & Colotla, V. A.   Stimulus function in errorless simultaneous discrimination. *Perceptual and Motor Skills*, 1971, **33**, 759-764.

Bloomfield, T. M.   A peak shift on a line-tilt continuum. *Journal of the Experimental Analysis of Behavior*, 1967, **10**, 361-366.

Deutsch, J. Discrimination learning and inhibition. *Science*, 1967, **156**, 988.

Guttman, N., & Kalish, H. I. Discriminability and stimulus generalization. *Journal of Experimental Psychology*, 1956, **51**, 79-98.

Hearst, E., Besley, S., & Farthing, G. W. Inhibition and the stimulus control of operant behavior. *Journal of the Experimental Analysis of Behavior*, 1970, **14**, 373-409.

Rilling, M., Richards, R. W., & Kramer, T. J. Aversive properties of the negative stimulus during learning with and without errors. *Learning and Motivation*, 1973, **4**, 1-10.

Skinner, B. F. *Verbal behavior.* New York: Appleton-Century-Crofts, 1957.

Terrace, H. S. Wavelength generalization after discrimination learning with and without errors. *Science*, 1964, **144**, 78-80.

Terrace, H. S. Discrimination learning and inhibition. *Science*, 1966, **154**, 1677-1680.

Emotional Behavior: Introduction

The emotions and how to define them have plagued psychology for years. The question is asked: "How is emotional behavior different from any other behavior?" The intelligent layman's answer is not only that it is different from other behavior but also that he can name the emotion involved. This statement does not stand up under close scrutiny. When the layman names a given emotion, he usually is using stimuli in the situation other than those provided by the person producing the emotional behavior. It is this knowledge of other stimuli that allows man to name emotions. Deprived of this knowledge, his description of the emotion is often faulty. An animal trainer may produce a show of teeth in a chimpanzee by pinching the animal strongly. If we do not see the pinch, we may label this emotion as joy, when in fact the behavior exhibited is anything but joyful. Knowledge of the eliciting stimulus, in this case, the pinch, improves our labelling.

It is of interest, however, to examine what a person means when he says either that he is behaving emotionally or that someone else is. As is all behavior, emotional behavior is exhibited by an organism to certain stimuli in the environment. The stimuli that produce emotional behavior are usually physically strong. For instance, touching a hot stove may be followed by limb withdrawal, cursing, and the application of medicine to the burn. Plunging the hand into warm water will likely be followed by none of these things. The cursing in the former example probably would be labelled emotional behavior.

Up to this point, behavior has been discussed as being conditioned by either respondent (stimulus pairing) or operant (response-dependent stimulus presentation) methods. Some care has been taken to present the methods separately as this facilitates student discriminations between them. A discussion of emotional behavior necessitates the discussion of both systems simultaneously, for although respondents and operants may be conditioned differently, it is clear they may occur together.

Identifying Emotional Behavior

Emotional behavior is simply operant behavior occurring together with strong respondent behavior. In general, for it to be concluded that an emotional behavior has been exhibited, the discrimination of this strong respondent component is necessary. This discrimination is made either by the individual of his own behavior, or the individual of another's behavior. The discrimination of respondent behavior rarely undergoes independent validation exclusive of the operant behavior exhibited. For example, we take an individual's word that he is happy or sad even though crying may be exhibited in both cases. We often infer the presence of emotion based on the strength of the operant behavior we observe. Independent verification requires the presence of strong respondents as well, and these are usually not measured but simply inferred.

Usually a knowledge of extraneous stimuli suffices for the layman to conclude an emotion exists. For instance, we have seen the cherry-red

color of the stove element, and therefore we feel sure the individual who touched it is exhibiting emotional behavior when he curses.

Respondent Components of Emotional Behavior

In general, respondents involved in emotional behavior are produced by the action of the autonomic nervous system. The actions of the *sympathetic* branch of this system generally result from physically intense environmental stimulation. This system is often said to prepare the individual biologically for emergency action. For example, digestive processes stop, the adrenal glands secrete adrenalin, heart rate increases, respiration quickens, and blood pressure rises. These physiological responses — which are all respondents — when acting together in this fashion have been called the **ACTIVATION SYNDROME**. It is the action of this part of the nervous system that defines the presence of anxiety, or feelings of "uptightness." Operant behavior may occur along with the activation syndrome. If it does, it may be called emotional behavior. If the activation syndrome is present and operant behavior is not, it is difficult to conclude that emotional behavior is taking place. Similarly, if operant behavior takes place without the respondents of the activation syndrome, it cannot be called emotional.

The actions of the *parasympathetic* branch of the autonomic nervous system produce feelings usually described as pleasant and relaxing. Digestive processes are active; the adrenal glands secrete noradrenalin;

heart rate and respiration are slow, and blood pressure is lowered. Again, for emotional behavior to be recorded, it is assumed that the actions of this system will be taking place along with some observable operant behavior. For example, the individual may laugh and be joyful while eating.

Operant Components of Emotional Behavior

We have seen above that two general kinds of autonomic activity are possible given sufficient stimulation. This same stimulation can produce operant behavior, which means that unconditional or conditional eliciting stimuli can also function as discriminative stimuli for operant responding. Thus, in our hot stove example, in the presence of a burned finger, shaking the hand may be paired with pain reduction and, hence, may be negatively reinforced. Similarly, cursing may also be negatively reinforced when it occurs in the presence of a painful stimulus because of the associated reduction in pain. Cursing may additionally be reinforced by quickly gaining the attention of another individual who may be empathic. The stimuli that produce respondent behavior may also function discriminatively for operants. These operants can be modified as a function of their consequences.

Development of Emotional Behavior

The implications of the above analysis are for two types of emotional development. First, the respondents involved in emotional behavior pose some interesting issues. We have spoken of general classes of respondents occurring as a result of sympathetic or parasympathetic nervous system action. The respondents involved in emotional behavior are likely to be present throughout much of life in a rather unchanging fashion. What can we mean by respondent development then? Simply, that the actions of the autonomic nervous system are conditioned in the usual classical (respondent) manner to stimuli throughout life. Although the respondents involved in emotional behavior undergo little or no change throughout life, the conditional stimuli for those respondents may, through pairing with other stimuli or repeated exposure without such pairings, undergo successive conditionings and extinctions. Thus, emotional development in terms of respondents has to do with the respondent conditioning of formerly neutral stimuli that, through pairing with eliciting stimuli, gain the power to elicit the classes of respondents that comprise part of emotions.

A child may hear a dog bark but little change in respondent activity may initially take place. If, however, a dog's bark is paired with the child being bitten by the barking animal, barking occurring in the future may elicit increased heart rate, heightened blood pressure, and increased secretion of adrenalin. Continued barking by dogs over a period of time with no further biting may result in the extinction of the above respondents. Additional bites (or other stimuli provided by the animal that function as eliciting stimuli, e.g., snapping or baring the teeth) may recondition these respondents to the conditional stimulus — barking.

In addition to respondent development, there is the development of operant behavior comprising the emotions. This development takes place through the processes of operant conditioning and extinction. Hence, an operant component of some emotional behavior may be strengthened by reinforcement or weakened by extinction. If the natural dependencies undergo shifts, the topography of the behavior will shift with it. In the young infant, operant components of emotional behavior may simply involve increased random activity, while in the adult, the behavior may be extremely precise. For example, it may involve a well-defined motor response such as stamping the foot, striking one palm with the closed fist of the other hand, and so forth. There is no implication that these specific behaviors are conditioned by their occurrence with emotional respondents. On the contrary, they will be shaped by their consequences both during emotional and nonemotional behavior episodes. However, operants are present in the individual's repertoire, and conditional or unconditional stimuli producing emotional respondents may also function as discriminative stimuli, setting the occasion for the occurrence of these operants.

To continue with the emotional behavior engendered by the canine example above, we can consider the operant development that may occur. In the young child, the dog's bite may set the occasion for screaming and running away from the animal. Both these responses may be strengthened if there is success in escaping the dog. However, these responses may be suppressed if they produce further attacks by the dog and the resulting (negatively reinforced) operant may be standing still. Operant development during emotional episodes, therefore, is a function of the same variables as during nonemotional times.

Anxiety

The word *anxiety* is troublesome because its meanings are many. We will use the term to indicate the presence of the respondents produced by increased action of the sympathetic nervous system, along with the person's discrimination of these types of bodily feelings. He may further learn to say he is anxious in the presence of these feelings. The word *fearful* appears a reasonable synonym. Most individuals find these feelings unpleasant and will engage in behavior either to escape them or avoid them altogether. A great many deviant behaviors may be the result. For instance, a person fearful of snakes may also be anxious of all the stimulus circumstances that are paired with the presence of snakes — zoos, grassy places, deserts, and the like. Fear may even be produced by a picture of a snake or by saying the word *snake*. The person may then avoid many of these environments, some of which may be necessary parts of the person's existence. For example, a man may be a real-estate salesman and be unable to show customers undeveloped land because of his fear of meeting a snake.

Conditioned Suppression

Very early in the history of conditioning psychology, Pavlov documented procedures which generated emotional behavior experimentally in the dog. The behavior was so powerful that it disrupted the conditioned performance of the animal for a long period of time.

Considerable rest from the experimental apparatus was necessary, and considerable reconditioning at a later date to bring an animal back to his earlier level of performance.

Briefly, the animal was taught a respondent discrimination, let us say, between a circle (CS$^+$) and an ellipse (CS$^-$).[1] Pavlov then reduced the longer axis of the ellipse, making it more circular. Eventually, a point was reached where the discrimination became very difficult (ellipse axes having a ratio of 9:8), and it was at this point that the dog's discrimination broke down. The animal would strain at its harness, bark furiously, and bite the connections of the experimental apparatus. These reactions were named *experimental neuroses* (Pavlov, 1960). Thus, it has been clear for some time that emotional behavior by animals could be studied in the laboratory.

Other conditioning psychologists have used the activity of the rat in an open field to infer the amount of emotion (i.e., fear). Rats that are less fearful move about more and defecate less in an open field than rats that are more fearful. Thus, emotion (which is inferred only) is given objective status in terms of visible behavior, such as the number of grids the rat crosses in the open field and the number of fecal boluses the rat leaves in a given period of time. Occasionally also, the amount of time in which an animal freezes, or the number of vocalizations it emits, is also used to infer emotion.

Operant conditioners have studied emotion most commonly with a single technique, **CONDITIONED SUP-PRESSION.** In the typical conditioned suppression experiment, a pigeon may be responding for grain reinforcement on a variable-interval schedule. After its behavior is stable, a tone is presented for a few seconds in the experimental chamber and the bird's behavior is observed. Typically, very little happens; that is, the tone is not functional with respect to the bird's responding. The stable response rate of the variable-interval schedule continues. In a second condition, however, the experimenter follows these tone presentations immediately with a brief, *unavoidable* electric shock. This tone-shock pairing may be repeated every few minutes of the session. Eventually the bird will slow its responding and then finally almost stop responding altogether when the tone is presented; this will occur even when the shock is no longer presented at the end of the tone. The bird's behavior during the tone is suppressed via a conditioning technique; (the pairing of two stimuli) hence, **CONDITIONED SUPPRESSION.** The dependent variable often employed here is the degree of suppression, that is, the amount of reduction in response rate during the tone compared with the response rate during a comparable no-tone period.

In an operational way, emotional behavior can be studied with this technique, if several assumptions are made: 1) Shock, being a very aversive stimulus, is an emotion-producer; 2) the

[1] A respondent discrimination is conditioned in the following manner: The CS$^+$ is always paired with the UCS as in the basic classical conditioning paradigm; however, another stimulus (CS$^-$) is presented on some trials, but is never paired with the UCS. After repeated exposure to this regimen, on test trials an animal will respond to the CS$^+$ presented alone (e.g., by salivating copiously) but will not respond to the CS$^-$ when it is presented for a test trial (see Bykov's experiment, Unit 4).

association of tone and shock makes the tone also an emotion-producer; and 3) the degree of suppression is related to the amount of emotion experienced. However, we must be careful of this kind of speculation. If we consider the tone as a generator of "anxiety," the conditioned suppression technique can be used to study the effects of drugs on anxiety. But we may be in for some surprises. For example, given an injection of tranquilizer (reserpine, alcohol, or chlorpromazine), will a rat suppress its behavior less in the presence of the tone than if it were not tranquilized? The answer is no, it will not. Interestingly, on the other hand, injections of stimulants such as amphetamine will enhance conditioned suppression (Lauener, 1963). Thus, we must be cautious not to conclude too quickly that we are studying a technique that produces "anxiety."

Surprisingly little is known about why conditioned suppression occurs (Millenson & de Villiers, 1972). However, we can indicate some important variables that are related to conditioned suppression. First, there is the baseline incentive condition; given two reinforcers, one of which is qualitatively superior to the other (e.g., 32 percent sucrose solution *vs* 8 percent sucrose solution), suppression will be less during times when the superior reinforcer (i.e., 32 percent sucrose) is available for responding. Second, the subject's deprivation level must be considered. Less suppression occurs when an animal is deprived of food than when it has just been fed. Third, amount of suppression may depend on where in a schedule of reinforcement the suppressing stimulus occurs. For example, suppression is more complete immediately after reinforcement on

fixed-interval and fixed-ratio schedules than it is just before reinforcement on the same schedules. Utilizing this evidence, Millenson and de Villiers (1972) suggest that a most important consideration of the effects of a suppressing stimulus on operant behavior will be the "reinforcing value" of the baseline on which the subject is responding (p. 124). The term *reinforcing value* translates to the experimental conditions described above and to several others which we have not considered.

Illustration

S. Schacher, & J. E. Singer, Cognitive, social, and physiological determinants of emotional state. *Psychological Review*, 1962, **69**, 379-399.

In the illustration for this chapter, these scientists attempted to answer the question of why an individual labels an emotional state in the manner he does. Does the individual use the feelings generated by his body's systems when in a so-called emotional state? Or does he react to his milieu? Is it possible that the latter helps him describe his emotional state?

Schachter and Singer suspected that the individual does not react primarily to his physiological state. As we mentioned earlier in this unit, underlying physiological states accompanying emotional behavior do not lend themselves to easy division into the large number of emotions a person feels he experiences. Where research has shown that there are several physiological patterns that can be distinguished as emotional states, the differences between them are quite subtle. Schachter and Singer concluded:

". . . that the variety of emotion, mood, and feeling states are by no means matched by an equal variety of visceral patterns" (p. 380). Thus, they turned to the possibility that an emotional state may be due not just to some physiological state but also to what the individual labels the state. This labelling is a function of the individual's past experience. One hypothesis they made was that if the individual could not appropriately explain his feelings, he would call the experience of a physiological state (say, arousal) "emotional," and label it based on recent environmental circumstances.

But what of individuals who know the reason for their state of physiological arousal? (For example, they know it is caused by an injection of adrenalin?) These individuals, said Schachter and Singer, would have no need to label the state they felt as "emotional" because an explanation was available — the injection itself.

Finally, the experimenters reasoned that an individual might have emotion-provoking experiences to which to react and no underlying physiological state of arousal. They hypothesized that these latter individuals would not report their feelings as emotional.

To confirm these hypotheses, Schachter and Singer ran the following three-stage experiment. Male college students were told the effects of a "vitamin" injection (called *Suproxin*) on their vision would be evaluated if they submitted to an injection of the so-called vitamin. Actually, of the more than 100 who agreed to be injected with *Suproxin*, some were injected with epinephrine (adrenalin) — a sympathomimetic drug which increases blood pressure, raises heart rate, in-

creases respiration, cuts down blood flow to the skin, and generally mimics a sympathetic nervous system discharge — while others were injected with a placebo. The placebo was an injection of saline solution, a "catch" condition controlling for the effects of the injection itself on later behavior, because saline in small quantities has no known effects on physiological or behavioral change.[2]

Secondly, after injection, the subjects were told either that the *Suproxin* might have some temporary side effects and these were accurately described (face flushed, trembling hands, heart pounding — this was the informed group) — or they were misinformed by being told that the side effects would make their feet feel numb, their bodies itch, and give them slight headaches. Finally, some of the

[2] It is possible that this experiment could not be run today in the prevailing climate of informed consent in human experimentation, because of the experimental necessity of misinforming the subjects of the reasons for the research. This issue is far from resolved, but the government has strongly suggested that it will not fund research using human beings, where total information is not available to the subject. Further, current prototypic guidelines not only demand total subject knowledge, but also require that the experimenter state that there are no possible detrimental outcomes of his procedures, and preferably that there be therapeutic outcomes. Knowing as little as we do about the effect of a single experience (in humans) on responses at a much later time, either of these statements is difficult to assert with much validity. A possible outcome, one we will be discouraged to see, is that human behavior will be much less studied in the future than it has been in the past. Important knowledge may be denied mankind thereby. The issue has by no means been settled and the American Psychological Association is giving much attention to a discussion of the implication of the "informed consent" doctrine.

epinephrine-injection group were left ignorant by being told that the *Suproxin* would have no side effects. Saline-injected subjects were told that there would be no side effects to their injection.

In the third stage of their experiment, the two investigators decided to determine if states of euphoria and anger could be induced in their subjects by exposing them to stooges who socially attempted to produce these states. Anger and euphoria were chosen as emotions because of the difficulty of confusing them with one another. The stooge was introduced as another "subject" who was to wait with the injected subject for 20 minutes while the *Suproxin* was absorbed. In his euphoric act, the stooge would doodle on paper, make paper airplanes and fly them at the subject, shoot at the wastebaskets with paper balls, make a rubber-band gun and shoot paper wads, and work a hula hoop. All this was done with great animation and was completely standardized. Never, by his comments, did the stooge directly solicit the subject's inclusion in the activities.

In the anger condition the stooge complained to the subject about being injected. A questionnaire left by the experimenter for answering became the focus of his anger. He complained about its length, the requirements of the answers, invasion of privacy, lack of correct possible answers for some items, and finally ripped the questionnaire to shreds and stamped out of the room.[3] This act was also completely standardized.

Finally, the experimenter re-entered the room and asked each subject to fill out a short questionnaire that attempted to tap the subject's mood (e.g., "How irritated, angry, or annoyed would you say you feel at present?"). This was requested as a further clarification of the possible effects of the *Suproxin*. In addition to the above anger question, the questionnaire contained a question on degree of happiness, several other mock questions, and some on the individual's awareness of his own bodily state (e.g., "Do you feel any tremor of the hands, arms, or legs?").

After the questionnaire was answered, the experimenter fully debriefed each subject, explaining the necessity for the deception involved, and the subject then answered a few more questions regarding any suspicions he had of the experiment.

Schachter and Singer reported that the epinephrine *(Suproxin)* worked to increase pulse rate in individuals injected, and that individuals in the epinephrine groups reported experiencing more palpitation and tremor than those individuals given the placebo injection. Thus, they concluded the epinephrine injection produced a sympathetic nervous system reaction.

Note that this is a necessary preliminary outcome. Epinephrine groups must be physiologically different from placebo groups in order for the critical data of the experiment to be sensibly understood. If there were no significant body-state changes, one

[3]The questionnaire really contained some obnoxious questions: for example, "With how many men (other than your father) has your mother had extramarital relationships" (p. 385)? For this question the smallest answer was: "4 and under."

component of emotional behavior, critical to the definition of that behavior, would be absent.

But which subjects became most angry? or most euphoric? **Table 16-1 presents some of the results of this experiment. Graph the results for the Activity Index and the Acts-Initiated columns of the table. Use one set of coordinates for each and use bars to depict each condition, choosing a different bar (striped, filled, etc.) for each one. Conditions should be arrayed along the abscissa. Stack the coordinates so that the two sets of data are comparable; that is, the Activity Index for the Epinephrine-Informed group should be vertically above the Acts-Initiated result for the same group, and the kind of bar chosen for the Epinephrine-Informed group should be the same in each case.**

In Table 16-1, the Activity Index is a scoring system which the two investigators used to determine the degree of involvement (and hence, emotion) the subject was experiencing. Thus, the higher the score, the more active the subject (e.g., hula hooping was scored highest, followed by shooting with a slingshot, paper airplanes, doodling, and doing nothing). These scores were determined by observers who monitored the subject's behaviors when he was with the stooge. The score for the kind of behavior the subject exhibited was then multiplied by the estimated time the subject spent doing the behavior. Finally, each of these products was summed to produce the Activity Index (a measure of behavioral euphoria) for each subject. Acts Initiated was a score derived by examining how frequently the subject

Table 16-1

Behavioral indications of two emotional states. Data taken from Schachter, S., & Singer, J. E. Cognitive, social, and phsyiological determinants of emotional state. *Psychological Review*, 1962, 69, 379-399.

Condition	Activity Index	Mean Number of Acts Initiated
Epinephrine		
Informed	12.72	0.20
Ignorant	18.28	0.56
Misinformed	22.56	0.84
Placebo	16.00	0.54

commenced euphoric acts of his own (e.g., stood on a table and shouted how happy he was). This score was derived by counting the number of these "original" euphoric acts and dividing by the total subjects in each group.

Note that your graph should show a similar order effect for each of the two measures depicted. That is, each group is in a similar position with respect to the other groups independent of the measure graphed. Carefully scrutinize which conditions produced the highest activity level and the greatest number of acts initiated; ascertain also which conditions produced the fewest acts initiated and the lowest increase in activity level.

Think about what results to expect from the hypotheses presented earlier. Recall that the informed group knew there could be side effects of the injection and thus could "explain" any feelings they may have had. However, the remaining two groups either expected different feelings (Epinephrine-Misinformed) or perhaps expected no feelings at all (Epinephrine-Ignorant). Thus, these individuals would not have ready "nonemotional" explanations for their behavior and their feelings.

Although we did not depict them for you, Schachter and Singer found similar results with scores reflecting anger in the groups who experienced the angry stooge.

Schachter and Singer's results conclusively show that we are more likely to label a state "emotional" if we have some underlying physiological state change (in their case, sympathetic nervous system arousal) and no good explanation for the physiological change, than if we have some explanation. They also show very succinctly that where there is no explanation available for the feelings experienced, the individual will use his current environment to explain the "emotion" he feels. In other words, the emotion is a joint function of the underlying state, and the current external environment.

Interestingly also, their data suggest that an individual who does not have an explanation for his current feelings may be more amenable to having his behavior shift as a function of environmental input than an individual who knows why he feels the way he does. Thus, those ignorant or misinformed of the reason for their feelings in this experiment were more likely to become angered or euphoric as a result of the stooge's behavior than individuals who were informed of the possible effects of the injection.

Therefore, our emotional labels are very much determined by what we think are the reasons for our feelings, and these reasons exist largely in our own environments outside our integuments.

The serious study of emotional behavior began with William James in 1890. James proposed, contrary to commonsense analysis, that we see a bear, run and thereafter are frightened, rather than see a bear, therefore are frightened, and run (James, 1950).

For James, running produced the physiological changes the individual felt as fear. We need not argue how the physiological changes were actually produced, that is, either: 1) by seeing the bear; 2) by running from him; or 3) by an injection as in Schacter and Singer. Critical here is the perception of these changes by the individual. For James, this perception itself was

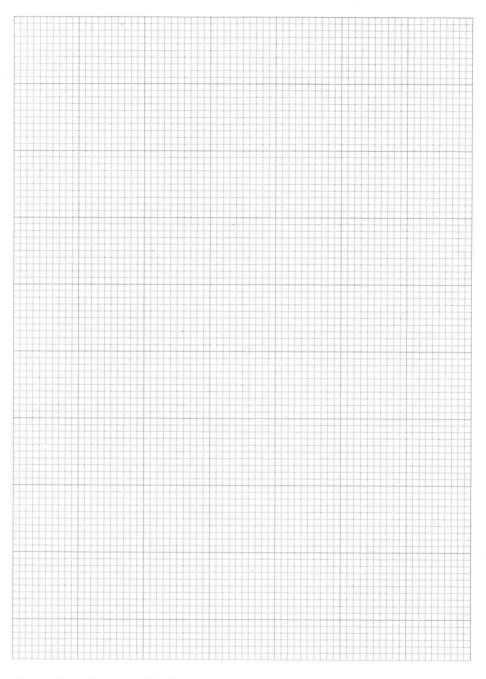

Figure 16-1   Behavioral indications of two emotional states. The Activity Index
(upper set of coordinates) is a summed product of the time an individual spent in
one of several stooge-imitated "euphoric" behaviors such as hula-hooping.
Initiated acts were those the subject produced that were original but still could be
classed as euphoric.

*

emotion (p. 449). He went on to say that because we have so many perceptions that we call emotions there must, therefore, be a great many physiological states which accompany them.[4] Research data have not supported this contention. Still it is possible that we somehow perceive different body states which instruments have failed to measure. But assuming that we experience few different body states, we are nevertheless left with the fact that many emotional labels exist for these few states. The James-Lange theory provides no basis for understanding this surplus of labels. However, we can now understand *how* the labelling occurs, having read Schachter and Singer's experiment.

[4]Independently stated at the same time by Professor C. Lange of Copenhagen and commonly known today as the James-Lange theory.

Exam

1. What is emotional behavior?
2. What is meant by the "development" of emotional behavior?
3. Describe a particular emotion specifying its operant and respondent components.
4. What is the activation syndrome?
5. State why the operant component of emotional behavior may change in topography while the respondent behavior does not. How do the respondent components of emotional behavior change?
6. State Schachter and Singer's three major hypotheses.
7. Describe the three main parts of Schachter and Singer's experiment; that is, the three independent variables.
8. What is a placebo?
9. What does Figure 16-1 show? Which group initiated the most euphoric acts? Which group became most involved with the stooge (Activity Index)?
10. How can we interpret Schachter and Singer's results with respect to how our emotions are determined? (Be careful: Emotions are determined jointly by the presence of at least two events.)
11. State and describe an operant conditioning technique used to study emotional behavior. How might an investigator using this technique determine the effects of an unknown drug that he suspects may function as a tranquilizer?
12. What is an "experimental neurosis"? Describe the procedures which could generate this condition in a dog.
13. Describe several experimental operations that may affect the "reinforcing value" of an intermittently reinforced operant. How might these operations relate to the suppression of that response in the conditioned suppression preparation?

References

James, W. *The principles of psychology.* New York: Dover Publications, 1950.

Lauener, H. Conditioned suppression in rats and the effects of pharmacological agents thereon. *Psychopharmacologia,* 1963, 4, 311-325.

Millenson, J. R., & deVilliers, P. A. Motivational properties of conditioned anxiety. In R. M. Gilbert & J. R. Millenson (Eds.), *Reinforcement: Behavioral analyses.* New York: Academic Press, 1972. Pp. 97-128.

Pavlov, I. P. *Conditioned reflexes.* New York: Dover Publications, 1960.

Schachter, S., & Singer, J. E. Cognitive, social, and physiological determinants of emotional state. *Psychological Review,* 1962, 69, 379-399.

Emotional Behavior: Kinds and Application

In the preceding unit we stated that intense stimuli could elicit autonomic activity and that other stimuli with which these elicitors (UCSs and CSs) were paired could also come, through respondent conditioning, to elicit autonomic activity.

One type of stimulus that may be strong, given appropriate deprivation conditions, is the consequence for operant behavior. Thus, reinforcers and punishers, both conditioned and unconditioned, may not only increase or decrease the operant responses they follow, but also elicit subsequent respondents which the individual calls emotions.

To make a conditioning analysis of emotional behavior as relevant as possible, we can label emotions as a result of knowing how a consequent stimulus (reinforcer or punisher) functions with respect to some operant behavior the individual emits.

Presentation of Strong Positive Reinforcers

Positive reinforcers functioning additionally as unconditional or conditional eliciting stimuli produce feelings variously called euphoria, happiness, joy, and contentment. While the feelings elicited in one reinforcing situation are the same as those elicited in another, the operant components may be vastly different. A student may just smile upon answering a question correctly, while a pitcher completing a no-hit, no-run baseball game may leap in the air and jump on the backs of his teammates. If the question answered by the same student resulted in the presentation of a substantial sum of money to him (e.g., $64,000), he might also jump in the air and on the backs of his colleagues.

Withdrawal of Strong Positive Reinforcers

Loss of a strong positive reinforcer may produce what we call grief, sadness, or sorrow (Mowrer, 1960). Well-known examples are the loss of a mate to many species of mammal, especially man, or the loss of a financial empire to a tycoon. Loss of a strong positive reinforcer (punishment, Type II) may also result in the overall decrease in behavior that is characteristic of depression. Mowrer (1960) has suggested this condition may produce anger if the loss is perceived as temporary, sorrow if the loss is irrevocable.

Presentation of Strong Aversive Stimuli

A strong aversive stimulus produced by an operant can function three ways: 1) It may suppress further occurrences of the operant (punishment, Type I); 2) it may elicit strong respondents, which are typically called anger, rage, or fear; and 3) it may be discriminative for alternative operants. Take an example in education. If a child is corporally punished in school for disobedience, the future amount of disobedience may be decreased. However, punishment itself, functioning as an unconditional stimulus, may elicit fear and rage.

Further, the punishment is associated with many other stimuli that are part of the school environment: for example, other teachers and the classroom. This association may be sufficient to: 1) produce conditional fear or rage respondents, and 2) produce alternative operants such as escape from or counteraggression toward the conditioned aversive stimuli. For example, an adolescent may drop out (escape) from school because many strong aversive stimuli are presented therein. Given that the truant officer forces him to school, receipt of this punishment may result in an attack on the surroundings, such as vandalism or beating the teacher, or, as has been suggested, the ultimate vandalism — failure to support his country's educational systems (Skinner, 1968).

Withdrawal of Strong Aversive Stimuli

Response-dependent withdrawal of aversive stimuli — negative reinforcement — will result in an increase in the frequency of the operant behavior producing the withdrawal. Removal of these aversive stimuli produces respondent feelings often called "relief." For example, having successfully climbed a tree to escape a bear, the climber may say he feels considerably relieved. Use of the word *relief* usually implies a cessation of fear or anxiety-producing stimuli. Usually some operant (e.g., tree climbing) produces this cessation.

The foregoing analyses are based on the four possible consequences of a response (Unit 8). Mowrer (1960) has also developed a fourfold classification of emotional responding, stressing a "situational" analysis of emotion (p. 167). Mowrer's classification is similar to the present authors' except that he further defines the emotion based on whether the individual's response is followed by a presentation or withdrawal of an *unconditioned* positive or aversive stimulus or a *conditioned* positive or aversive stimulus. Where a conditioned positive reinforcer follows behavior, Mowrer has suggested that this produces the emotion of "hope." Where a conditioned positive reinforcer is withdrawn, Mowrer suggests the emotion is "disappointment." Where a conditioned aversive stimulus is withdrawn, the emotion is "relief," although he suggests this may also produce hope (hope, we suppose, that the stimulus will not occur again). These relations are depicted in Figure 17-1.

Extinction

A given behavior has resulted in positive reinforcement in the past, but now the behavior no longer produces positive reinforcement. The respondents elicited by this occurrence and the operants emitted are said to be a result of "frustration." If a person continually gets emergency signals or the wrong number when he dials the phone, he may swear at it, fiercely jiggle the on-off switch, and finally slam down the receiver (see Unit 7 for a discussion of extinction-produced aggression).

Barker, Dembo, and Lewin (1943) provide an illustration of the effects of frustration on child behavior. In a classic study, they took 30 children from 25 to 61 months of age to a playroom in which three free-play situations

Unconditioned Stimuli

	S^{R+}	S^{R-}
Present	Joy; Euphoria; Happiness;	Anger; Fear
Remove	Anger; Sorrow	Relief

Conditioned Stimuli

	S^{r+}	S^{r-}
Present	Hope	Fear
Remove	Disappointment	Relief; Hope

Figure 17-1

Fourfold dependency tables with correlated emotions resulting from stimulus consequences which are unconditioned (top panel) or conditioned (bottom panel) reinforcing stimuli.

existed. Each free-play situation consisted of a few ordinary toys (telephone, boat, etc.) arrayed on a piece of paper. The experimenter showed the child how each toy could be used and thereafter observed the child's play for 30 minutes. At the next session a sliding partition hiding another room was lifted. In this room there were luxurious toys (e.g., a large doll house with electric lights, a miniature lake with sailboats, and a tea-party set), and the experimenter allowed the child to play with these toys for 5 to 15 minutes. After this time, the experimenter collected the free-play toys from among the luxurious items, redistributed them on the paper squares, took the child to the paper squares saying, "And now let's play at the other end" (p. 446), and lowered a screen again dividing the room in two. However, the screen allowed the child to see the luxurious toys, although it denied access to them. The child was then observed for 30 more minutes in the free-play situation. After this time the child was asked if he was ready to leave. When he said he was, the experimenter lifted the divider and allowed the child free access to the luxurious toys until the child was ready to leave on his own.

The children's play behavior was rated in the free-play situation for "constructiveness" both before and during the barrier-present situation. By constructiveness was meant how involved, detailed, and inventive each child's play behavior was. Using just a truck and trailer as an example, minimal constructiveness was simply taking both in hand; slightly more constructive play was moving them from one place to another; much more constructive play was using the truck and trailer to haul something. The addition of descriptive or explanatory verbal behavior evidencing an original plan was rated even higher (e.g., the child said he was loading trailer for a trip and then did it, explaining the loading step by step). The children's emotional behavior was also noted as a function of the conditions.

Twenty-two of the 30 children were less constructive in their play after being frustrated, 3 showed no change, and 5 increased. While 22 children showed a reduction in the use of

imagination, complexity, and structure of their play, the older children showed greater reductions in these measures than the younger children. For instance, an older child who showed highly original play with the truck and trailer might now just hold them. A younger child who had used the truck and trailer to haul something might now just run them from place to place. The authors also noted changes in emotional behavior. There was a decrease both in (monologue) play-talk and friendly conversation with the experimenter. Unhappy expressions increased while happy expressions decreased. The experimenters also noted an increase in restlessness and aggressiveness during frustration conditions. The study shows that the nonavailability of reinforcers, after a period of sampling them (extinction), may produce emotional behavior.

A hypothetical generalization may be illustrative. Ghetto children may be frustrated by sampling reinforcers available to them outside the ghetto when these reinforcers are not available in their own environment. If television is available at home to allow these children to sample many reinforcing activities symbolically, but not in actuality, these conditions may serve to promote frustration because of confinement to a deprived environment. Barker et al. might suggest here that we should expect a reduction in constructiveness and a decrease in social interactions when these children are exposed to unattainable reinforcers. Does this sound like a familiar description of a child of poverty?

We should re-emphasize the speculative nature of our analysis in this unit. There is very little human evidence of any kind in this area.

However, as Mowrer has suggested, it seems very useful to operationalize our language of emotions in this way. Understanding is fostered and we gain a framework in which to do research having a more standardized notion of what emotional behavior is.

Application

J. Wolpe, Isolation of a conditioning procedure as the crucial psychotherapeutic factor: A case study. *Journal of Nervous and Mental Disease*, 1962, 134, 316-329.

One of the problems facing a practicing clinical psychologist is the inability of a patient to engage in a class of behaviors because of an irrational fear. This is called a **PHOBIA**. Many people have demonstrated fears that make them unable to behave in a large number of environments. These have included fear of heights, fear of snakes, fear of dogs, fear of cutting oneself, fear of sexual intercourse, fear of automobiles, fear of open spaces, fear of small spaces, and so on.

Some individuals who have these fears may never seek the services of a psychologist because they rarely come in contact with the stimuli producing the phobic-avoidance responses. For example, an individual may never learn he is deathly afraid of heights because he has never been in a tall building or in an airplane. Or if he does know of his fear, his life may be little curtailed by it because he may live in a rural setting where he need not ride in airplanes or look out from tall buildings. However, for a large number of people, the inability to perform certain behavior may mean the loss of some very strong reinforcers and the individuals may worry about their failing to deal effectively with their environments.

In order to cope with the respondents produced by phobic stimuli, a technique called **SYSTEMATIC DESENSITIZATION** has been formulated. Principally, it is a way to change stimuli which function to elicit strong fear respondents, so the stimuli elicit respondents that are incompatible with fear.

Joseph Wolpe, a psychiatrist, is responsible for the development of this technique which is loosely based on **RECIPROCAL INHIBITION**, a neurological phenomonon first discussed by C. S. Sherrington (1947). Sherrington showed that a muscle contracting in response to a stimulus could be inhibited from contracting (i.e., made to relax) by another stimulus applied at the same time. Thus, the second stimulus overrides or inhibits the response produced by the first stimulus. Sherrington's work employed spinal reflexes — nerves and muscles attached to the spinal cord.

From this evidence, Wolpe generalized to ideational behavior, and some say this generalization is unjustified (Davison, 1968; Wilson & Davison, 1971). However, the generalization results in the following hypothesis: There are behaviors occurring as a result of prior stimulation and these behaviors can be inhibited by providing a second stimulus, which produces a response that precludes the earlier response.

Figure 17-2 provides a stylized representation of this behavioral generalization of the reciprocal inhibition concept. In Panel A we see that some stimulus, S_1, leads to a response, R_1, and that another stimulus, S_2, leads to a response, R_2. Thus, each stimulus leads

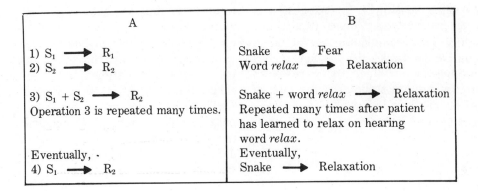

A	B
1) $S_1 \longrightarrow R_1$ 2) $S_2 \longrightarrow R_2$	Snake $\longrightarrow$ Fear Word *relax* $\longrightarrow$ Relaxation
3) $S_1 + S_2 \longrightarrow R_2$ Operation 3 is repeated many times.	Snake + word *relax* $\longrightarrow$ Relaxation Repeated many times after patient has learned to relax on hearing word *relax*.
Eventually, · 4) $S_1 \longrightarrow R_2$	Eventually, Snake $\longrightarrow$ Relaxation

Figure 17-2

Stylized representations counterconditioning by reciprocal inhibition.

to its own response; but if S_1 and S_2 are presented together, S_1 fails to produce R_1; instead, R_2 occurs. R_2 (and therefore, S_2) inhibit the occurrence of R_1. Panel B of the same figure suggests how this is hypothesized to operate in a common stimulus-response relation, such as seeing a snake and becoming fearful. In our stylization the individual is taught how to relax large muscle groups by intoning the word *relax*. Wolpe postulated that relaxation was incompatible with fear. Thus, presumably, $R_{(fear)}$ and $R_{(relaxation)}$ should not be able to occur simultaneously. If the snake stimulus were presented to a client along with his cue to relax, only one of the two responses should follow. If the relax stimulus and subsequent relaxation are strong enough (or the fear weak enough), the relaxation response should be prepotent and occur. After numerous pairings of this sort, the snake stimulus itself should lead to relaxation. Where this latter substitution occurs and S_1 now produces R_2, **COUNTERCONDITIONING** is said to

have occurred, and this is another term for systematic desensitization by reciprocal inhibition.[1]

In clinical practice, systematic desensitization is conducted in the

[1]Counterconditioning is an example of an additional way by which it has been proposed that stimuli and responses can become functionally related. Proponents of this school of thought have argued that reinforcement is not necessary for stimuli and responses to become related. Rather, the critical condition simply is the juxtaposition (i.e., contiguity) of the stimulus and response (Guthrie, 1935). However, this very simple notion raises many more questions than it answers (Estes, Koch, MacCorquodale, Meehl, Mueller, Schoenfeld, & Verplanck, 1954).

We have now presented three possible ways in which a stimulus can become functional with respect to a response: 1) stimulus pairing (also called *stimulus-stimulus contiguity*) as in respondent conditioning and the formation of conditioned reinforcers; 2) stimulus-response pairing (also called *stimulus-response* contiguity, as above); and 3) the consequation of a response in the presence of a stimulus, which makes the stimulus discriminative and reinforcing — the reinforcing function probably due to the operation in 1).

following fashion. The patient, with the help of the therapist, describes scenes which involve his phobia. A large number of these are gathered and ranked in a hierarchy from most frightening to least frightening. This is called an **ANXIETY HIERARCHY**. The patient is taught by the therapist how to relax physically. This involves opposition of large muscle groups, breathing, and other exercises. After mastery of the relaxation procedures, which may take a number of sessions and additional practice at home, the patient is able to relax upon the occasion of a self-generated stimulus (e.g., he tells himself to relax). The therapist then presents the least frightening scene in the anxiety hierarchy, with the patient instructed to relax. If the scene begins to produce fear, the patient signals the therapist and the scene is withdrawn. While the patient is relaxed, the scene is presented by the therapist and the patient is instructed to imagine the scene's details. Over a number of sessions, patient and therapist proceed through the hierarchy from the least frightening to the most frightening scene.

The result of this procedure is that the patient may imagine a formerly fear-producing situation and now remain completely relaxed. This procedure may allow him to engage in behaviors which were formerly impossible due to his irrational fear. Useful adjuncts of this procedure have the patient actually experience the graded stimulus situations rather than simply imagining them. This latter procedure provides a direct measure of the success of the treatment because the therapist observes the patient engaging in the feared behavior.

Wolpe used these techniques in the case of a woman who was involved in a traffic accident while riding with her husband in their automobile. A truck ran a red light hitting their car, knocking her out of the car and causing serious injury. After this incident, the patient feared riding in cars, crossing streets, and even imagining doing these things. A hierarchy of 36 scenes was established utilizing the patient in various relations to automobiles. For the first scenes, cars imagined were at some distance, travelling slowly, and driven by people the patient knew; these cars approached and stopped safely at decreasing distances. Very specific stimulus situations were quite fear-provoking. For example, the patient became fearful when imagining making a left turn if an oncoming car were anywhere in sight. The lateral approach of any automobile was extremely frightening. The imagination of these scenes without fear was accomplished by having the patient imagine a large distance between the cars, slow speeds, and someone driving the other automobile whom she trusted. Slowly, the distances between cars were decreased, automobile speeds increased, and unknown drivers substituted for known ones. In addition, the patient also imagined cars in various relations to herself walking across an intersection.

Each scene in the hierarchy was repeatedly presented until it evoked no anxiety, most scenes from 25 to 40 times, but some scenes over 100 times. In all, nearly 1,500 presentations were made. At the end of therapy (around 60 to 70 sessions) the patient felt normal in nearly all traffic situations. At one point during therapy, she was taken out in an automobile and allowed to cross intersections by herself. This procedure provided an actual test of her ability to engage in the previously feared behaviors.

Figure 17-3 contains the space for graphing the results of a portion of the foregoing procedures. This graph shows the distance at which the patient could imagine (without fear) an automobile oncoming, while the patient's car was making a left turn. Use the data in Table 17-1 to complete Figure 17-3. Note that the successive columns of the table correspond to differences in the same basic scene. Each should be graphed using a different line and point code. These are supplied in the table at the top of each column. Spaces on the abscissa are intervals during which no treatment was given; break the graphed lines across these intervals. When the table gives two points for a single session, it means that the distance changed during the session, and this will produce a vertical graphed line.

Exam

1. Define the following terms:

   a. counterconditioning
   b. contiguity
   c. anxiety hierarchy
   d. conditioned aversive stimulus
   e. extinction-produced aggression
   f. "disappointment" (according to Mowrer)
   g. stimulus-stimulus contiguity
   h. stimulus-response contiguity

2. What kind of operation usually generates frustration?

3. Name the procedure that may produce anger or rage.

4. What are the four procedures that strengthen or weaken operant behavior that also produce emotional behavior?

5. What is systematic desensitization? (Describe the procedures involved.)

6. What is a phobia? Give an example of one which would interfere with a person's life.

7. How might systematic desensitization be used to overcome fear of snakes? Construct a hypothetical hierarchy of phobic stimuli which might be used in treatment of this condition. Seven items should suffice for your example.

8. In the Wolpe study, cite two pieces of evidence that indicate improvement in the patient's phobia.

9. Summarize the Barker, Dembo, and Lewin study. What are the implications of their results?

10. Describe an everyday instance of how a child might be frustrated by an older brother. What behaviors might you expect to see as a result of the frustration?

11. Present an operational definition of Sherrington's reciprocal inhibition concept.

12. Construct a 2 x 2 table inserting names for emotions generated by the response-dependent presentation or withdrawal of unconditioned and conditioned positively and negatively reinforcing stimuli.

13. Describe three sets of operations that make a stimulus functional with respect to a response.

References

Barker, R. G., Dembo, T., & Lewin, K.   Frustration and regression. In R. G. Barker, J. S. Kounin, & H. F. Wright (Eds.), *Child behavior and development.* New York: McGraw-Hill, 1943. Pp. 441-458.

Davison, G. C.   Systematic desensitization as a counterconditioning process. *Journal of Abnormal Psychology*, 1968, **73**, 91-99.

Estes, W. K., Koch, S., MacCorquodale, K., Meehl, P. E., Mueller, C. G., Jr., Schoenfeld, W. N., & Verplanck, W. S.   *Modern learning theory.* New York: Appleton-Century-Crofts, 1954.

Guthrie, E. R.   *The psychology of learning.* New York: Harper, 1935.

Mowrer, O. H.   *Learning theory and behavior.* New York: John Wiley and Sons, Inc., 1960.

Sherrington, C. S.   *The integrative action of the central nervous system.* Cambridge: Cambridge University Press, 1947.

Skinner, B. F.   *The technology of teaching.* New York: Appleton-Century-Crofts, Inc., 1968.

Wilson, G. T., & Davison, C. G.   Processes of fear reduction in systematic desensitization: Animal studies. *Psychological Bulletin*, 1971, **76**, 1-14.

Wolpe, J.   Isolation of a conditioning procedure as the crucial psychotherapeutic factor: A case study. *Journal of Nervous and Mental Disease*, 1962, **134**, 316-329.

Table 17-1

Change in the imagined distance of a phobic stimulus for a patient with an automobile phobia. Data estimated from Wolpe, J.   Isolation of a conditioning procedure as the crucial psychotherapeutic factor: A case study. *Journal of Nervous and Mental Disease*, 1962, 134, 316-329.

Session	Distance from Approaching Car in Sixteenths of a Mile			
	A* (−)	B (. − .)	C (o − o)	D (x − x)
1	16,12			
2	12,7	16	14	
3	7,5	16,8	14,12.5	
4	5,4	8,6	12.5,12	
5	4,3.5	6,5.5		
No Active Treatment				
6		9,7.5	12,8	
7	7.5,4	8		
8		4	8,6	
9		4,3	6,4	12
10		3,2	4,3	12,10.5
11		2,0,1.8	3,2.5	10.5,8
12		1.8	2.5	8,5
13		1.8	2.5	5
14		1.8,1.5	2.5,2	5
15		1.5,1.3	2,1.8	5,4
16			1.8,1.5	4,3.5
17				3,2.5
18				2.5,2.0
No Active Treatment				
19				2,1.8
20				1.8,1.5
21				1.5,1.2

*A=brother driving patient's car; Dr. G. the other.
 B=same, with stranger driving other car.
 C=husband driving patient's car; Dr. G. the other.
 D=same, with stranger driving other car.

Figure 17-3 Progress in the desensitization treatment of a woman who feared riding in an automobile. The figure describes the distance, across therapy sessions, the woman was able to imagine without fear between an automobile in which she was riding and an automobile which was approaching her imagined automobile.

*

Punishment, Type I

18

PUNISHMENT, TYPE I is defined as the presentation of a negative reinforcer dependent upon a response. Recall that a negative reinforcer is a stimulus of proven effect; therefore, punishment will necessarily result in a decrease in the rate of responding. Given the above operation, it is incorrect to use the term *punishment* when the behavior does not, in fact, decrease.

Recent experiments by Azrin and Holz (1966) and their co-workers have told us much about the effects of punishment and have unraveled some of the puzzles surrounding this procedure. Edward Thorndike, a pioneer psychologist who formulated the "Law of Effect" (in brief: "satisfiers" stamp in behavior; "annoyers" stamp out behavior), later revised this law based on his research with humans. He found that the word *wrong*, supplied after an incorrect choice on a multiple-choice test, was not very effective in altering a subject's choice next time through the test. He concluded that punishment did not weaken behavior (see Thorndike, 1935, Chapter 6 for a summary of his position on punishment).

We now know that this conclusion was incorrect. Punishment, especially severe punishment, can permanently eliminate a response (Appel, 1961; Azrin, 1960). However, the effects of a "punishing" stimulus depend so much on the conditions under which punishment is administered, that without a careful specification of these conditions, it is not possible to make general statements about the nature of punishment. For example, suppose a hungry pigeon is pecking a key for food and we decide to make him stop pecking by giving him an electric shock every time he pecks. Will an 80-volt shock be sufficient? Not necessarily. It all depends on how the pigeon is introduced to the shock. Read on.

Some Problems with Punishment, Type I

Tolerance for punishment. Azrin, Holz, and Hake (1963) found that the manner in which punishment was introduced — either gradually raising the intensity or starting at the maximum intensity — was critical in determining whether a given stimulus would act as a punisher. They were successful in permanently eliminating a key-pecking response in a pigeon by administering a brief 80-volt shock every time the pigeon responded. The pigeon was responding for food on an FR 25 schedule of reinforcement. However, if the initial intensity of the shock was low, say 30 volts, and it was gradually increased over sessions, the bird would continue to respond. This procedure would result in a pigeon that will not stop responding even though it receives 130 volts every time it responds! If you did not know this subject's history, you would probably conclude that punishment simply does not work.

Aversive stimuli as discriminative for positive reinforcement. A response-produced aversive stimulus can be paired with positive reinforcement and become discriminative for that rein-forcement. Holz and Azrin (1961) reinforced pigeons with food on a VI 2-min schedule and later shocked (60-volts ac) the birds for each response. Response rates were halved over what they were during non-shock periods, showing that shock was a punishing stimulus. Subsequently, they alternated periods where responses were reinforced and shocked, with periods where responses were neither shocked nor reinforced (the traditional procedure for establishing a discrimination). After 3 weeks, the pigeons continued to respond at steady rates throughout the reinforcement-shock condition, while responding during the no-reinforcement-no-shock condition was virtually eliminated.

Later in the experiment, sessions were run in which shock was presented for responses during one 10-minute period of the session. *No responses were ever reinforced during these entire sessions* (i.e., *extinction*). During periods when responses produced shock, response rates abruptly accelerated to the rate that was present during earlier sessions where responses were reinforced! Rates continued low during periods when responses did not produce shock. Here we have an interesting paradox. The pigeon responds more when it is shocked than when it is not shocked, and yet it is clear that the shock is an aversive stimulus. This result clearly shows that an aversive stimulus, which is functioning as a punisher to reduce response rates, can concurrently have an additional function. The stimulus may also be discriminative for positive reinforcement, and under special conditions may actually raise the rate of responding.

In many crowded institutions, attention by the staff (usually a positive reinforcer) is a precious commodity and is often given only to the troublemakers. Rosenhan (1973) found that most of the normal behavior of patients in mental hospitals is ignored by the staff (see the illustration in Unit 21 for a full discussion of typical staff-patient interactions). However, deviant behavior such as fighting or throwing things brings an immediate response — one or more aides come rushing up to intercede with the disputants or otherwise interact with the troublemaker. The interaction is usually aversive. The individual may be "roughed up," placed in restraints, and put in isolation. At the same time, though, he also recieves the attention of several persons. If this is the only way this person can receive attention, he may continue to misbehave even when the "punishment" is increased in severity. The solution to this problem, of course, is to provide the positive reinforcer, attention, for some desirable behavior and to administer punishment without undue attention. The patient's behavior (spitting, fighting, etc.) can become a discriminative stimulus for positive reinforcement — in this case, attention — just as the shock became discriminative for food to the pigeon.

Elicitation of respondents. The procedure of punishment, Type I is not easy to use effectively for a variety of reasons. One reason is that punishment by painful stimulation elicits respondent behavior. For instance, rats will frequently bite and defecate; monkeys bite and vocalize; children yell and cry. All species will attack another organism in close proximity in response to painful stimulation. In most cases, a person administering punishment is angry. Under these circumstances, it is difficult to teach a child what he should have done in the situation in which he was just punished. The parent will have to wait until both he and his child are calm again before he can attempt to teach anything. Have you ever noticed how difficult it is to deliver a positive reinforcer to anyone with whom you are angry?

Aggression. The use of punishment, Type I may also lead to two forms of aggression, neither of which is desirable. The first form, mentioned above, is called **PAIN-ELICITED AGGRESSION** (Ulrich & Azrin, 1962). When two animals such as mice or rats are placed in a small cage and both are subjected to a painful stimulus, such as an electric shock, they attack each other. Their fighting (which is stereotyped) does nothing to reduce or eliminate the shock, but still they fight. Pain-elicited aggression has been observed in a variety of species from reptiles to primates, so it appears to be a reliable phenomenon. While humans have not been studied in this situation, for obvious reasons, you can provide your own verification of this phenomenon by recalling your reactions when you hit your head on a cupboard door after you suddenly raised your head. Did you ever slam the door? Strike out at it? Or yell at the person next to you? In a calmer moment, you may have wondered why you behaved so stupidly.

The second form of aggression is operant in nature. Operant aggression is either positively or negatively reinforced. A child who pushes another child away from a toy, so that he obtains it for himself, is positively reinforced for his aggressive act. When a person aggresses against a person administering punishment, he may sometimes be successful in getting the agent of the punishment to stop. This sequence of events negatively reinforces aggression with the result that the attempted control of the original behavior has been lost. Here, we see another reason why punishment, or the threat of it, is not a good technique of control in the long run. When a boy, for example, becomes a teenager, he will have the size and strength of an adult, and he may discover that the threat of counteraggression on his part is sufficient to avoid punishment. If his parents have relied heavily on punishment as a means of control, they may lose that control when their son's physical status changes.

Punishment and teaching. If you have spanked your child frequently for engaging in some undesirable behavior and are puzzled because he does not learn to behave "correctly," you are forgetting that in order to teach you must specify behavior that the child should do. Consider a learning situation with 100 possible alternatives, only 1 of which is correct. If you punish your child for making a mistake, you have taught him very little; there are still 98 wrong responses that can be made. Reinforcement for the correct response tells the child exactly which response is the correct one. Hence, in situations where there are many possible responses and only 1 correct alternative, punishment is a poor way to teach.

Punishment reinforces the punisher. If punishment is fraught with so many problems, why is it in common use and why is it the prime way society controls its members? The reason for this is that punishment reinforces the punisher *immediately*. If a child is playing with a knob on the television and won't respond to a request to stop, a slap is immediately effective in getting him to stop, even though it results in crying, running from the room, and so on. Punishment, much more so than positive reinforcement, immediately reinforces the administrator, and immediate consequences are much more effective than delayed consequences in learning. Hence, administrators of punishment learn to use punishment to attain short-term effects. This is unfortunate because a heavy reliance on punishment as a technique of control leads to side effects which make long-term behavioral management difficult or impossible. The boy who receives little but punishment when attending school will eventually learn, among other things, to hate school, books, teachers, and "authority" in general. He may escape from all the controlling practices of school officials by refusing to attend school.

At this point, some of you may be wondering whether you should ever slap or spank a baby. The answer is yes. A quick slap administered with the word "NO!" is very effective in establishing "NO" as a conditioned aversive stimulus. Obviously, what is needed is some combination of procedures. Punishment of undesired behavior administered concurrently with positive reinforcement for desired behavior is extremely effective in changing behavior (see Unit 19). An exclusive reliance upon physical punishment (or the threat of it) is not an effective means of behavioral control in the long run, and it produces as many problems as it eliminates.

In the following section, punishment was used because the self-destructive behavior the child engaged in occurred so frequently that it was impossible to teach him anything. In this case, punishment was useful because it eliminated behavior that the child must not do.

Application

O. I. Lovaas, & J. Q., Manipulation of self-destruction in three retarded children. *Journal of Applied Behavior Analysis*, 1969, 2, 143-157.

If you visit an institution for retarded or emotionally disturbed children, you will probably see two or three children on every ward walking around with football helmets on. These are self-destructive children and they are the "lucky" ones. These children may walk about, and some attempt is probably being made to teach them the rudiments of self-care. Others, much less fortunate, are kept in restraints 24 hours a day. They are untied only when the bed clothes have to be changed or when they are fed.

Self-destructive or autistic children bang their heads against walls (hence the need for football helmets), bite themselves, hit themselves with clenched fists, bang their elbows or knees together, and so on. It is difficult to convey the distress one feels in observing one of these children. The child appears to be in the worst state of anguish and there is nothing one can do to help. If you attempted to console, sympathize with, or to prevent the child from hitting himself, your attempts would be rebuffed. In fact, the child would not even look at you. Autistic children appear not to acknowledge the existence of other people. When left alone, if they are not hitting themselves, they spend hours engaged in self-stimulatory behavior, such as rocking back and forth or twirling their fingers at a high rate.

It might be thought that autistic children can't really be hurting themselves. But this is not true! If not restrained, some children will actually pull their hair out by grabbing a handful and yanking as hard as they can; or they will bite off their fingers and nails. One girl in the present experiment had bitten her little finger so many times and so severely, that it had to be amputated at the first joint. Although the authors worked with three children, we will report the results of their research with only one child because they found essentially the same thing with the other two subjects.

John was 8 years old and diagnosed as mentally retarded, with no organic basis for his retardation. He lacked speech, could respond only to simple commands, was not toilet trained, could not dress himself, and did not imitate. His self-destructive behavior started when he was 2 years old, and for 6 months prior to this treatment he had been in physical restraints. Tranquilizers had been tried, but they had no effect on his self-destructive behavior. Out of restraints, John had to be prevented from destroying himself.

The experiments were done in simply furnished rooms, and the child's behavior was observed from an adjoining room through a one-way mirror. Observers kept a continuous record of self-destructive responses as well as other annoying behaviors such as whining and resisting contact with adults.

Extinction. In one condition of the study, the authors attempted to eliminate self-destruction by extinction. It was suspected that the attention the child received when he engaged in self-destructive behavior may have been the reinforcer maintaining that behavior. So John was placed on the bed, with the restraints removed, and the adults left the room. The sessions were conducted in the morning and lasted for 90 minutes.

Table 18-1 shows the frequency of self-destructive responses over the 11-day extinction phase of the study. Plot these data in the form of histograms using five squares for each bar. Note how much self-destructive behavior was emitted in extinction.

Table 18-1

Frequency of John's self-destructive behavior during extinction. Data taken from Lovaas, O. I., & Simmons, J. Q. Manipulation of Self-destruction in three retarded children. *Journal of Applied Behavior Analysis,* **1969, 2, 143-157.**

Days	Self-Destructive Responses
1	2750
2	1750
3	1425
4	1825
5	625
6	600
7	125
8	50
9	10
10	0
11	0

Punishment. The extinction sessions in the morning were carried out in only one of the experimental rooms, the bedroom, and while his self-destructive behavior was eliminated in the bedroom, it still occurred in other situations. In sum, the extinction treatment did not generalize. The authors then decided to use punishment in an attempt to determine which treatment was more effective. In one situation, John was placed on the lap of one of the nurses with his restraints removed. He was held so that he had as much freedom as possible but could not easily get off her lap. The number of times John hit himself was recorded every day during a 5-minute observation period. Baseline observations were collected over 15 days. During these sessions, his self-destructive responses did not systematically change in this situation even though they were decreasing in the bedroom.

On Day 16, punishment was introduced. As soon as John hit himself, he was given a 1-second shock delivered by a hand-held shocking device. The experimenter had tried it on himself and reported that it definitely was painful, but that the pain stopped as soon as the shock ended. John was given 12 shocks in all, spread over four sessions. **The data in Table 18-2 show the results of this punishment. The table also shows the sessions in which shock was given as well as which one of the four experimenters delivered the shock. Plot the data in Table 18-2 and indicate by an arrow ($\uparrow$) those sessions in which shock was delivered. On the abscissa and right below the days of the experiment, write in which of the experimenters (E_1, E_2, E_3, or E_4) was present with John.**

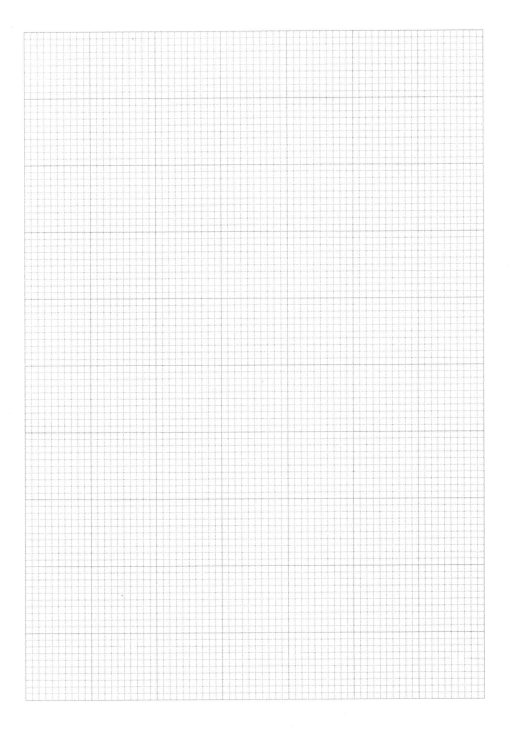

Figure 18-1   Frequency of self-destructive responses in the bedroom of a ward across an 11-day extinction period for John, a retarded boy.

*

Table 18-2

Frequency of John's self-destructive behavior while sitting on a nurse's lap for 5 minutes. During the days that are circled, a brief shock was delivered when he made a self-destructive response. The second column lists which of the four experimenters was present for that session. Data taken from Lovaas, O. I., and Simmons, J. Q. Manipulation of self-destruction in three retarded children. *Journal of Applied Behavior Analysis*, 1969, 2, 143-157.

Days	Experimenter	Self-Destructive Responses
1	1	105
2	1	110
3	1	305
4	1	280
5	1	240
6	1	260
7	1	180
8	1	210
9	1	155
10	1	260
11	1	240
12	1	330
13	1	Data missing
14	1	180
15	1	260
(16)	1	10
17	2	50
18	3	100
(19)	1	5 or less
20	1	5 or less
21	3	5 or less
22	1	5 or less
23	2	30
(24)	1	5 or less
25	2	155
26	3	140
27	4	145
28	1	5 or less
29	1	5 or less
(30)	3	5 or less
31	2	5
32	4	5
33	3	5 or less
34	2	5 or less
35	4	5
36	1	5

As John's self-destructive behavior was being punished in one situation, sitting on the nurse's lap, it was being recorded in still another situation — a dormitory room. **Table 18-3 shows the frequency of his self-destructive responses in this room. Plot these data on Figure 18-3. Label the abscissa as you did in the previous graph, starting from Day 1. Notice that there are no data for the first 7 days. Recording in the dormitory room started on Day 8 of the project, so plot your first data points here. John was given four shocks over days 28 and 29 and this treatment was effective in decreasing his self-destructive behavior. As in the previous graph, indicate by an arrow the sessions in which shock was given.**

There are several effects of punishment in this experiment that should be emphasized. First, not only did punishment reduce the frequency of self-destructive responses but it also eliminated whining and avoidance behavior. At the beginning of treatment, John squirmed and fought to get off the nurse's lap. Later on, he remained relatively quiet and the amount of eye contact with adults increased. This result was an unexpected benefit of the procedure because eye contact and lack of fussing would make it much easier to establish smiles, approving looks, and praise as conditioned reinforcers for later instructional programs.

A second important point is that self-destructive behavior and related maladaptive behaviors were engaged in so frequently that the child had no time to do anything else. Hence, he did not have the opportunity to come in contact with any positively reinforcing stimuli

Table 18-3

Frequency of John's self-destructive behavior in a dormitory room. On the two circled days, John was shocked for self-destructive responses. Baseline measurements were begun on Day 8 of the study. Data taken from Lovaas, O. I., & Simmons, J. Q. Manipulation of self-destruction in 3 retarded children. *Journal of Applied Behavior Analysis*, **1969, 2, 143-157.**

Days	Self-Destructive Responses
1	—
2	—
3	—
4	—
5	—
6	—
7	—
8	200
9	195
10	275
11	270
12	200
13	205
14	255
15	230
16	225
17	240
18	215
19	260
20	220
21	245
22	275
23	150
24	180
25	285
26	250
27	160
㉘	2
㉙	2
30	0
31	0
32	0
33	0
34	0
35	0

Figure 18-2   Frequency of John's self-destructive behavior while sitting on a
nurse's lap. A brief shock was given for self-destructive responses on the days
marked by arrows. The numbers on the abscissa under the days of the project
indicate which of four experimenters was present.

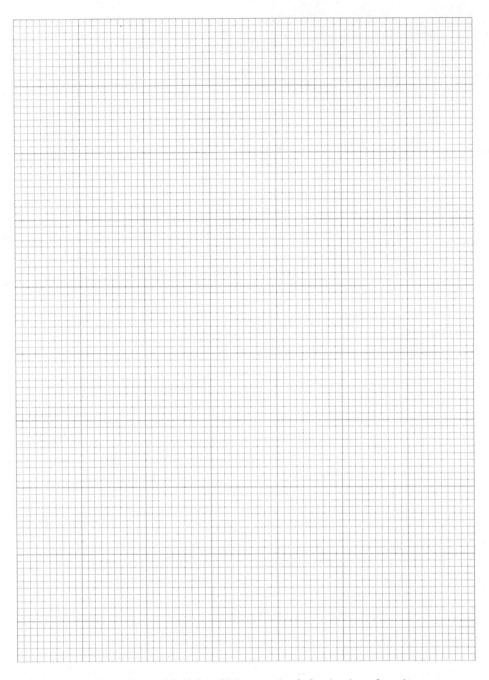

Figure 18-3   Frequency of John's self-destructive behavior in a dormitory room. Although John's self-destructive responses were being measured in a bedroom and while on a nurse's lap from Day 1 of the project, measurements were not begun until Day 8 in John's dormitory. On days 28 and 29, shocks were given for self-destructive responses.

in his environment. When self-destructive behavior was reduced, other behaviors were strengthened by natural reinforcers. John discovered the pleasures of water and played in the bathtub. He also began running up and down the hallways. These were activities he could not do prior to treatment because he was always restrained.

Although the effect of the shock did not generalize completely to other situations, there was some transfer of effect across situations. The authors reported that after they had eliminated self-destructive responses in the dormitory room, only a few more shocks were required to eliminate the self-destructive behavior in other wards and in the street. Generalization was also effected across persons in this experiment by having more than one experimenter administer shock. This was done in order to prevent a discrimination among experimenters which had begun to develop by Day 19 (see Figure 18-2). This made the treatment completely effective.

Caution. Punishment by presentation of shock was effective in eliminating self-destructive behavior in this study, but it was administered by professionals. We do not advocate the use of strong punishers, such as shock, by laymen because the consequences of the misuse of punishment can be serious; for example, alienation of the subject from the controlling agency, and physical damage. Other techniques can be used to control behavior which rely on a combination of procedures and which will be effective for most of the problems the lay person is likely to encounter.

Exam

1. Define the following terms:
   a. punishment, Type I
   b. conditioned aversive stimulus
   c. pain-elicited aggression
2. Distinguish between operant and respondent aggression. State two ways that operant aggression can be reinforced and provide an example of each.
3. Describe three disadvantages in the use of punishment.
4. Not all the effects of punishment are disadvantageous. Describe two advantages and give examples of each.
5. Under what conditions might you suggest to a mother that punishment, Type I would be preferable to extinction as a treatment plan?
6. A child's parents tell you that they have systematically used punishment at home and have succeeded in eliminating their child's tantrums. The child's teacher complains that the child is still acting up in class and insists that the parents are not doing their job well at home. How might you explain this child's behavior to the satisfaction of both parties? What additional procedure would you suggest?

7. Examine Figure 18-1. Would you say that the extinction procedure was successful? In light of results obtained from the rest of the study, how would you answer this question?

8. Refer to Figure 18-2. How would you explain the results obtained on days 17 and 18? (Hint: Who was the E?)

9. How might you explain the fact that only four shocks were needed to eliminate self-destructive responses in the dormitory room (Figure 18-3)?

10. Based on the evidence provided in this unit, what might you say to an individual who claims, "Shocking autistic children for **any** behavior is morally indefensible"? You should be able to marshal several arguments in favor of using shock in a treatment program designed to eliminate self-destructive behavior.

References

Appel, J. B.   Punishment in the squirrel monkey *saimiri sciruea*. *Science*, 1961, **133**, 36.

Azrin, N. H.   Effects of punishment intensity during variable-interval reinforcement. *Journal of the Experimental Analysis of Behavior*, 1960, 3, 123-142.

Azrin, N. H., & Holz, W. C.   Punishment. In W. K. Honig (Ed.), *Operant behavior: Areas of research and application*. New York: Appleton-Century-Crofts, 1966.

Holz, W. C., & Azrin, N. H.   Discriminative properties of punishment. *Journal of the Experimental Analysis of Behavior*, 1961, 4, 225-232.

Lovaas, O. I., & Simmons, J. Q. Manipulation of self-destruction in three retarded children. *Journal of Applied Behavior Analysis*, 1969, **2**, 143-157.

Rosenhan, D. L.   On being sane in insane places. *Science*, 1973, **179**, 250-258.

Thorndike, E. L.   *The psychology of wants, interests and attitudes*. New York: Appleton-Century, 1935.

Ulrich, R. E., & Azrin, N. H.   Reflexive fighting in response to aversive stimulation. *Journal of the Experimental Analysis of Behavior*, 1962, **5**, 511-520.

Punishment, Type II

19

Definition and Some Illustrations

PUNISHMENT, TYPE II is defined as the removal of a positive reinforcer dependent upon a response. It is sometimes difficult to provide an example of this type of punishment. How does one take away a positive reinforcer such as food once the animal has it? It is obvious that if one did try to reach into a rat's cage to remove a piece of food, he or she would probably get bitten. Perhaps if we think of the environment growing "worse" dependent on a response, it would make this concept easier to understand. For instance, fines are a commonly used example of punishment, Type II. Here, an individual has some money, which is a generalized, positive reinforcer, and loses some of it dependent on doing something illegal, such as parking in the wrong place.

Going back to our rat example, we could make an analogue to the use of fines in human society by first establishing a conditioned reinforcer and then removing some or all of it dependent on a response. We might train a rat to press a lever under conditions in which each lever press turns on a light in a panel of lights. There are 10 lights in the panel and when all 10 are lit, the rat is fed. The lights will eventually become conditioned reinforcers; if we later wished to punish the animal for responding, we could turn off one light when he pressed the lever. In this situation, a response would make things worse; we would soon observe a decrement in the rat's rate of lever pressing. Such a procedure has been called **RESPONSE COST** and has been systematically studied by Weiner (1962, 1963). Weiner has found that a point loss is as effective as a point gain in controlling human behavior.

In addition to fines, or response cost, a **TIME OUT (TO) FROM POSITIVE REINFORCEMENT** dependent upon a response is punishment, Type II and is a common procedure used in natural settings by parents and behavior modifiers. Sending a child to a room for a few minutes when he misbehaves would be an attempt to use a TO from positive reinforcement. It is imperative, if this procedure is to be effective, that the activity from which the child is being excluded is, in fact, positively reinforcing. A high-school student, who is sent out of a class he dislikes because of some prank, does not receive a TO from positive reinforcement, but instead is escaping an aversive situation (negative reinforcement) which will maintain his pranks.

A second possible problem with this procedure is that the TO environment may be as reinforcing as the activities the subject is being excluded from. A parent may send his misbehaving child to the child's room, which contains all the child's toys and games. All the parent may be doing is sending the child from one reinforcing activity to another, and we would not expect any improvement in the child's behavior under these conditions.

Third, even when the activity the subject is excluded from is positively reinforcing and the environment to which he or she is sent is not, there is the problem of the attention the subject receives on the way to the TO situation. Most mothers, on witnessing their children's misbehavior, feel compelled to lecture and explain the punishment.

In addition, there is the guilt that mothers may feel when having to use punishment. (This tends to produce the "explanations" mentioned before.) Solicitous attention on the way to the TO environment may negate the effects of TO. In a now classic study, Wolf, Risley, and Mees (1964) found why TO was unsuccessful in reducing the tantrums of Dicky, a 3-year-old severely disturbed boy. For the first 4 months of the study, the TO was ineffective. The authors discovered, after examining reports, that the attendants were giving Dicky long, involved explanations as they were taking him to his room, the TO environment. When he was released from the TO room, they proffered " . . . tender, practically tearful apologies and fondling . . . " (p. 140)! Eventually, these solicitations dropped out and, with a few other changes in the experimental program, the TOs became effective in eliminating the tantrums.

Advantages of Punishment, Type II

One advantage of punishment, Type II is that no physical pain is involved, thus, it avoids some of the problems associated with punishment, Type I. If a male nurse in a mental institution uses physical force on a patient who breaks a rule, it is possible for the staff member to administer a severe dose of punishment — a thrashing — because he is angry at the patient or because the patient fights back. Such an instance is unfortunately not uncommon in large institutions with relatively untrained staff.

Further, if aggression or force is one of the primary methods of controlling behavior in the institution, then the male nurse serves as a model for the patients who witness his aggression. Aggression (if you can get away with it) becomes the acceptable mode of resolving interpersonal conflicts. One of the tragedies of the "battered-child syndrome" is that the children who survive such parents tend to beat their children as they were beaten. One of the things these child victims may learn from growing up in this extreme environment is that force or aggression is *the* means of controlling one's offspring.

Punishment, Type II, permits the administration of a consequence with a minimum of side effects. For example, in a token economy, where patients earn tokens for special privileges, a fine can be levied for misbehavior. This practice is desirable because the exact amount of the fine for each offense is **determined beforehand and both staff and patients know what the** consequences for the patients' misbehaviors will be. There is not as much opportunity as with punishment, Type I for an out-of-sorts staff member to inflict more punishment than is warranted.

Alternative-Response Procedure

One of the most effective ways to use punishment is in combination with positive reinforcement — the **ALTERNATIVE-RESPONSE PROCEDURE.** The idea is to provide the individual with some behavior other than the undesirable one and make sure that we reinforce this behavior frequently, while concurrently punishing the undesirable behavior. The individual will learn very quickly to stop making the undesirable response. Some of the laments about the failure of punishment to effect a change in a misbehaving child are related to the lack of opportunity for the child to do something correctly that obtains as much reinforcement as the misbehavior. Parents' complaints sound something like this: "I punish him every time I catch him at it (whatever *it* is) more now than when I started punishing him, and he still does it." There may be several reasons why these parents are not effective in controlling their child's behavior. One possibility is that a parent will attend to the child when he is administering punishment (especially a spanking), and the parent's attention can be and usually is a powerful reinforcer. Thus, the child's misbehavior has more than one consequence. It produces both a positive reinforcer and a punisher (attention and spanking). Attention may be a very strong reinforcer, especially if the child rarely receives attention for his other, more desirable behaviors.

Patterson and his co-workers (1970) have found that one of the common threads running through families with delinquent or deviant children is that the mother does not give as much positive reinforcement or attention to her children as do the mothers of normal children. In fact, these mothers rely almost exclusively on techniques of aversive control not only to control their children but also to control adults. (Patterson has called this the *"Xanthippe syndrome"* after Socrate's wife who was reputed to be a terrible scold.) A typical response from one of Patterson's Xanthippes, when the therapist pointed out to her that she did not reinforce her child's good responses was, "That is what he ought to do (coming home on time, for example). Why should I reward him for that" (p. 248)?

An Experiment Using the Alternative-Response Procedure

An experiment by Azrin and Holz (1966) illustrates how effective the alternative-response procedure can be. Pigeons were first trained to peck a key for grain on an FR 25 schedule. When the animal was working at a steady rate, shock was introduced for every response. The pigeon still received food every so often on the FR 25 schedule, but he was receiving shock every time he pecked the key. The following data are taken from Azrin and Holz's experiment and Table 19-1, Column 3, shows what happened to the pigeon's rate of responding under these conditions.

In the next part of the experiment, a second response key was made available. The pigeon had seen this second key before, had pecked it a few times, but had shown a preference for the first key, the one he was receiving shocks and food for pecking. The

Table 19-1

Rate of responding for a pigeon at various shock intensities. During the shock conditions every response produced a shock, while every 25 responses produced food. The third column shows the rates of responding on the punished key when no alternative key was available. The last column shows the rates of responding on the punished key when an alternative key was available. Data estimated from Azrin, N. H., & Holz, W. C. Punishment. In W. K. Honig (Ed.), *Operant behavior: Areas of research and application.* New York: Appleton-Century-Crofts, 1966. Pp. 380-447.

| | | Rate of Responding (Rs/min) | |
Condition	Shock Intensity (in volts)	Single-Response Situation	Alternative-Response Situation
1	0	250	220
2	10	250	220
3	20	240	220
4	30	250	220
5	40	240	240
6	50	215	5
7	60	175	15
8	70	125	10
9	80	10	10

situation was now changed so that the nonpreferred key provided food on the same FR 25 schedule as the regular key, but responding on the nonpreferred key did not produce shock. The conditions on the regular key remained unchanged; food was delivered on the FR 25 schedule and every response was shocked. The data for this phase of the experiment are presented in Table 19-1, Column 4.

Plot the data on a single piece of graph paper using a different code for the two main conditions: Punishment without an alternative response available, and punishment with an alternative response available. When you examine the two curves, it should be clear that the combination of punishment and providing an alternative response that is *not* punished leads to greater suppression of the punished response at lower shock intensities.

This finding has also been generalized to humans. Herman and Azrin (1964) reinforced three male mental patients on a VI 60-second schedule with cigarettes for responding on either of two manipulanda. In one part of the experiment, one manipulandum was locked and a 96 db[1] white noise was produced by each response on the unlocked manipulandum. In another part of the experiment, both levers were operable and noise was produced

[1]The abbreviation *db* stands for decibel which according to Webster's *New International Dictionary* (3rd ed.) is "a unit for measuring the relative loudness of sounds equal approximately to the smallest degree of difference of loudness ordinarily detectable by the human ear the range of which includes about 130 decibels on a scale beginning with 1 for the faintest audible sound" (p. 585).

for every response on only one of the manipulanda. Suppression of responding was greatest in the alternative-response condition; in fact, almost no responses occurred on the manipulandum that produced the loud noise in the alternative-response condition. Notably, there was only partial suppression of the punished response in the single-response situation.

Application: Fines or Response Cost

T. J. Stachnik, The use of behavior modification by individual classroom teachers. In R. Ulrich, T. Stachnik, & J. Mabry (Eds.), *Control of human behavior*, Vol. III. Glenview, Ill.: Scott, Foresman, 1974, Pp. 96-106.

Carol, a second-grade teacher, had a class of 19 students and a common problem: The students talked out of turn, did not raise their hands before talking, and called out in loud voices to the teacher or to other students. She elected to use fines in an attempt to lower the number of these outbursts, which totalled between 35 and 45 per half-day session. She decided to use a free-time period and a recess period as the activities the children could earn by reducing their frequency of outbursts.

After recording a baseline for 5 days, she informed the class that they would start each day with 40 points. She made two large charts with the numbers from 1 to 20 written on each. If any of the children in the class made an outburst, she would cross out one of the numbers on the charts. If she crossed out 20 numbers, the class lost its free-time period. If she crossed out the 20 numbers on the second chart, the class would lose the recess time for the next session as well. The teacher had made two signs which hung below the charts. On the recess chart, the sign read, "Yea! Recess," as long as the class had fewer than 20 outbursts. If the class had exceeded 20 outbursts, the teacher flipped the sign over and it read, "Sorry. No Recess." A similar sign was displayed under the free-time chart. Children could tell from glancing at the charts where they stood at any moment and whether they had earned a free-time period or a recess period during the next session. In addition to these fines, the teacher increased the magnitude of the reinforcing activities during free-time and recess by telling the children they could bring their favorite games to school to play with during these times. Later on she attempted to make the playtime activities even more fun by having children suggest things they would like to do, such as taking walks and having longer recesses.

The results of the teacher's study are presented in Table 19-2. Note that at Session 12, the criterion was made more stringent by having only 10 outbursts lead to a loss of an activity. In Session 20, the criterion was lowered to 5 outbursts. **Plot these data on Figure 19-2 and be sure to label the points at which the dependencies were changed.**

The results show that the fines were an effective method of reducing disruptive talking. The teacher also reported other beneficial effects of her program. One such effect was the absence of any ill-feeling by the students when they made an outburst. The teacher reported, "When I witnessed disruptive behavior, I would calmly and quietly mark off a number. The child who caused the disruption did not become angry or sullen — common in the case of being reprimanded — but usually smiled or indicated a 'whoops, I goofed' reaction" (p. 104).

She went on to say that the class appeared more attentive in group discussions and that they kept a scrupulous record of their outbursts in another class and during a study period. This suggests that the children had learned to identify their disruptive behavior and to control themselves in new situations (generalization of treatment), which is especially important if a behavior change is to become permanent.

Application: Time Out

J. Zeilberger, S. E. Sampen, & H. N. Sloane, Modification of a child's problem behaviors in the home with the mother as therapist. *Journal of Applied Behavior Analysis*, 1968, 1, 47-53.

Rorey was a five-year-old boy with a history of behavior problems in nursery school and his home. At the time of the study, his behavior was only a problem at home, having been changed to acceptable levels in the nursery school. Rorey had four problem areas: He bossed other children, yelled and screamed at them, enforced his bossing by punching, kicking or slapping, and he was disobedient to his parents. In preliminary observations, the authors found that when his mother noted Rorey's undesirable behavior, she reinforced it with excessive attention. She was also inconsistent in the consequences she administered, and the dependencies set down by her were not clear. She frequently resorted to long instructions after a misdeed. Since both

Figure 19-1 Rate of a pigeon's key pecks as a function of the intensity of punishment (voltage level) under two conditions. In one situation, there was only 1 key the pigeon could peck for food and the animal also received a shock each time it pecked the key. In the other situation, an alternative key was available which provided food without shock.

*

Punishment, Type II

Table 19-2

Frequency of disruptive outbursts for a second-grade class of 19 children under several conditions. Data estimated from Stachnik, T. J. The use of behavior modification by individual classroom teachers. In R. Ulrich, T. Stachnik, & J. Mabry (Eds.), *Control of human behavior*, Vol. III. Glenview, Ill.: Scott, Foresman and Co., 1974. Pp. 96-106.

Half-Day Sessions	Number of Outbursts	Condition
1	45	
2	39	
3	38	Baseline
4	44	
5	36	
6	34	
7	17	
8	18	20 outbursts lead to
9	8	loss of an activity
10	Missing data point	
11	14	
12	9	
13	9	
14	14	
15	8	10 outbursts lead to
16	10	loss of an activity
17	10	
18	1	
19	8	
20	5	
21	4	
22	5	
23	4	5 outbursts lead to
24	5	loss of an activity
25	4	
26	5	
27	1	

parents were concerned about Rorey's behavior and were willing to cooperate in a treatment plan, and because the problem behavior occurred mostly at home, it was decided to use the mother as the therapist.

One-hour sessions were established on weekday afternoons and Rorey was free to play in his yard or his house at this time with his playmates, as he usually did. In order to keep the same children coming each day to play with Rorey, his mother put an inflatable swimming pool in the yard along with other toys. The experimenters also received cooperation from other mothers in the neighborhood who encouraged their children to stay the entire afternoon session.

The experimenters observed and recorded all four classes of Rorey's misbehavior during a 9-day baseline period, but elected to modify only the more serious: physical aggression such as hitting, biting, or scratching other children and following (or not following) instructions given by his mother.

Rorey's mother was instructed to administer a 2-minute TO after she witnessed a misdeed. Immediately after Rorey was aggressive or disobedient, Rorey's mother was to put him in one of the family bedrooms in which things that might be of interest to him had been removed. She was also instructed not to lecture Rorey or attempt to explain away her actions. Instead, as she was accompanying Rorey to the TO room after he hit a playmate, for instance, she was instructed to say simply, "You cannot stay here if you fight." She was also told to time the 2-minute TO period from the moment Rorey stopped crying. (This is important! If Rorey were taken out of the TO room while he was still crying, his crying would be negatively reinforced. Such a mistake would tend to establish crying in the TO room.) Finally, and most importantly, Rorey's mother was told to reinforce desirable, cooperative play once every 5 minutes and to reinforce him *every time* he obeyed an instruction from her. The mother was prompted by the experimenter-observer when necessary.

Table 19-3 shows some of the results of the treatment program. The percent of instructions followed in the first baseline period ranged from 11 percent to 53 percent with an average of 30 percent. "Instructions-followed" increased to 100 percent during the last session of the first experimental condition, with an average of 78 percent over this phase of the experiment. Column 3 shows the number of TOs given Rorey during the two experimental conditions, and Column 4 gives the average duration of the TOs.

Plot these data on Figure 19-3. Observe that this graph has two ordinates: The left ordinate is for the percent of instructions followed and the right ordinate is for both the number of TOs and the average length of the TOs. Use a solid line for the "Percent Instructions" data, a dashed line for the "Average Length of TO" data, and a histogram (bar graph) for the "Number of TOs" data. Allow two squares for each bar of the histogram and fill in the bars so that they are easy to see. Label each of the conditions.

In addition to decreasing Rorey's disobedience and aggressiveness, the TO procedure, in combination with positive reinforcement for desirable behavior, also affected Rorey's yelling

Figure 19-2 Frequency of disruptive outbursts in a second-grade class over several conditions. After the baseline period, the class was fined 1 point for each outburst and if enough points were lost, the class lost a free-time period or recess.

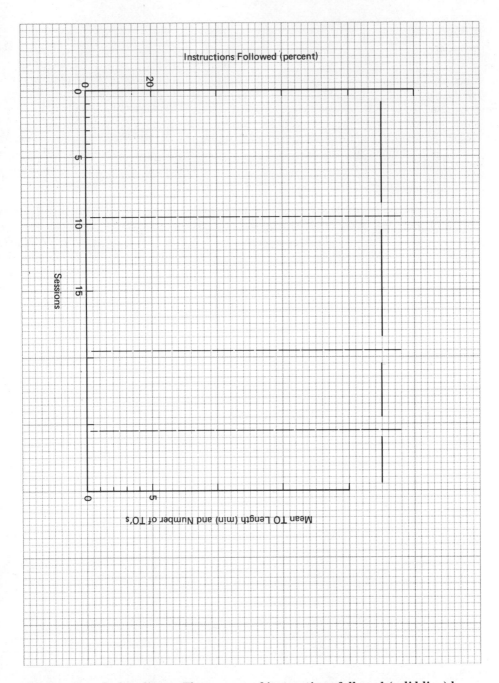

Figure 19-3 Left ordinate: The percent of instructions followed (solid line) by a five-year-old boy during periods without (baseline) and with (**experimental**) a TO. Every instance of a disobedient response led to an immediate **TO of 2 minutes**, while each obedient response led to positive reinforcement. Right ordinate: The number and average length of TOs given during the experimental periods.

Table 19-3

Percent of instructions followed during baseline and experimental conditions by a 5-year-old boy with several behavior problems. During the experimental sessions, a 2-minute TO for aggressive or disobedient behavior was in effect. The number and average length of the time outs is given in columns 3 and 4, respectively. Data estimated from Zeilberger, J., Sampen, S. E., & Sloane, H. N.   Modification of a child's problem behaviors in the home with the mother as therapist. *Journal of Applied Behavior Analysis*, 1968, 1, 47-53.

Session	Instructions Followed (%)	TOs	Average Length of TOs (min)	Condition
1	42			
2	53			
3	40			Baseline$_1$
4	11			Mother uses verbal
5	33			explanations in attempt
6	22			to control undesirable
7	23			behavior.
8	30			
9	13			
10	50	1	19	
11	19	2	7	
12	32	2	8	
13	85	1	2	Experimental$_1$
14	50	1	8	Undesirable behavior
15	50	2	7	leads to 2-min TO
16	100	0	0	
17	91	1	3	
18	67	3	3	
19	100	1	4	
20	67			
21	39			
22	39			Baseline$_2$
23	35			Same conditions as in
24	50			Baseline$_1$
25	25			
26	68	2	6	Experimental$_2$
27	82	2	3	Same conditions as in
28	88	0	0	Experimental$_1$

which was a behavior not directly manipulated. Yelling dropped from an average of 26 percent in the beginning of the experiment to an average of 3 percent in the final three sessions. The changes in all of Rorey's misbehaviors were clearly noticeable to those who knew him, and the authors reported that several neighbors commented favorably on his improved behavior.

Although this experiment was not designed to change the mother's undesirable behavior (giving Rorey attention when he misbehaved), her inappropriate attention did decrease over the course of the program. This was one beneficial side effect of using the mother as a therapist. As the child's behavior improved, his mother regarded him more positively. Thus, the improvement in Rorey's behavior, which his mother could see by observing the data, reinforced her new skills as an effective parent and guaranteed positive social interactions in the future.

Many attempts at modifying an undesirable behavior have been only partially successful because the therapist has failed to consider that the environment (the social environment, in this case) needs to be modified at the same time. If it is not, the dependencies which shaped and maintained the original misbehavior will do so again (see Tharp & Wetzel, 1969, for an excellent discussion of this point). As the authors of this study pointed out, other advantages of using the mother as therapist were that the program continued after the experimenters went home and was in effect as long as the child was awake.

Summary:
Making Punishment Effective

Now that you have studied punishment in Units 18 and 19 you can see that, although it can be an effective technique of controlling behavior, its successful application requires a thorough understanding of other variables. Table 19-4 summarizes some of the more important rules which maximize the effectiveness of punishment and provides an example of the way that rule is typically violated. Study this table and try to construct your own list of examples.

Table 19-4

Procedures which maximize the effectiveness of punishment (adapted from Azrin & Holz, 1966). The left column gives the rule and the right column an example of how the rule is commonly violated.

Rule	Example of Violation
1.) Unauthorized escape from the punishing stimulus should be prevented.	Boy who puts his schoolbook in the seat of his trousers to minimize the blows of the birch rod.
2.) Punishing stimulus should be as intense as possible.	Elderly aunt who attempts to "spank" hulking, teenaged nephew. Nephew smiles while receiving "punishment."
3.) The punished response should be punished very frequently — after every response if possible.	A boy makes about 20 aggressions against his peers during the day. Only one of his teachers punishes him. Most of his bad behavior goes unpunished. This type of program is also poor because it may teach the child to discriminate between those who punish and those who don't, rather than to teach him to change his misbehavior.
4.) Punishing stimulus should be delivered immediately after a response.	Mother says to child who misbehaves, "That does it. Just wait till your father gets home. He'll fix you good!" Father arrives home 6 hours later and mother has to reconstruct the "crime." In addition to the ineffectiveness of the punishing stimulus after 6 hours, the child is punished for the wrong behavior, for example, greeting his father cheerfully.
5.) Punishing stimulus should not be introduced gradually but at an intensity as high as ethically possible.	Mother is shopping in a supermarket with her child who is pouting and whining for candy. Mother starts by saying *No* in a soft whisper. Child continues to whine; mother repeats word *No* in louder, desperate whispers. After a half-hour, 50 or more *Nos*, and a few shakes on the child's arm, the mother loses her temper, shouts, "No!" and hits the child hard. Mother is shaping a beautiful tolerance for punishment.

Table 19-4 (Continued)

Rule	Example of Violation
6.) Punishing stimulus should not be delivered with positive reinforcement. Otherwise the punishing stimulus may become a conditioned reinforcer.	Solicitations and lengthy explanations given by adult while taking child to a time-out room. The case of the autistic boy, Dicky, and the ineffectiveness of the TO procedure for the first 4 months of the study is a prime example.
7.) Degree of motivation to make the punished response should be reduced as much as possible.	Spanking a hungry child for stealing food. (Punishment of food stealing will be more successful when the child is not hungry.)
8.) An alternative response should be provided which yields as much positive reinforcement as the punished response and is not punished. (This is a very important rule which can make even mild punishment very effective in eliminating undesirable behavior.)	Punishing a teenage girl for shoplifting by "grounding" (not allowing her to see her friends). She shoplifts in the company of her two closest friends, and it seems clear that peer attention is maintaining her shoplifting. (If the parents provided the girl with frequent opportunities to reinforce her friends in socially-approved ways while punishing shoplifting by loss of a privilege not associated with peers, they would be using the alternative-response procedure.)

Exam

1. Define:
    a. punishment, Type I
    b. punishment, Type II
    c. generalized reinforcer
    d. alternative-response procedure
    e. Xanthippe syndrome
    f. TO
    g. response cost
2. What is the difference between the procedure of extinction and the procedure of punishment, Type II?
3. What is one advantage of punishment, Type II over punishment, Type I?
4. What is one possible reason why a particular punishment plan is ineffective? (Hint: Review the alternative-response technique.)

5. How would you answer the question: "Is 50 volts of shock a punishing stimulus for a pigeon?" (Examine your graph, Figure 19-1.)

6. Summarize the Stachnik study using fines. Why didn't the teacher start with the criterion of 5 outbursts instead of 20 outbursts?

7. Give an example, not in the text, of a TO procedure. What are three problems that may arise with this technique?

8. Why should the beginning of a TO interval be timed from the moment a child stops crying rather than from the time he or she is placed in the TO room?

9. How might you answer a concerned mother who wants to stop her child's aggression toward his playmates but is afraid that punishment (a TO) would just lead to tantrums, which would only compound her problems. Assume that you have Figure 19-3 in front of you when answering this mother. What could you tell her to expect in terms of the length of the treatment? How long might a tantrum last? What might you tell her about increasing desirable behavior?

10. What are two advantages to using a parent as the therapist for the child instead of a professional?

11. What are five rules which, if followed, will make punishment maximally effective? Give an example of how these rules are violated. (Try using examples not given in the text.)

References

Azrin, N. H., & Holz, W. C.   Punishment. In W. K. Honig (Ed.), *Operant behavior: Areas of research and application*, New York: Appleton-Century-Crofts, 1966. Pp. 380-447.

Herman, R. L, & Azrin, N. H.   Punishment by noise in an alternative response situation. *Journal of the Experimental Analysis of Behavior*, 1964, **7**, 185-188.

Patterson, G., McNeal, S., Hawkins, N., & Phelps, R.   Reprogramming the social environment. In R. Ulrich, T. J. Stachnik, & J. Mabry (Eds.), *Control of human behavior*, Vol. II. Glenview, Ill.: Scott, Foresman, 1970. Pp. 237-248.

Stachnik, T. J.   The use of behavior modification by individual classroom teachers. In R. Ulrich, T. Stachnik, & J. Mabry (Eds.), *Control of human behavior*, Vol. III. Glenview, Ill.: Scott, Foresman, 1974. Pp. 96-106.

Tharp, R. G., & Wetzel, R. J.   *Behavior modification in the natural environment.* New York: Academic Press, 1969.

Weiner, H.   Some effects of response cost upon human operant behavior. *Journal of the Experimental Analysis of Behavior*, 1962, **5**, 201-208.

Weiner, H.   Response cost and the aversive control of human operant behavior. *Journal of the Experimental Analysis of Behavior*, 1963, **6**, 415-421.

Wolf, M., Risley, T., & Mees, H.   Application of operant conditioning procedures to the behavior problems of an autistic child. *Behavior Research and Therapy*, 1964, **1**, 305-312.

Zeilberger, J., Sampen, S. E., & Sloane, H. N.   Modification of a child's problem behaviors in the home with the mother as therapist. *Journal of Applied Behavior Analysis*, 1968, **1**, 47-53.

Escape And Avoidance Conditioning

UNIT

20

The Distinction between an Escape and an Avoidance Response

As you recall from Unit 8, termination of a negative reinforcer is one of the ways a response can be increased or maintained in frequency. Conditioning which relies on the *termination* of a stimulus dependent upon a response is called **ESCAPE CONDITIONING** and the response is labelled an **ESCAPE** response. In **AVOIDANCE CONDITIONING,** the response *prevents* or *postpones* the onset of a negative reinforcer and is called an **AVOIDANCE** response.

Most often researchers have used shock as the aversive stimulus primarily because its characteristics (duration and intensity) can be better specified than other aversive stimuli (e.g., loud noise, smoke, or blows). In escape conditioning, the shock might be programmed to come on at regular intervals. If the subject emits the operant — for example, a bar press or wheel turn — the shock is terminated and remains off for a specified period of time. Once the shock comes on, it stays on until the subject makes the escape response. Eventually, subjects learn to respond rapidly at the onset of shock, and the latency of the escape response is often used as one measure of learning.

There are two procedures used in avoidance conditioning: In one procedure, we warn the subject that an aversive stimulus is about to be delivered — this is called the **DISCRIMINATED AVOIDANCE** procedure — and in the second we do not warn the subject. This is called the **NONDISCRIMINATED AVOIDANCE** procedure. We will discuss these procedures in the order mentioned primarily because it is easier to understand what keeps a rat or a pigeon responding in the nondiscriminated avoidance situation when the escape and discriminated avoidance situations are understood. Before we turn to some representative experiments in each of these areas, some everyday examples of escape and avoidance responses might be helpful.

Some Common Examples of Escape and Avoidance

A visit to the dentist. Suppose you are visiting your dentist and he is in the middle of an extended drilling operation on one of your molars (horrible thought). Though you have been given an anesthetic, you have had enough of the infernal drilling. You leap out of the chair and head for home without so much as a buy-your-leave. This is an escape response. You are presently in a situation that is aversive and you end the aversiveness by leaving.

Suppose further that the startled dentist, being the conscientious professional that he is, calls you and asks you to return next week so that he can finish the job he started on your tooth. You agree to come next week, but the day before your appointment you "discover" something imperative that you must do, and so you phone and make a new appointment. The response of phoning and postponing the dental visit is an avoidance response. The unconditioned aversive stimuli (pain

and discomfort) are not presently being experienced but they are uncomfortably close, and you can push the appointment into the distant and forgettable future by the simple response of making a phone call. This avoidance response brings temporary relief and may become more likely as the time to the new visit approaches.

Sometimes, though, the designation of a response as escape or avoidance is not so easy — an operant may serve both functions, as in the following illustration.

Nagging. A fairly typical social interaction between parent and child based on aversive control is nagging by the parent. It starts by the parent making a request. The child does not perform the task required. The parent then repeats the request more insistently (i.e., nags). The child escapes the mother's nagging by complying with the request or by some other escape response. The following example of a mother trying to get her reluctant child off to school in the morning is illustrative:

Mother: "Susan, brush your teeth."
Susan: (who is in the living room out of her mother's sight, watching television) "OK."
Mother: (a few minutes later and growing impatient because she has not heard toothbrushing sounds.) "Susan, brush your teeth, NOW!"
Susan: (still intently watching television says in a louder voice) "OK!"
Mother: (still later, growing exasperated, yells the classic line) "HOW MANY TIMES DO I HAVE TO TELL YOU TO DO SOMETHING?"
Susan: (on hearing her mother leaving the kitchen, jumps up, meets her mother on the

way to the living room, sees the storm on her mother's face and lies) "I already brushed my teeth."

—

The child's responses in the above dialogue are both escape and avoidance responses. The child's OKs signal compliance with the mother's request, so they escape the mother's nagging. Observe that this response also permits the child to continue watching television. The lie which is emitted in the presence of parental wrath is an attempt to escape the anger and to avoid a further aversive consequence such as a spanking. Sometimes the lie is not detected, which, of course, negatively reinforces lying. All of you at different times have probably played either one of these roles: the "nagger" or the "naggee." As you can surmise from this example, much of our behavior is controlled through escape and avoidance dependencies. Now that you have some feeling for the distinction between the terms *avoidance* and *escape*, and for how these responses can develop in everyday life, let's examine some representative research.

Escape Conditioning

In schedules of negative reinforcement, as in schedules of positive reinforcement, we specify either a number or time dependency with respect to the delivery of a consequence. In these schedules, however, the stimulus consequence is the reduction or termination of an aversive event. On a CRF escape schedule, a single response terminates the aversive stimulus; on ratio escape, a number of responses are necessary to terminate the stimulus; on interval escape, the first response after a period of time terminates the stimulus. Although it is not difficult to condition CRF escape, it has been difficult to obtain escape on intermittent schedules. If you put yourself in the subject's place for a moment, you can see the problem. Assume that after initial training on a CRF schedule, we program an FR 5 for escape from shock. Previously, a press on the lever was followed immediately by the removal of a painful stimulus. On the FR 5 schedule, nothing happens after the first press; the pain and discomfort resulting from the shock are still present. The response is suddenly not effective and other behaviors — jumping on the bar, for instance — may result.

It could be argued that the same experience occurs on an intermittent food schedule, and, to some extent, it does. A transition from CRF for food to an FR 5 is disrupting for a while. Eventually, however, animals produce stable rates and patterns of responding on intermittent, appetitive (e.g., food or water) schedules. This smooth performance does not develop on intermittent escape schedules. Thus, we suspect that there are basic differences between appetitive and aversive schedules. One difference is that pain resulting from shock has an immediacy that hunger established by twenty-four or forty-eight hours of food deprivation does not. In other words, the motivational properties of pain may be different than the motivational properties of hunger. Another difference is that shock, per se, can be disruptive. Shock elicits respondents such as muscle rigidity and freezing, which can interfere with operant performance.

This discussion is included to inform you that some aversive stimuli, such as shock, may have special properties which make the acquisition of intermittently scheduled behavior difficult. This difficulty has in the past been annoying to scientists, for we would like to find that the principles that hold in one part of a discipline also apply to the rest of the discipline. A principle with wide generality confirms the scientist's view of the way things work and ought to work in the field. This is why the difficulty of obtaining and maintaining behavior on intermittent escape schedules was bothersome to scientists working on escape conditioning. Why wouldn't subjects such as rats and pigeons produce the same rates and patterns on an FR 20 schedule when the reinforcer was **negative** as they did when it was **positive?**

Intermittent Escape

Winograd (1965) trained three rats to escape shock which was delivered through bars on the floor. After the rat was placed in the chamber, a 1-milliampere shock was given.[1] This was strong enough to make the rat respond swiftly. When the rat pressed the lever, the shock was turned off and remained off for 2 minutes. If the rat happened to be holding the lever down (a common practice of rats in avoidance and escape experiments), it had to release the lever and depress it again before the shock was terminated. Fifty

trials were given per session and 16 sessions were run on this CRF schedule. After this initial training, the schedule was changed to an FR 5, then to an FR 10, and finally to an FR 20.

While Winograd did find some consistencies between the escape performances and comparable appetitive performances, he experienced difficulties. One of his three subjects developed a postural response which competed with lever-pressing when the schedule was increased to an FR 5. For this subject, the intensity of the shock had to be doubled before it resumed responding. This rat was only given 2 sessions at each of the schedule values used while the other two animals had approximately 10 sessions at each value. Winograd also found that increasing the ratio requirements disrupted lever pressing for the first few sessions in all subjects.

In addition to the difficulties in acquisition, the final performance on the fixed-ratio schedule was not typical for the two rats which completed the experiment. Cumulative records for these subjects showed breaks in responding at FR 10 and FR 20. This is not typical of performance on fixed-ratio schedules that use positive reinforcers. Once the animal makes the first response on appetitive fixed-ratio schedules, the remaining responses are emitted at a uniform rate. Breaks in the "ratio run" occur only under extreme circumstances, as when the size of the ratio is increased by too large a step (e.g., from FR 5 to FR 100). After summarizing the difficulties other researchers have had in generating reliable escape responding on intermittent schedules, Winograd concluded that ". . . it remains a somewhat delicate procedure" (p. 124).

[1] The milliampere is one-thousandth of an ampere, the unit of electric current.

Titrated Escape Procedure

As mentioned previously, one of the problems with using shock in escape training is that the shock itself elicits behavior (e.g., freezing) incompatible with the operant escape response (lever pressing). Some investigators have reasoned that if the motivational properties of shock could be kept while eliminating the incompatible respondents associated with shock, there would be no difficulty in maintaining escape behavior on intermittent schedules (Weiss & Laties, 1959; Khalili, Daley, & Cheney, 1969). They have thought it might be possible to approximate an intermittent schedule by gradually reducing the amount of shock-free time.

Khalili et al. suggested that allowing a subject even a small amount of reinforcement for each response might help in the transition to an intermittent schedule. Suppose that on an FR 10 escape schedule, the 10th response produces a 30-second time out from shock, but that each response produces a shorter time free from shock, say 10 seconds. Perhaps after the subject has had some experience with this schedule, the shorter time outs from shock could be reduced to 5 seconds and eventually eliminated, thereby leaving a full-fledged intermittent schedule. This is exactly what Khalili and his associates did, and it worked.

The subjects were guinea pigs and rats, and they were first shaped to press a lever to terminate a shock. After one session in which each response was negatively reinforced with a 30-second time out from shock, the subjects were placed on several schedules. On an FR 40, the shorter time outs were 20 seconds for several sessions, then 15 seconds, 10 seconds, 5 seconds, 3 seconds, 1 second, 0.5 second, and then 0.0 second (or simply FR 40). This procedure was labelled a **TITRATION SCHEDULE** because of its loose similarity to a titration procedure in chemistry in which progressively less and less of a chemical is added to a solution until a desired point has been reached. Figure 20-1 shows sample cumulative records of several schedules for two rats and four guinea pigs after the CRF time outs had been eliminated. The top three records show an FR 20 with a rat (A), an FR 40 with a guinea pig (B), and an FR 60 with a rat (C). The bottom two records show a VI 30-sec (D) and VI 60-sec (E) with guinea pigs.

Khalili et al. reported that the only difference between the rats and the guinea pigs was that the final performance of the guinea pigs was not as smooth as that of the rats. This may have been due to differences in the topography of the operant: Rats pressed the lever with either of their forepaws and guinea pigs pressed with their chins. In spite of this difference, the overall patterns of responding were very similar to those found in appetitive schedules. In contrast to the results of earlier studies, the subjects in this experiment were maintained on the various schedules over an extended number of sessions. Figure 20-1, Record A, was the 168th session at FR 20 without the short time outs from shock!

In conclusion, the use of a titration procedure in acquisition allows the experimenter to maintain intermittent escape indefinitely. Thus, the demonstration that performances on intermittent schedules of negative reinforcement closely resemble

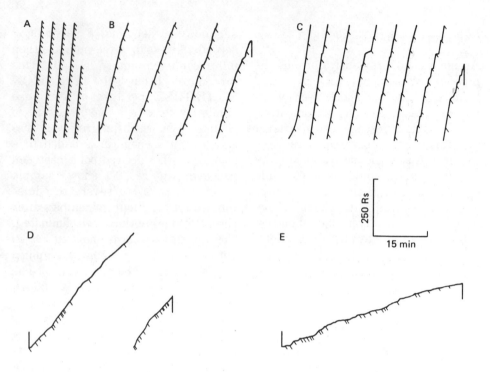

Figure 20-1

Cumulative records of steady-state responding under several schedules of
negative reinforcement. The top three records show an FR 20 (A), FR 40 (B),
and an FR 60 (C) for a rat, guinea pig, and a rat, respectively. The bottom two
records show performances under VI 30-sec (D) and VI 60-sec (E) schedules for
guinea pigs. From Khalili, J., Daley, M. F., & Cheney, C. D.   A titration
procedure for generating escape behavior. *Behavior Research Methods and
Instrumentation*, 1969, 1, 293-294.

performances on intermittent schedules
of positive reinforcement greatly
extends the generality of our
knowledge.

Discriminated Avoidance

In the following experiment, the
authors (Miller, Banks, & Ogawa, 1962;
1963) were mainly interested in
communication among monkeys, but
their basic procedure was discriminated
avoidance so it will serve as an
illustration. The scientists were looking
for a procedure that would allow them
to study the communication of emotions
in primates. They were interested in
whether one monkey's facial expression
could act as a cue for another monkey.

Rhesus monkeys were put in specially constructed primate chairs and allowed to adapt to the chairs for 5 days.
On the 6th day, discriminated-
avoidance training was begun. A
stimulus panel occasionally displayed a

colored light. After the colored light had been on for 6 seconds, a shock was delivered to the ankle of the monkey. However, if the monkey pressed a lever when the light was on, the light terminated and the shock was avoided. The time between presentations of the light (warning stimulus) was varied around 2 minutes, so the monkey had no way of telling when the next trial would begin. The subjects were given 20 trials a day over a 10-day period under these conditions.

After this training, two monkeys were placed in their chairs facing each other and "cooperative avoidance" conditioning was begun. One monkey was given the stimulus panel but no lever with which to avoid the shock. His partner was given the lever but no stimulus panel, so this monkey could not tell when the shock was due. If the monkey with the lever did not make an avoidance response during the 6-second warning stimulus, both monkeys received shock. The problem facing the two monkeys was this: The monkey with the stimulus panel had to signal the monkey with the lever that the warning light was on. Did they solve this problem?

Table 20-1 shows the number of avoidances of shock over 32 days of the cooperative avoidance condition. Since there were only 20 trials per day, the maximum number of avoidances was 20 per day. The column labelled "Estimated chance avoidances" needs some explanation. One solution to the problem facing the monkeys, which may have occurred to you, was to respond at a high rate. That is, if the monkey with the lever responded at a rapid rate throughout the session, both monkeys would avoid shock. Thus, the monkey with the lever would ignore any

"message" its partner was sending and avoid shock if it worked very hard for the entire 45-minute session. The authors anticipated that the "responder" monkey might increase its rate of responding throughout the session, and they devised a way of estimating whether the avoidance response just happened to fall during the 6-second warning stimulus or whether it was a "signalled" avoidance. For example, on Day 1, the responder responded at such a steady rate that all (100 percent) of the three avoidance responses were due to the high rate and not to a discriminated performance.

Plot the data on Figure 20-2 with the number of avoidances on the left ordinate and the estimated chance avoidances on the right ordinate. Let two squares equal 1 day on the abscissa. For the left ordinate, set two squares equal to one avoidance. For the right ordinate, set one square equal to 2 percent. Note that after Day 22, the monkey's roles were reversed; the one that previously had the lever now had the stimulus panel and vice versa. Indicate this change on your graph as well as those days in which a screen was placed between the subjects.

The authors report that the behavior of the monkeys changed after they had been in the social situation for a few days. When the warning stimulus was presented, the "stimulus" monkey squirmed, slapped its chair, and grimaced. The responder learned to observe the stimulus monkey closely and respond very quickly, typically emitting a burst of responses when its partner was observing the warning stimulus. You might be wondering whether the monkeys used sound or visual cues to signal the warning

Table 20-1

Number of shock avoidances by a pair of Rhesus monkeys in a cooperative avoidance situation (2nd column), and estimated percent of those avoidances that were due to chance (3rd column). One monkey had the stimulus panel which signalled impending shock and the other had a lever which, if depressed during the warning stimulus, terminated the warning stimulus and avoided shock. Failure to make an avoidance response during the warning stimulus resulted in shock for both monkeys. Data taken from Miller, R. E., Banks, J. H., & Ogawa, N. Communication of affect in "cooperative conditioning" of Rhesus monkeys. *Journal of Abnormal and Social Psychology*, 1962, 64, 343-348.

Day	Number of Avoidances (20 possible per day)	Estimated Chance Avoidance (%)	Condition
1	3	100	
2	17	100	
3	17	83	
4	19	90	
5	18	100	
6	19	20	
7	14	44	
8	16	68	
9	19	35	Monkey 120 had
10	19	54	stimulus panel.
11	19	28	Monkey 132 had
12	19	38	lever.
13	18	47	
14	18	17	
15	15	29	
*16	15	17	
*17	16	6	
*18	15	5	
19	Apparatus failure		
20	Apparatus failure		
*21	15	9	
*22	16	7	
23	19	12	
24	19	9	
25	18	4	Roles reversed:
26	19	3	Monkey 132 had
*27	18	3	Stimlus panel.
*28	20	1	Monkey 120 had
*29	18	3	lever.
*30	20	3	
**31	20	0	
**32	19	11	

*Partial screen placed between subjects — face visible only
**Complete screen placed between subjects — no visible cues available.

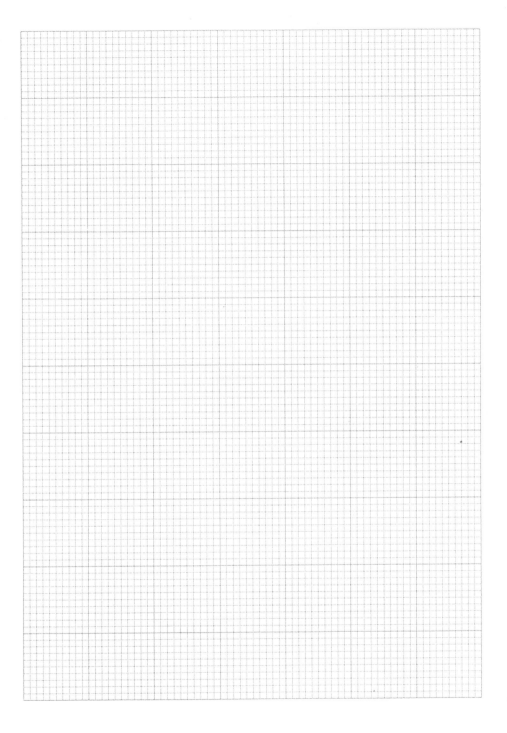

Figure 20-2   Number of avoidances by a pair of monkeys in a "cooperative avoidance" experiment.

*

stimulus. In a second experiment, the monkeys were placed in separate rooms and the stimulus monkey's facial expression was displayed on a television monitor for the responder monkey. With auditory cues removed, the authors found that facial cues were just as effective as both cues together in signalling a warning stimulus.

Non-Discriminated Avoidance

Until the 1950s typical escape and avoidance studies used a warning stimulus. In one sense, the discriminated-avoidance procedure is really escape conditioning. The model is based on straightforward Pavlovian conditioning. A neutral stimulus (e.g., a light) is presented a few seconds before an unconditional aversive stimulus (e.g., a shock). After several pairings of the neutral stimulus with the unconditional stimulus, the neutral stimulus becomes a conditional aversive stimulus. The animal's response in the presence of this warning stimulus terminates it. The only difference between escape conditioning and discriminated-avoidance conditioning is that in the former, the subject escapes from an *unconditional* aversive stimulus (shock), while in the latter, the subject escapes from a *conditional* aversive stimulus (light). Both procedures are escape procedures.

Sidman (1953) questioned whether the warning stimulus was necessary in an avoidance task. For over a decade, he carried on an extensive, systematic investigation of avoidance behavior in situations without warning stimuli. The procedure is called **NONDIS-CRIMINATED AVOIDANCE** or,

after its developer, Sidman avoidance. Here is how it works. At fixed intervals, for instance every 10 seconds, a brief shock is delivered. If the animal does nothing, it will receive a shock every 10 seconds. The time between the shocks is called the **SHOCK-SHOCK** interval and is controlled by one of two timers. If the animal responds, each response postpones the shock for a fixed period of time. The second timer programs this time, which is called the **RESPONSE-SHOCK** interval. Only one timer is working at a given time; when the animal makes a response the next shock will be delivered by the response-shock timer; if the animal does not make any further responses, the shock-shock timer will deliver the next shock. The response-shock interval can be greater than, equal to, or less than the shock-shock interval.

Can the subject avoid all shocks under this procedure? Let's look at an example in which the shock-shock interval is 5 seconds (S-S = 5 sec) and the response-shock interval is 20 seconds (R-S = 20 sec). If the rat does not press the lever, it will receive 12 shocks a minute, that is, 1 shock every 5 seconds, but since each response postpones shock 20 seconds, 3 or 4 well-spaced responses per minute are all that is required to *avoid shock completely*. In actuality, under the S-S and R-S values used in this example, animals tend to respond at higher rates than are required by the schedule. Figure 20-3 shows a cumulative record of a rat responding during the first session on just such a schedule. In the first hour of acquisition, the rat's rate increased and stabilized at between 10 and 12 responses per minute. Avoidance responding remained at this rate for the duration of this 7-hour

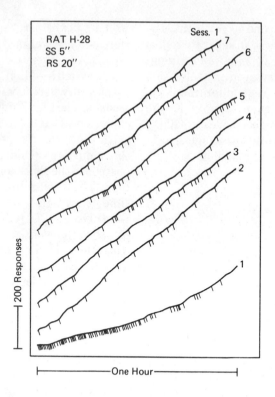

Figure 20-3

Rate of avoidance responding for a rat
during an initial 7-hour conditioning session.
The cumulative record for the session has
been cut into 1-hour segments and stacked
for ease of comparison. The S-S interval was
5 seconds and R-S interval was 20 seconds.
From Sidman, M. Avoidance behavior. In
W. K. Honig (Ed.), *Operant behavior: Areas
of research and application*. **New York:
Appleton-Century-Crofts, 1966. Pp. 448-498.**

session, which was about two or three
times the rate necessary to avoid all
shock if the responses had been spaced
about 20 seconds apart.

Even at this high rate, the rat did not
avoid all shocks. Its performance was
still quite effective, however. From the
3rd to the last hour, this rat received
about 33 shocks per hour. If it had not
responded at all, it would have received
720 shocks per hour or 3,600 shocks in 5
hours. In fact, it only received about 165
shocks in the last 5 hours.

Acquisition of the avoidance response
is more rapid if the R-S interval is long
relative to the S-S interval than if the
reverse is true. Thus, a lever press is
associated with a much longer period of
shock-free time than not pressing the
lever. Another consistent finding is

that, as the R-S interval grows short relative to the S-S interval, the rate of avoidance responding increases. The subject responds more frequently because each response produces less shock-free time. However, the rate of responding increases only up to the point where the S-S and R-S intervals are equal. When the R-S interval is shorter than the S-S interval animals produce *more* shocks by responding than by not responding and, under these conditions, soon learn to stop making the avoidance response.

A Theoretical Problem

Ever since Sidman introduced the nondiscriminated avoidance procedure, theorists have been thoroughly exercised in trying to account for the subject's conditioning. What reinforces the avoidance response in this situation? When there is no warning stimulus that is terminated by the response, there is no visible, immediate consequence for the avoidance response. In the dependencies discussed so far in this text, a stimulus change has always immediately followed a response. Psychologists have thoroughly demonstrated that immediate consequences are more effective than delayed consequences in conditioning, hence the problem: How can the acquisition and maintenance of an avoidance response be explained when there is no observable, immediate consequence?

Theorists have suggested that internal stimuli mediate the time between a shock (S-S interval) and the next shock or between a response and the next shock (R-S interval). These internal stimuli supposedly act as a rough kind of clock informing the animal how close the next shock is. As time to the forthcoming shock approaches, these stimuli become increasingly aversive. The animal reduces the aversiveness of these stimuli by responding and the internal clock starts over again. This explanation maintains the idea of an immediate consequence (escape from internal aversive stimuli) as an explanation but hides the warning stimulus inside the subject where it is difficult to study. How do we know that such a "clock mechanism" develops in this avoidance situation? How can we test whether such a formulation is correct? Whenever a key explanatory construct is put inside the skin of the subject, it causes problems for experimenters and theorists alike. The mechanism inside the subject can be made to do all kinds of clever tricks to account for any experimental findings — but by doing so it accounts for nothing.

Suppose we give a tranquilizer to a rat responding in a nondiscriminated avoidance situation, with the notion that the drug would make the internal aversive stimuli correlated with the passage of time less aversive. We might expect the rat's rate of responding to decrease and that the animal would experience many more shocks with the drug than without. Let us say we do this experiment and discover that at dosages which usually show an effect in rats, the avoidance behavior remains unchanged. The theorist argues that the drug did not act on the muscles, glands, or part of the brain, that make up the internal timing mechanism, so, of course, the rate of avoidance responding would not change. This is called *post-hoc* reasoning and theorists who rely on it have an uncanny way of being correct. Every time a drug or other independent variable fails to affect avoidance behavior, the theorists will claim that it has failed to affect the "internal clock." Every time avoidance behavior is affected, so too must have been the clock. In each case, the change or lack of it in the internal clock is wholly redundant with the change or lack of it in the avoidance behavior. The internal clock explains nothing. With a little practice, the student can become very adept at generating his own internal mechanism and could be well on the way to becoming a "good theorist." Actually, a good theoretician is fully aware of the dangers of *post-hoc* reasoning and the illegitimate use of unverifiable constructs, and tries to formulate theories and hypotheses that have the potential of being proved wrong. Nevertheless, an experimental finding such as that posed by the maintenance of avoidance responding in Sidman's procedure causes consternation (and loose theories) among scientists when the finding goes against well-established principles. Fortunately, Sidman (1962) suggested a plausible account for the maintenance of the avoidance response, and shortly after this account, Herrnstein and Hineline (1966) tested Sidman's hypothesis in an elegant experiment. This account does not appeal to a hidden mechanism but it does require us to change our views about the nature of the consequences that can produce learning.

Reduction of Shock-Frequency as a Reinforcer

Herrnstein and Hineline (1966) examined the results of many nondis-criminated avoidance experiments and generated several reasons why a reduction in shock density or frequency might be a good candidate for the main reinforcer in this procedure. First, subjects learn to avoid very quickly when the S-S interval is much shorter than the R-S interval and a response noticeably changes the environment for the better. If the S-S interval were 1 second and the R-S interval were 60 seconds, a single response would dramatically improve the subject's environment. Second, subjects will not respond when the R-S interval is less than the S-S interval because they produce an increase in shock frequency by responding. The increase in shock frequency acts as a punisher. It follows that a decrease in shock frequency should be a reinforcer.

Herrnstein and Hineline used rats and had two separate shock timers as in the usual Sidman procedure. The shock-shock timer programed shocks at a rate of nine per minute on a *random* basis throughout the session, a variable S-S interval. The response-shock timer randomly programed three shocks per minute, a variable R-S interval. Making these intervals variable eliminated the possibility of the rat using a fixed-time period as a discriminative stimulus for the avoidance response. When the rat pressed a lever, it shifted the program from the higher to the lower density of shocks. When a shock eventually occurred, the high-density, shock-shock program went into effect and presented shocks at the high rate until the next response. It is important to note that the rat could not avoid all shocks. The best the animal could do was to respond as soon as it received a shock and stay in the low-density, response-shock program. Thus, there was no immediate consequence explicitly programed for a response — a response might be remote from a shock, or a shock might occur just after a response had been made.

Seventeen of the 18 rats acquired the avoidance response even though the acquisition of the response was slow and erratic. It required about 30, 100-minute sessions for the majority of subjects to reach a stable rate of six to nine responses a minute. Table 20-2 gives the entire experimental history for one rat, M-1, which had an exceptionally long extinction period.

Plot these data on Figure 20-4 and determine the asymptote of the extinction curve. Use a scale of one square for 500 minutes on the abscissa and one square to 1,000 responses on the ordinate. Label the first and third parts of the figures as "Avoidance" and the middle portion, "Extinction". Since each session lasted 100 minutes, the scale on the abscissa is easily converted to sessions.

The authors summarized their findings by saying that the reduction of shock frequency is a negative reinforcer

Table 20-2

Cumulative number of responses made by a rat in a nondiscriminated avoidance situation. In conditioning phases, a response reduced the frequency of (but did not completely eliminate) shocks. Data taken from Herrnstein, R. J., & Hineline, P. N.   Negative reinforcement as shock-frequency reduction. *Journal of the Experimental Analysis of Behavior*, **1966, 9, 421-430.**

Cumulative Time (min)	Cumulative Responses	Condition
2,500	4,000	Avoidance conditioning:
5,000	20,000	Reponse lowers shock
6,500	30,000	frequency: 9 per minute to 3 per minute
7,500	35,500	
10,000	42,500	
12,500	45,500	Extinction:
15,000	48,500	Response does not change
17,500	50,500	shock frequency: 3 per
20,000	51,000	minute.
22,500	51,000	
23,000	51,000	
25,000	54,000	Re-conditioning: Response lowers shock frequency: 9 per minute to 3 per minute.

in Sidman avoidance. Their research is in the best tradition of the experimental analysis of behavior. Sidman removed the warning stimulus and showed that it was not necessary for avoidance. Because the time between shocks was fixed in his procedures (either from a shock or from a response), it was argued by others that stimuli correlated with the passage of time could serve as warning stimuli. Herrnstein and Hineline's procedure invalidated this explanation by showing that time-correlated stimuli were not necessary for avoidance. A response-dependent change in the frequency of aversive stimuli was sufficient to maintain avoidance responding. This implies that consequences which come into existence over a period of time can be effective, and it expands our conception of what makes a stimulus functional. A change in shock rate cannot be an immediate consequence because in order to define a change in rate, we need several points along the continuum of time. Yet a change in shock rate was shown to be functional in this experiment. This study nicely demonstrates the non-necessity of any speculative, internal mechanism.

Extinction of Avoidance Behavior

Avoidance behavior is interesting because of its great resistance to extinction. Why should avoidance behavior be any more resistant to extinction than appetitive behavior? Think for a moment about how you would place an animal on extinction after it had been conditioned to avoid. In an appetitive situation, we would disconnect the feeder. A response which was previously followed by a bit of food is no longer followed by food. An analogous procedure in Sidman avoidance would be to disconnect the programmers delivering shocks. Immediately we can see some problems. If the subject is successfully avoiding and is not receiving any shocks, how will it discover that shocks are no longer forthcoming? As long as the subject continues to respond, the conditioning and extinction situations are identical. Of course, animals like rats, pigeons, and monkeys gradually slow down their responding, and, while conditioning is in effect, they receive an occasional shock. The shock not only motivates them, but it also informs them that the shock is still programmed. Characteristically, avoidance responding is cyclic, and perhaps you can see why this is so. An animal that always responded at a rate which prevented all shock would be at a disadvantage when compared with an animal which responded at a lower rate and occasionally received a shock. The first subject would never learn that the shock had been turned off. This is analogous to a child who is very afraid of the dark and will not go into a dark room by himself. The child has to go into the room while it is dark in order to learn that there is no monster lurking there.

Notice that the rat in Figure 20-4 was placed on extinction not by disconnecting the shock programmer but by making the response ineffective in lowering the shock frequency. The rat was shocked, no matter what it did, at a rate of 3 shocks a minute. As you can see from M-1's extinction curve, it took a considerable period for this rat to discriminate that the shock rates were no longer different. In fact, the authors found that as the difference between the two shock rates used in conditioning diminished, the number of responses in

Figure 20-4 Cumulative number of responses made by a rat in an avoidance conditioning experiment. In conditioning, the rat's response reduced the average shock rate from 9 to 3 shocks a minute. In extinction, responses had no consequences. The subject received an average of 3 shocks a minute.

Figure 20-5 Number of meals eaten by Mary, a mental patient who had a history of refusing to feed herself. During treatment, nurses who fed her spilled food on her dress occasionally. Mary could avoid messy clothes by feeding herself.

extinction increased. Where a response only reduced the shock rate by an average of 3 shocks a minute, the number of responses in extinction was high, 16,000, and more. Where a response reduced the shock rate a large amount, by an average of 12 shocks a minute, extinction responding was low, about 1,000 responses, a considerable drop. This illustrates an important relation: The more similar the conditions of extinction and conditioning, the greater the resistance to extinction.

Illustration

T. Ayllon & J. Michael, The psychiatric nurse as a behavioral engineer. *Journal of the Experimental Analysis of Behavior*, 1959, 2, 323-334.

One of the more difficult staff problems in a mental institution involves the refusal of patients to eat. Some patients have to be led to the dining room or even spoonfed by a nurse. Ayllon and Michael (1959) successfully treated two female patients with eating problems using escape and avoidance conditioning. The two patients would not feed themselves, so the nurses had to spoonfeed them, which was time-consuming and inefficient. Imagine the difficulties of spoonfeeding an entire ward of patients! These patients had little contact with others and did not engage in many activities which might have served as positive reinforcers for feeding themselves. However, they always dressed neatly and took pains with their appearance. This fact gave the authors an idea. They told the nurses who fed them to be a bit careless in their feeding and to

occasionally spill some food or soup on their dresses. The nurses were instructed not to be mean or indifferent but to get across the notion that it is cumbersome to spoonfeed an adult.

The nurses' program consisted of giving each patient one or two spoons of food and then spilling some food on the patient's dress. The nurses continued this schedule until the meal was completed or until the patient took the spoon away from the nurse and fed herself (escape). The aversive stimulus, spilled food and a messy dress, could be avoided if the patient took the spoon and fed herself from the beginning of the meal. In addition to the escape-avoidance schedule, the nurse was instructed to sit with the patient and chat with her for a few minutes after the patient started eating on her own. This social attention was used in an attempt to positively reinforce self-feeding.

Table 20-3 reports the number of meals consumed each week by Mary, one of the two subjects. The column labelled "Self-Feeding" gives the number of meals which Mary ate without assistance, and the column labelled "Spoon-Feeding" gives the number of meals in which she was fed by the nurse. Plot these data on Figure 20-5 using a different code for each feeding condition. Place an asterisk over the data points for Week 6; at this time the authors discovered that Mary may have learned that the "food spilling" was intentional and this might have accounted for Mary's refusal to feed herself for a few days during this week.

The program was a success in more ways than one. Mary was admitted to the hospital because she refused to eat, claiming her food was being poisoned. As a consequence of the treatment, she

Table 20-3

Number of meals eaten without assistance (self-feeding) or with assistance (spoon-feeding) for Mary, a female mental patient. After the baseline week, an escape-avoidance schedule was used to condition self-feeding. Data taken from Ayllon, T., & Michael, J. The psychiatric nurse as a behavioral engineer. *Journal of the Experimental Analysis of Behavior*, 1959, 2, 323-334.

Week	Self-Feeding	Spoon-Feeding by Nurse	Condition
1	5	12	Escape-Avoidance Conditioning:
2	8	12	Nurse spills food
3	12	8	on patient's dress.
4	21	0	Patient can avoid messy
5	18	2	clothes by feeding
6	7	11*	herself.
7	16	2	
8	19	0	

*Patient may have been told that the foodspilling was not accidental.

ate without assistance, gained 21 pounds, and no longer made statements about poisoned food. There was little reason to keep her in the institution after this, and she was discharged. The authors inform us that no special program was undertaken to deal with her disturbed verbal behavior (poisoning of food). These statements stopped as she started feeding herself.

Exam

1. Define:
   a. escape conditioning
   b. discriminated avoidance conditioning
   c. nondiscriminated avoidance conditioning (Sidman avoidance)
2. Describe an example not in the text, which illustrates the differences between an avoidance and an escape response.
3. In a situation in which a mother nags her child to perform a task, describe what might be some of the escape and avoidance dependencies controlling the child's behavior.
4. In what ways are an intermittent appetitive schedule and an intermittent escape schedule similar? Different?

5. Why was it desirable (Or was it!) for scientists to extend the procedures of intermittent reinforcement to escape conditioning?

6. What were some problems that Winograd encountered in his experiment?

7. What is the titrated-escape procedure? Summarize the Khalili et al. experiment using this procedure. How would you compare their results (Figure 20-1) to results with positive reinforcement schedules (see Unit 11)?

8. Summarize the Miller et al. experiment. When could you say the monkeys had solved the problem? (Examine Figure 20-2 and determine at what place the chance avoidances were low relative to the overall avoidances. This will require you to make an arbitrary judgment, but pick a point and try to defend it.)

9. Was an efficient performance established as fast when the monkeys' roles were reversed (examine Figure 20-2)? How do you explain these results?

10. How does the nondiscriminated avoidance procedure differ from the discriminated avoidance procedure?

11. It has been argued that escape conditioning and discriminated avoidance conditioning are both escape procedures. How can this be?

12. After examining Figure 20-3, someone could claim that the rat still had not learned to avoid. It received a number of shocks even in the 7th hour, and one could argue that only when the subject receives no shocks has learning taken place. What would you say to this argument?

13. Why is avoidance responding in the nondiscriminated avoidance procedure cyclic?

14. Avoidance behavior is said to extinguish slowly. How would you account for this?

15. Why does the animal stop responding when the R-S interval is shorter than the S-S interval in nondiscriminated avoidance?

16. What is wrong with an explanation of avoidance responding that relies on internal stimuli to account for the reinforcer?

17. Describe Herrnstein and Hineline's experiment. What consequences did a response have in this study? What was the main conclusion of their study? How long (in sessions or minutes) was required for M-1's avoidance response to extinguish? (Use the asymptote of the extinction curve as the end point, and the last session of conditioning as the starting point to make this determination.) How many responses were made in extinction?

18. What was the relation between the amount of reduction of shock and the resistance to extinction in the Herrnstein and Hineline experiment?

19. What did Ayllon and Michael do? Of what general significance was it that the patient re-learned to feed herself?

References

Ayllon, T., & Michael, J.   The psychiatric nurse as a behavioral engineer. *Journal of the Experimental Analysis of Behavior*, 1959, **2**, 323-334.

Herrnstein, R. J., & Hineline, P. N.   Negative reinforcement as shock-frequency reduction. *Journal of the Experimental Analysis of Behavior*, 1966, **9**, 421-430.

Khalili, J., Daley, M. F., & Cheney, C. D.   A titration procedure for generating escape behavior. *Behavior Research Methods and Instrumentation*, 1969, **1**, 293-294.

Miller, R. E., Banks, J. H., & Ogawa, N.   Communication of affect in "cooperative conditioning" of Rhesus monkeys. *Journal of Abnormal and Social Psychology*, 1962, **64**, 343-348.

Miller, R. E., Banks, J. H., & Ogawa, N.   Role of facial expression in "cooperative avoidance conditioning" in monkeys. *Journal of Abnormal and Social Psychology*, 1963, **67**, 24-30.

Sidman, M.   Avoidance conditioning with brief shock and no exteroceptive warning signal. *Science*, 1953, **118**, 157-158.

Sidman, M.   Reduction of shock frequency as reinforcement for avoidance behavior. *Journal of the Experimental Analysis of Behavior*, 1962, **5**, 247-257.

Sidman, M.   Avoidance behavior. In W. K. Honig (Ed.), *Operant behavior: Areas of research and application.* New York: Appleton-Century-Crofts, 1966. Pp. 448-498.

Weiss, B., & Laties, V. G.   Titration behavior on various fractional escape programs. *Journal of the Experimental Analysis of Behavior*, 1959, **2**, 227-248.

Winograd, E.   Escape behavior under different fixed-ratios and shock intensities. *Journal of the Experimental Analysis of Behavior*, 1965, **8**, 117-124.

Behavior Modification

21

Behavior modification signifies the employment of conditioning techniques to change behavior. The phrase is now employed by nearly everyone, and this wide use has resulted in meanings not intended in the original use of the term. In this unit we shall define the term, discuss the techniques that result in behavior modification, and discuss the philosophy underlying the use of behavior modification.

What Is Behavior Modification?

Behavior modification is the systematic employment of techniques derived from conditioning principles to increase or decrease the frequency of desirable and undesirable behaviors in human beings, and to bring those behaviors under the control of appropriate stimulus conditions. A necessary component of the definition is that the psychologist employ a conditioning technique of some kind. If no conditioning technique is used, then by definition, behavior modification has not occurred (some other kind of therapy might have, though). Most often, the conditioning techniques will be those that affect the frequency of the operant behavior of the individual; however, an important portion of the published literature also deals with changes in respondent behavior in the form of emotions and phobias. Techniques employing respondent conditioning operations, or derived therefrom, are often called behavior *therapy* rather than behavior modification.

The term *behavior modification* further implies that the behaviors modified will be socially relevant. If this social significance exists, as well as the use of a conditioning technique, the response changes being produced can appropriately be thought of as behavior modification.

In 1949, a psychologist reinforced a profoundly retarded adolescent with squirts of condensed milk in the mouth for raising his arm (Fuller, 1949). The result was a threefold increase in arm raising — a powerful demonstration of the possible successes available to researchers utilizing conditioning techniques with the retarded. By our definition, this work would not be considered behavior modification, principally because the social significance of arm raising by a retarded youngster is not readily apparent. This project might best be conceived as a demonstration or as applied research, although the adjective *applied* often is considered to connote social relevance (Baer, Wolf, & Risley, 1968). If Fuller had extended the arm movement control to self-feeding, this would certainly have had social relevance and could be considered behavior modification.

Behavior modification also connotes that the psychologist or the patient himself will be measuring *overt* behaviors that are well-defined.[1] The major datum will be the frequency of the behavior's occurrence. This generally means that the psychologist will be graphing or otherwise charting the course of the modification. He may be counting the frequency of out-of-seat behavior in a classroom, cueing a mother to ignore a deviant behavior of one of her children, or counting the number of times a father attends to his child's deviant behavior. In many situations he will be counting all these responses and more.

Our definition disagrees with that of Paul (1969), who lumps all kinds of treatments — pastoral therapy, sleep therapy, emotional re-education, and others — under the heading of behavior modification. By doing this, the term *behavior modification* can mean just about anything with regard to behavior change. This sloppiness of meaning is one reason for defining behavior modification more precisely.

What Behavior Modification Isn't

Obviously behavior modification is not the converse of some of the examples given above. Behavior modification does not occur where conditioning techniques are not being employed; it does not occur where responses, consequences, and stimuli are not objectively defined and recorded. Thus, the operations and their results

---

[1] A new area in psychology is self-management. Here a patient may count responses that can only be observed by himself — that is, they are *covert*. These may be thoughts, feelings, fears, or the like (see Unit 7, Illustration). Self-management is behavior modification if the person managing his own behavior applies conditioning techniques to that behavior in a systematic and objective fashion. Thus, after pinpointing the response, he may record occurrences and reinforce or punish the covert response.

While there is no difficulty in incorporating self-management into behavior modification, there are problems in studying covert responses

together define whether behavior modification is being engaged in, and occurs.

The rigorous recording of responses and detailed specification of procedures differentiates behavior modification from many current areas of applied psychology and psychiatry. Psychoanalysis, reality therapy, and encounter groups all may produce behavior change. However, these changes are not documented as is necessary in our definition and, hence, do not constitute behavior modification procedures. As there is little documentation of both response changes and procedures in the latter cases, it is usually difficult to point to the behavior changes these procedures may have produced. Furthermore, this failure to document makes the evaluation of the procedures used impossible from a scientific standpoint. This statement doesn't argue with the popular success of some of these techniques. It simply implies that the reasons for successes cannot be ascertained, at least within a scientific framework, until such documentation takes place.

We also note that for the most part, traditionally understood testing and diagnostic procedures do not constitute behavior modification. For one thing, their purpose is not to modify any behavior per se; they merely classify. Secondly, they may not even specify any behavior to be modified. (Some behavior change may take place as a function of taking a test itself, but this is not to be understood as behavior modification.) Testing of this sort can scientifically. The major one is that covert responses are usually observable only to one individual at a time and not subject to consensual verification — a basic tenet of scientific method. There appear to be at least two ways to circumvent this problem; one is to make the response, or events functionally related to it, observable via instrumentation so that consensual verification can occur. Humans can lower their blood-pressure if blood pressure decreases provide feedback (e.g., a bell ringing). Here we do not know what response the individual makes to produce a blood pressure decrease and it may not be parsimonious to ask if there is such a response. (This latter kind of speculation usually involves psychologists inferring neural events on the basis of behavior.) But the individual will usually be unable to produce the blood pressure decrease unless he is given a way of detecting it (e.g., the bell). In this instance, consensual verification is possible because a covert response, not even observable to the person producing it, has been made overt. While there may be another underlying response (often called a mediating response — in this case what the individual *does* to produce a blood pressure decrease), we may not need to measure it to produce reliable changes in the response we made overt.

A second way to bring covert responses under study is a little more risky. It involves inferring the presence of the response from other observable aspects of the environment that are well-correlated with the response. For example, we reasonably accept that an individual with a swollen jaw has a toothache if he so reports. We might also accept that a patient has more positive thoughts when he has arranged his environment so that he rewards himself handsomely each time a positive thought occurs, especially if we have no reason to believe the patient involved knows anything about what positive reinforcement does. The difficulty in these two cases is the correlation. There will be individuals with swollen jaws, whose teeth don't ache, who report toothaches; and individuals who report increases in the frequency of positive thoughts, without experiencing the increase. This is a big problem because we don't know all the variables governing the control of the verbal report. When we do we should be in a better position to infer whether the report results from the detection of the covert response or some other response.

often lead to the belief that no further action is necessary. One of the authors has recorded the following type of interaction on a number of occasions when a teacher was having difficulty with a specific child:

Psychologist: "You wished to see me?"
Teacher: "Yes, Johnny won't obey me; I want him tested."
Psychologist: "Why should we test him?"
Teacher: "Because he doesn't obey me; he always causes trouble; you could find out his problem."
Psychologist: "You have already stated his problem; he doesn't obey you."
Teacher: "Well, maybe he isn't capable of obeying."
Psychologist: "Why don't we see if he's capable?" (Launches into his behavior modification spiel.)

Quite likely, the teacher's part in the above is an attempt at an escape response. In that sense the testing does provide a kind of solution for her. However, the luxury of being without a disruptive Johnny in this case may be temporary, especially if Johnny learns he can escape the classroom by being disruptive.

Additionally, the teacher would appear to be suggesting that the psychologist engage in testing to locate the underlying "personality structures" that make Johnny the little bastard he is. When these tests have been given, the psychologist who said he would test Johnny could return to the teacher and say:

Psychologist: "Johnny, we have discovered, is neurotic; call again when we can be of further help."
Teacher: "Hey, wait a minute . . . "

The point of this is that teacher and psychologist eventually have to deal with Johnny's *behavior* to do their jobs. More than likely the behavior dealt with will *not* be test behavior, nor will it be the descriptor of the behavior (e.g., neurosis).

The Medical Model

We have been led to believe by the philosophical ethic of our culture and the disease model of medicine that there are two levels to the actions of men. The first or overt level is what is seen; the second or covert level is not seen and is considered by many to direct overt behavior. How has this conceptualization come about? Psychology historically evolved from philosophy and this same notion is recorded there as *dualism*. This conception described man as a physical and mental being. The mental life of man in this framework was considered inaccessible and unmeasurable, hence, not amenable to overt controls. The physical side simply involved man's motor behavior in which, it was thought, he was little different than other animals.

The medical model is the application to behavior of concepts of disease action on the body. In medicine, a virus or germ causes physical illness which may be seen overtly as changes in an individual's vital signs. Fever is a common example, although any number of changes could be measured. In medicine, treatment is not directed to the outward sign or *symptom* of the illness, but instead the underlying disease is treated. Treating the underlying disease successfully produces a remission of the symptom. If the symptom itself is treated, it may be temporarily remitted but the basic problem is not likely to be solved by this action; therefore, the symptom is likely to return shortly after treatment ceases. For example, taking aspirin may reduce fever but have little effect on the disease entity producing the fever, say, the virus that produces influenza. (We often mistakenly attribute the "feeling-better" condition that comes with aspirin — reduced headache pain and fever — to some action of the aspirin on the disease producing these effects.)

This same approach, without further consideration, is considered to be applicable to disordered behavior as well. The model assumes that there is an underlying cause for any deviant behavior. Behavior itself is only a symptom of the underlying cause. Therefore, treatment of the overt behavior itself is incorrect because it ignores the underlying cause. If the overt behavior is treated, it might disappear but another would occur in its place because the underlying pathology has not been dealt with. This is the doctrine of *symptom substitution*.

Pathology underlying disordered behavior was initially considered to be physical in kind, so there was good reason for utilizing the medical model. More often than not, however, this pathology could not be located. The historical result was that the pathology did not become less real — it was still assumed to be there — it was just given different properties. The pathology became "mental pathology." Freud synthesized these developments and it became understood that the individual was ruled by underlying forces which were balanced energy systems making up a total (closed) system — the personality. As long as the balance was maintained among this system's parts, behavior was normal; imbalances produced abnormal behavior. As Freud was a physician, it might be thought normal that he would conceive a behavioral system of this sort. Few questioned the fact that these systems — now reified — had never been measured independently of behaviors they produced. We would suggest that popular acceptance was due to the prevailing view in the West of man as a "dual" being.

Some results of accepting this medical model are that the person with the deviant behavior is medically labelled. He becomes a *patient*; he is called *sick* or otherwise *ill*. His mental *health* is impaired. He is *hospitalized*, not infrequently. Doctors of medicine are considered experts in his treatment. As a result of his behavior being a supposed function of underlying, unspecified causes, he is not responsible for his actions; therefore, he is denied many of the rights of the "responsible" citizen (e.g., voting). If the deviant behaviors disappear ("remission of symptoms"), the patient is still called "sick" because the underlying difficulty has not been removed. (The fact that no one has ever seen, measured, or otherwise interacted with these underlying forces seems not to trouble those holding this view.) If the individual gains help outside the hospital it is time-consuming and expensive, because no one can specify when the underlying pathology has been corrected.

Not incidentally, many practitioners who adhere to the sort of modern dualism that the medical model invokes are forced by their beliefs to conclude that a part — the hidden part — of man's behavior cannot be known utilizing scientific techniques. The forces of the personality, they would say, are unmeasurable and unobservable. The result is that psychology cannot be a science for these individuals, because science deals only with observables and measurables. Because a large portion of man's nature is nonobservable and nonmeasurable in their view, it follows that behavior is neither predictable nor controllable. Of course, this analysis reduces to the fact that nobody should deal with man's behavior because it cannot be dealt with. The remainder of this book and the now extensive literature on behavior modification and conditioning are testimony to the incorrectness of this point of view.

The Psychological Model

An alternative to the medical model is the model emphasized throughout this book. This model considers that most of man's behavior is a function of: 1) the present environment in which it occurs; 2) past environments; and 3) his genetic makeup and, as part of this, his species characteristics. Environments contain stimuli which are antecedent and consequent to behaviors. The juxtaposition of these stimuli with behavior in time results in changes in that behavior. While primary control resides in the current environment, behavior will also be a function of control by stimuli of past environments, with the most recent past having the largest effect. In addition, boundary conditions of species membership and genetic inheritance set limits on man's behavior.

According to a psychological model, behavior is deviant for three reasons: 1) Its relative occurrence in the culture as a whole; that is, behavior will be labelled deviant if its normative frequency is low and an individual emits a higher frequency of it. Conversely, behavior will be called deviant if its normally occurring frequency is high and our example individual doesn't emit enough of it. 2) If stimulus control is faulty or control by appropriate stimuli is lacking, behavior will be labelled deviant. Stimuli in the environment control certain kinds of behavior. Given the presence of a stimulus, failure of a response following it may be called deviant, as in the failure to answer when spoken to. If a given behavior occurs in the presence of stimuli that ordinarily don't produce that response, such as disrobing on a street corner, this may be labelled deviant behavior. Finally, 3) behavior will be labelled deviant if other individuals collectively wish to punish, not reward, it.

The psychological model does not dichotomize man's behavior into knowable and unknowable halves. As man is a natural being, his behavior is considered a function of natural laws; therefore, it is potentially understandable. If there are aspects of man's behavior that still are unpredictable, it is because the laws or principles governing those behaviors are still unknown, not that they are unknowable. The model also results in a single psychology, a psychology of (human) behavior, rather than special psychologies of "abnormal" behavior. This doesn't result in the advocacy of terminating Abnormal Psychology classes on university campuses around the country. Better, these courses might be taught as History, or better yet, might be used to discuss the special environmental conditions which produce non-normal behavior.

The psychological model also questions a number of assumptions of the medical model. First, the medical practitioner may not be the best-equipped individual to deal with behavior problems. The practice of labelling individuals as sick, or deranged, and as requiring hospitalization, is questionable at best. Labelling allows the possibility of self-fulfilling hypotheses — the label leads people to expect deviancy and the individual is thereby treated as deviant. Further, the need for expensive, one-to-one treatment over a long period of time is an assumption we also question.

Emphasis in the psychological model is on the very overt behaviors (no longer symptoms) the medical model chooses to ignore. It is these behaviors which must be changed. If they are a function of the environment, then it follows that environmental changes will produce changes in these behaviors. This approach draws on a 50-year data base in experimental psychology.

Behavior Modification Techniques

Behavior modification reduces to a collection of procedures that are systematically employed to change the frequency of behavior (either increasing or decreasing a behavior's occurrence) and the environment in which a behavior occurs. Washing one's hands after going to the bathroom or before eating a meal may produce a hand-washing frequency of 3-6 times per day. Most individuals who washed their hands many hundreds of times per day would be exhibiting non-normal frequencies of this behavior. If a client complained to us of this "compulsive" behavior, one part of the modification plan would be to reduce the frequency with which he washes his hands. Similarly, lowering one's pants in the bathroom is behavior controlled appropriately by stimuli in the environment, that is, rectal-sphincter tension, the presence of a lavatory, and so forth. However, engaging in the same behavior on a city street would be punished because it occurs in an environment in which others are unwilling to accept it. The task in the last case is less one of changing the frequency of the behavior than it is one of modifying the controlling stimuli so that the behavior occurs in a societally approved environment. In practice, however, both frequency and stimulus control enter into all behavior modifications.

As the reader might guess, because of earlier applied examples and the definition of behavior modification in the present unit, he is already familiar with the principal techniques of behavior modification. They are nothing other than conditioning procedures systematically and objectively applied to behaviors that have social significance. Consequently, we will limit our discussion of the techniques and only briefly mention some examples of the populations and behaviors with which they have been employed.

Strengthening behavior: Positive reinforcement. Recall that this procedure involves following a response with a stimulus that raises the frequency of the behavior; or it may involve manipulating high-probability behaviors in such a way that they follow

low-probability behaviors (Premack's Rule).

One outstanding set of examples of the former involved a program utilizing a nursery school setting at the University of Washington in the 1960s. This program used adult attention to change the frequency of a large number of child behaviors. One case involved a child who was a social isolate. The teachers attended to him only when he was playing with at least one other child. All other activities of this child were ignored. The result was a substantial increase in the amount of time this youngster spent playing with other children (Allen, Hart, Buell, Harris, & Wolf, 1964). Adult attention in this case functioned as a social reinforcer. In another case a child's activity level with respect to climbing was increased (Johnston, Kelley, Harris, & Wolf, 1966). Before the teacher began to attend to the child, he stood passively and was very inactive. When teacher-attention was made dependent on climbing, the child's activity level increased. Another child who could walk, but spent much of her nursery school time crawling, was attended to only when in an upright position (Harris, Johnston, Kelley, & Wolf, 1964). On-feet behavior (viz., walking) became more frequent.

The reader should note that while these are simple applications to talk about and understand, carrying them out requires considerable skill. In this case the teacher assigned to a particular child would have to be on her toes to catch (i.e., attend to) every bit of specified desirable behavior that occurred, and concurrently to guard against attending to undesirable behavior that may also be occurring. Not many of us are used to monitoring our own behavior this precisely, and gaining the skill of doing so requires a systematic program of reinforcement.

Application

Osborne (1969), using Premack's Rule, attempted to change the behavior of six retarded deaf girls. The presenting problem was out-of-seat behavior, even when the teacher was teaching! As this was occurring at a high rate, it might be considered a high-probability behavior. Conversely, in-seat behavior was infrequent. Thus, it was decided to make out-of-seat behavior (5 min) dependent on in-seat behavior (15 min). That is, remaining seated could earn each girl 5 minutes of free time (out-of-seat). **Table 21-1 contains the data for this application. Graph the data on the sheet provided and be prepared to answer the unit exam questions regarding the outcomes of this experiment. Use a separate set of coordinates for each subject. Stack the coordinates one above the other starting with S_6 on the bottom, S_5 next, and so on. You can determine how much space is necessary for each subject's points by finding the largest number for that subject and making your ordinate big enough to contain this number. Each abscissa will require 27 points.**

Osborne first took a 5-day baseline of out-of-seat occurrences. Thereafter, for 5 days the above dependency was in effect; that is, being in-seat for 15 minutes was followed by 5 minutes of free time. Osborne then made another manipulation which does not concern us here, and this is the reason the table does not show days 11 through 15. On days 16 through 50 the time required to

Table 21-1

The mean number of out-of-seat responses for each of six deaf girls. Data are from Osborne, J. G. *Free-time as a reinforcer in the management of classroom behavior. Journal of Applied Behavior Analysis*, 1969, 2, 113-118.

Condition	Day	S_1	S_2	S_3	S_4	S_5	S_6
Baseline	1	0.00	2.00	0.88	2.11	1.25	0.38
	2	0.10	0.80	0.80	1.20	1.60	1.40
	3	1.65	1.50	1.12	1.25	0.80	1.00
	4	0.27	1.18	0.55	1.09	1.18	1.82
	5	0.36	1.09	0.82	1.36	1.36	1.73
Free-time	6	0.09	0.27	0.09	0.27	0.27	0.00
	7	0.00	0.08	0.00	0.00	0.08	0.00
	8	0.00	0.08	0.00	0.00	0.00	0.30
	9	0.10	0.10	0.00	0.20	0.00	0.00
	10	0.11	0.00	0.11	0.00	0.11	0.11
	11-15			Omitted			
Free-time	16	0.10	0.25	Absent	0.25	0.17	0.00
	17	0.00	0.08	0.10	0.11	0.00	0.17
	18	0.00	0.00	0.00	0.08	0.00	0.08
	19	0.00	0.00	0.00	0.00	0.00	0.00
	20	0.00	0.08	0.00	0.10	0.00	0.00
	21	0.08	0.08	0.00	0.08	0.00	0.08
	22	0.00	0.00	0.08	0.00	0.00	0.00
	23	0.25	0.13	0.00	0.00	0.00	0.00
	24	0.00	0.00	0.00	0.00	0.00	0.00
	25	0.00	0.00	0.00	0.00	0.00	0.00
	26	0.00	0.00	0.00	0.00	0.00	0.00
	27	0.00	0.09	0.09	0.09	0.00	0.00
	28	0.00	Absent	0.00	0.00	0.00	0.00
	29	0.09	0.00	0.00	0.00	0.00	0.00
	30	0.00	0.00	0.00	0.00	0.00	0.00
Follow-up		0.00	0.00	0.00	0.00	0.00	0.00
Reversal		0.50	0.63	0.38	0.63	0.75	0.38

be seated was 15 minutes, while after Day 50, the in-seat requirement was raised to 25 minutes. (Data are not included beyond Day 30.) At the end of the study, Osborne left the teacher on her own for about 6 weeks and then the teacher recorded out-of-seat responses for one more day (follow-up). **These data should be placed after Day 30 on your graphs as separate points.**

Finally, a dependency reversal was employed to demonstrate that the controlling consequence was free time. During this 1-day period, students had to be out-of-seat once per 15-minute class segment to gain free time. **Place these points next to the follow-up points but do not join them.**

Positive reinforcement procedures have been used successfully with mentally retarded children, brain-damaged children, deaf children, blind children, schizophrenic women, juvenile delinquents, and businessmen, to name but a few populations. Responses manipulated have included: reading, using adjectives, performing work, doing homework, playing, and so on.

Behavior Modification Techniques Continued

Negative reinforcement. This technique has not systematically been used a great deal, most likely because its successful use may mean that the subject of the technique may behave to escape the purveyor (the modifier) of the aversive stimuli necessary to carry out the technique (Unit 20). To utilize this technique, the therapeutic agent would present an aversive stimulus, and the behavior the subject emits to escape the aversive stimulus will be strengthened. Usually, if the behavior that escapes the stimulus is desirable, the behavior modifier will positively reinforce that behavior, in addition. Thus, Lovaas and his associates (Lovaas, Schaeffer, & Simmons, 1965) employed electric shock to the feet of severely autistic children to condition them to come to, and make physical contact with, the behavior modifier. Autistic children do not

react socially, so there was little else that could be done to get the children to emit this behavior. When a child made contact with the therapist, shock terminated. The therapist then embraced the youngster. After a few sessions and very few shocks, the stimuli presented by the behavior modifier — arms out, calling the child to come — controlled approaching by the child, which was in turn maintained by the conditioned negative reinforcement of being embraced by the therapist. Later in the program, the therapist was paired with many powerful positive reinforcers and his own stimulus function changed to that of a conditioned positive reinforcer.

The Ayllon and Michael study (1959), also used negative reinforcement to strengthen self-feeding in schizophrenic women.

Weakening behavior: Extinction. Using this technique, the behavior modifier first locates what he considers to be the reinforcer(s) maintaining the client's behavior. As extinction is the operation of precluding reinforcement for a given response, the modifier attempts to cut off the source of reinforcement. For much deviant child behavior, as one example, this may just mean eliminating the attention a parent gives to some obnoxious behavior. This can be done by having the parent monitor the number of times a day he or she attends to this behavior. Review the temper-tantrum case by Williams (1959) in Unit 8; it provides a classic example of the use of extinction.

Ayllon and Michael (1959) also provide an example. A schizophrenic woman on their ward had for two years pestered the on-duty nurses by entering their station to chat and otherwise

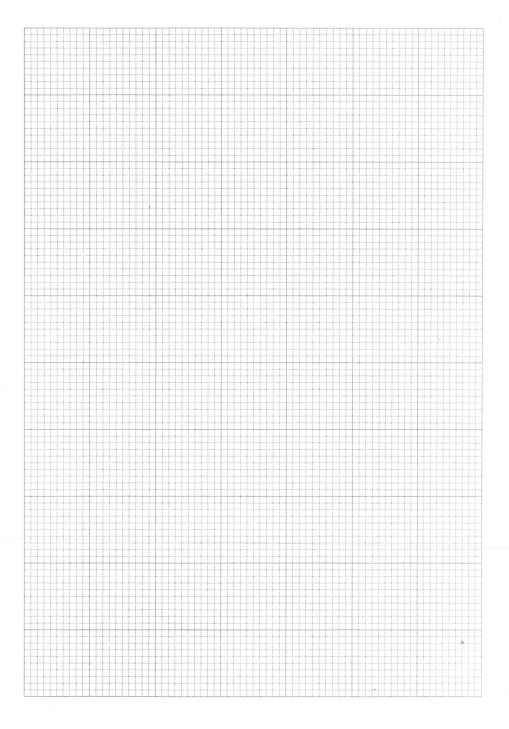

Figure 21-1   The mean number of out-of-seat responses for 6 deaf girls reinforced for remaining seated.

*

be around while the nurses attempted to work. It seemed fairly obvious that the nurses' attention to the woman maintained her high frequency of visits. The nurses agreed not to interact with the woman in the station. Within a few weeks, the behavior of entering the nurses' station had substantially diminished.

Punishment, Type I. The use of strong aversive stimuli dependent on the occurrence of deviant behavior is infrequent, and it is a technique of last resort. Its use generally connotes that a deviant behavior is so strong that a behavior modifier has little chance to help the individual by reinforcing behaviors incompatible with the deviant behavior or by using extinction. In the first case the individual may have *no* desirable behaviors to reinforce, because of the high frequency of undesirable behaviors. In the second case, extinction may take so long that injury may result to the individual or to others near him. Extreme aggressiveness by an adult or severe self-destructive responses by a child are examples of these kinds of behaviors. In cases like those above, faradic (electric) shock has been used. The application is brief, immediately following the occurrence of the undesired behavior. If the child hits his head against any solid object, a few shocks are often sufficient to suppress this head-banging. Generally, the behavior modifier will also attempt to pair himself and significant others in the individual's environment with the punishing stimulus (Lovaas & Simmons, 1969). This can make all of them conditioned punishers. Risley (1968) applied shock to influence a

young girl's dangerous climbing. Each time he did so, he shouted, "No!" Later he was able to suppress other responses the girl emitted (e.g., autistic rocking) simply by shouting, "No!" Every effort in these cases is made to employ unconditioned aversive stimuli (e.g., shock) sparingly. The transfer of control to a conditioned punisher in the above example is one such illustration.

We also would like to emphasize in concluding this section that punishment is defined functionally (as are most other terms we have used). Spanking a child is not punishment unless the behavior that produced the spanking is thereby suppressed. Many of the difficulties of understanding some of our institutional systems' goals could be eliminated if this functional approach were adopted uniformly by society. Incarceration for committing a crime is defined a priori, by those who believe the approach to be successful, as punishment. The figures on recidivism, however, indicate that for the average prisoner in this country, prison is not *functionally* a punishing stimulus.[2] If it were, criminal behaviors would be suppressed by incarceration. They are often not.

Punishment, Type II: Time out from positive reinforcement. Punishment can also occur by making deviant

[2]A few years ago the national average for recidivism for first offenders was 30 percent. Of course, repeat offenders are even more likely to continue their pattern of crime, and so the figure rises substantially here. In addition, some states have recidivism rates that deviate sharply from the national figures. For example, in Alabama, estimates are that 70 percent of first offenders become recidivists (The Rehabilitation Research Foundation, 1970).

behavior result in the withdrawal of some available reinforcers. This technique is an unusually successful one because it combines extinction and the loss of all positive reinforcement for behavior for a period of time. Wolf, Risely, and Mees (1964) provide a now classic example. Dicky, three years old, had undergone a cataract operation for occluded lenses. If he didn't wear his glasses he would become functionally blind due to lack of retinal stimulation. However, he had extreme temper tantrums whenever anyone tried to put his glasses on him or otherwise thwarted him. Wolf et al. incarcerated Dicky in his room at the hospital (cutting off all social contact with staff and others) whenever Dicky had a tantrum. Dicky was allowed out of his room 5 minutes after the tantrum ceased. In 4 months, tantruming was suppressed to zero and the modifiers were able to advance to and deal with the wearing of glasses and other deviant behaviors that Dicky exhibited. Remember that the length of time necessary for this modification was likely due to unauthorized changes in the procedure by ward staff (Unit 19).

There are possible problems with this technique that any user must be aware of. First, it is used to reform the behavior of the punished individual rather than to provide an escape from his aversive behaviors to a teacher or parent. Long seclusion is not usually necessary, but the behavior producing the punishment must have ceased prior to allowing the individual back into contact with the original environment.

Second, if the environment the individual is put into, is, on balance, less aversive, or more reinforcing, than the one he is withdrawn from, the technique will not work; in fact, employing it may be detrimental. If a child is put in his room with toys when he misbehaves at home, he could be reinforced by playing with the toys. The child may actually increase the frequency of any deviant behavior that results in his being sent to his room. Likewise, if a classroom environment is very aversive, removing the child from it dependent on some unwanted behavior may negatively reinforce the behavior rather than punish it. Again, the reader will note, that while the principles are simple, their application takes considerable skill.

Punishment, Type II: Response cost. Rather than removing the individual for a *time* from all positive reinforcement as in time out, a number of positive reinforcers could be withdrawn from the individual dependent upon the occurrence of some undesirable behavior. Response cost is an effective punishment procedure provided the individual has something to lose. Fines are an example of society's use of response cost. Burchard and Barrera (1972) employed fines in a token economy to manage the behaviors of institutionalized, adolescent retardates. They were able to produce some suppression of swearing, physical assault, property damage, and related behaviors. In their experiment a larger response cost (30 tokens) produced greater suppression than a smaller response cost (5 tokens). When they compared time out and response cost they found similar amounts of suppression by each procedure.

There is at least one possible advantage to response cost over time out. If the situation the individual is timed-out from is important to his eventual welfare, his time away from that environment is effectively lost time. Response cost allows the individual to stay in the environment where his desirable behaviors can continue to be strengthened.

Systematic desensitization. This technique is somewhat different than the above techniques in terms of the fact that it: 1) usually deals with behavior in a setting removed from where the behavior occurs; 2) acts on covert responses the subject makes. It is applied mainly to phobias which are unreasonable fears that stop an individual from performing a significant behavior.

Typically, there are three major operations in systematic desensitization: 1) A heirarchy of feared stimuli (phobic scenes) is constructed; 2) the patient is taught to relax as the response incompatible with fear; and 3) the therapist verbally presents individual phobic scenes which the client visualizes while in a state of relaxation.

As an illustration of this technique Freeman and Kendrick (1960) cured a particularly severe case of cat phobia. The patient was a 37-year-old woman who had been terrified of cats all her life. This fear kept her from going out at night, hanging up wash outside where a cat might be, entering a room where there was a cat, wearing fur gloves, and in fact, even touching fur. She reported her greatest fear was the sight of a live cat, followed by the thought that a cat might leap at her, and the thought of going out at night where she might encounter cats. She was also frightened by toys that looked like cats and by furry objects.

Instead of the verbal presentation of imaginary scenes involving cats, as would be done in typical desensitization procedures, these therapists confronted the woman with three graded hierarchies of feared stimuli. The first hierarchy began with the handling of fur initially unlike cat fur. The patient handled each fur piece until she reported no fear in so doing. Subsequently she handled fur progressively cat-like in texture. The second hierarchy involved pictures of cats and a toy cat. This was extended from usual practices (i.e., use of imaginal stimuli, restriction of procedures to the therapist's office) to include hanging pictures of cats around her home. A third hierarchy was very clever: The patient was given and had to care for a baby kitten. As the kitten grew slowly into a full-grown cat, it traversed the hierarchy to the most-feared stimulus.

The woman successively coped with each of the first two hierarchies in approximately 3 weeks, and reported she was prepared to handle a live kitten. The kitten was introduced to her in the therapist's office while being held by a nurse. By the end of this session she was able to stroke the kitten while it was in her lap. She indicated that this was a great day in her life and she was happy at being successful. For 2 more days she cared for the kitten at the clinic, subsequently taking it home. Three years later she owned the same cat and was occasionally taking care of another one. She had no further distress.

As this is being written, there is considerable controversy over the necessary and sufficient conditions for desensitization. Observe that Freeman and Kendrick did not use relaxation training, although the client handled the phobic stimuli until she was able to do so comfortably. Further, they presented real phobic stimuli rather than representations in imagination. Suffice to say that a number of variations on this basic procedure have been successful. While *experimental* studies may show that some aspects of the traditional procedure are not necessary to successful outcomes, these aspects of the procedure may be practical for *clinical* reasons. For example, relaxation training may alleviate the client's distress to such an extent that he desires to continue in therapy, whereas without this training, confronting the feared stimuli may drive the client away.

Modeling (Imitation). In modeling, the client watches another perform some desired behavior and sees the outcomes for it. The client then performs the behavior himself. To be successful, given that a complex set of responses are to be emitted, the model can emit portions of the entire behavioral act, after which the client emits each portion. Successfully emitted responses can be reinforced by the behavior modifier as they occur.

There are not many published experiments regarding the use of modeling in the applied setting. Quite likely modeling a behavior provides discriminative stimuli for the observing organism. These stimuli may indicate whether identical responses will be reinforced, punished, or extinguished.

Bandura, Grusec, and Menlove (1967) used modeling to change the behavior of dog-phobic children. In one condition children who were afraid of dogs went to a party where they saw another child play fearlessly with a large dog. A second group of children went to a party but did not have the model interact with the dog. Subsequent measures showed that the first group of children was much more likely to interact with the dog than the latter group.

Bandura and his associates (Bandura, Blanchard, & Ritter, 1968) also compared modeling and desensitization procedures in snake-phobic adults. One group saw a movie of a model interacting with and handling a snake fearlessly (symbolic modeling). This group could control their exposure to the movie. A second group was given desensitization procedures which involved only *imaginal* contact with snakes. A third group was given modeling with "guided participation." In this treatment subjects saw an assistant handle a snake. They were then helped to make a similar response with the aid of the assistant. Initial response requirements were made the least fearful (e.g., putting the patient's hand on the assistant's hand which was on the snake; gradually touching the snake itself while the assistant held the snake's head and tail. Further respones were graduated in difficulty until eventually the patients could handle the snake freely, pick it up, let it crawl over their bodies, and so forth.

Tests were given all groups which involved approaching and touching a live snake. A larger percentage of the group getting the modeling treatment with guided participation was able to do this than those getting systematic desensitization or symbolic modeling. However, both these latter groups showed improvement and were significantly better than a third group which experienced no treatment (and did not improve).

Thus, modeling procedures can be employed to get rid of phobic responses. Although direct applied evidence is lacking, modeling might also be used to disinhibit severely inhibited responses; there is some experimental evidence that the technique can function this way. For example, inhibited sexual responses might be disinhibited by seeing them being reinforced when emitted by a model.

Aversive counterconditioning. This technique is operationally inseparable from punishment, Type I, though it is differentiated theoretically. A stimulus may lead to the emission of a deviant response that is powerfully reinforcing; aversive counterconditioning changes the valence of the stimulus so that it does not lead to the deviant response, and instead leads to a response incompatible with the deviant response. Usually this incompatible response is very aversive.[3]

The use of drug-induced nausea in alcoholics is an example. Since thinking of drinking is reinforced by getting a drink and its subsequent effects (getting high; avoiding or escaping

delirium tremens), the modifier may start with the patient thinking about having a drink. The patient is given a nausea-inducing drug. When the drug begins to take effect the patient is instructed to engage in responses preliminary to actual drinking, such as smelling liquor, thinking about having a drink, pouring one, and actually taking a small amount to taste (but not swallow). After a number of these sessions, these behaviors, which previously led to imbibing, will lead to nausea without the drug. Similar revulsion is reported when shock is paired with these same behaviors. The most successful outcomes of this type of therapy are those in which the patient is re-treated at irregular intervals subsequent to the main treatment.

This treatment would seem applicable in any cases where the deviant behavior is strongly reinforcing, such as in drug use or in deviant sexual behavior. Its effect is to suppress the frequency of the deviant behaviors by making stimuli which prior to treatment led to the deviant behavior, lead to incompatible responses. However, the effect is one of response suppression, and the temporal relations of thinking about or emitting deviant behavior leading to aversive feelings (nausea, etc.) are the defining operations and effects of punishment, Type I.

[3]This technique is a theoretical twin of systematic desensitization. In systematic desensitization, the juxtaposition of a stimulus that usually leads to a phobic response (e.g., fear) with a response incompatible with this phobic response (e.g., relaxation) is thought to reciprocally inhibit the fear response and allow the stimulus to lead only to the adaptive response. In aversive counterconditioning, a stimulus again leads to an unwanted response (e.g., an erection), and if paired with an incompatible response (e.g., nausea), reciprocally inhibits the unwanted response and thereafter the stimulus will produce only the incompatible response.

Illustration

D. L. Rosenhan, On being sane in insane places. *Science*, 1973, **179**, 250-258.

We have suggested that various stigma occur as a consequence of medically labelling behavior. One of these is psychiatric hospitalization. But is the psychiatric hospital the best place to modify the behaviors of deviantly behaving individuals? Further, do the individuals who are hospitalized deserve hospitalization? That is, are they so different that the hospital is necessary for them? One would guess that hospital staffs and administrations would answer these questions resoundingly in the affirmative. Of course, they would say, individuals in mental hsopitals are different from those who don't belong there, and they can be detected from the normal individual. Concurrently, while complaining about inadequate budgets, they may also suggest that the mental institution is the best location for a mentally ill person because that institution is geared to provide the individual the treatment he needs. Our illustration for this unit suggests that these last statements may be wrong.

An ingenious natural experiment was conducted by Rosenhan (1973). He took eight volunteers with a wide variety of backgrounds who agreed to become pseudo-patients in a number of public and private mental hospitals across the country. These pseudo-patients called their respective hospitals for appointments and when the appointment was kept, complained of hearing voices. The voices, the pseudo-patients explained, were often unintelligible, but sometimes sounded like they said, "empty," "hollow," or "thud." These pseudo-patients evinced this symptom only. They falsified their names, vocations, and employment but made no further changes in any of their personal statistics. That is, when asked, they reported family and other histories exactly as they had occurred. Rosenhan reports

that none of these histories was pathological in any way; rather, the pseudo-patients' lives contained a normal assortment of good and bad times. After the initial interview, the pseudo-patients never mentioned the voices again and emitted no symptomatic behavior, although most reported initial nervousness at the possibility of being accused of carrying out a charade. The pseudo-patient participated fully in hospital life — reporting for meals, following staff instructions, and the like. As there is little to do in a hospital, each of the pseudo-patients talked with staff and patients and made notes of his observations.

All eight pseudo-patients were admitted to the hospitals; all but one were diagnosed schizophrenic. All were discharged, 7 to 52 days later, with the diagnosis: *schizophrenia, in remission. In remission* is psychiatric terminology meaning the symptoms of the illness are no longer present, but the underlying pathology probably is, even though it cannot be detected; that is, the patient is temporarily well. Rosenhan thus concluded that our institutions for the mentally ill are incapable of differentiating the sane from the insane. *Not one pseudo-patient was exposed for what he was.* Interestingly, while staff failed to discriminate the sane from the insane, the patients themselves frequently approached a pseudo-patient with the claim that the latter was not really a patient, but was more likely a journalist or a professor.

A hospital, not involved in the first study, did not believe Rosenhan's findings and agreed to participate in a second study. The hospital stated that their procedures could detect the sane. So their staff was told that one or more pseudo-patients would seek entrance in the following 3 months. The staff was asked to rate admissions during the 3-month period on a 10-point scale with a 1 or 2 reflecting high confidence that the rated patient was, in fact, a pseudo-patient. Rosenhan sent no pseudo-patients to the hospital during this time. However, 41 patients were rated by at least one staff member as being pseudo-patients. Twenty-three were so rated by at least one psychiatrist and 19 by one psychiatrist and one staff member. Therefore, Rosenhan was able to conclude that psychiatric hospitals are also incapable of differentiating the insane from the sane.

Some additional evidence that Rosenhan presents is equally disturbing. It concerns the experience of psychiatric hospitalization. As we asked earlier: Is the hospital, as currently structured and operated, a good place to treat deviant behavior? One measure of the possible efficacy of psychiatric treatment might be the amount of patient-staff contact in a hospital and the relevance of that contact to the patients' difficulties. In most hospitals, patients and staff quarters are physically separated. Even on the wards this is the case. Staff often have a small, island-like area that is glassed, allowing them to work inside and, if they desire, to observe the patients on the ward. Rosenhan's pseudo-patients measured the time hospital staff spent outside this area. Note that this could be time during which no patient interactions were occurring — the staff could be watching television or doing something else — but it was the only measure that the pseudo-patients found reliable in four public hospitals because staff-patient contacts were few.

Attendants spent only 11.3 percent of their time outside this area. Daytime nurses left this area 11.5 times each shift; afternoon and evening nurses 9.4 times a shift. Physicians left this area just 6.7 times per day. Rosenhan's pseudo-patients counted the number of times out of the cage for nurses because their forays were so brief that it "... proved impossible to obtain a percent mingling time for (them) ... " (p. 254).

These data suggest that staff-patient contact in the psychiatric hospital is minimal. The data further imply an inverted state of affairs: Assuming that patients would profit most from interacting with physicians (the most highly trained staff member), these were individuals with whom patients had the least frequent contact. The patients had the most frequent contact with the least-trained individuals — the attendants. A strong inference from these data must be that psychiatric hospitals, as currently designed and operated, do not provide adequate treatment for those with behavior problems.

Rosenhan presents still further data buttressing this inference. Common sense (and the model for behavior change presented in this book) would lead us to believe that behavior change procedures might be begun and carried out in the two-person situation. That is, when staff and patient interact should be the best time for initiating and accomplishing behavior change, because it is at that time that staff can socially influence the patient's behavior. Staff could, for instance, smile and discuss a subject of interest to the patient if the patient produced an appropriate greeting ("Good morning, Dr. X; How are you today?"). Or staff could instruct the patient to emit certain behaviors, after which social reinforcement could occur. To determine whether these opportunities were being appropriately used by staff members, Rosenhan's pseudo-patients initiated staff contacts by asking sensible questions such as, "Excuse me, could you tell me when I might be eligible for a grounds pass?" Remember that these were the pseudo-patients who were asking and that the questions were in no way "bizarre or disruptive."

In the four hospitals in which these data were gathered, Rosenhan reports the overwhelming response was " . . . either a brief response to the question, offered while they were 'on the move' and with head averted, *or no response at all*" (p. 255; italics ours). Rosenhan reports the following as a common encounter (p.255):

Pseudo-patient: "Pardon me, Dr. X., could you tell me when I am eligible for grounds privileges?"
Physician: "Good morning, Dave. How are you today?" (Moves off without waiting for a response.)

In fact, in the psychiatric hospitals in the sample, just 4 percent of the psychiatrists stopped to talk and 0.5 percent of the nurses or attendants did so. Comparatively, Rosenhan had a young lady question faculty members at Stanford University with regard to information about the school. Faculty were chosen if they seemed to be purposefully headed toward an engagement. Fully 100 percent stopped to talk, an interesting statistic considering anecdotal feelings that the university environment and its faculty are too busy to attend to the student. Similar data were obtained in a University Medical Center, unless the young lady asked for a psychiatrist. In the latter case cooperation in her endeavor was lower. In these latter two environments, the individuals questioned made considerable eye contact with the questioner. The opposite was true in the psychiatric hospital.

Rosenhan's article is a powerful indictment of the medical model and that model's overwhelming emphasis on diagnosis and hospitalization. Given the model of the present book, Rosenhan's results are particularly disturbing. They lead to the belief that the psychiatric hospital may be perpetuating and encouraging the very problems it is supposed to be ameliorating.

Exam

1. Define the following terms and give an applied example:

   a. positive reinforcement
   b. negative reinforcement
   c. extinction
   d. punishment, Type I
   e. punishment, Type II
   f. systematic desensitization
   g. modeling
   h. aversive counterconditioning
   i. self-managment
   j. response cost

2. What is the doctrine of symptom substitution?

3. What are the components of an operation that lead us to call it behavior modification; for what reasons would we *not* call a procedure behavior modification?

4. Suggest reasons why people who exhibit non-normal behaviors are called "ill" or "sick."

5. What is the psychological model and how does it differ from the medical model in regard to viewing and treating human behavior?

6. In Osborne's study, what can you conclude with regard to the effect of the dependencies he employed? That is, what happened to the behavior of the six girls? What was the result of the follow-up? The reversal? What technique was applied in this case?

7. Who did Rosenhan find had most contact with patients in a psychiatric hospital? Who had least?

8. Consider what behavior modification technique a psychiatrist is (unconsciously) using when he ignores a normal greeting by a patient. Given other evidence of this same technique, what is a possible outcome of its continued use in this fashion? Relate your answer to the possible de-personalizing effects this technique may have on a patient's behavior.

9. What do Rosenhan's data suggest about diagnosis within the medical model? Why may he have obtained the results he did? Relate this answer to the medical model.

10. In what two ways does the conduct of systematic desensitization differ from other behavior modification procedures?

11. Summarize Freeman and Kendrick's case study. How did the kitten approximate a graduated hierarchy of fear stimuli?

12. Discuss three problems associated with psycho-diagnostic testing.

13. What are the logical consequences of assuming the doctrine of the medical model?

14. In the psychological model what three observations lead to the conclusion that behavior is deviant?

15. A mother brings her child to the clinic. The presenting complaint is that the child is dog-phobic. Design two different programs that would rid the child of this phobia.

16. What "catch" conditions did Rosenhan use to demonstrate that the "sane" are not detectably different from the "insane"? That the setting for interpersonal actions determined the nature of the interaction?

References

Allen, K. E., Hart, B. M., Buell, J. S., Harris, F. R., & Wolf, M. M. Effects of social reinforcement on isolate behavior of a nursery school child. *Child Development*, 1964, 35, 511-518.

Ayllon, T., & Michael, J.   The psychiatric nurse as a behavioral engineer. *Journal of the Experimental Analysis of Behavior*, 1959, 2, 323-334.

Baer, D. M., Wolf, M. M., & Risley, T. R.   Some current dimensions of applied behavior analysis, *Journal of Applied Behavior Analysis*, 1968, 1, 91-97.

Bandura, A., Blanchard, E. B., & Ritter, B.   The relative efficacy of desensitization and modeling approaches for inducing behavioral, affective, and attitudinal changes. Unpublished manuscript, Stanford University, 1968. As cited in: A. Bandura, *Principles of behavior modification*. New York: Holt, Rinehart & Winston, 1969.

Bandura, A., Grusec, J. E., & Menlove, F. L.   Vicarious extinction of avoidance behavior. *Journal of Personality and Social Psychology*, 1967, 5, 16-23.

Burchard, J. D., & Barrera, F.   An analysis of timeout and response cost in a programmed environment. *Journal of Applied Behavior Analysis*, 1972, 5, 271-282.

Freeman, H. L., & Kendrick, D. C.   A case of cat phobia. *British Medical Journal*, 1960, 2, 497-502.

Fuller, P. R.   Operant conditioning of a vegetative human organism. *American Journal of Psychology*, 1949, 62, 587-590.

Harris, F. R., Johnston, M. K., Kelley, C. S., & Wolf, M. M.   Effects of positive social reinforcement on regressed crawling of a nursery school child. *Journal of Educational Psychology*, 1964, 55, 35-41.

Johnston, M. K., Kelley, C. S., Harris, F. R., & Wolf, M. M.   An application of reinforcement principles to development of motor skills in a young child. *Child Development*, 1966, 37, 379-387.

Lovaas, O. I., Schaeffer, B., & Simmons, J. Q.   Experimental studies in childhood schizophrenia: Building social behavior in autistic children by use of electric shock. *Journal of Experimental Research in Personality*, 1965, 1, 99-109.

Lovaas, O. I., & Simmons, J. Q.   Manipulation of self-destruction in three retarded children. *Journal of Applied Behavior Analysis*, 1969, 2, 143-157.

Osborne, J. G.   Free-time as a reinforcer in the management of classroom behavior. *Journal of Applied Behavior Analysis*, 1969, 2, 113-118.

Paul, G. L.   Behavior modification research: Design and tactics. In C. M. Franks (Ed.), *Behavior therapy: Appraisal and status*. New York: McGraw-Hill, 1969. Pp. 29-62.

Risley, T. R.   The effects and side effects of punishing the autistic behaviors of a deviant child. *Journal of Applied Behavior Analysis*, 1968, 1, 21-34.

Rosenhan, D. L.   On being sane in insane places. *Science*, 1973, 179, 250-258.

The Rehabilitation Research Foundation.   *An experimental and demonstration manpower project for training and placement of youthful inmates of Draper Correctional Center at Elmore, Alabama: Final Report*, Elmore, Alabama, P.O. Box 1107, 1970.

Williams, C. D.   The elimination of tantrum behavior by extinction procedures. *Journal of Abnormal and Social Psychology*, 1959, 59, 269.

Wolf, M. M., Risley, T. R., & Mees, H.   Application of operant conditioning procedures to the behavior problems of an autistic child. *Behavior Research and Therapy*, 1964, 1, 305-312.

How to Do Behavior Modification

22

In the present unit we will present a general approach to behavior modification, discuss some problems often encountered in carrying out behavior modification, and offer a method for modifying your own behavior.

Carrying Out Behavior Modification

A major difference between behavior modification and other approaches to behavior change is the degree to which behavior modification constitutes a systematic approach. We can tell you how to do behavior modification successfully, whereas other therapeutic approaches have considerable difficulty specifying what a therapist should do and when he should do it. Some of these approaches (e.g., psychotherapy) suggest that it is impossible to carry out the therapy's procedures unless the individual has thoroughly experienced the technique as a patient himself.

The following steps can be used to set up and carry out a behavior modification.

Steps in Behavior Modification

Define behavioral goals. How will the subject of the modification be behaving when you are finished? Within this framework the response must be operationally defined and objectively stated. Saying that Johnny will do his mathematics homework at the end of the program is insufficient. What *is* mathematics homework? When will he do it? Where will he do it? How much will he do? How long will he do it? What exactly will he do? This is called pinpointing the response. In terms of the above example, we may specify:

a) **The response (what he does:** single-digit addition, subtraction problems.[1]

b) How much will he do: 10 problems of each, correctly.

c) For how long: 6 weeks.

d) Where: at his desk, in his room.

e) When: from 4:00 to 6:00 P.M. or from 7:00 to 9:00 P.M. Sunday through Thursdays, inclusive.

When these criteria are adequately specified, success, or lack thereof, can be accurately judged. Without criteria it is often difficult to tell what has happened, and, if the criteria are not made explicit, they can shift without the participants' awareness. Johnny, for example, insists he has fulfilled his contract; Dad on the other hand, says he has not.

It is important that the goals of a project be realistic. Novice behavior modifiers often err in demanding too big a change in the subject's repertoire at one time. Homework completion in mathematics for Johnny may be unrealistic if he does not have all the behaviors in his repertoire appropriate to adding and subtracting. Or completion of 100 percent of the mathematics homework may be unreasonable, if Johnny is currently doing no homework and the reinforcers his family can provide are weak.

Collect baseline data. The second step of any modification procedure is to ascertain the baseline rate or operant level of the response. This information tells the modifier what the current state of affairs is with respect to the response to be modified. Perhaps everyone was wrong: Johnny is actually doing his mathematics homework 50 to 75 percent of the time. Baseline data will indicate the frequency of the behavior prior to commencing the project and provide a perspective from which to view later changes in the behavior. Without a baseline, the modifier cannot easily determine the success of his project. If possible, enough baseline data should be gathered so that the modifier is convinced it is a stable, valid sample of the target's behavior. In the case of our homework example, this may be as few as 8 to 10 school nights where homework is issued or longer if there are large fluctuations in the data.

Choose a behavior modification technique. Is the behavior to be increased or decreased in frequency?

---

[1] In specifying the response, choose an action, not a non-action; the latter are difficult to count. Consider the child whose room is perennially messy. Counting instances of "not-picking up toys," you can see, would be very difficult. The child may say he is going to pick them up. When do you count an instance of "not-picking up?" It would be much simpler to tabulate and reinforce instances of "picking up" in the child's room. Lindsley (1968) has labelled the test of the adequacy of response definition, the "dead man test." If a dead man can perform the response — not picking up his room — the specification of the response is probably inadequate.

Are the conditions under which a behavior occurs to be narrowed or broadened? Answers to these questions will direct the modifier to one of the techniques presented in Unit 21. Continuing with the above example, Dad decides Johnny's homework completion needs to be increased, and he chooses positive reinforcement as a procedure. In addition he decides a written contract between Johnny and him will make the terms of the procedure well known to them. He considers that if Johnny reaches the program's goal, he can select a strong reinforcer of his choice (for middle-class purposes, let's say, a bicycle). Dad constructs a chart on which gold stars will be placed for every occasion that Johnny reaches the criterion (10 problems of each) under the above conditions. Dad, if he is smart, might also consider pairing his own praise with the delivery of stars, as well. In any case, he has chosen a positive reinforcement procedure by determining how he will relate the behavior to be changed and the consequences for it. That is, he has specified the dependency involved.

Conduct the modification. The individuals who control the dependencies now bring the consequences to bear on the behavior. The dependencies may be explained to Johnny at this point, especially if he is a lad amenable to verbal control; however, while this is often facilitory, it is not absolutely necessary to the success of a project.

Chart the results. Charting is an extremely important part of any behavior modification. It is necessary to provide feedback to the modifier regarding how his procedures are succeeding. Often, changes may be so slight that the modifier may be unaware they have occurred. Charting may alleviate this uncertainty and provide feedback to the modifier. Charting may also be informative to the subject as well, by making him aware that his behavior is changing, and this can facilitate progress. A record allows accurate communication of the results upon completion of the modification.

Verify the procedure. If the modifier is interested in proving that it is his program that accounts for the subject's behavior change, he must engage in further manipulation. This can take the form of a *reversal probe*, in which the dependency is withdrawn for a period and then re-instituted. This often resolves to instituting an extinction period after a reinforcement period and, subsequently, returning to a reinforcement period. In our example, Johnny's Dad may no longer place stars on Johnny's chart for homework responses. If Johnny's rate of responses decreases during this period and increases when stars are again dependent on those responses occurring, Dad has proved that the stars are maintaining Johnny's homework and are therefore functioning as positive reinforcers. This is called an **ABA REVERSAL DESIGN**, where A = the reinforcement condition and B = the extinction condition. B is the "catch" condition on which proof rests. Other types of B conditions are possible. For example, the behavior modifier could choose, during

B conditions, to reinforce a behavior incompatible with the behavior he is reinforcing during A conditions. Recall that Osborne (Unit 21) reinforced the deaf girls for standing in one condition of his study. This was incompatible with being seated, and being seated decreased while standing increased. As the major response was being seated, this demonstrated that the free-time dependency could control either being seated or standing.

Using this kind of reversal, Dad might pay Johnny for something incompatible with homework for a while. If doing homework decreases, he could conclude that the stars were truly reinforcers. Of course, Dad would not want to stay in this condition very long and should ensure that he returns to the A conditions; that is, doing homework produces stars.

A second method would be to take other responses Johnny makes and show that they are similarly affected by the stars. This is known as the **MULTIPLE BASELINE TECHNIQUE.** If, in addition to not doing his homework, we suspect that Johnny does not make his bed, we can record the frequency of bed making while we are reinforcing homework completion, to determine the operant level of bed making. After determining this operant level, we may consequate bed making with stars, too. If bed making does not change while we are reinforcing homework completion (i.e., it is not part of the same response class as homework), but does increase when we consequate its occurrence with stars, we can assume the stars are reinforcers. Our case is strengthened by each new response we treat the same way and thereby produce the same results.

Common Problems in Behavior Modification

Lack of control. Control problems result when unknown or uncontrollable reinforcers exist apart from the modifier's reinforcers. Situations in which the behaviors are to be modified should be observed for these reinforcers prior to commencing the modification; this can be accomplished during measurement of the operant level. If the reinforcers cannot be removed, and are strong, the individual might be removed from them; that is, the modification could be carried out in another environment.

Another source of poor control involves specifying stimuli as consequences for behavior which turn out to be either nonfunctional or to have an incorrect function with respect to the modification desired. Let us say that in the example above, Dad decides to consequate Johnny's homework completion by allowing him to watch television. Let us also assume that Johnny, who is outdoors every chance he gets, hardly ever watches television. Chances are that television will be nonfunctional with respect to homework completion; it may even function to punish, that is, reduce, the frequency of doing homework. Careful scrutiny of anyone's behavior should provide us with clues regarding that person's reinforcers. In the above example, Johnny has effectively told us what is reinforcing to him — to be outside. In that case, making going outside dependent upon homework completion may be successful. One rule of thumb is to see what the individual does when he is free to do whatever he wants (cf., Unit 12). He will likely do something he finds reinforcing. A second rule of thumb is to ask the individual what he would like to do. Often, children and adults are able to specify reinforcing events for themselves. Initial client interviews can be used to accomplish this function ("If you could do whatever you want to this Saturday, what would you do?").

Yet another source of diminishing control involves presenting the individual with too much reinforcement of a given kind. If the individual begins to tire of the reinforcer, he will emit less and less of the behavior to be strengthened. This is the problem of *satiation*. Circumventing satiation is tricky, but not impossible. After initial strengthening of the behavior, satiation can be delayed by scheduling reinforcers intermittently. At successive stages of the program this intermittency can be increased. Dad may give Johnny a star for homework assignments completed each night for the first 3 weeks; thereafter, stars may be dependent on completion of an average of three assignments each night for 3 weeks, and then only after an average of five completions each night for 6 weeks. In each case the modifier must make sure the behavior is strong enough to occur with less reinforcement for it. Some skill is involved. Sudden decreases in output may necessitate decreasing the reinforcement intermittency until the behavior again becomes stable.[2]

[2]Contracts must be fair. Dad should refrain from changing the contract after it is firm. Instead, this type of program change might be included in the initial contract.

Another method of delaying satiation is to employ either a wide variety of unconditioned reinforcers, conditioned reinforcers, or, best of all, a strong generalized reinforcer (money, points, tokens). The latter type of reinforcer, as we explained earlier (Unit 9), becomes largely independent of specific states of satiation.

Finally, control is weak if there are reinforcers available to a subject that are not under the control of the behavior modifier. For example, a teacher may attempt to withhold her social reinforcement for a child's deviant behavior within her class only to find that the behavior is maintained by the attention of the child's peers. A second problem of a similar nature exists where the behavior modifier can specify the consequences for a behavior but is not in a position of controlling the dependencies. In the latter case, the modification should be carried out by an individual in the subject's environment who has this control; for example, a wife for a husband whose problems occur in the home, or an employee's boss for a problem that occurs on the job. In the first classroom example, the problem of surreptitious reinforcement can be dealt with by including the other children in the modification procedure. Perhaps they could be reinforced for extinguishing the subject's deviant responding. A second solution would be to remove this other source of reinforcement by making a physical change; for example, the deviant child is removed from the class.

Generalization. The problem of generalization is formidable but it should be not unexpected. Briefly stated, it is the problem of changing behavior in one environment and having that behavior occur in another, somewhat different environment. A classic failure or two may illustrate: An individual is incarcerated in a federal hospital as a heroin addict; he undergoes withdrawal and remains in the hospital until the administration decides he can go back on the streets. Successful generalization would entail the survival of the repertoire he has acquired in the hospital back on the street. Frequently this doesn't occur. Generalization failure is also one problem of the prison system. In the laboratory we learned (Unit 15) that the amount of generalization depends on the similarity among the various stimuli to which the organism is exposed. Responding by a pigeon is more likely to a hue of 560 nanometers than 590 nanometers when it was formerly reinforced for responding to a hue of 550 nanometers. Generalizing from this laboratory finding to our hypothetical addict, we might assume that drug use for him would be least likely to occur in environments similiar to where he was treated, for instance, other hospitals. There is, however, considerable difference between the hospital and the street, and we should not expect generalization from one circumstance to the other. Behavior-modification research exemplifies this quite clearly (see Lovaas & Simmons, 1969, in Unit 19).

Fortunately, some answers are at hand regarding the generalization problem, but they are easier to write about than carry out. To begin with one could actually program generalization's occurrence in the modification. In the Lovaas and Simmons study, recall that the children were shocked in other rooms of the hospital and additional therapists administered the shock. This made the shock effective in a variety of settings by a variety of people. Thus, some rudimentary generalization programming has been successful.

A second way to produce generalization is to shift the subject to reinforcers for his new behavior that exist naturally in the environment. Thus, a program might start with artificial reinforcers, tokens, and be shifted to social reinforcement that occurs without programming in the subject's regular environment. Recall the Unit 15 application where teachers first reinforced a nursery school child for interacting with his peers. After he was primed and reinforced for interacting a number of times, the natural reinforcers were sufficient to maintain these interactions when the teachers stopped their reinforcement program.

Finally, and perhaps the most reasonable way to make a behavior modification endure, is to change the behavior in the actual environment in which it occurs. Thus, if addiction is highly likely in the ghetto, behavior-change programs might achieve the best results when accomplished in the ghetto environment. This latter idea doesn't solve the generalization problem, it just rather nicely avoids it.

Other Techniques of Behavior Modification

The techniques described in Unit 21 constitute the main devices of the behavior modifier. However, the field is growing rapidly and we expect that new techniques will evolve regularly as new principles of conditioning are discovered. An example of this is the response-deprivation hypothesis (Unit 12). Its significance has not yet been ascertained by behavior modifiers, but is potentially great. Its use appears not to be restricted to specific operants or specific situations and its cost may be minimal.

Both basic and applied research will continue to provide us with new, more parsimonious explanations of behavior which will improve the steps in our procedures. We can look for some new steps to be added, others to be deleted, and still others to be combined in new ways. The current interest in biofeedback — self-management of the autonomic system in controlling blood pressure, heart rate, and so forth — is an example of a new technological application. The prevailing controversy over the necessary and sufficient conditions for systematic desensitization may result in the deletion of non-necessary steps in that procedure. For example, it has already been shown that systematic desensitization procedures can be automated, suggesting that a "live" therapist is not necessary to the success of the procedures (Lang, 1969).

One way of elaborating behavior modification techniques is to combine several known procedures to produce a more effective technique. For example, punishment of a deviant behavior is never carried out without concomitant reinforcement of desirable behavior. Similarly, reinforcement is almost never used without simultaneously employing extinction to weaken other responses. Further, extinction can often be supplemented by occasional punishment of those responses being extinguished.

A good example of a combination of procedures to produce a more powerful technique has recently been documented by Azrin and his associates (Azrin, Sneed, & Foxx, 1974). They were able to cure childhood enuresis in a very short time. Prior to their system, treatment for enuresis was only moderately successful and required considerable time. The procedures systematically employed: 1) the traditional alarm apparatus which buzzed when the child wet the bed; 2) training of the child to inhibit urinations; 3) positive reinforcement for correct urination; 4) training in rapid awakening; 5) self-correction of accidents (requiring practice in walking from the bed to the toilet); and 6) mild punishment (verbal disapproval) for accidents. In addition, the program included corrective loops for failures to meet specified criteria. With the program, Azrin was able to toilet train children in 24 hours (Azrin & Foxx, 1974). Once trained, the children have stayed trained, a powerful technique, indeed.

A good exercise for yourself would be to compare behavior modification techniques to determine which most readily work together. Consider the fact that the combined techniques can be focused on a single behavior, (e.g., to lower the frequency of an undesirable behavior) or can be used simultaneously on different behaviors (e.g., to raise the frequency of desirable behaviors and lower the frequency of undesirable behaviors at the same time).

Application:
Project in Self-Management

If you wish to modify your own behavior, the first step is to make a record of the behavior. This can be accomplished with a response counter and daily logging of response totals on graph paper (Unit 2). Using the counter, you can measure food intake (in bites or mouthfuls) if you are interested in weight-loss or weight-gain, nosepicking, or any personal behavior. Sometimes simply counting the behavior will change its frequency. This may be because we evaluate the behavior when we count it (e.g., "Damn, that's my 20th cigarette today! I simply must slow down."). Chances are, though, that the behavior may not continue to change in a desired direction; if this is the case, program reinforcers for yourself that are dependent upon reaching certain goals on your graph. For example, in a weight-loss program, after cutting down to and maintaining a certain number of bites per day for a number of days, a new dress (in a smaller size) might help you continue to keep bites down. If the behavior to be counted is weak, frequent immediate reinforcement may be necessary. If a

behavior is strong, reinforcement of incompatible behavior needs to occur for each incompatible response.

Table 22-1 and Figure 22-1 are to be used for a self-management project of your choice. Follow the steps outlined at the beginning of this unit. First determine a behavior that you would like to increase or decrease in frequency. Pinpoint the response and specify the criteria for deciding when you have successfully changed. (Joan's procedures in Unit 2 for reducing swearing provide helpful hints.) Gather baseline data and record them in Table 22-1. If you run out of space in this table you may construct additional sheets yourself. At the same time, graph the baseline data in Figure 22-1. Label the ordinate with the response you are counting and the abscissa with the days of the project. Carry out the program tabulating and charting the data each day of the project. Have fun!

Exam

1. List and describe the steps necessary to engage in behavior modification. Illustrate each step with examples.

2. What are three common problems in behavior modification that restrict the modifier's control over the subject?

3. What is the generalization problem in behavior modification? State several ways that it may be alleviated.

4. Describe the self-management project you have chosen to carry out. List the potential difficulties and describe ways to circumvent them.

5. How does behavior modification differ from other techniques of behavior change with regard to carrying out the change itself? (Hint: Compare behavior modification with psychotherapy.)

6. What is the "dead-man test"? Why is it important to response specification?

7. How would you define "attention span"? Specify at least three responses and a criterion for each with which you could measure attention span. Would changing three responses convince anyone that you had changed attention span? Why or why not?

8. What is an ABA design? Give an example.

9. What is the multiple baseline procedure? Give an example.

10. What is the problem of satiation and how may it be circumvented?

11. Describe three ways in which behavior modification techniques are likely to evolve and give examples of each.

12. Summarize the findings in Figure 22-1. What problems did you encounter that you did not list in Question 4? What might you do differently next time?

References

Azrin, N. H., & Foxx, R. M. *Toilet training in less than a day.* New York: Simon & Schuster, 1974.

Azrin, N. H., Sneed, T. J., & Foxx, R. M. Dry-bed training: Rapid elimination of childhood enuresis. *Behavior Research and Therapy*, 1974, **12**, 147-156.

Lang, P. J. The mechanics of desensitization and the laboratory study of human fear. In C. M. Franks (Ed.), *Behavior therapy: Appraisal and status.* New York: McGraw-Hill, 1969. Pp. 160-191.

Lindsley, O. R. Procedures in common described by a common language. Paper presented at the University of Kansas Ninth Annual Institute for Research in Clinical Psychology, July, 1968. Cited by R. B. Stuart, Behavior modification techniques for the education technologist. In R. Ulrich, T. Stachnik, and J. Mabry (Eds.), *Control of human behavior*, Vol III. Glenview, Ill.: Scott, Foresman, 1974. Pp. 18-39.

Lovaas, O. I., & Simmons, J. Q. Manipulation of self-destruction in three retarded children. *Journal of Applied Behavior Analysis*, 1969, **2**, 143-157.

Table 22-1

A simple record sheet for a self-management project.

Days	Responses	Remarks

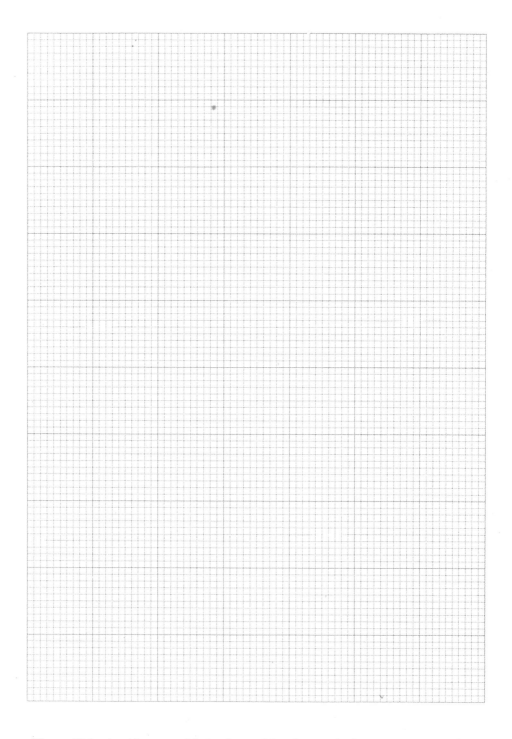

Figure 22-1   A self-managed behavior and its changes in frequency as a result of self-delivered consequences.

Social Behavior: Cooperation

23

The Definition of Cooperation

The term *cooperative* has been used in a variety of contexts: A behavior may be cooperative, a person may be cooperative, even a group or nation may be cooperative. As an area of study, cooperation has been treated as both an independent variable and a dependent variable. As an independent variable, cooperation might be manipulated by telling some experimental groups to concentrate on "working as a team," while in other groups, each individual would be told to work only for himself or herself. In such an experiment, the investigator might be interested in how well the individuals, who worked at the same time on a task, liked each other after completing the task. As a dependent variable, the degree of cooperation might be measured in an experiment in which two children are reinforced every time they share a toy. The increase in the number of occasions upon which they share would be taken as an increase in cooperation.

The term is also value laden; for example, for nations or groups to cooperate is said to be good and international competition is said to be bad. When a term is used in so many different ways, it is said to have surplus meaning, and its value as a scientific term is considerably reduced. In order to communicate effectively with other scientists, it is necessary to introduce another term or to redefine the original term so that its meaning is more precise. We will define **COOPERATION,** then, as the linked behavior of two or more individuals which produces reinforcement for those individuals. By linked, we mean that Person A's behavior is in some way related to Person B's reinforcement. For example, John comes over to Mary's house to help her move furniture because it frequently takes two people to move bulky chairs and sofas around. With John's help, Mary redesigns her rooms, which is reinforcing to her. To take another example of linked behavior that will be familiar to teachers, consider grading a stack of papers. Mary has 100 papers to grade and another teacher, John, takes half of her stack to do himself. The job of grading the 100 papers will be completed much faster with John's help. It is necessary to add that the linkage must be reciprocal. If John can do something which reinforces Mary and she cannot or does not reciprocate, then John's behavior is not called cooperative but **ALTRUISTIC.**

The Distinction between Cooperation and Altruism

Altruism does not mean that a person behaves without reinforcement, as is sometimes implied, but rather that he or she receives no visible reinforcer from the person he or she is reinforcing. For example, John might have ministered to Mary while she was in the hospital. If John does not know Mary very well, and if he also ministers to other patients, it is likely that some individual would call John's actions altruistic, especially when they observe John helping the more truculent patients. That is, a casual observer watching John might say to himself, "Look at that guy helping those patients day-in and day-out and no one bothering

to thank him! All they do is to complain." This observer might wonder what benefit John receives from this interaction and would be at a loss in attempting to account for John's helping behavior. It is under conditions like these that the observer resorts to terms like *altruistic, saint,* or *martyr.* The observer is forgetting that there are many sources of reinforcement available for John's behavior and that they need not come from the beneficiaries of John's actions. For example, John may belong to a religious community which places great value on charity. (The community dispenses frequent and large amounts of **reinforcement for helping others.**) In **any case, cooperation requires that the** participants in the interaction all receive reinforcement and that each person's behavior is linked to the reinforcers that all receive, while altruism refers to a reinforcement relation that is uni-directional (A reinforces B; B does not reinforce A). However, as suggested above, if A persists in behavior which reinforces B and B does not reciprocate, we can look outside the interaction between A and B for agents which reinforce A. Now, let's look at some types of cooperative dependencies.

The And Dependency

In the **AND** dependency, person A must engage in some behavior *and* person B must also do some specified behavior. Simplified and put in the form of a diagram, the *And* dependency could be specified like this:

$$A_{FR\ 10} + B_{FR\ 10} \longrightarrow S^{R+}{}_{A,B}$$

This diagram would be read: When A makes 10 responses and B makes 10 responses, then and only then, both receive reinforcement. An example of this type of dependency in the real world would be two workmen confronted with a heavy desk to move. Neither of them by himself can move the desk, but if each lifts, simultaneously, the desk can be moved with ease.

Azrin and Lindsley (1956) studied the development of cooperation in children using an *And* dependency. Each child had a panel with three holes in it. The children's task was to place a stylus into one of the three holes simultaneously. When the stylus of each child was placed in the same hole of their respective panels — for example, both in the middle hole — a piece of candy was delivered into a cup that each child could reach. A wire screen separated the children from each other and kept them from operating each other's panel.

The experiment lasted an hour and during the first phase, each cooperative response was reinforced. Next, cooperative behavior was extinguished. Reconditioning of cooperation followed. All the teams of children learned to cooperate and they did so without requiring special instructions. Most of the pairs of children divided the candy they received equally within a few trials. In one team, however, one child took all the candy for several trials, but shortly thereafter, he began to share the candy with his partner. (Can you construct an account of what happened in this team that eventually lead to cooperation?) The main conclusion of this study was that cooperative responding was susceptible to reinforcement in much the same way as individual responding. The authors also suggested that cooperation could be maintained without delivering a reinforcing stimulus to each member of a team each time.

There is a problem with the reasoning in this last conclusion, however. These children had a history of sharing and so the single piece of candy occasioned no problems; the children simply took turns. But there were no experimenter-controlled dependencies which required the children to share, so it was possible that one child would continue to take all the candy, at least for a while. If this happened, cooperative behavior might not develop. The child who was receiving no candy for responding might simply stop responding.

The Backscratch Dependency

Suppose that you have complete control over a reinforcer for me and, similarly, that I completely control your reinforcers. Such a relation might be called a **BACKSCRATCH** dependency and might be diagrammed like this:

$$A_{FR10} \longrightarrow S^{R+}{}_B$$
$$B_{FR10} \longrightarrow S^{R+}{}_A$$

This diagram reads: When A makes 10 responses, B receives a reinforcer; when B makes 10 responses, A receives a reinforcer. Will an enduring pattern of exchange develop with this dependency? This question has been examined by Boren (1966) with animals and by several investigators with humans (Powers & Powers, 1971; Sidowski, Wyckoff, & Tabory, 1956; Sidowski, 1957). Let's look at Boren's study first.

Illustration

J. J. Boren, An experimental social relation between two monkeys. *Journal of the Experimental Analysis of Behavior*, 1966, 9, 691-700.

Boren first trained monkeys to press a lever for banana pellets. Then each subject was trained to wait for a variable period of time for its food (delay-of-reinforcement training). When the two monkeys were placed together, one monkey would be required to work while the other would have to wait for the pellet its partner would deliver. In the delay-of-reinforcement condition, each animal was taught to press the lever when a white light was on and then wait up to 30 seconds for its banana pellet in the presence of a red light. When both monkeys had learned this task well, their two cages were placed together and a **BACKSCRATCH** dependency was put into effect. Now, when "Al" made 32 responses in the presence of the white light, its partner, "Si," received a banana pellet in the presence of a red light. As soon as Al completed its fixed-ratio requirement, its white light changed to red and this monkey waited for its pellet which was provided by Si's responding (Alternation Condition). The two monkeys could see and touch each other but could not operate each other's levers. The fact that the subjects could see and hear each other was important. As Boren later found, when one monkey was removed from the situation or when a door was placed between the two, their performance deteriorated. This suggests that an important source of stimuli for each animal's behavior was social.

There were several manipulations that were made after this preliminary training. In the alternation condition with the stimulus lights telling each monkey when to work and when to eat, each worked at a high rate and provided its partner with a steady supply of food. With the lights turned off so that each monkey could respond at any time (Free-Responding Condition), their behavior changed dramatically. Within a few sessions their rate decreased almost to zero. Even when Boren extended their sessions to an entire day, the number of pellets each was providing was very low and not enough to maintain the animals in good health. At this point, Boren intervened and returned the subjects to the alternation condition. Their rates then returned to a level where each was supplying the other with most of their daily food ration. **Plot the data in Table 23-1 which lists the rates of responding for both monkeys under the alternation and free-responding conditions. Use a different colored pencil or pen for each subject and separate the experimental conditions so that changes in rates under each of the conditions can be easily seen.**

A Backscratch Experiment with Retarded Children

Powers and Powers (1971) placed retarded children on a backscratch FR 15 schedule and found results similar to those that Boren found with monkeys. Response rates were consistent and high when the children worked on individual FR 15 schedules. The rates, once the backscratch dependency was in effect, fell very quickly, and in one team, one child (Bingo) did no work

Table 23-1

Rates of responding (responses/minute) for two monkeys (Si and Al) responding on a backscratch dependency. In the alternation condition, different colored lights "told" the animals when to respond and when not to respond. In the free-responding situation, the stimulus lights were removed and the monkeys could respond at any time. Data estimated from Boren, J. J. An experimental social relation between two monkeys. *Journal of the Experimental Analysis of Behavior*, 1966, 9, 691-700.

Alternation (red & white lights)			Free Responding (no stimuli)			Free Responding (run 24 hours a day)			Alternation		
Session	Si	Al	Session	Si	Al	Session	Si	Al	Session	Si	Al
80	142	108	84	83	64	102	1	10	112	2	2
81	139	99	85	62	37	103	0	9	113	20	8
82	118	106	86	80	5	104	6	2	114	82	68
83	105	95	87	64	10	105	2	6	115	64	40
			88	5	42	106	1	1	116	72	28
			89	7	19	107	1	1	117	75	26
			90	10	20	108	1	1	118	86	42
			91	23	48	109	2	2	119	96	24
			92	12	45	110	2	1	120	70	64
			93	3	60	111	2	1			
			94	4	70						
			95	2	58						
			96	9	50						
			97	0	75						
			98	0	68						
			99	1	48						
			100	1	49						
			101	0	21						

during an entire session. During the second session on the backscratch schedule. Bingo received several tokens while merely standing in front of his response panel. When his partner slowed down and momentarily stopped Bingo's tokens, Bingo demanded another token by pointing to his token tray and by verbally asking for another token. Bingo soon learned that he could request tokens from his partner and he did little work for the remaining sessions until the dependencies were changed. In both of the retarded teams studied, communication (verbal requests and hand signals) affected the number of tokens each of the team members received and, in this respect, these findings differ from those of Boren, who did not find that the monkeys attempted to influence each other. It is not clear how much control over cooperative responding was exerted by the communication that developed in the retarded children's teams.

Why Cooperative Behavior Breaks Down in the Free-Responding Backscratch Dependency

After reading about Boren's monkeys and the retarded children, you might wonder what events caused cooperative behavior to break down. In both experiments, the deterioration started when one of the participants received a reinforcer when he was not working. The delivery of a reinforcer reinforced behavior other than lever pressing and controlled behaviors associated with the food pellet or the token — that is, eating in the case of the monkeys, and picking up the token, depositing it, and eating candy in the case of the children. These consummatory responses interfered with responding, and frequently the organism who was eating received another pellet (or candy) before he could make a response. This continued the consummatory chain and reinforced the organism for whatever behavior occurred prior to the receipt of the reinforcer. So the first step in the deterioration is that one participant receives reinforcement for not working.

Second, the organism that was not receiving reinforcement and was still responding was on extinction. The rate of responding increased for a short time (one of the initial effects of extinction), which increased the number of reinforcers the partner received for "loafing." Eventually, of course, the overworked member of the pair ceased to respond. At this stage, both of the participants were not working, but for different reasons: One, because he was handsomely paid for *not* working; and the other, because he received no payment for all the work he did.

To cement the collapse of cooperative behavior even further, the subject who had not made any responses while he was receiving reinforcers would sometimes start responding when his reinforcers stopped. This, of course, reinforced the previous hard worker for not working and subjected the "loafer" to extinction for his work. This final social dependency insured that neither of the subjects would respond in this situation in the future.

The Minimal Social Situation

In both of the studies described so far, the subjects responded in each others' presence so that the social nature of the situation was salient for each individual. Suppose the subjects were not aware of each other's existence; would cooperation develop in a backscratch situation? Sidowski and his colleagues placed college students in what they termed a "minimal social situation" and found that pairs of subjects would learn to reinforce each other consistently. Each subject was placed in a room by himself and given instructions that he was to try and earn as many points as he could by pressing either one of the two buttons on a response panel. Unknown to the subject, his response panel was connected to an identical panel in another room, where another subject was given the same instructions. When Subject A pressed his red button, his partner received a point. When A pressed his black button, his partner received a shock. The same dependencies were in effect for Subject B. On any trial[1] there

[1]In the first experiment conducted with the minimal social situation, a free-operant procedure was employed. Later research has generally adopted a restricted trial procedure, so the account in the text is based on the restricted trial procedure.

Figure 23-1   Rates of responding for 2 monkeys on a backscratch dependency.
Alternation condition: Lights controlled responding and not responding. Free
responding: Subjects could respond or not at any time.

*

were four possible outcomes: point-point $(+, +)$; point-shock $(+, -)$; shock-point $(-, +)$; and shock-shock $(-, -)$. If we assume the general rule that a reinforced response will be repeated and a punished response will not, then no matter how the pair initially responds, they will eventually give each other points, and this is what Sidowski found. Let's work through one of the four possible combinations following the general rule: "win-stay; lose-change."

Table 23-2 shows a sequence of three plays in the minimal social situation. In the first play, A gives B a point and B gives A a shock. A switches to his other response (shock button) and B stays with the button he has just pressed (shock button), so both receive a shock on the second trial and switch to the other response (point button) for the third trial.

Note that the conditions in this minimal social situation differ in an important way from the two previous experiments. In the minimal social situation, shocks as well as points were used. Sidowski et al. (1956) found that a group of subjects who experienced strong shock as well as earned points locked into a stable cooperative exchange, while a group experiencing weak shock did not. In a second experiment, Sidowski (1957) found that the combination of reinforcement and punishment was more effective than either shock alone or points alone in leading to a cooperative exchange. If the studies with the monkeys and the children had incorporated a punishment lever in the free-responding situation, a cooperative exchange might have developed and been maintained. Sidowski's experiments demonstrate that it is not necessary for the subjects in a social interaction to communicate in order for them to cooperate. The consequences of their interaction, per se, are sufficient to lead them into a mutually reinforcing pattern of responding. It is no doubt true,

Table 23-2

Hypothetical sequence of plays in the "minimal social situation" where each subject can reinforce or punish his partner.

Trial	Subject A	Subject B	Results
1	Plays + Receives −	Plays − Receives +	B was reinforced, so he repeats. A was punished, so he changes.
2	Plays − Receives −	Plays − Receives −	Both A and B were punished so they both change.
3	Plays + Receives +	Plays + Receives +	Both A and B were reinforced so they stay and game reaches stable exchange of positive reinforcers.

however, that communication can greatly facilitate the development of cooperation.

The Or Dependency

All of you have at one time or another been involved in some group endeavor, such as a car wash to raise money for a dance or some other activity. The dependency in this situation is called an **OR** dependency and may be diagrammed in the following way:

$$A_{RX} + B_{RX} = 100\ R \longrightarrow S^{R+}_{A,\ B}$$

The diagram is read: When 100 responses have been made by either A or B or both, then both receive reinforcement.

In the example of the car wash, the more cars that are washed, the more money the group earns. Notice that this dependency does not specify any behavior for an individual. It does not say, for instance, that Joe must wash seven cars to fulfill his obligation. Such a dependency is called an *Or* dependency because no one person must do so much work. A given amount of work (a group quota) produces a reinforcer for all members of the group or organization. Under these conditions, it is possible for most of the work to be done by a few individuals and, if this happens, there is usually some resentment among those who did more work than others. There are other problems with dependencies which do not specify any behavior for an individual, and we can look at one series of experiments which studied an *Or* dependency intensively.

Glaser and Klaus (1966) examined the performance of two- and three-member teams which were arranged in *And* and *Or* structures. Two of the team members were called monitors and their task was to watch a stimulus panel and to report, by pressing a lever, the kind of stimulus presented. A third team member was called the operator, and he received the reports from the monitors and then indicated whether they were correct or not. When the *team* made a correct response, a buzzer sounded and points were recorded on a large wall counter that all members could see. Team members could see each other but could not talk to, or otherwise communicate with, each other.

Subjects were first trained on the monitoring task as individuals until they reached a stable level of correct responding. Then each monitor was given training with the operator as a two-man team until a predetermined level of proficiency was reached. After this training, three-person teams were formed with each team consisting of two monitors and the operator with whom each had worked. It is important to note that the team members did not receive individual feedback about their performance while they operated in a team. Thus, a correct team response gave Collective Reinforcement and an incorrect team response produced Collective Extinction.

In order to make the results of this study understandable, the rationale for adding a third member to a team needs some discussion. Suppose that the monitoring task were an important one, such as observing a radar screen for the possibility of enemy planes or missiles. A commonsense approach would suggest that we add another monitor to increase the overall level of the team's proficiency. That is, if Monitor A has a

50 percent chance of being correct and Monitor B also has a 50 percent chance, then the chance of the team making a correct response should be higher with two monitors than with one, and it is. With the percentages we have used, the chance that at least one of the monitors would be correct would be 75 percent — a substantial gain over the two-person team.[2]

Following an initial increase in the proficiency of the three-person teams, four of the six teams lost accuracy with continued training contrary to commonsense expectations. In two teams, the three-person team finished performing at levels lower than either of the individual monitors when they were working only with their operator in a two-person team. Why did this happen?

With the addition of the third member, a condition was created in which a monitor could be reinforced for an incorrect response. Suppose on a given trial that Monitor A is correct, Monitor B is incorrect, and that the operator is correct. The team will receive reinforcement. For Monitor A and the operator this event could be called appropriate reinforcement. For Monitor B, though, the reinforcement is inappropriate. He receives reinforcement for the wrong response, which will tend to increase the number of wrong

responses he makes. If a monitor's proficiency begins to drop, the overall team proficiency will also tend to decrease. Since either monitor is exposed to these dependencies, it is possible that both monitors' proficiency will decrease. In fact, for 8 of the 12 monitors, the ratio of inappropriate to appropriate reinforcement did increase over the course of the experiment, indicating that they were receiving an increasing percentage of reinforcement for making the wrong response. Under the conditions used in this experiment, these results go against the logical idea that adding redundant members to a team will improve team performance. As in the other experiments reported so far, any time that a social structure permits reinforcement for inappropriate behavior, performance of the individuals will deteriorate and, unless there are other dependencies operating, the social unit (group or team) will be in danger of collapsing.

Maximizing Cooperative Behavior

After reading about the types of dependencies that can occur in cooperative situations and some of the problems that arise with each of these dependencies, you might ask how we can generate a cooperative relation that will last. From the material presented in this unit, two general rules emerge:

1) *Specify the response requirements for each member of the social unit.* This may be done by specifying the amount of work to be done for each individual or the kind of work done; for example, Person A will wash 10 cars or Person A will wash all the car windows while Person B empties the car ashtrays, and

[2]With a single individual, there are two possible outcomes; he can be correct or incorrect on a given trial. Thus, the probability of a correct response is 1/2 or 0.50. There are four possible outcomes with two monitors; John and Sam can both be correct; both can be incorrect; John can be correct and Sam incorrect; and Sam can be correct and John incorrect. Three of these four possibilities contain *at least* one correct response. Therefore, the probability of a correct response in a two-monitor team is 3/4 or 0.75.

so on. If an individual does not do what is specified, it is obvious to all members of the social unit (including the individual himself), and appropriate consequation can be administered.

2.) *Provide individual consequation for each member of the social unit.* In social arrangements where the behavior of the members is linked and the reinforcement is a team or unit product, reinforcement and nonreinforcement may be nonspecific. An individual football player's actions may have been outstanding even though his team lost. If the team's outcome (a loss, which is not reinforcing) is the only consequence he receives, his appropriate behavior may weaken. To prevent the weakening of his appropriate behavior, he should be reinforced for his play. On the other side of the coin, when the team wins, a player who plays poorly should be punished for his play.

Application

J. N. Hingtgen, B. J. Sanders, & M. K. DeMeyer, Shaping cooperative responses in early childhood schizophrenics. In L. P. Ullmann and L. Krasner (Eds.), *Case studies in behavior modification.* New York: Holt, Rinehart and Winston, 1965. p. 130-138.

Children diagnosed as schizophrenics do not interact with their peers and, hence, miss the opportunity to learn and be reinforced by others of their age group. These authors designed a program in which schizophrenic children had to cooperate in order to receive reinforcement. Since four of the six children had no speech and none of them were controlled by instructions, the experimenters had to shape the final cooperative behavior in stages.

To begin with, each subject was placed in the experimental room and trained to press a lever on an FR 15 schedule of reinforcement. For every FR 15 completed, the child was given a coin. The child could then deposit the coin in a vending machine for food. After two members of a pair reached a stable rate of lever pressing, the two were placed in the experimental room together and cooperative behavior was shaped in four stages: 1) During this stage, the two children were free to operate the coin lever at any time. When Subject A operated the coin lever, a red light lit the response panel, and when B operated the lever, the light was green. 2) In the next stage, Child A could operate the lever only when the red light was on, while B could operate it only while the green light was on. The experimenter alternated the red and green lights so that the children were responding in turn. 3) In the next step, another response panel was placed in the room and Child A had to press this new lever when it was red in order to turn on his red light over the old response panel. When the red light was lit over the old panel, he could obtain a coin by making 15 responses as in the second stage. 4) In the final stage, when A pressed the new lever, B's light came on over the old response panel. The same dependency held for B.

The final complex series of behaviors looked like this: Child A would go over to one side of the room and respond on the new panel when his stimulus light was lit. A's response would turn on the stimulus light for B, and this child could then go over to the old panel, make 15 responses, receive a coin, deposit it, and collect a goody. The light on the new panel would change, and Child B would then return to the new panel and make a response so that A could work and eat.

The final cooperative response was shaped in an average of 23 sessions. Although the rates of responding decreased when the subjects went from the third to the final cooperative stage, they continued to respond frequently enough so that each child received from 4 reinforcers (lowest cooperative rate) to about 13 reinforcers (highest cooperative rate) during the 25-minute session.

In addition to the establishment of cooperative behavior, the authors noted that in each team, the children attempted to communicate with or otherwise influence their partners. In one pair, during the condition in which children were free to respond in any order, one of the children was responding at a very low rate on the coin lever. Mary could not receive her coin until her partner finished so she started to pull the slow responder back to the lever whenever he paused. On one occasion, after a long pause in his rate, she slapped him and his rate increased. This girl continued to slap her partner whenever he started to dawdle during the emission of his fixed-ratio responding. After one of these slaps, however, the boy began to cry and refused to respond. After a while, Mary went over to him, hugged him, and led him back to the lever. His rate on the lever increased and, thereafter, she used both slaps and hugs to increase his rate.

The point to remember about the development of this social interaction is that the person who controls the reinforcement in an interaction will be the one who receives communications and attempts at influence. Autistic or schizophrenic children in institutions will initiate contacts with adults but not with other children. In these settings, it is the adults who have all the reinforcers. This experiment illustrates the fact that when his peers control access to a reinforcer, the child will learn to direct communications to them. When each member of a pair controls some reinforcement for the other, communication and influence will be reciprocal and the possibility of a stable social bond will be created.

Exam

1. Define the following terms:
   a. cooperation
   b. altruism
   c. *And* dependency
   d. *Backscratch* dependency
   e. minimal social situation
   f. *Or* dependency
   g. collective reinforcement
   h. collective extinction
2. Use an example not in the text which illustrates the difference between cooperation and altruism.

3. Give an example of each of the three cooperative dependencies. Use examples not presented in the text.

4. Why did cooperative behavior break down in the free-responding phase of Boren's study?

5. Describe the changes in the rate of responding under the first free-responding condition in Boren's experiment (Figure 23-1). What would you say the reinforcement schedule was for Si during sessions 92 to 101? What was Al's schedule during the same time?

6. What happened during the second free-responding condition in Figure 23-1? What were their respective schedules now?

7. What is the minimal social situation? What did the results of Sidowski's experiments demonstrate?

8. A plant manager suggests setting up a factory-wide quota system for increasing the productivity of his factory. Bonuses in the form of extra money will be given to every employee for every month the quota is exceeded. Can you suggest two problems that this manager might have with such a system?

9. Describe the dependencies used by Hingtgen et al. in establishing cooperation in schizophrenic children. How do you account for the fact that communication developed between the children of a pair?

10. What is one plausible explanation for why communication does not develop between schizophrenic children in an institution?

11. A teacher has two children in her class who neither share nor interact with each other or other children. Design a program in which cooperative behavior is strengthened in these two children. Explain why you do what you do for each part of your program.

References

Azrin, N. H., & Lindsley, O. R.   The reinforcement of cooperation in children. *Journal of Abnormal and Social Psychology*, 1956, 52, 100-102.

Boren, J. J.   An experimental social relation between two monkeys. *Journal of the Experimental Analysis of Behavior*, 1966, 9, 691-700.

Glaser, R., & Klaus, D. J.   A reinforcement analysis of group performance. *Psychological Monographs*, 1966, 80 (Whole No. 13).

Hingtgen, J. N., Sanders, B. J., & DeMyer, M. K.   Shaping cooperative responses in early childhood schizophrenics. In L. P. Ullmann & L. Krasner (Eds.), *Case studies in behavior modification*. New York: Holt, Rinehart and Winston, 1965. Pp. 130-138.

Powers, R. B., & Powers, E.   Responding of retarded children on a backscratch schedule of reinforcement. *Psychological Aspects of Disability*, 1971, 18, 27-34.

Sidowski, J. B.   Reward and punishment in a minimal social situation. *Journal of Experimental Psychology*, 1957, 54, 318-326.

Sidowski, J. B., Wyckoff, L. B., & Tabory, L.   The influence of reinforcement and punishment in a minimal social situation. *Journal of Abnormal and Social Psychology*, 1956, 52, 115-119.

Child Development

24

Large sections of introductory psychology textbooks are often devoted to developmental psychology. However, from the point of view of a functional analysis of behavior, a much smaller section can suffice. Usually under this heading, "heredity versus environment" issues are discussed, and maturation is given serious consideration as a "cause" of behavior. In this unit we point out the futility of the heredity-environment issue, the correlational nature of maturational variables as they relate to behavior, and, most important, how a functional approach conceives development.

A Functional Definition of Development

Throughout this book we have dealt with what we consider the proper business of a science of psychology, functional relations between stimuli and responses, or more commonly, environment-behavior relations. These relations between stimuli and responses have been those of consequation, elicitation, discrimination, or a combination thereof.

The formation of new functional relations. We define development in two ways: the formation of new functional relations between stimuli and responses, and progressive changes in these relations (Bijou & Baer, 1961). In the first case, any example where a neutral stimulus becomes functional with respect to a response is an example of development. When a baby begins to suck (CR) at the *sight* (CS) of the bottle or breast as a function of repeated pairings of this stimulus with an unconditional stimulus for sucking (e.g., nipple in the mouth), a new S-R relation has been formed, and some development has taken place. Making a neutral stimulus (NS) a conditional eliciting stimulus (CS) through pairing it with an already functional eliciting stimulus (i.e., performing respondent conditioning) results in the formation of a new functional relation between environment and behavior. The conditional sucking example given in Figure 24-1 illustrates this. Note that the arrows between S and R indicate the presence of the relation. Much emotional development can be considered in the same fashion, that is, as the development of stimulus-response relations in which the stimulus has an *elicitation* function.

If a neonate reliably learns to turn his head (an operant) in one direction rather than another when an auditory signal (S^D) is presented, and turning in that direction is always followed by the presentation of milk (S^R+), a relation between the auditory stimulus and the head turn results (Figure 24-2). This is also evidence of development, because it is evidence of the formation of a new functional relation. In this example, the pairing of a neutral stimulus (auditory signal) with a response, and with the response's subsequent consequation, gives the stimulus a *discriminative* function. Evidence for the discrimination is a head turn reliably following the sound of the buzzer. Here again a formerly neutral stimulus is made functional by correlating it with responding and response consequences. This can be considered development, as a new stimulus-response relation is formed.

The development of discriminative relations such as the above are the ones most likely to be interpreted by parents and others as intelligent behavior. For example, a child might begin to verbalize names of objects in his environment. The training conditions for this discrimination are usually parents' reinforcing statements after correct naming and correctional statements (i.e., extinction, and a

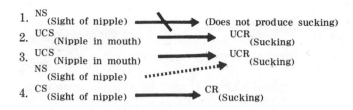

Figure 24-1

The formation of a new functional relation via respondent conditioning as evidence of one aspect of development in the neonate.

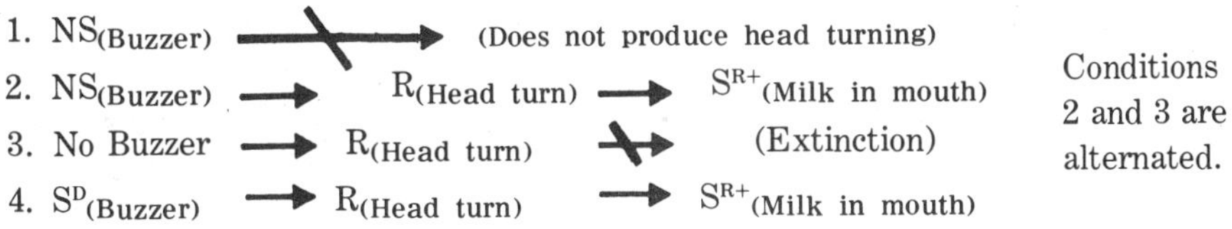

1. $NS_{(Buzzer)}$ ⟶̸ (Does not produce head turning)

2. $NS_{(Buzzer)}$ ⟶ $R_{(Head\ turn)}$ ⟶ $S^{R+}_{(Milk\ in\ mouth)}$

3. No Buzzer ⟶ $R_{(Head\ turn)}$ ⟶̸ (Extinction)

4. $S^D_{(Buzzer)}$ ⟶ $R_{(Head\ turn)}$ ⟶ $S^{R+}_{(Milk\ in\ mouth)}$

Conditions 2 and 3 are alternated.

Figure 24-2

The formation of a new functional relation: $S^D_{(Buzzer)}$ ⟶ $R_{(Head\ turn)}$ via differential reinforcement in the neonate as one aspect of development.

further S^D for correct responses) after incorrect naming. The stimuli — dogs, cats, brothers, sisters, parents, utensils, and so forth — initially are neutral with respect to verbal responses. However, verbal responses in the presence of these stimuli produce social reinforcers from happy parents. The conditions exist, then, for objects to become discriminative stimuli for naming responses. Thus, a large number of new relations are formed when the child begins to "develop" language. The child who has an extensive naming vocabulary is often considered more developmentally advanced than a comparison child of the same age who knows fewer names. (Further discussion of a functional analysis of verbal behavior will be presented in Unit 25.)

Giving a stimulus a conditioned reinforcing function by pairing it with unconditioned or other conditioned reinforcers may also be considered as development because a new relation results. A child may hold a blanket and carry it everywhere because the blanket has been paired with: 1) reinforcing tactual sensation; 2) sleep; 3) feeding; 4) temperature regulation;

and 5) being held by mother. Thus, the blanket may maintain a considerable number of responses which result in it being handled, and it thereby figures as the reinforcing stimulus in a large number of response-stimulus relations. Illustrative of this line of reasoning are common anecdotal reports of children crying until their blanket is given them (not a very desirable relation) and climbing anywhere to get it. The conceptual formation of this relation is diagrammed in Figure 24-3.

We have just dealt with the formation of functional relations due to the consequences of pairing stimuli with positive reinforcement. However, another entire class of relations would result from the pairing of neutral stimuli with aversive stimuli. If a child hits his head each time he tries to stand erect under a low structure like a table, behaviors which result in lower frequencies of head banging will result. The table will become a conditioned aversive stimulus for other behaviors which avoid unpleasant stimulation such as a head bang. In the present example, this other behavior might still be locomotor, but its form would now be crawling rather than upright walking.

1. $R_{\text{(Holding blanket)}} \longrightarrow S^{R+}_{\text{(Sleep)}}$
   $R_{\text{(Holding blanket)}} \longrightarrow S^{R+}_{\text{(Tactile sensations)}}$
   $R_{\text{(Holding blanket)}} \longrightarrow S^{R+}_{\text{(Being warm)}}$
   $R_{\text{(Holding blanket)}} \longrightarrow S^{R+}_{\text{(Feeding)}}$

These relations may not be dependent: e.g., holding blanket may occur when baby is being fed but does not truly *produce* feeding. The results are the same in either case, only the temporal sequencing is important.

2. $S^{D}_{\text{(Sees blanket)}} \longrightarrow R_{\text{(Holds blanket)}} \longrightarrow S^{R+}_{\text{(One of the above)}}$

3. $R_{\text{(Climb)}} \longrightarrow S^{r+}_{\text{(Sees blanket)}} \longrightarrow R_{\text{(Holds blanket)}} \longrightarrow S^{R+}_{\text{(One of the above)}}$

4. $R_{\text{(Whines)}} \longrightarrow S^{r+}_{\text{(Sees blanket)}} \longrightarrow R_{\text{(Holds blanket)}} \longrightarrow S^{R+}_{\text{(One of the above)}}$

Figure 24-3

Illustration of how a single stimulus, the blanket, may produce a number of reinforcers, and figure in the generation of new S-R or R-S relations.

Progressive changes in functional relations. So far, we have equated development with the resultant behavior changes (new relations specifically) that are due to conditioning procedures. Because this definition is synonymous with conditioning itself, not many developmental psychologists would agree to it. This is largely because of the redundancy, but also because we have been talking about changes which can take place in a very brief span of time. Typically, the developmental psychologist is interested in changes in these relations over longer spans of time, indeed some over the entire life span of the human being. The reader can imagine that the difficulties of studying behavior over long periods of time are an increasing function of the length of time involved. The longer one wishes to study individuals the more difficult it is to do it. People move, they die prematurely, they disappear, they no longer wish to participate, and so on.

However, it is important to conceptualize the second part of our definition of development regardless of the difficulty of proof. This part simply has to do with changes in already existing relations that occur when those relations are further modified by conditioning techniques. In one case, a response may produce a stimulus and the stimulus does not lead to a subsequent response. Later in time, the initial response may lead to many subsequent responses via a stimulus-response chain. Thus, one progression is the change of a single S-R relation to a chain of S-R relations (i.e., S-R-S-R). For example, a baby may simply spit out any disagreeable food to escape the unpalatable taste. A toddler may spit out the food, grimace, and escape future encounters by telling his mother he doesn't like the food. The task of a developmental psychology is to explain the ways these changes take place. In Figure 24-4, a stimulus-response chain involving the response of getting the blanket is conceptualized. The initial relation involves a single stimulus and response. Upon further conditioning,

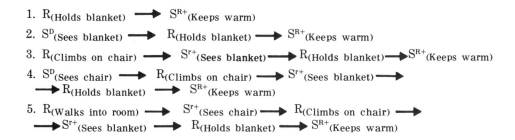

1. $R_{\text{(Holds blanket)}} \longrightarrow S^{R+}_{\text{(Keeps warm)}}$

2. $S^D_{\text{(Sees blanket)}} \longrightarrow R_{\text{(Holds blanket)}} \longrightarrow S^{R+}_{\text{(Keeps warm)}}$

3. $R_{\text{(Climbs on chair)}} \longrightarrow S^{r+}_{\text{(Sees blanket)}} \longrightarrow R_{\text{(Holds blanket)}} \longrightarrow S^{R+}_{\text{(Keeps warm)}}$

4. $S^D_{\text{(Sees chair)}} \longrightarrow R_{\text{(Climbs on chair)}} \longrightarrow S^{r+}_{\text{(Sees blanket)}} \longrightarrow$
   $\longrightarrow R_{\text{(Holds blanket)}} \longrightarrow S^{R+}_{\text{(Keeps warm)}}$

5. $R_{\text{(Walks into room)}} \longrightarrow S^{r+}_{\text{(Sees chair)}} \longrightarrow R_{\text{(Climbs on chair)}} \longrightarrow$
   $\longrightarrow S^{r+}_{\text{(Sees blanket)}} \longrightarrow R_{\text{(Holds blanket)}} \longrightarrow S^{R+}_{\text{(Keeps warm)}}$

Figure 24-4

Successive links in a complex S-R chain depicting the development of the chain *qua* development in the infant.

three functional relations are linked together. (Recall from Unit 9 that a stimulus in a chain has two functions — it is reinforcing for preceding responses and discriminative for subsequent responses.)

Another progression in functional relations occurs when a stimulus initially leads to a single response but at a later time leads to more than one response occurring concurrently. This is best seen when a new relation has been formed. At that time it may be the only one occurring. For instance, when a child begins to walk, that may be all he does while walking occurs. Later on, he may simultaneously talk, carry a toy, and do other things as well. This development — an increasing number of relations tied to the same stimulus — is graphically shown in Figure 24-5.

We should also note that because development is defined as progressive changes in the above relations, one type of change would be a decreasing of the length of these chains and a lowering of the number of responses occurring at one time. Conceivably, these changes could occur through extensive extinction or punishment conditions. That is, a chain could get shorter, or eventually cease to exist, and fewer responses might take place in the presence of a single stimulus rather than more. Extinction and punishment are often seen in impoverished or

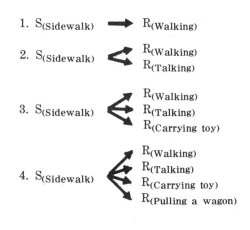

1. $S_{\text{(Sidewalk)}} \longrightarrow R_{\text{(Walking)}}$

2. $S_{\text{(Sidewalk)}} \Big\langle \begin{array}{l} R_{\text{(Walking)}} \\ R_{\text{(Talking)}} \end{array}$

3. $S_{\text{(Sidewalk)}} \Big\langle \begin{array}{l} R_{\text{(Walking)}} \\ R_{\text{(Talking)}} \\ R_{\text{(Carrying toy)}} \end{array}$

4. $S_{\text{(Sidewalk)}} \Big\langle \begin{array}{l} R_{\text{(Walking)}} \\ R_{\text{(Talking)}} \\ R_{\text{(Carrying toy)}} \\ R_{\text{(Pulling a wagon)}} \end{array}$

Figure 24-5

Development as an increase in the number of responses to the same stimulus performed simultaneously.

otherwise abnormal environments, and lengthy exposure to them can retard or slow development. Disease and crippling injuries can function similarly. A child who has a heart condition, and whose physical activities have to be restricted for several years, may not acquire some of the typical behaviors his peers do such as riding a bicycle or learning to swim. Acquiring these skills later in life may prove difficult, perhaps because reinforcement for them may be weak or nonexistent or because attempts may be punished.

A final kind of development is that known as skill. A functional approach considers the development of skill to be a combination of: 1) discrimination formation (Unit 14); 2) response differentiation; and 3) shaping. All three occur through reinforcement and extinction.

RESPONSE DIFFERENTIATION involves the narrowing of a specific response class by extinction of members of the class and the concurrent strengthening by reinforcement of other members of the class. A good experimental example of response differentiation is the illustration in Unit 6 by Herrick. Recall that he successively narrowed the zone in which a lever could be placed by a rat for reinforcement. Hitting a baseball with a bat provides a good human example. Consider first that the ball comes to the same location each time. Swings which miss the ball in this location are extinguished, while those which connect solidly are reinforced by a number of consequences (e.g., sound, feel, sight, teammates, etc.). Thus, swings which miss the ball should decrease in frequency while those which hit the ball increase. The class of responses narrows to those which hit the ball, and the topography of the response shifts to make this more likely. Note, however, that we considered the ball to be always in the same location relative to the batter. When the ball changes position, we consider this to be a new problem (i.e., a new stimulus). The bat may need to be swung higher, although much of the rest of the response topography will be the same. The problem in this latter case, and in each new location of the ball, is one of discrimination formation, that is, stimulus control. Each new position of the ball comes, through differential reinforcement, to control swings in its vicinity as a batter is repeatedly reinforced and extinguished for successful and unsuccessful swings, respectively. Although we have conceptualized them for you separately, response differentiation and discrimination formation take place concurrently.

There is a highly technical difference between response differentiation and shaping, both of which are accomplished through differential reinforcement. In response differentiation the operant to be strengthened is already in the repertoire of the subject (e.g., swings of the bat); however, the response class may have very wide boundaries. That is, almost any instance of the response is reinforced (cf., Herrick's experiment). Response differentiation narrows the boundaries of a response class, selectively strengthening reinforced operants within those narrowing boundaries. Shaping, on the other hand, involves shifts in the boundaries of the response class that do not necessarily include narrowing it. These shifts make new operants more likely, and only after the terminal responses are observed and strengthened are the response-class boundaries narrowed.

The difference between response differentiation and shaping can be illustrated in terms of the response-class called walking. Where walking doesn't occur in the young child, shaping is necessary to produce it. You can't tell a child to walk when he doesn't know how; that is, he doesn't have the response in his repertoire. Where walking does occur and differential reinforcement improves the way in which walking takes place, we can consider this response differentiation. Some components of the walking response class initially will be: 1) standing while holding onto a stationary object; 2) later, standing alone; and 3) still later, taking a step. In the final response class, standing while holding onto an object for support will not be reinforced. When we are shaping, our initial response class may include standing holding onto an object because this operant makes taking a step more likely. Response differentiation of walking may involve differential reinforcement for a smoother gait (e.g., less effort is involved and the subject may get where he's going more quickly). Where response differentiation takes place, all responses are already part of the final class; however, shifts will take place in their relative strengths.

These changes, which are traditional evidence of motor development, involve progressive changes in relations between behavior and environment. To take the simplest example: Parents will strongly reinforce a child when he initially can stand in an upright position, and parental reinforcement and standing may be functionally related. Later, parents no longer reinforce a child just for standing if he's already walking (or if they consider he should be walking). Thus, other stimuli in the environment must control standing at this later time if standing continues to occur (e.g., it's part of a chain preliminary to walking; it allows the child to see the goodies that are usually on tables, much to the chagrin of many mothers). There has been a change in the controlling events in this example demonstrating that skill development also involves a progressive change in functional relations between behavior and environment.

Maturation as Development?

It is not possible to prove that maturation "causes" behavior. Maturation refers to development of parts of the body both structurally and functionally, not the development of relations between behavior and environment. To prove that maturation causes behavior, we would have to manipulate the speed of maturation, but these procedures are not applicable to humans. Thus, we are stuck with a variable that can only be correlated with behavior, not functionally related to it. As an example, we can correlate the presence of walking and age (say 2 years) and find a high positive value. That is, at age 2 years, walking is likely to be present. This finding, however, tells us nothing about the variables that produce walking; thus, it has limited explanatory power.

The present approach considers conditions such as maturation to be boundary or limiting conditions, making it possible or impossible for behavior to occur. Thus, the infant will be unlikely to walk prior to the time when his bones and muscles are capable of supporting him. However, simply having this developed musculature is not sufficient for walking to occur, albeit necessary. A more extreme boundary condition is species membership. Walking would be precluded if we belonged to a species that did not develop legs. It is further necessary for there to be reinforcement for responses that approximate walking and, eventually, for walking itself, for this response to become strong. Maturation does not cause behavior, but is related to whether the behavior can or will occur. Within the present approach, causes of behavior are produced by antecedent and consequent stimuli.

The Heredity-Environment Issue

The question was historically asked, and is being asked again with renewed vigor: Which is a more important determiner of behavior, one's genes, or one's environment?

Answers obtained to this question at this time are unsatisfactory. It has finally been concluded that to ask a related question — Is a specific behavior due to heredity or environment? — is nonsense. Genes and environment cannot be separately conceptualized. Man and other animals cease to exist without genes, and every behavior that occurs, occurs in some environment. Thus, behavior cannot be conceived as occurring without the possibility of the environment acting on it, and the genes cannot be considered

to direct behavior independently of the environment as the latter is always present. A better conception is that both contribute to behavior. Our initial question — Which contributes most? — evolves from the resolution of this pseudoproblem.

Currently, there is considerable interest regarding this issue with respect to the complex of behaviors we describe as intelligent. Reputable psychologists have stated that approximately 80 percent of intelligence is genetically determined, with only 20 percent the result of possible environmental circumstances. The issue is a hot one as long as differences exist between the average (measured) intelligence of people of different ethnic groups, especially when the majority are the ones on the high end of the scores, and they are the ones who make up the tests![1]

There is at least one facet of the above that is anathema to the authors, regardless of the correctness of the above assumptions. If any behavior or group of behaviors is concluded to be not amenable to environmental manipulation, two things happen: 1) The behaviors fall outside the purview and expertise of psychology. That area is defined as the study of behavior and environmental relations; if no relations exist, psychology ceases to exist as we

[1]Note the huge problem here. Intelligence appears to be a culturally defined construct, evidence for which is performance on some intelligence test. Most cultures define intelligence in some manner but their definitions need not relate with one another. Further, there is no such thing as a "culture-fair" or "culture-free" intelligence test. It can be argued that simply using paper and pencil may bias the results of an intelligence test for or against members of a particular culture depending on their experiences with paper, pencils, and test-taking in general.

conceptualize it. If, for example, eugenics becomes popular, it will likely become the speciality of geneticists, although a change of roles of the psychologist to behavior geneticist has been made successfully by some researchers. 2) A defeatism sets in. This is very subtle. If the environment is responsible for behavior, then those who know how to manipulate the environment correctly assume some of the responsibility for the occurrence or nonoccurrence of behavior. Thus, if a teacher, cannot teach a child to read, it may be argued that the teacher and his/her techniques were inadequate, not the child himself. Another try at producing effective reading techniques might then be made. But, if the child is incapable — genetically — there is nothing the teacher or anyone else can presently do to change this state of affairs. If the latter is the case, no one need produce a new reading program for those with a genetically determined reading problem. However, rather than just being restricted to genetically determined cases, the expectation of failure usually generalizes to much broader classes of children. We may begin to believe we can change the circumstances of the mentally retarded, for example, very little. In fact, a not uncommon conclusion, in the literature of the 1950's, dealing with the retarded was that they were incapable of certain tasks. An investigator may have designed a task specially for the retarded on which a percentage of them still fail, new program or not. To describe this failure is good science; to conclude incapability from it is not. An equally good explanation is that the new program was inadequate. At least that conclusion may lead to further work.

The Relevance of Environment

We have presented one reason for not thinking that heredity alone accounts for behavior. A second equally good reason involves the design of the studies said to support the conclusion that heredity is more important than environment. Examples exist with respect to intelligence and the disposition of schizophrenia. Families in which schizophrenia has been diagnosed are more likely to contain relatives in earlier generations who were similarly diagnosed. Statistically, those with above-average I.Q.'s are more likely to produce offspring with above-average I.Q.'s. In all of these studies, the environment is assumed to play all possible roles, and thus not produce any specific effect. An equally good alternative conclusion is that the environment produces very specific effects. Here is an example: Identical twins are genetically identical. If they behave more similarly on I.Q. tests than fraternal twins — that is, regular siblings born on the same occasion — it is concluded a true genetic determiner has been isolated. To bias the conditions further away from the heredity position, only identical twins are examined who, through circumstances, have been raised apart from each other. These are compared with fraternals who have been raised together. *Assumption*: Environments in the same household will be more nearly alike for two fraternals, than environments in different households for two identicals. *Results*: On I.Q. tests, identicals reared apart have more nearly identical I.Q. scores than fraternals reared together. *Conclusion*: Regarding I.Q., heredity is a stronger determiner than

Table 24-1

Data demonstrating formation of a functional relation between infant vocalizing and adult social reinforcement. Data taken from Rheingold, H. R., Gewirtz, J. L., and Ross, H. W. Social conditioning of vocalizations in the infant. *Journal of Comparative and Physiological Psychology*, 1959, 52, 68-73.

Mean Vocalizations per 3-Minute Period

Day	Experiment 1	Experiment 2
1	13	15
2	14	14
3	19	18
4	25	25
5	18	16
6	17	14

well known that parents treat their subsequent offspring differently than the first. They may be more assured of their own capabilities now that they are experienced with children, and so forth. Thus, the greater difference in I.Q. of the fraternals may result from being treated differently within the same household.

The error being made is a common one, again having to do with our physical-functional dichotomization of stimuli in Units 3 and 13. The physical identity of a single home is equated with functional identity. We suggest this functional identity has been unmeasured and likely does not exist. The assumption is also made with respect to twins reared apart. Here, two physically different environments are assumed (again unmeasured) to be functionally different as well.

environment. *Fact*: No one has independently measured the degree of similarity or difference between environments in the reared-apart homes or the reared-together homes in these studies.

Several suppositions: 1) Suppose that regardless of the physical locale in which an individual was raised, the environment tended to treat him a certain way because of his physical attributes (color, height, weight, etc.); the environment may treat two identical individuals much more similarly than two nonidentical individuals. *Alternative conclusion*: Identical twins may grow up in functionally identical environments even though physically located apart. 2) Suppose the environment within a single home differed for the individuals therein; for example, it is

Illustration

H. L., Rheingold, J. L., Gewirtz, & H. W. Ross, Social conditioning of vocalizations in the infant. *Journal of Comparative and Physiological Psychology*, 1959, **52**, 68-73.

The following study illustrates the formation of functional relations involving an operant response (vocalization) and its consequences (social and physical contact with an adult human).

Rheingold and her colleagues chose 21 institutionalized infants whose median age was 3 months. Vocalization was defined by agreement between the experimenter and an observer; they ruled out respondent vocalizations such as coughs, grunts, and snorts.

Days 1 and 2, and 5 and 6 were baseline days. During these periods, the experimenter positioned herself

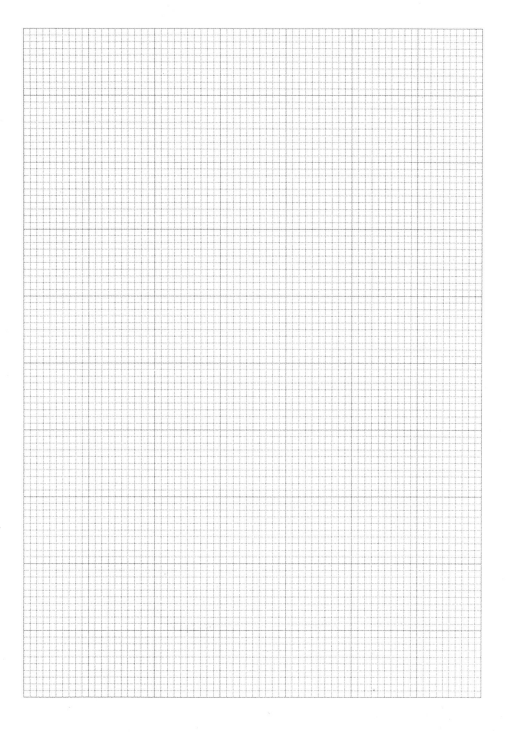

Figure 24-6 The formation of a functional relation between infant vocalization and adult social reinforcement.

over the subject's crib and looked at the subject with an expressionless face. The second observer counted any vocalizations.

Days 3 and 4 were conditioning days. On these days too, the experimenter looked at the subject, but if the subject vocalized, the experimenter smiled, said, "Tsk, tsk, tsk," and touched the infant's abdomen. For the most part, each response was reinforced, but as the rate of responding increased, occasionally only every second or third response was reinforced.

Each infant was seen for nine 3-minute periods each day. These periods were grouped in blocks of three and separated by rest periods of 2 minutes. The three blocks of periods were spread across each day.

Table 24-1 contains the data of this study. The subjects were run in two groups on different occasions as a way of assessing reliability. On these occasions, the experimenter and observer reversed roles. Hence, there are two data points for each day.

Construct a graph using the "Mean Number of Vocalizations Per 3-Minute Period" as the ordinate and "Days" as the abscissa. Separate the various conditions of the experiment by not joining the lines between days 2 and 3, and 4 and 5. Carefully inspect the graph to enable yourself to answer the exam questions at the end of this unit. Use one point code for the data of Experiment 1 and a different code for Experiment 2.

Exam

1. Define development from the point of view of a functional analysis of behavior.

2. Give an example of the development of a discriminated operant (one controlled by an S^D) and one example of the development of a conditional respondent in the neonate.

3. Produce an environmental explanation of retarded development based on the functional analysis presented in the book.

4. What is meant by the word *maturation*?

5. Why do we say maturation does not "cause" behavior?

6. Provide an environmental explanation for the finding that identical twins reared apart have I.Q. scores closer together than fraternal twins reared together.

7. What humanitarian reasons are there for adopting an environmental approach to the heredity-environment issue with regard to the developmentally retarded?

8. Look at Figure 24-6. Where do the greatest numbers of vocalizations occur? How would you characterize response rates during baseline and experimental periods relative to each other? During beginning and ending baselines?

9. Why can we conclude a functional relation has been formed in the Rheingold et al. experiment? (Hint: The answer has to do with the variation in response rate

with the experimental conditions.) What is the relation that has been formed in S-R terms?

10. What is the difference between response differentiation and shaping? Illustrate the differences between these two procedures with an example.

11. As traditionally stated, the heredity-environment issue is a pseudoproblem. Why?

References

Bijou, S. W., & Baer, D. M. *Child development: A systematic and empirical theory*. New York: Appleton-Century-Crofts, 1961.

Rheingold, H. R., Gewirtz, J. L., & Ross, H. W. Social conditioning of vocalizations in the infant. *Journal of Comparative and Physiological Psychology*, 1959, **52**, 68-73.

Verbal Behavior

25 One of the least explored frontiers in psychology has to be in language development. How and why does language occur? Prior to Darwin's theory of evolution, man was considered separate from other animals. Supposedly, man was divinely created. Darwin's theory suggested that man evolved naturally from a line of ancestors who were other primates. Many of those who believed man to be distinctly separate from other living animals took recourse in man's language. Seemingly of infinite complexity, it again appeared to provide a quantum distance between man and other animals. As we will discuss later in this unit, even this distance may be bridged, as it may be shown that animals can be taught to use rudimentary languages. But what of man himself? How does he acquire language? We will attempt to develop the position that language can be considered a result of conditioning processes. There are other schools of thought, and they will be discussed briefly. We will also present an abbreviated description of how language develops in the human infant and how it can be produced in nonhuman animals as well.

Two Opposing Philosophies of Language Development

There are two major schools of thought regarding language development in humans. The first, the behavioristic, underlies the thinking of this book; the second is a nativistic position. The behavioristic position, proposed by B. F. Skinner (1957), states that language, or more appropriately, verbal behavior, may be conceptualized as a learned phenomenon. Like any operant behavior, verbal behavior will be a function of its consequences, events which have been thoroughly explored in earlier units. The nativistic position, espoused by Noam Chomsky (1957), a linguist, considers that language is an innate phenomenon to which all humans are predisposed. The fact that the same language is not common to all humans is inconsequential to this position. The general rules common to all languages are maintained to be innate. It is the job of the linguist to discover these rules.

Also aligned with this approach is E. Lenneberg (1967). He has suggested that language is a biological phenomenon: Given the natural conditions for its development (e. g., normal physiology and anatomy), language occurs. The reader can see that this also is a nativistic position. Lenneberg has superbly documented boundary conditions which affect language development. A *boundary condition* provides a limit to the phenomenon under study. Species membership is such a condition. Because, as humans, we do not grow wings, conditioning flight (unpowered, unaided) is not possible. Operationally, a boundary condition in most conditioning studies is the *state* of the subject. Deprivation of food for a certain period of time may be considered a boundary condition for the study of relations where food is to be employed as a reinforcer. Lenneberg has described many boundary conditions which limit language development. Among them are defects in physiology and anatomy such as those which produce profound hearing losses. It is well known that a hearing impairment, which results in a severe restriction of stimulus input through the auditory system, without special habilitative procedures, is a sufficient condition to restrict language generation.

Chomsky's position is essentially rationalistic while Skinner's is empirical. Thus, Chomsky is in the business of building knowledge about language via deduction from a priori principles, theories which he, himself, has generated. This statement must be tempered by the fact that there are now a great many psychologists who are empirically testing Chomsky's theories. Skinner's proponents maintain basically an informal atheoretical position, and attempt to show how language is conditioned like any other response.

Language Development in the Human

The human infant begins life with the capacity to emit a great deal of sound, as most beleaguered new parents find out. The infant has the elements of a very broad response class already in his repertoire. Very recent evidence can be used to infer that language development may begin immediately after birth.

Condon and Sander (1974), using high-speed photography, have shown that newborn infants synchronize their movements with adult speech.[1] The

[1] This area is called the study of *micro-kinesics*. It involves correlating stimulus inputs to a human with the same individual's motor responses fractionated into small components by viewing individual frames of motion-picture film shot at

neonate's movements are more likely to begin and end with the change from one **PHONEME** to another in the adult's speech than during a phoneme itself. A phoneme is the smallest unit of speech that distinguishes one utterance from another. The word *come*, for example, can be divided into three phonemes, *kk*, $\curlywedge$, and *mm*. Condon and Sander, present a movement-pattern example for one 2-day-old child in conjunction with the sentence, "Come over and see who's over here" (p. 100). During the 0.07-second interval in which the voice says, the *kk* of come, the infant moves his head a little, extends his left elbow, rotates his right and left shoulders and right hip, and flexes his toes. During $\curlywedge$ and *mm*, which last for 0.10 second, the left elbow, right hip, and head movement continue, the left hip begins to rotate, and the toe movement ceases. Right and left shoulder movement continue but change form at the end of "come." A new pattern begins with "over," and yet other patterns with remaining words and phonemes of the utterance. There is no claim in this work that the infant produces the *same* movements repetitively to an adult speech input. Simply the infant is more likely to begin and end his movement with the beginnings and endings of phonemes in human speech, whatever the infants' movements are.

To insure that infant movements were not just randomly synchronized with speech, Condon and Sander employed a control condition. Another film of the same infant was taken to fit this same speech episode in length. The film was made during a period of infant

high speed (e.g., 30 frames/second). Movements taking place across fractions of seconds can be correlated with associated environmental events.

movement when there was no speech input. Then the previous speech episode was superimposed on the film and the synchrony searched for. Under this condition, where there was no speech input, similar synchrony in the infant's movement and adult speech did not exist. This synchronization of movement appears specific to the rhythmic pattern of the human voice, because the presentation of a nonhuman rhythmic stimulus (such as taps on a wood block) or isolated vowel sounds does not produce the synchrony.

Further evidence of the newborn's capacity for language comes from an analysis of the sounds he emits. Infants typically produce a complete range of phonemes in their babbling during the first year, that is, sounds common to all languages. In the beginning all sounds are not emitted with equal frequency, however. Vowels appear first, and their kinds increase up to about 30 months while consonants appear second. At about one year, the frequency of consonants catches up with and surpasses the frequency of vowel sounds. The first vowels to appear are those made in the front and middle of the mouth, followed by those made in the back; consonants formed in the back of the mouth appear first, and those made in the front appear last. This sequence appears very regular. The infant emits more and more kinds of sounds during the first year and then begins to restrict himself mainly to the sounds of his own language.

If language is a learned phenomenon, questions about its development should begin at this point. The Condon and Sander study suggests the possibility that the infant is "tuned" to other humans very early in his life. From their data, we cannot say unequivocally that this "tuning" is specific only to language stimuli, although that thought is certainly suggested. We might ask if there have been conditioning studies that have modified the early behavior of the infant. Is he conditionable? The answer is most definitely yes. Conditioning of several behaviors (e.g., sucking, head-turning) is possible within the first three days of life (Kaye, 1967; Lipsitt & Kaye, 1964; Siqueland & Lipsitt, 1966). A similar question can then be asked about prelanguage behaviors, such as vocalizing, and the answer is again affirmative. Recall from the illustration in the last unit that Rheingold and her colleagues were able to reinforce vocalizations socially in the 3-month-old infant (Rheingold, Gerwitz, & Ross, 1959). While everyone seems sure that prelanguage vocalizations must relate to later language responses, at this time it is not fully clear just how they do. Thus, it can be argued that while the young infant can be operantly conditioned to vocalize more frequently, how (or even *if*) this affects his language is unknown.

Language development in our exposition thus far has been confined to the development of sound (phonology). Development of language is also conceived in terms of **SYNTAX** and **SEMANTICS**. Syntactical development refers to the ordering of words in a language and their interrelations. It is well known that a child's first word usually appears around 1 year of age. Two-word utterances, the basic syntactical study unit, appear around 18 to 24 months. These appear to be systematic, containing one word in one position (the pivot) and a number of words in the other (open) position (*See boy*; *See Mommy*; *See dog*; or *Bird gone*; *Cat gone*; *Daddy gone*). The next expansion is to three-word utterances that have more complex form (e.g., pivot-open-pivot: *See dog gone*). Adult structures follow rapidly, but little is known of the nature of the transition from simple child grammars evidenced by two-and three-word utterances to those of the adult. However, adult grammar can be observed, and the emergence of adult syntactical forms in the child's language can be studied (e.g., use of the negative or interrogative) and used to infer development. First negatives appear when mean utterance length is 1.4 to 1.9 **MORPHEMES**, and these usually have the form of an appended *No* prefixing the utterance (e.g., *No play*; *No sleep*). A morpheme is the smallest unit utterance an individual can make that has meaning. This may be smaller than a word, though often it is a word. From this point, several additional stages may be charted in terms of mean utterance length. The development of the interrogative occurs at about the same time as the negative.

SEMANTIC development refers to the development of meaning in language, and has been little studied in children. The role of semantics is best illustrated in sentences that can have more than a single meaning, for example, "*The behaviorist and the psycholinguist are trying to understand*" (Catania, 1972, p. 10). We can consider at least two meanings of this sentence. One meaning connotes that these individuals are people who are *difficult* to comprehend; that is, it is a very trying business to understand them. Another meaning suggests that they are *working toward* understanding something. As the sentence stands, though, its specific meaning is ambiguous. These kinds of sentences can be used by the psycholinguist to see what variables produce one or the other meaning. In Chomsky's terms, the sentence has a *surface* structure (what it looks like) and a *deep* structure (its meaning). It is of semantic interest to the psycholinguist because it has more than one deep structure in the sense of the two meanings presented.

Semantic development has been studied by inserting nonsense words in sentences and then determining if children can pick the word the nonsense word is equivalent to. Werner and Kaplan (1952) inserted nonwords such as *corplum* in series of sentences successively presented (e.g., *A* corplum *may be long or short, thick or thin, strong or weak*; *A wet* corplum *will not burn*; and so forth). The child had to indicate after each sentence what he thought a *corplum* was and why it had the particular meaning he gave it. Werner and Kaplan employed 12 different nonsense words in all, each embedded in its own series of six sentences. Children improved with age on this task, but the results suggested that sementic development is anything but a simple process.

A Functional Analysis of Language Development

Differential reinforcement and the shaping of speech. Reinforcement aids us in conceptualizing language development in terms of conditioning principles. The young infant can be considered an organism ready to be acted upon by his environment. Most neonatal vocalizations are respondent in nature. That is, they are elicited by unconditional stimuli in the child's environment: Being made uncomfortable in

any of a number of ways leads to vigorous crying. This discomfort is usually reduced by an adult human ("Mother"), and we can see that the operations for negative reinforcement exist in Mother and baby's earliest interactions.[2] Mother also is an important source of unconditioned, positive reinforcement. She cuddles her offspring, feeds him, cleans him, makes him warm, talks to him, brings him in contact with novel stimuli, in fact, pairs herself with many reinforcers. The operations exist, therefore, for mother to become a powerful generalized reinforcer for her child's behavior. Mother's verbal behavior may function as reinforcement for her child's verbal behavior. Rheingold et al.'s findings support this reasoning.

[2]There are a number of responses of the human newborn that appear to be both respondent *and* operant. That is, they can be elicited regularly by antecedent stimuli where no history of conditioning exists, but their frequencies can be modified after their initial elicitation by the stimulus consequences the response produces. Sucking is one such response. It can be elicited by the insertion of nearly any object into a neonate's mouth, and can thereafter be reinforced by the delivery of milk. Head-turning and crying may also be responses of this sort. The procedures (i.e., the "catch" conditions) necessary to determine which type of conditioning has occurred with these responses are beyond the scope of this text.

Note that it seems adaptive in an evolutionary sense to have an organism constructed in this fashion. Being initially responsive in a reflexive manner insures that the organism will produce behavior that can be further affected by the environment after it occurs. If there were no way that operant behavior could be initially brought forth, operant conditioning could never take place. Of course, this analysis is speculative and is reinforcing to the writers primarily because it fits their point of view.

In all probability, parents differentially reinforce their infants for approximations to better and better speech. Initially, the infant receives attention for almost any sounds he makes. Thereafter, he receives attention only for cooing or emitting any pleasurable sounds; many infants also continue to receive parental attention when they cry. Slowly, parents reinforce babbled sounds that approximate words of the culture's language. While there is no direct evidence to support this analysis, the naturalistic data are congruent with it. The fact that an infant emits almost all the sounds of every language when he begins to babble makes it look like he is innately built to produce any language. The fact that sounds of his own language become relatively more frequent, while those of other languages tend to decrease are what one expects from the differential reinforcement of any response class.

At this same time, parents are also differentially reinforcing the infant for his understanding of their language. He is asked to come to his mother and when he does, she is especially pleased with him; when he doesn't come, she retrieves him, tells him to listen better, and perhaps is mildly punishing. Conditions exist, therefore, for the establishment of operant stimulus control of the infant's behavior, where the controlling stimuli are the verbal responses made by another person to the infant.[3] Concurrently, the infant

[3]The reader should consider the fact that the *responses* of one individual in a social interaction are *stimuli* to another individual in the same interaction. Further, an individual who is listening to himself talk (Skinner, 1957) is an individual whose responses are also functioning as stimuli to himself for further behavior he may emit.

learns that verbal responses of another are important consequences for his own behavior along with learning to produce that same verbal behavior.

To separate verbal behavior from other kinds of behavior, Skinner (1957) has defined it as behavior the reinforcement for which requires the mediation of other individuals. This definition stands without reference to the response's topography as long as the behavior is a function of socially mediated consequences. Thus, verbal behavior will include, among other responses, vocal behavior, writing, gesturing, and tapping a telegraph key. For the infant, however, primary shaping will include speech responses.

Echoic behavior. Quickly and justifiably the reader should argue that there is a great deal of time when the infant is by himself. No one is reinforcing him during these times for vocalizing. Why does he do so? There are at least two possible explanations using conditioning principles for the analysis. The most obvious and parsimonious is that of intermittent reinforcement. After a number of reinforcers for verbal behavior, the behavior should carry on without further continuous reinforcement. Occasional reinforcement after initial strengthening should continue verbal behavior's occurrence and perhaps even raise its rate. This accounts for the maintenance of verbal behavior in the absence of extrinsic reinforcement.

It is also possible that the infant reinforces himself. This self-reinforcement becomes obvious later in the speech of the toddler. As an example of self-reinforcement, one author (RBP), who is currently enjoying his second

(2-year-old) offspring, has noted that his son will often applaud himself or say, *"Good boy."* This utterance will occasionally occur when the child has been asked to do something, has complied, and has not received the same utterance from his parents. However, his parents have said, *"Good boy"* to him on many similar occasions in the past.

Yet a large problem remains. Given that much of the infant's time is spent where others are not reinforcing him for better speech, why does his speech become so rapidly adult-like? One explanation is that the infant shapes his own verbal behavior during times when he is alone. The analysis goes like this: The verbal behavior of those in the infant's environment is reinforcing to him because it has been associated with many unconditioned reinforcers. If he can produce this same verbal behavior, he can reinforce himself. Thus, functioning as both speaker and listener, he can shape some of his own verbal behavior. Further, the analysis implies that the more similar his verbal behavior is to what he has heard, the more reinforcing it is.

Mommy doesn't grunt or cry at her baby when she feeds him, even though babies grunt and cry a lot. However, mother may say "baby" in the infant's presence frequently. Thus, the word *baby* is frequently paired with mother's reinforcing attention to the infant, while grunting and crying are not. If the infant emits a sound approximating *baby*, this should be reinforcing, while if he emits a grunt it should not. It is reinforcing because it sounds similar to how his mother sounds. Sounds approximating those of the language associated with his parents should therefore increase in frequency, while sounds which are not similar should

decrease. This looks very much like the results of a shaping procedure, and the infant's speech development can be so conceptualized. We need not consider that the infant is consciously processing what he hears. Knowing, as we do, that reinforcement is automatic, any verbal response that is similar to those he has heard in the past should increase in frequency, regardless of whether the organism is aware of the dependency.

In fact this analysis accounts for the **ECHOIC**, a verbal response which resembles its stimulus. In the above account the stimulus would be the responses made by mother or the baby himself.

Generalized imitation. Is infant echoic behavior actually reinforcing? How can we demonstrate that similarity is reinforcing? The reasoning behind questions such as these has stimulated an entire area of research by conditioning psychologists. Baer and Sherman (1964) first demonstrated that similarity might function as a reinforcer for children's imitative behaviors. They reinforced children for imitating three responses emitted by a puppet. The puppet dispensed social reinforcers. It also emitted a fourth behavior, a bar press, to which it never referred and for which the children were never reinforced. Seven of the 11 children studied pressed their bar without reinforcement when the puppet pressed its bar, several of them even imitating the rates of responding produced by the puppet. When reinforcement was withdrawn for the reinforced imitations, responding on the unreinforced lever became less likely. Because responding on the lever which had never been directly reinforced changed along with the reinforced imitations, it was assumed that this unreinforced response was a member of the same response class as the reinforced responses (a class of imitative responses). Imitation must have generalized to this other response, hence the term, **GENERALIZED IMITATION**. This term refers to the occurrence of an unreinforced operant having the topographical properties of its evoking stimulus (i.e., the model's response). In this experiment the unreinforced imitative response happened not to be verbal; if it had been verbal, it would have been an echoic.

There followed demonstrations using echoics in the position of the response to be imitated, but not reinforced. One such study was done by Brigham and Sherman (1968). They reinforced normal preschool children for the imitation of English words. Sometimes, however, the experimenters modeled Russian words which were never reinforced. There were two basic conditions in the study: 1) The children were reinforced immediately with candies, tokens, and social praise for correct English imitations; and 2) the children were reinforced 5 seconds after an imitation of an English word or, in a second condition, for not imitating; in both cases, Russian words, which were interspersed among the English words, were *never* reinforced. The second condition was used as a control to decrease the frequency of English imitations in order to observe whether the correctness of Russian pronunciation decreased concomitantly.

The results for a single subject of Brigham and Sherman's experiment are presented in Table 25-1. Graph them in the usual manner using one point code for English words and one point code for Russian words. (There is only an English point for Session 1 because Brigham presented no Russian words during this session. Rather it was used to screen out children who would not imitate at all and therefore would not qualify for the experiment.) Note that you will use a single ordinate — Percent Correct Responding — but that it must be labelled twice because scoring was different for English words than it was for Russian words.

The child was scored correct on the English word if the experimenter understood the child's word as an imitation of the word he had presented. (This judgment had to occur immediately so that the subject could be reinforced immediately.) However, the Russian words were scored later for pronunciation of each syllable by two individuals who rated audio-tapes made during the sessions. Each Russian word was divided into letters and syllables; the former were counted one point if correctly pronounced, the latter were counted three points for each correctly pronounced. These points were totaled, divided by the number it was possible to achieve, and multiplied by 100 to produce a percent correct pronunciation score.

Carefully scrutinize your graph for: 1) trends in the data of each condition, and 2) changes across conditions. The results lend support to the hypothesis that matching (nonreinforced) verbal responses produces the conditioned reinforcer of "similarity," because when English verbal imitations are extrinsically reinforced, and become more and more correct, nonreinforced Russian imitations increase in correctness also. When reinforcement for English verbal imitations is delayed,

Table 25-1

Percent correct verbal imitative responses of a 4-year old preschool boy. Data taken from Brigham, T. A., & Sherman, J. A. An experimental analysis of verbal imitation in preschool children. *Journal of Applied Behavior Analysis*, 1968, 1, 151-158.

Session	English Words (Correct/Total Presented)		Russian Words (Degree of Correctness/ Total Presented)	
1	75			
2	80	English	72	Russian
3	100	Imitations	88	Never
4	80	Reinforced	82	Reinforced
5	100		96	
6	100		97	
7	100		87	Russian
8	78	Delayed	83	Never
9	50	Reinforcement	66	Reinforced
10	75		74	
11	80	English	100	Russian
12	85	Imitations	100	Never
13	88	Reinforced	100	Reinforced

English correctness decreases as does the correctness of nonreinforced Russian verbal imitations. Thus, the two kinds of responses appear to be a function of similar variables and are members of the same response class even though their topographies are different. Consider as an example the Russian word for book. It is pronounced *ka nēe ga*. Obviously this is vastly different in spoken topography from *buk*, yet the two words are members of the same functional response class.

Two other major hypotheses attempt to explain generalized imitation. In the first, it has been suggested that subjects simply fail to discriminate which imitations they are reinforced for and which imitations they are not reinforced for (Bandura, 1969). The second hypothesis states that there is no such thing as generalized imitation, rather that the children used in most studies as subjects are under the social control of the adults in the experiments. This hypothesis suggests that the response class truly being studied is that of instruction-following, and children who follow instructions without reinforcement are exhibiting generalized instruction-following (Martin, 1971). Current research is directly evaluating the relative merits of these positions.

A final hypothesis, and perhaps the most parsimonious one, has been suggested by Gewirtz (1971). This might be dubbed the *intermittent reinforcement hypothesis*, and was alluded to above. Once an operant is reinforced, it can thereafter occur without further reinforcement for a time (i.e., in extinction). Further, intermittent reinforcement of the operant can make it occur frequently when only a few instances of the many responses occurring are reinforced. Gewirtz suggests that children imitate in the absence of reinforcement because of this.

Gewirtz has also suggested that the imitation (modeling) paradigm can be considered the analogue of the laboratory matching-to-sample procedure (cf. Unit 13). In imitation, a response to be imitated is presented to the subject; in matching-to-sample, the subject is also presented a stimulus (the sample). In imitation, the subject chooses a response from his entire repertoire of responses which *matches* the response of the model; in matching-to-sample, the subject chooses one stimulus from a group of stimuli presented to him which matches the sample. Superficially, the two procedures appear analogous; however, in imitation the topographical representation of the response may be more important than in matching. As Bandura (1969) has suggested, it is one thing to be able to match (i.e., indicate) which of a group of musical pieces presented is a Wagnerian aria and still another, when presented the aria, to perform it. Conceptually, however, the two procedures are very similar and research will indicate where they differ.

The tact. One of the ways a child learns the meaning of language is to associate words with the stimuli the words represent. Skinner (1957) has suggested we use the word **TACT** to signify this. "A tact may be defined as a verbal operant in which a response of given form is evoked (or at least strengthened) by a particular object or event or property of an object or event" (pp. 81-82).

The tact, in its simplest form, is easy to understand. It is exemplified by naming or labelling responses and is conceptualized in the three-term dependencies diagrammed in Figure 25-2. In Skinner's analysis it is important to note that the tact represents a stimulus-controlled, verbal operant which is independent of deprivation conditions such as hunger, thirst, and so on. That is, the primary control of the tact lies in the environmental stimulus. (As you will see shortly, this is necessary to differentiate the tact from the mand.) In all the examples in the figure, a number of tacts equal to the number of stimulus aspects of the object or event is theoretically possible, and the third example shows this.

The tact is developed through differential reinforcement, and this development is diagrammatically explored in Figure 25-3. Given your experience with the development of stimulus control (cf. Unit 14), you should have a good idea about how this analysis of the tact will proceed. In fact, it might be a good exercise to try it on your own before reading Figure 25-3 and the following text. Then you can check yourself and perhaps provide a little self-reinforcement for a good generalized response.

A number of studies have been accomplished which support a functional analysis of the development of the tact and help support a

Figure 25-1   Percent correct verbal imitative responses of a 4-year-old boy to English words (reinforced) and Russian words (nonreinforced). In the delayed reinforcement condition reinforcement followed 5 sec after the last English imitative response.

*

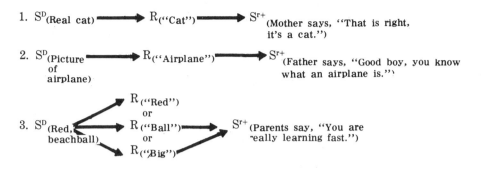

1. $S^D_{(Real\ cat)}$ ⟶ $R_{("Cat")}$ ⟶ $S^{r+}_{(Mother\ says,\ "That\ is\ right,\ it's\ a\ cat.")}$

2. $S^D_{(Picture\ of\ airplane)}$ ⟶ $R_{("Airplane")}$ ⟶ $S^{r+}_{(Father\ says,\ "Good\ boy,\ you\ know\ what\ an\ airplane\ is.")}$

3. $S^D_{(Red,\ beachball)}$ ⟶ $R_{("Red")}$ or $R_{("Ball")}$ or $R_{("Big")}$ ⟶ $S^{r+}_{(Parents\ say,\ "You\ are\ really\ learning\ fast.")}$

Figure 25-2

Three-term dependencies which are examples of the developed tact. The third example shows that specific aspects of a single object or event may control particular tacts.

behavioristic viewpoint of semantic development of the child's language. An often seen difficulty in exceptional children is poor language. In fact, it is not uncommon to find children who are not deaf (where you might expect language problems) but are developmentally retarded, brain damaged, or otherwise injured, who have little or no language. Obviously language is important to at least one aspect of their habilitation as productive citizens. Applied operant conditioners have been in the forefront of the movement to build language into such children. Recall the case of Dicky (Wolf, Risley, & Mees, 1964) which we reported in Units 19 and 21. After Wolf et al. were successful in suppressing tantrums and strengthening the wearing of glasses, they began to work on Dicky's speech which was bizarre. Dicky could sing the complete lyrics to *Chicago* but had no other appropriate verbal behavior. He was reinforced for correct tacts of five pictures by bites of

his breakfast and lunch.[4] An aide would present a picture, say, "This is Santa Claus. Now say Santa Claus," and

[4]It is extreme to deprive a human being of the necessities of life (e.g., food) to make that necessity a reinforcer, and then subsequently use it to condition desirable behavior. Rarely is this done and then only after all else fails in the most extreme of cases. (In the future it may be impossible to do it at all. Cf. footnote 2, Unit 16, and Wexler, 1973.)

Where food deprivation appears necessary, several prior procedures are followed. First, the range of possible reinforcers that are not necessities of life are sampled. (With Dicky, the therapists tried candy and fruit and found these were not reinforcers.) Secondly, naturally occurring deprivations are utilized. For example, the child is not deprived of several meals in order to make a subsequent meal more reinforcing. However, a child goes naturally from dinner to breakfast without food, and, therefore, approximately 12 hours of deprivation for food exist at breakfast time. It is likely that the child will respond in order to obtain bites of breakfast for desirable behavior. The authors know of no work with children where the subjects have been explicitly deprived of food.

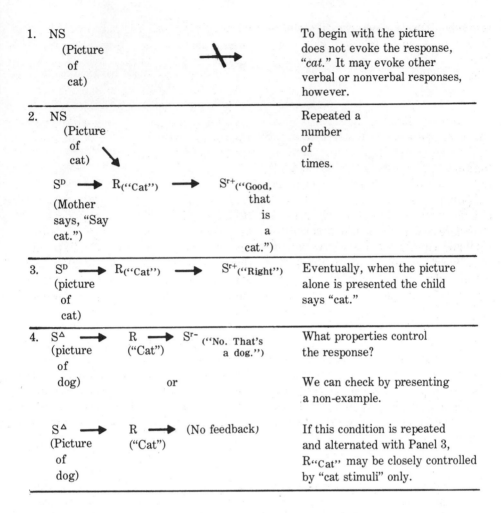

1. NS
    (Picture
    of
    cat)

    To begin with the picture does not evoke the response, "*cat*." It may evoke other verbal or nonverbal responses, however.

2. NS
    (Picture
    of
    cat)

    $S^D \longrightarrow R_{(\text{"Cat"})} \longrightarrow S^{r+}_{(\text{"Good,}}$
    (Mother
    says, "Say
    cat.")
    that
    is
    a
    cat.")

    Repeated a number of times.

3. $S^D \longrightarrow R_{(\text{"Cat"})} \longrightarrow S^{r+}_{(\text{"Right"})}$
    (picture
    of
    cat)

    Eventually, when the picture alone is presented the child says "cat."

4. $S^\Delta \longrightarrow R \longrightarrow S^{r-}$ ("No. That's
    (picture   ("Cat")   a dog.")
    of
    dog)   or

    What properties control the response?

    We can check by presenting a non-example.

    $S^\Delta \longrightarrow R \longrightarrow$ (No feedback)
    (Picture   ("Cat")
    of
    dog)

    If this condition is repeated and alternated with Panel 3, $R_{\text{"Cat"}}$ may be closely controlled by "cat stimuli" only.

Figure 25-3

The development of the tact by differential reinforcement.

reinforce with a bite of food when Dicky imitated the response. After a while, the aide was able to drop the verbal prompt and merely present the picture and wait. Thereupon, Dicky would tact the picture and be reinforced. It took 3 weeks to get him to respond correctly to approximately 10 pictures! After that, Dicky progressed to picture books, household objects, and finally remote events (e.g., "What did you do outside?"). Note that the "remote-event" response is still a tact, under the control now, we assume, of internal stimuli (memories) representing the event. Eventually, the parents helped broaden Dicky's repertoire at home. More than a decade later Dicky is in school functioning normally, where he continues to be followed closely by interested behavior modifiers (Nedelman & Sulzbacher, 1972).

The mand. Skinner has also coined the term *mand*, to describe another verbal response class important in language development. "A **MAND** [is] . . . a verbal operant in which the response is reinforced by a characteristic consequence and is therefore under the functional control of relevant conditions of deprivation or aversive stimulation" (p. 36). Requests, commands, orders, advice, prayers, entreaties, demands, imperatives, exhortations — all may be conceptualized as mands. Importantly, the mand is not under the control of environmental stimuli such as pictures or objects, but is related to a particular reinforcer. Thus, the thirsty child may say, *Milk!*" or *"Milk, please!"* because this verbal behavior is reinforced by the presentation of milk. Note that reinforcement is still socially mediated even though it is, in this example, an unconditioned reinforcer. Earlier we presented the first syntax seen in children's language as the pivot-open phrase. The examples used were mands. *"See Daddy!" "See doggy!" "See truck!"* can be thought of as mands (not tacts) when the child is under the control of the reinforcing properties of these objects rather than their discriminative properties. For example, if the child could not see out the window, and his Father had just left home to walk to work, *"See Daddy!"* would probably be a mand, the reinforcer for which would be mediated by Mother who holds the child to the window permitting him to see his father. However, if in the presence of Daddy the child says *"Daddy!"*, in the sense of identifying him, this response is a tact, not a mand.

Note that the reinforcement for the mand is the thing, event, or such that is manded by the speaker. When the child mands milk, the reinforcer is the milk, not mother's attention.

Intraverbal behavior. **INTRAVERBAL** behavior has no topographical, or as Skinner says, "point-to-point correspondence" with the verbal stimuli that set the occasion for it. Intraverbals are responses that follow almost automatically, as if they are evidence of memorization or rote learning. For example, the response, *4*, is an intraverbal to the stimulus, *2 + 2 = .* The response, *Mister*, to the stimulus, *Monsieur*, is an intraverbal as will be most translation. Intraverbals also are evidenced by automatic phrases in our language. *"How are you?"* is almost always the occasion for *"Fine, thank you"*; when it is not, and the answering individual begins to expostulate on his current ills, the speaker of the greeting is often quite surprised. His surprise may be punishing to the person asked, making it less likely for him in the future to discuss his maladies when asked *"How are you?"* and more likely to emit the intraverbal, *"Fine, thank you,"* which may be reinforced by the first speaker (*"Nice to see you"*). Intraverbals will often exist as stimulus-response chains, as in a child's recitation of a Mother Goose rhyme (viz., "Old King Cole"). The controlling stimuli will be at the beginning of the chain; if the child is stopped in the middle of his recitation, he may be unable to start successfully from where he stopped. The stimuli in the middle of the chain (i.e., "And a merry old soul was he") may only occasion further responses if the child approaches them from the beginning of the chain.

Intraverbals are established similarly to other verbal responses. In the presence of a specific verbal stimulus (*7 x 7 =*), a specific verbal response (*49*) is reinforced; other verbal responses emitted in the presence of the stimulus are extinguished or mildly punished. Eventually the verbal stimulus occasions a precise response; however, a single intraverbal response may be evoked by a large number of stimuli as, for example, *100* can be evoked by; a) *10 x 10 = ?*; b) *97, 98, 99,?*; c) *103, 102, 101,?*; d) *60, 70, 80, 90,?*; e) *130, 120, 110,?*; f) *10² = ?*; g) $\sqrt{10,000} = ?$; h) *What is the reciprocal of 1/100?*; and so on.

The intraverbal may represent one simple aspect of a behavioristic definition of knowledge. It represents the case where an automatic stimulus-response relation is produced in which it is evident that the relation is an arbitrary one and is not naturally produced by the environment. By arbitrary, we mean that societies (other men) are responsible for its formation. We could prove this by reinforcing a child for "wrong" answers until he became thoroughly proficient at producing these answers. Some of the language studies described below contain features such as this.

The autoclitic. The **AUTOCLITIC** is a verbal response by the speaker that is a response to verbal stimuli either he or

another individual has generated (i.e., another verbal response). Its function is to affect the listener with regard to the strength of the speaker's verbal behavior, by describing a controlling relation for the listener — the relation of the speaker's verbal response to its conditions of production. Thus, a speaker may say, "*I BELIEVE in behaviorism.*" The autoclitic, *I believe*, indicates that the speaker is discriminating (correctly or incorrectly) why he behaves in a given way toward some subject matter (i.e., behaviorism), and so informs the listener. Autoclitics will frequently begin with *I* because the speaker attempts to describe some of his own behavior verbally. An autoclitic can: 1) describe the type of verbal behavior it is associated with; for example, "*I SEE that John has failed*"; "*I HEARD that John failed*"; 2) describe the strength of the associated verbal behavior, for example, "*I DOUBT that he is correct*"; "*I AM POSITIVE he is correct*"; 3) be used by the speaker to relate what he is saying to other verbal behavior, for example, "*I AGREE with John on this matter*"; "*I ADMIT John is correct*"; and 4) indicate the speaker's emotional state, for example, "*I AM SAD to tell you . . .*"; "*I AM PLEASED to inform you . . .*"

In general, autoclitics modify what the individual says, informing the listener of the speaker's qualifications about his verbal behavior. Autoclitics will be generated in a language community by verbal stimuli that set the occasion for a self-referring statement. "*What do you think of our new car?*" occasions, "*I THINK it looks very nice,*" which is reinforced by smiles from the owners of the new car.

Illustrations: Human Research

D. Guess, W. Sailor, G. Rutherford, & D. M. Baer, An experimental analysis of linguistic development: The productive use of the plural morpheme. *Journal of Applied Behavior Analysis*, 1968, 1, 297-306.

Language generation where none exists. We have already mentioned that children can be reinforced for correctly imitating some verbal responses, and other unreinforced verbal responses will increase in accuracy of pronunciation (Brigham & Sherman, 1968). We have also alluded to the fact that children with deficient language repertoires can have their language repertoires strengthened. But what of the child who does not speak at all? Baer, Peterson, and Sherman (1967) taught three severely retarded children who initially had no language (just grunts) and no imitative behavior, to produce nonverbal imitations. Food at mealtimes was used as the reinforcer for imitating the experimenter, as in the following sequence: "Do this"; the experimenter models a response; the subject imitates; the experimenter dispenses a bite of the meal. A large number of imitative responses was learned by each subject, and subjects learned imitations presented later in training more quickly than those presented early in training. Initial training included manual-guidance prompting in order to have first imitations occur and be reinforced. After two of the children had completed the nonverbal imitation program successfully, verbal imitations were developed. In one, this was accomplished by " . . . chaining together motor and vocal behaviors and then fading out the motor components" (p. 414). After 20 hours of training this child could imitate 10 words. In the other subject, 7 hours of training produced imitation of 7 vowels and consonants.

Strengthening the use of descriptive adjectives. Hart and Risley (1968) conditioned the use of color adjectives in the speech of disadvantaged preschool children. At the beginning of the school year the children rarely used color-noun combinations — a condition the observers recorded during free-play time. The teachers first used a procedure during a time when the children were in a group in which they reinforced color naming of objects. Teacher: "This truck is blue"; Child: "That truck is blue"; Teacher: reinforces child. Then the teacher would pick an object and a child and have the child identify it and its color. This procedure produced accurate color naming within the group session by nearly all the children. However, no general change occurred in the use of color names in the free-play setting. After this, the children were only given play or work materials or food if they asked for the item and included its color. Prompting took place early ("What color doll dress do you want?") and was dropped after several days. Children were praised whenever they correctly used the adjective-noun combination and were given the items sought.

There was a dramatic increase in the use of color-noun combinations during free-play periods. When the dependency between food, materials, and color naming was removed, there was some decrease in the use of color naming, but use still remained well above that recorded during the original baseline. This study suggests that reinforcement dependencies can affect specific language usage of children.

Generating use of plural morphemes. The subject for this experiment was a 10-year-old severely retarded girl who had a verbal repertoire of a few words and simple phrases (Guess, Sailor, Rutherford, & Baer, 1968). This repertoire was due to an earlier operant training program she had experienced. Her verbal behavior itself, as well as her history, showed that she did not use the plural form. She was asked, "What do you see?" and shown a single object; then 2 objects were shown her and the question was asked again. No instance of plural usage was noted using 10 different objects. During training, the girl was shown single objects and asked, "What do you see?" If she named the object, she was reinforced with a bit of food. If she failed to label the object, the experimenter named it, and it was presented again after a brief period. When the child incorrectly labelled an object, the experimenter said, "No," and re-presented the object. In the next stage of training 2 objects of a kind were presented and the child was reinforced for emitting the plural form. The experimenter said "No," whenever the child responded with a singular to 2 objects. In a final stage, the child was shown an intermixed array of single and multiple objects and reinforced for correct singular and plural responses. In all, 44 objects were presented in this experiment. In each session the girl was trained on 1 object only; and in each session one new item-pair which was not trained was presented.

Two control conditions were employed by Guess et al. to prove that the subject's newly acquired plural usage was a function of the reinforcement program. During a reversal period, the subject was reinforced for responding with a singular in the presence of 2 objects and a plural in the presence of a single object. In another condition the girl was presented objects whose plurals were irregularly formed (e.g., *man-men, leaf-leaves*). She was not trained in the use of these irregular plurals. In the first of these control conditions (the reversal), the girl's use of plurals regularly in the presence of single objects and the converse would be grounds to conclude the importance of the reinforcement dependencies. In the second control condition, regularly formed plural responses to the irregular-type objects (i.e., *leaf-leafs*) would substantiate: 1) the absence of the correct form from the child's repertoire; 2) the presence of the class of responses strengthened by the experimental program; and 3) evidence that the child had developed a simple grammatical rule.

The study also allowed the experimenters to determine when the subject actually became grammatically generative for plural usage. This was determined by recording the number of occasions on which the girl correctly produced a plural, the *first* time she was presented with a pair of objects on which she had received only singular training. This generalization is a powerful demonstration of the effects of a conditioning procedure, especially one which apparently produces a rule or a concept the subject follows. The rule here might be loosely stated: When I see more than one object, I should add /s/ or /z/ to the word. (Whether the child says something like this to herself is incidental.)

Table 25-2 presents the results of this experiment. Construct a graph of these data in the following way. Use a set of coordinates having "Sessions" on the abscissa (1 to 44) and on the lefthand ordinate — "Percent Correct" (0 to 100). Add a righthand ordinate labelled "Number of Plural Shifts" drawn from the right-most edge of your abscissa. Make the length for the right-hand ordinate equal to the length of the left-hand ordinate. Next, cumulate the number of plural shifts in the fourth column of Table 25-2. The sum you obtain will be the final number of this ordinate and should be located on the same horizontal line as 100% (however, it will be spaced to the right-hand side). Remember to graph both sets of data from left to right. Use a different point code for the points in the reversal condition and the same code for points in normal usage. Graph the plural shifts *cumulatively*. (Refer to Unit 3 if you have forgotten how to construct a cumulative record.)

To begin with, the girl used no plurals. When reinforced for it, plural use increased. When the dependencies were reversed, the subject again used the singular when presented with 2 objects and the plural when presented

Table 25-2

The plural-usage performance of a 10-year-old, severely retarded girl presented with single and multiple objects. The second column depicts the percent of correct plurals formed during three training conditions, while the third column displays the number of occasions on which the subject correctly produced a plural the *first* time she was presented with an object-pair. Data taken from: Guess, D., Sailor, W., Rutherford, G., & Baer, D. M. An experimental analysis of linguistic development: The productive use of the plural morpheme. *Journal of Applied Behavior Analysis*, 1968, 1, 297-306.

Sessions	Percent Correct	Plural Shifts	Cumulative Plural Shifts	Condition
1	80	0		Reinforcement for
2	85	0		normal plural
3	100	1		usage.
4	100	1		
5	100	1		
6	100	1		
7	100	1		
8	100	1		
9	100	1		
10	100	1		

Table 25-2 (continued)

Sessions	Percent Correct	Plural Shifts	Cumulative Plural Shifts	Condition
11	38	0		Reinforcement for
12	23	0		reversed plural
13	55	0		usage.*
14	55	0		
15	80	0		
16	75	0		
17	65	1		
18	90	0		
19	75	0		
20	100	1		
21	100	1		
22	100	1		
23	80	1		
24	100	1		
25	88	1		
26	100	1		
27	88	1		
28	100	1		
29	100	1		
30	90	1		Reinforcement for
31	100	1		normal plural
32	100	1		usage.
33	95	1		
34	100	1		
35	100	1		
36	90	1		
37	100	1		
38	100	1		
39	100	1		
40	100	1		
41	100	1		
42	92	1		
43	100	1		
44	100	1		

*Percentages indicate the subject produced the singular form when shown two objects.

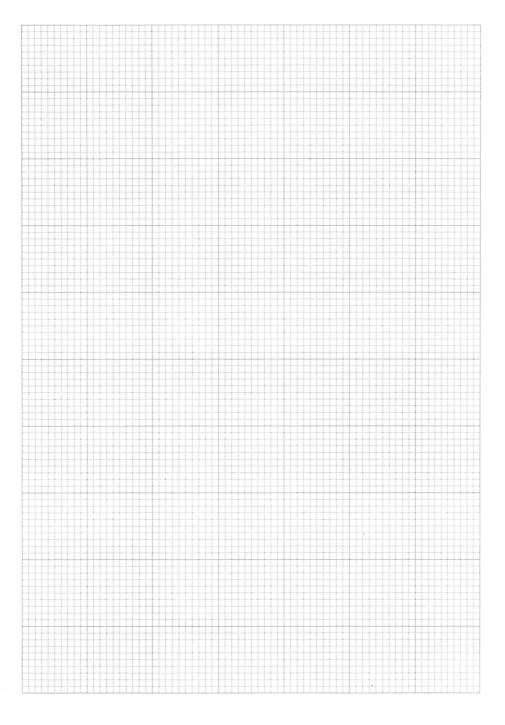

Figure 25-4 Percent correct responses and the number of correct shifts of a 10-year-old severely retarded girl.

*

with a single object. When the dependencies were finally made congruent with normal usage again, the girl used plurals when presented with 2 objects and the singular when presented with 1 object.

In the generalization test, the girl initially responded to the item-pair with the singular form but rapidly began to use plurals, even though she was never reinforced for doing so on these pairs. When the dependencies were reversed, she continued to produce plurals to these items but after awhile began to say the singular. When the dependencies were returned to normal usage, she immediately switched back, correctly identifying the item-pairs with the plural form. It is worth re-emphasizing that on these item-pairs there was no reinforcement for either type of response, yet the response was a function of the dependency in effect on the trained items.

The fact that the girl still made errors in using irregular plurals (e.g., leafs, sheeps, mouses, etc.) attests to the complexity of the English language rather than any deficiency on her part; most young children do not use the correct plural form for irregular plurals. Another set of rules could have been taught her for correct use of irregular forms.

How far can we generalize from these data? There are a large number of rules in language and the study has dealt with only one. Further, the study was carried out on a retarded individual. It is possible (but not likely) that normal children acquire such rules differently. Finally, the study involved a single case and until it is replicated with other individuals, we must remain cautious. In spite of these limitations, however, the results of the study are highly significant in suggesting the possible role of conditioning in the language development of children.

In fact, the original Guess et al. results have been replicated in several important ways. Guess (1969) replicated his earlier finding with two retarded boys. These boys were first conditioned to point to single and paired objects when instructed (e.g., "Point to the cup; now, point to the pencils."). This is equivalent to demonstrating *receptive* language in these youngsters. They understood what was being said to them after this training. Throughout the training Guess probed for whether the boys could correctly say the plural forms as a function of the receptive training. Their *expressive* language during the probes was faulty. (Expressive language connotes language construction — an individual generates verbal behavior.) Subsequently, both boys were trained as the girl had been to produce plurals expressively, so these results replicate and extend Guess's earlier finding. In addition, the results suggest receptive and expressive language response classes may be independent of each other, at least in so far as the plural morpheme is concerned.

Other results. A question the reader should have is the following: Should we generalize to other aspects of language development with regard to conditioning principles when all this text does is describe the usefulness of conditioning principles in: 1) generating speech; 2) increasing use of adjectives; 3) generating use of the plural morpheme; and 4) producing generalized imitation? The answer is no, we should not. Yet each additional conditioning demonstration in the area of language is grounds for generalizing a little further about the power of this explanation. Also, there are other studies which show the relevance of conditioning techniques to various aspects of verbal behavior, selectively including: 1) the operant conditioning of reading responses (Staats, Staats, Shutz, & Wolf, 1962); 2) the respondent conditioning of meaning (Staats & Staats, 1957); 3) the operant conditioning of verb (tense) usage (Schumaker & Sherman, 1970); 4) the operant conditioning of syntactical relations (Garcia, Guess, & Byrnes, 1973; Wheeler & Sulzer, 1971); and 5) the receptive use of adjectival inflections (−er and −est) (Baer & Guess, 1971).

Illustrations: Animal Studies

Particularly exciting is the demonstration of language behavior in nonhuman animals using conditioning procedures. Scientists have been interested in animal capabilities for a long time. George John Romanes (1848-1894), a personal friend of Darwin, defended the latter's theory by locating and describing episodes of animal behavior that allowed a conclusion that the animals were functioning intelligently. In this fashion an attempt was made to describe the continuity between man's and and animals' behavior. Romanes, however, frequently tended to *anthropomorphize*, that is to interpret animal behavior in terms of human behavior. C. Lloyd Morgan (1852-1936) saw this error and attempted to ensure its removal from the study of animal behavior. His formal statement, that a higher level explanation (e.g. a mental process) should not be used to explain a phenomenon if a lower level explanation

(e.g., a habit) would suffice, has become known as **LLOYD MORGAN'S CANON**. Lloyd Morgan was critical that Darwin's followers read "mind" into much animal behavior, and that, in fact, similar interpretations occurred of one man's behavior by another. Lloyd Morgan had an important influence on E. L. Thorndike, a pioneer in conditioning research with animals, and J. B. Watson, the titular head of the school of psychology known as Behaviorism.

The comparison of animal and human behavior continues to the present day with respect to language. In recent times chimpanzees have been raised in homes essentially as human children are raised (Kellogg, 1968) to facilitate this kind of comparison. However, no one has reported success in manipulating the chimpanzee's vocalizations. Four differentiable sounds have been the maximum number reported that approximate human sounds. One possible reason why chimpanzees don't learn to vocalize human sounds is that their vocal apparatus is not designed to allow the production of complex sounds. This is a good example of a boundary condition. The evidence on this point is equivocal because chimpanzees emit a wide variety of sounds in their natural environments. A second possible reason is that vocalization approximating human sounds in the chimpanzee is not conditionable. The failure of behavior scientists to produce vocal language in the chimpanzee led two psychologists to a more easily manipulable response. Casual observation indicates the chimpanzee can make a wide variety of responses employing its hands. Beatrice and Allan Gardner (1971) raised an infant chimpanzee (Washoe) in a house trailer. Washoe was exposed only to humans who communicated by

American Sign Language (ASL), the language of many deaf individuals throughout the world. ASL is a gesture language in which words are formed by moving the hands in space in various ways. Thus the sign for "drink" is a fist clenched with thumb extended, in which the thumb is brought in proximity to the mouth and the fist is rotated around a horizontal axis parallel to the face. The movement is similar to tilting a can of beer with the fist playing the role of the can.

Washoe's handlers used shaping, manual guidance, and imitation to produce an expressive vocabulary by the chimpanzee. After 3 years of training that vocabulary exceeded 160 signs! Washoe also learned to put her signs together in strings that were combinations she had never been actually taught. One combination she especially liked to use was *Gimme tickle*, which manded being tickled by one of her handlers. The Gardners eventually gave Washoe to one of their graduate students who was also one of Washoe's teachers. The Gardners' work has rekindled interest in the possibility that other mammals are capable of sophisticated language behavior. Their students are interested in whether two chimpanzees, each given ASL training, will spontaneously communicate using this method with one another or with their offspring. An early answer to this is not yet possible.

Two other, more formal experiments round out the current work with language in chimpanzees. Premack (1971) taught a chimpanzee (Sarah) to manipulate plastic figures used as language symbols. The magnetized figures could be attached to a board allowing Premack to construct vertical arrays (like Chinese) and reinforce construction of similar arrays by his animal. There are a number of advantages to this system: a) The language of the chimpanzee is less evanescent than is a sign; b) questions asked also can be more permanent; c) the experimenter can control the number of words in the animal's language because he makes them; and d) because the words can be presented for long durations, variables such as memory are controlled for.

Sarah was first given a small vocabulary. This was done by having the chimpanzee exchange plastic pieces for fruit. Each plastic piece corresponded to a specific fruit. Next, another piece of plastic was added and systematically changed with the donors of the fruit (i.e., the trainers). These pieces became the names of the trainers. This allowed tests where: 1) The name of the donor remained constant but the available fruit changed; and 2) the fruit available remained constant and the donor's name changed. Thus, Sarah would have to "write" *Michael apple* when the donor was Michael, but *Mary apple* if the donor was Mary, and *Mary banana* (not *Mary apple*) if the fruit was a banana. Of course, the fruit reinforcer was supplied by the trainer only if the animal's language was correct. When this pivot-open stage was reached part of the dependency between receiving fruit and producing language was syntactical (i.e., word order). In order to receive fruit the chimp had to say, *Mary apple*, not *apple Mary*.

In addition, Sarah was taught the use of the interrogative. This was done by reinforcing the animal for placing one marker (*same*) between pairs of objects that were similar (e.g., two cups), and another marker (*different*) between two objects that were different (e.g., a cup and a spoon). When performance was accurate, Premack added a *?* between the two objects to be compared and let the animal answer with either the *same* or *different* marker. It was then possible to determine if this capability could generalize to other pairs of objects that had not been part of training.

One of the hallmarks of language is that the language-competent individual can learn new concepts through language alone, without direct experience with the real-world stimuli that the language stimuli represent. Sarah eventually became capable of producing a sentence using a marker to indicate *is name of*. Thus, shown the marker word for apple, an apple, and the interrogation marker, Sarah could respond: *Apple* (marker) *is name of* (marker) apple (real one). This allowed Premack to teach Sarah later that one word was equivalent to another without showing the chimpanzee the actual referrent of the word. Premack refers to the use of language to teach further language as *metalinguistics*.

Sarah was also taught: 1) dimensional classes of words such as color, shape, and size; 2) to use these dimensional classes metalinguistically where the animal had not experienced the actual objects (e.g., where Sarah had experienced *chocolate* and *color of* as words but not *brown*, the chimpanzee was successfully taught *brown is color of chocolate*); 3) to discriminate word order (i.e., syntax) important to using the preposition *on*. (*Cup on saucer* connotes a considerably different relation than *saucer on cup*.) Sarah could produce sentences conforming to displays of this nature that were presented; 4) the conditional, *if-then*. This was more difficult for Sarah. The chimpanzee learned that, presented

with the sentences: *(If) Sarah take apple then Mary give Sarah chocolate* and *(If) Sarah take banana then Mary no give Sarah chocolate*, she could choose the apple and always get a chocolate. To complete the discrimination however, two more tests were necessary reversing the relations in the above sentences. These read: *(If) Sarah take apple then Mary no give Sarah chocolate* and *(If) Sarah take banana then Mary give Sarah chocolate*. Sarah made considerable errors while learning this discrimination but after reaching criterion the animal generalized easily. Given *(If) Mary take red then Sarah take apple* and *(If) Mary take green then Sarah take banana*, Sarah was able to observe these sentences and carry out the correct response observing what Mary did without being trained with these stimuli.

In addition, Sarah was taught how to compose a compound sentence. This was accomplished by teaching the chimpanzee to react first to the individual sentences eventually making up the compound, for example, putting a banana in a pail, and an apple in a dish. Subsequently, redundant parts of the two sentences were deleted so that: *Sarah insert banana dish* and *Sarah insert apple pail* became *Sarah insert banana dish apple pail* or *Sarah insert banana pail apple dish*. Sarah had no difficulty with all combinations of this arrangement.

A slightly different program has been carried out with yet another female chimpanzee (Lana) by Rumbaugh and his associates (Rumbaugh, Gill, & Von Glasersfeld, 1973). Using visual stimuli presented by a computer, they have taught Lana to read and complete sentences. Lana's console contained 25 word-keys on which symbols were rear-projected. When the animal pressed a symbol it was visually added in a left-to-right order to one of seven rear projectors displayed horizontally above the console. This horizontal display was the sentence. The left-most projector was reserved for *please*, *?*, *yes* or *no*, and the right-most projector for the *period*.

To begin with, Lana was reinforced with the object or event that signified a word in "Yerkish," the laboratory's language.[5] Thus, for example, simply pressing a key with an X on it produced a piece of banana; pressing a key with another symbol on it produced music; another produced an experimenter; yet others an outside view, movies, music, and juice. The equipment was designed so that Lana could operate it any time the chimpanzee felt like it. The next step was to chain in *please* and *period*, so that phrases producing *please music period* or some other request were honored with the fulfillment of the request. Then Lana had to press single keys that contained a holophrastic representation (i.e, the stimuli, such as *machine give juice*, were all combined on one key). This response also had to be preceded by *please* and followed by *period*. Next, Rumbaugh et al. fractionated the stimuli making up the holophrase by putting part of it on a separate key, and Lana had to press 1) *please* 2) *machine* 3) *give/m&m* and 4) *period*. Finally, Lana had to press all keys of a sentence in their correct order preceded by *please* and followed by *period* as in *please/machine/make/*

window/open/period. Following this, randomization of the stimuli among the 25 word-keys occurred and Lana had to select words from among all the others and press them in the correct order. If Lana miscalculated, a push of the period key "erased" the sentence.

Rumbaugh et al. report intriguing results. Lana quickly learned to press the period key whenever an error was made. The experimenters programed sentence beginnings on the horizontal projectors activated by Lana's keys. For example, they could write, *Please machine give* and then see if Lana could finish the sentence correctly. As in our language only certain endings to this sentence were sensible. *Please machine give Tim into room* would be wrong, while endings saying: 1) *piece of banana* (or *apple*); or 2) *m&m*, *juice*, or *water* would be correct. Lana scored very high on sentence completion of this sort. Further, when an incorrect sentence beginning was presented (e.g., *Please machine come*), Lana could press the period key for erasure. Thus, Lana could discriminate valid and invalid sentence forms. These data suggest that the chimpanzee can discriminate a form of syntactical relation.

Each of these experiments strengthens the notions of psychologists that conditioning principles can account for language development. There are many problems to overcome, however. One is the very definition of language itself. Certainly the behaviors of these animals are complex, and demonstrably under the control of complex stimuli, but this, in itself, may be insufficient to call the behavior language behavior (Mistler-Lachman & Lachman, 1974). However, the facts remain. Conditioning psychologists

---

[5]Named for R. M. Yerkes (1876-1956), an important investigator of animal behavior. His most significant work was with chimpanzees.

have been able to produce language-like behavior in animals including: 1) syntactical relations (choosing the correct endings, rejecting incorrect beginnings, forming sentences, use of prepositions); 2) rule-governed (concept) behavior (given a new word, the word is combined correctly with other words); 3) metalinguistical development (using words to teach about words); 4) the use of the interrogative; 5) the use of the conditional; and 6) the use of words themselves.

As Premack (1971) suggests, "Since man is required to teach the chimp language and not vice versa, we may continue to claim uniqueness" (p. 228). And, of course, so far that is true.

Exam

1. Define the following terms:
   a) syntax
   b) semantics
   c) microkinesics
   d) mand
   e) tact
   f) intraverbal
   g) autoclitic
   h) verbal behavior
   i) generalized imitation
   j) metalinguistics
   k) echoic

2. Describe Brigham and Sherman's (1968) results. Pay particular attention to whether the curves for English and Russian imitations correlate.

3. What do Brigham and Sherman's results suggest about the role of the echoic response in speech development?

4. Describe four hypotheses that purport to explain generalized imitation.

5. Present a behavioristic explanation of speech development in the human child.

6. Are matching-to-sample and modeling similar? Explain.

7. Diagram three, three-term dependencies which are evidence of a child tacting an object or event in his environment. Use examples not given in the book.

8. How does a functional analysis of behavior consider the tact is developed?

9. Give an example of a tact, a mand, an intraverbal, and an autoclitic not presented in this unit.

10. Describe what happened to the severely retarded girl in the Guess et al. experiment when she was: a) reinforced for correct plural usage; b) reinforced for reversed plural usage; and c) again reinforced for correct plural usage. Why did her correct plural use drop after Session 10?

11. What did Guess et al. mean by a "correct plural shift"? What was the highest rate of correct plural shifts that could occur each session? When did the subject begin emitting correct plural shifts in the experiment? What happened to plural shifts when the reinforcement dependencies were reversed? When they were reversed again?

12. What can we conclude regarding the role of conditioning procedures and the production of the use of the plural form? (Hint: Is the phenomenon necessarily innate? Can it be environmentally determined? Should we generalize very far from a single, special case?)

13. What is a boundary condition? Give an example not from the text.

14. What is Lloyd Morgan's Canon? Give an example of its application.

15. What does *anthropomorphization* mean? Give an example.

16. What language-like behaviors have chimpanzees been conditioned to produce? State at least four using examples.

17. Why must we be careful not to conclude too quickly that chimpanzees can be taught language? (Hint: What is language?)

18. What is meant by the surface structure of a sentence? The deep structure? Give an example of a sentence not in the text which has more than one deep structure (i.e., has ambiguous meaning).

References

Baer, D. M., & Guess, D.   Receptive training of adjectival inflections in mental retardates. *Journal of Applied Behavior Analysis*, 1971, 4, 129-139.

Baer, D. M., Peterson, R. L., & Sherman, J. A.   The development of imitation by reinforcing behavioral similarity to a model. *Journal of the Experimental Analysis of Behavior*, 1967, 10, 405-416.

Baer, D. M., & Sherman, J. A.   Reinforcement control of generalized imitation in young children. *Journal of Experimental Child Psychology*, 1964, 1, 37-49.

Bandura, A.   *Principles of behavior modification*. New York: Holt, Rinehart and Winston, 1969.

Brigham, T., & Sherman, J. A.   An experimental analysis of verbal imitation in preschool children. *Journal of Applied Behavior Analysis*, 1968, 1, 151-158.

Catania, A. C.   Chomsky's formal analysis of natural languages: A behavioral translation. *Behaviorism*, 1972, 1, 1-15.

Chomsky, N.   *Syntactic structures*. The Hague: Mouton, 1957.

Condon, W. S., & Sander, L. W.   Neonate movement is synchronized with adult speech: Interactional participation and language acquisition. *Science*, 1974, 183, 99-101.

Garcia, E., Guess, D., & Byrnes, J.   Development of syntax in a retarded girl using procedures of imitation, reinforcement, and modeling. *Journal of Applied Behavior Analysis*, 1973, 6, 299-310.

Gardner, B. T., & Gardner, R. A.   Two-way communication with an infant chimpanzee. In A. M. Schrier & F. Stollnitz (Eds.), *Behavior of nonhuman primates: Modern research trends*. Vol. IV. New York: Academic Press, 1971. Pp. 118-184.

Gewirtz, J. L.   The roles of overt responding and extrinsic reinforcement in "self-" and "vicarious-reinforcement" phenomena and in "observational learning" and imitation. In R. Glaser (Ed.), *The nature of reinforcement*. New York: Academic Press, 1971. Pp. 279-309.

Guess, D.   A functional analysis of receptive language and productive speech: Acquisition of the plural morpheme. *Journal of Applied Behavior Analysis*, 1969, **2**, 55-64.

Guess, D., Sailor, W., Rutherford, G., & Baer, D. M.   An experimental analysis of linguistic development: The productive use of the plural morpheme. *Journal of Applied Behavior Analysis*, 1968, **1**, 297-306.

Hart, B. M., & Risley, T. R.   Establishing use of descriptive adjectives in the spontaneous speech of disadvantaged preschool children. *Journal of Applied Behavior Analysis*, 1968, **1**, 109-120.

Kaye, H.   Infant sucking behavior and its modification. In L. P. Lipsitt & C. C. Spiker (Eds.), *Advances in child development and behavior*. Vol. III. New York: Academic Press, 1967. Pp. 1-52.

Kellogg, W. N.   Communication and language in the home-raised chimpanzee. *Science*, 1968, **162**, 423-427.

Lenneberg, E.   *Biological foundations of language*. New York: John Wiley and Sons, 1967.

Lipsitt, L. P., & Kaye, H.   Conditioned sucking in the human newborn. *Psychonomic Science*, 1964, **1**, 29-30.

Martin, J. A.   The control of imitative and nonimitative behaviors in severely retarded children through "generalized instruction-following." *Journal of Experimental Child Psychology*, 1971, **11**, 390-400.

Mistler-Lachman, J. L., & Lachman, R.   Language in man, monkeys, and machines. *Science*, 1974, **185**, 871-872.

Nedelman, D., & Sulzbacher, S.   Dicky at 13 years of age: A long term success following early application of operant conditioning procedures. In G. Semb (Ed.), *Behavior analysis and education –1972*. Lawrence, Kansas: The University of Kansas Support and Development Center for Follow Through, 1972. Pp. 3-10.

Premack, D.   On the assessment of language competence in the chimpanzee. In A. M. Schrier & F. Stollnitz (Eds.), *Behavior of nonhuman primates: Modern research trends*. Vol. IV. New York: Academic Press, 1971. Pp. 185-228.

Rheingold, H. L., Gewirtz, J. L., & Ross, H. W.   Social conditioning of vocalizations in the infant. *Journal of Comparative and Physiological Psychology*, 1959, **52**, 68-73.

Rumbaugh, D. M., Gill, T. V., & VonGlasersfeld, E. C.   Reading and sentence completion by a chimpanzee (*Pan*). *Science*, 1973, **182**, 731-733.

Schumaker, J., & Sherman, J. A.   Training generative verb usage by imitation and reinforcement procedures. *Journal of Applied Behavior Analysis*, 1970, **3**, 273-287.

Siqueland, E. R., & Lipsitt, L. P.   Conditioned head-turning in human newborns. *Journal of Experimental Child Psychology*, 1966, **3**, 356-376.

Skinner, B. F.   *Verbal behavior*. New York: Appleton-Century-Crofts, 1957.

Staats, A. W., Staats, C. K., Shutz, R. E., & Wolf, M. M. The conditioning of textual responses using "extrinsic" reinforcers. *Journal of the Experimental Analysis of Behavior*, 1962, **5**, 33-40.

Staats, C. K., & Staats, A. W. Meaning established by classical conditioning. *Journal of Experimental Psychology*, 1957, **54**, 74-80.

Werner, H., & Kaplan, E. The acquisition of word meaning: A developmental study. *Monographs of the Society for Research in Child Development*, 1952, **15**, (Whole No. 51).

Wexler, D. Token and taboo: Behavior modification, token economics, and the law. *California Law Review*, 1973, **61**, 81-109.

Wheeler, A. J., & Sulzer, B. Operant training and generalization of a verbal response form in a speech-deficient child. *Journal of Applied Behavior Analysis*, 1970, **3**, 139-147.

Wolf, M. M., Risley, T. R., & Mees, H. Application of operant conditioning procedures to the behavior problems of an autistic child. *Behavior Research and Therapy*, 1964, **1**, 305-312.

*

GLOSSARY

ABA reversal design A research design employed with one or few subjects in which the subject functions as his own control. The A conditions are the control conditions and the B conditions involve the instatement of the independent variable. The most classic general case is: operant level, *i.e.*, no reinforcement (A); reinforcement (B); operant level, *i.e.*, extinction (A). However, the ABA designation is not restricted to extinction, reinforcement, extinction. The proof that a given treatment was effective is determined by the repeatability of the effect. If the effect is present in the experimental periods (B) and absent during baseline periods (A), the independent variable under study causes the effect. (2)

abscissa The horizontal axis on a figure or graph, also referred to as the X axis. Time, trials, or sessions are usually plotted on this axis. Occasionally the values of the independent variable are plotted on this axis as well (*e.g.*, 12, 24, 36, 48, and 60 hours of deprivation). (2)

activation syndrome A rubric for the actions of the sympathetic nervous system. These changes prepare the body biologically for action, and include, but are not restricted to, increased adrenalin flow, raised blood pressure, cessation of digestive activity, and quickening of heart rate. (16)

aggression 1. Extinction produced: aggression directed toward an animate or inanimate object as a result of placing the organism on extinction.

2. pain-elicited: aggression directed toward an object, either animate or inanimate, which was elicited by a painful stimulus. This form of aggression is considered innate and thought to exist in many species, including man. (18)

alternative response procedure A technique of modifying behavior in which a positively reinforced, unpunished alternative response is made available to the organism at the same time an undesirable response continues to be punished. (19)

altruism Refers to social behavior which does not appear to be extrinsically reinforced. The term is misleading because it hides the source of control for the helpful behavior. (23)

American Sign Language An ideographic language produced by positioning and moving the hands relative to each other and the body. The language of the deaf in this country, and in various forms around the world. A gesture language. (25)

amplitude of the reflex One measure of the strength of a reflex. It refers to the size, intensity, or magnitude of the response. A knee jerk which traverses 40° of arc has a greater amplitude than one which traverses 10° of arc. (4)

And dependency A cooperative dependency which specifies the response requirement for each participant. Only when each has satisfied the requirement are the participants reinforced. (23)

anorexia nervosa A condition in which the patient eats very little and progressively loses weight. Can lead to malnutrition and even death. (12)

antecedent stimulus A stimulus that occurs prior to a given response that is related to that response. (13)

anthropomorphize To interpret and/or explain the behavior of nonhuman animals in terms of human behavior. (25)

anxiety The report of an individual that he is experiencing the action of the sympathetic branch of the autonomic nervous system, and verification that these respondents have occurred. Typically, clinical judgment is used to verify this state. (16)

anxiety hierarchy A group of feared stimuli ranked by patient and therapist in terms of the degree of fear produced by each stimulus. Used as the collection of stimuli to be individually counterconditioned in systematic desensitization. (17)

appetitive schedule A positive reinforcement schedule in which the reinforcer is consumable (*e.g.*, food). (20)

area shift A shift in the shape of the generalization gradient after discrimination training. The resulting post-discrimination gradient has a relatively greater concentration of responding on one side of the training stimulus (S^+) than was present in the generalization gradient. *Cf.* peak shift. (15)

asymptote The limiting value of a curve after which there is little or no further increase in the value of the curve. (7)

autism A complex of behaviors found in children characterized by some or all of the following: 1) physical self-destruction; 2) social nonresponsiveness; 3) excessive self-stimulation; 4) severe tantrums; 5) little or no language (often bizaare, if present); 6) lack of imitative behavior. (18)

autoclitic A type of verbal operant which affects the listener by describing the strength of the speaker's verbal behavior. The speaker describes the conditions controlling his verbal behavior. (25)

avoidance conditioning Conditioning in which a response prevents or postpones the onset of an aversive stimulus for a short time. The operant which postpones the aversive stimulus is called an avoidance response.

1. discriminated avoidance: an avoidance procedure in which a conditioned aversive stimulus such as a buzzer precedes the delivery of an unconditioned aversive stimulus such as an electric shock. A response during the conditioned aversive stimulus terminates it and postpones shock for a brief time. (20)

2. nondiscriminated avoidance (Sidman avoidance): An avoidance procedure in which a brief shock is presented at fixed times. A response postpones the shock for a fixed time. There is no warning stimulus used in this procedure. (20)

Backscratch dependency A cooperative dependency in which each subject controls the consequences for his partner; that is, responses made by subject A produce consequences for subject B and vice versa. Used in the minimal social situation. (23)

baseline period A period of time during which a behavior is systematically observed. During this time, no attempts are made to alter the behavior under study. Data collected during the baseline are used to assess the effects of the independent variable administered in the experimental period. (2)

behavior modification The systematic utilization of a conditioning technique with a human to produce a change in the frequency or the environmental control of a socially significant behavior. (21)

behavioral contrast A type of interaction between two or more simple schedules of reinforcement in which a manipulation in one of the schedules produces a behavioral change in one of the other schedules. Specifically, the rate in the unchanged schedule changes in a direction opposite that of the rate in the manipulated schedule. That is, one rate decreases while the other increases or vice versa.

1. negative behavioral contrast: A schedule interaction in which the response rate in the manipulated schedule increases and the response rate in the unmanipulated schedule decreases.
2. positive behavioral contrast: a schedule interaction in which the response rate in the manipulated schedule decreases and the response rate in the unmanipulated schedule increases. (14)

behaviorism A school for psychological thought circa 1913 that believed that all behavior was respondently conditioned, and that the business of psychology was to determine functional relationships between objectively defined and measured (i.e., overt) stimuli and responses. Headed by John B. Watson. *N.B.* There is no current school as such. (25)

boundary condition A generic term in science which describes the limits within which a particular phenomenon exists. Implies that the lawfulness of a phenomenon is dependent upon contextual factors. (24)

bribery Payment or promise thereof to engage in an illegal, immoral, or unethical action. (5)

catch condition A procedure in an experiment which permits a researcher to rule out some alternative explanations of his results. A good example was the pencil movements made in the Lady Wonder case ruling out extrasensory perception as a cause of the horse's performance. (1)

chain schedule A sequence of simple schedules in which unconditioned reinforcement occurs only after the final schedule is completed. There is a unique stimulus correlated with each schedule in the sequence. Each schedule must be completed before going on to the next one. (11)

circular reasoning Language in which one fact is used as the reason for a second fact and the second fact, in turn is used to explain the first fact. (1)

collective extinction Extinction of the behavior of two or more organisms simultaneously in a social situation. (23)

collective reinforcement Reinforcement of the behavior of two or more organisms simultaneously in a social situation. (23)

comparison (choice) stimuli In a matching-to-sample task, the stimuli from which the subject chooses a match to an earlier presented stimulus (the sample). (13)

conditional discrimination A discrimination task in which a reinforceable response depends on more than one stimulus, e.g., responding is reinforced in the presence of a vertical line only when the line is red.

conditional response (CR) The response component of a conditional reflex. After respondent conditioning, the CS will elicit the CR. The CR is not identical to the UCR. (4)

conditional stimulus (CS) The stimulus which, after respondent conditioning, can elicit the CR. If not occasionally paired with the UCS, it will lose its power to elicit the CR, hence its functionality is *conditional*. (4)

conditioned aversive stimulus A stimulus which has been made aversive by pairing with an unconditioned aversive stimulus and/or other conditioned aversive stimuli. (18)

conditioned reinforcer A stimulus which has acquired its reinforcing properties by association with an unconditioned reinforcer or other conditioned reinforcers. (9)

conditioned suppression A reduction of the rate of a free operant in the presence of a stimulus after repeated pairings of that stimulus with an unavoidable, aversive stimulus (e.g., electric shock). (16)

conjugate reinforcement Describes a reinforcing operation in which the magnitude of the response is positively correlated with the magnitude of the reinforcing stimulus. In the Rovee and Rovee experiment, greater leg movements by the infant subjects produced larger movements of the toy mobile. Originally coined by O. R. Lindsley. (5)

consequation The act of applying a stimulus, either positive or negative dependent on a response. (22)

consequent stimulus A stimulus which follows a response and has the effect of changing the likelihood of similar responses occurring in the future. (13)

contiguity The notion that the simple juxtaposition of two events in time (e.g., stimuli, responses) is sufficient to produce an association between them.
1. stimulus-stimulus contiguity: Making a neutral stimulus functional by pairing it with an already functional stimulus, as in respondent conditioning.
2. stimulus-response contiguity: A stimulus is thought to acquire the power to produce a response simply as a function of the response being made in the presence of the stimulus, e.g., as in stuttering only in the presence of a single person. (17)

contingency A correlational relationship between a response and a stimulus. The stimulus closely follows a response and may affect the response, but it is not produced by it. (5)

continuous reinforcement schedule (CRF) A schedule of reinforcement in which every response is reinforced. Also referred to as FR 1. (10)

control In psychology, the design of an environment to produce a specific likelihood that a certain behavior will occur over the long run. (1)

cooperation Behavior by two or more individuals which is linked to the reinforcement of those individuals. There are a variety of ways the behavior can be linked (see And, Or, and Backscratch dependencies). (22)

counterconditioning A technique in which a stimulus (S_1) is paired with another stimulus (S_2). S_2 typically produces an undesirable behavior (R_2). S_1 produces a response (R_1) which is incompatible with R_2; with repeated pairings, S_2 leads to R_1. See systematic desensitization. (17)

countercontrol The overriding of part or all of the control of an agency or institution by the individuals within that agency or institution. Prison culture is a good example. (1)

covert response A response directly observable only by the organism producing it. (1)

cumulative recorder An apparatus which records the responses of an organism over a measured period of time, i.e., response rate. It also reveals the pattern of responding in the periods between reinforcements as well as the pattern over an entire experimental session. (11)

dead-man test A test used to decide if a response has been adequately specified. If a dead man can perform the response (e.g., not cut down a tree), it has not been adequately defined. Coined by O. R. Lindsley. (22)

dependency A relationship between a response and a stimulus such that the response produces or causes the stimulus. It differs from a contingency in which the response is only correlated with the stimulus. (5)

dependent response In the response-deprivation hypothesis, the dependent response is the one whose base rate has been suppressed. Opportunity to make the dependent response becomes available when the instrumental response requirement has been met. For example, if the subject pushes a wheel ten revolutions, it can then obtain ten licks of water (dependent response). (12)

dependent variable A label given to the outcomes of an experiment; what the scientist measures to determine the effects of his/her manipulations. In psychology, the dependent variable is usually some aspect of responding, e.g., rate, magnitude, percent correct. (23)

deprivation A state operationally defined by withholding a reinforcer for specified periods of time, e.g., no food for 24 hours; also, the restriction of the opportunity to emit a response for a period of time. (12)

development, behavioral In terms of conditioning, the formation of new functional relationships between stimuli and responses and progressive changes in those relationships. (24)

Differential Reinforcement of High Rate (DRH) A schedule which specifies that a given number of responses must occur in a limited time in order for a response to be reinforced. If a rate of two or more responses a second is desired, the subject can be reinforced every time it makes twenty or more responses in ten seconds. (9)

Differential Reinforcement of Low Rate (DRL) A schedule in which responses must be separated by a fixed time in order for the response to be reinforced. A response which occurs prior to the end of the interval, say ten seconds, postpones the opportunity for reinforcement until another ten-second interval has elapsed without a response. (8)

Differential Reinforcement of Other Behavior (DRO) Reinforcement for any behavior other than the one specified. For example, as long as the subject does not press a lever, a reinforcer is delivered every ten seconds. Every lever press in this example would postpone reinforcement 10 seconds. (6)

dimensional control A type of stimulus control, evidence for which is differential responding to the stimuli presented the organism along a single stimulus dimension. (15)

discrimination index An arithmetical device to describe the quality of a discrimination; usually is calculated either as $S^D/S^\triangle$ or as $S^D/S^D + S^\triangle$. In the former case, as the ratio of S^D to $S^\triangle$ responses increases, the discrimination improves. In the latter case, as the discrimination improves, the fraction approaches 1.00. (14)

discriminative control The control of rates and patterns of responses by stimuli associated with reinforcing stimuli. Largely synonymous with stimulus control as used by conditioning psychologists. See discriminative stimulus. (13)

discriminative stimulus A stimulus that sets the occasion on which a response, if it occurs, will be consequated. There are two general classes: the S^D, signalling positive reinforcement and the $S^\triangle$ signalling punishment or extinction. (14)

dualism The philosophy suggesting two independent spheres of man's behavior; one sphere, the "inner man," directed by the "psyche," "soul," or "will" and the other, the "outer man," directed by the environment. The former is traditionally not thought to be knowable, measureable, or a function of natural law, while the latter is. (21)

echoic Verbal behavior which topographically resembles its controlling stimulus. Synonymous with verbal imitation. (25)

elicit To call forth or "cause" a response; used when referring to respondent behavior. The word elicit is close to the original meaning of stimulus — a goad or prod. It is appropriate for reflexive behavior because it is obvious (most times) that a specific stimulus (tap under knee) elicits the response (knee jerk). (4)

emit To make an operant: Operant behavior is said to be emitted because the stimulus controlling the operant is not always visible. Distinguish from *elicit* (to call forth) which is used in referring to respondent behavior. (4)

emotional behavior A complex response consisting of physiological respondents of the autonomic nervous system, the individual's discrimination of these respondents and the concurrent occurrence of operants. The operants are jointly occasioned by the stimulus properties of the respondents and the external environment. (16)

errorless discrimination 1. A technique in which S⁻ is made as physically unlike S⁺ as possible to minimize responding in its presence during the formation of a discrimination. Across training S⁻ is gradually made more and more like its final form and therefore, more like S⁺.

2. A discrimination formed by this technique where very few responses have been made in the presence of S⁻. (14)

escape conditioning Conditioning in which the *termination* of a stimulus (e.g., shock) is reinforcing. If the subject emits an operant such as pressing a lever, the aversive stimulus is removed for a short time. The operant which removes the aversive stimulus is called an escape response. (20)

exchange ratio The number of tokens that must be accumulated by a subject before the tokens can be exchanged for unconditioned reinforcers (e.g., banana pellets, candy, trinkets). (11)

experimental neurosis Emotional behavior produced by respondent discrimination procedures in which an organism's ability to make a discrimination is exceeded. First demonstrated by Pavlov. (16)

extended chain A chain schedule with many components as in a token reinforcement schedule. For example, if a subject must make ten responses to obtain one token (FR 10) and save thirty tokens before they can be exchanged,

the extended chain has thirty components. (11)

extinction 1. As an operant procedure, a reinforcer (stimulus) is no longer presented after a response. As a result, the operant eventually ceases to occur or occurs at a relatively low frequency (the operant level).

2. As a respondent procedure, the conditioned stimulus (CS) is presented repeatedly without the unconditioned stimulus (UCS). As a result, the CS no longer elicits the conditioned response (CR). (7)

expressive language Spoken and /or written language. (25)

fading The operations of successively making S⁺ and S⁻ more alike during discrimination training by progressively changing S⁻ along one or more dimensions. Also called stimulus shaping. *Cf.* errorless discrimination. (14)

fatigability of a reflex 1. The diminution of the strength of a reflex as a function of repeated elicitations of that reflex. Diminution is assessed in terms of: 1) increased latency; 2) decreased amplitude; and 3) increased threshold of the reflex.

2. The number of UCS presentations within a specified period of time necessary to produce reflex fatigue. (14)

fixed-interval schedule A schedule of reinforcement in which the first response after a fixed time is reinforced. On an FI 60-second schedule, the first response after 60 seconds is reinforced. On interval schedules (VI and FI) reinforcement is never delivered without a response. Only when the specified interval is completed, is the opportunity for reinforcement created and the subject must take advantage of that opportunity. (10)

fixed-ratio schedule A schedule of reinforcement in which every nth response produces reinforcement. On an FR 100, the 100th response would be reinforced. (10)

forgetting A decrement in performance due to the passage of time. To be distinguished from extinction which also leads to a decrement in performance but in which the behavior in question is emitted. (8)

functional relationship 1. In psychology, the reliable demonstration that a response varies predictably with changes in a stimulus or condition such as body states.
   2. The description of a relationship like that documented in 1. (3)

generalization gradient A curve composed of response rates or percent responding in the presence of a number of stimuli from one stimulus continuum e.g., brightness. Only one stimulus of the continuum was present during the subject's prior training. (15)

generalized reinforcer A conditioned reinforcer which is not tied to a specific deprivational state. Money is the best example of a generalized reinforcer. (9)

generalized imitation An imitative response that occurs without any direct, overt reinforcement of that response. (25)

histogram A bar graph which depicts the frequency of an event in intervals of a fixed size. Best used for data which occur in discrete categories such as living relatives versus nonliving relatives. (6)

hypothesitos Implicit hypotheses; hypotheses that are not formally stated; the implicit reason for conducting an experiment. (3)

independent variable A label given to the class of events a scientist directly manipulates in an experiment. In psychology, the manipulation of stimulus or state conditons, e.g., drugs, amount of reinforcement. (23)

induction A type of interaction between two or more simple schedules of reinforcement in which a manipulation in one of the schedules produces a behavioral change in one of the other schedules. Specifically, the rate in the unchanged schedule changes in a direction similar to that of the rate in the manipulated schedule. That is, both rates decrease (negative induction) or increase (positive induction). (14)

inhibitory stimulus A stimulus that develops the function during conditioning of decreasing the frequency of responding beneath that occurring when the stimulus is not present. (15)

inhibitory stimulus control A reduction of responding as a function of conditioning in the presence of a stimulus or a continuum of stimuli over that when the stimulus or members of the continuum are not present. (15)

instrumental response In the response-deprivation hypothesis, the response that the subject must emit in order to have the opportunity to make the dependent response. (12)

interresponse time (IRT) The time between the occurrence of one response and the occurrence of the subsequent response. (14)

intraverbal A verbal operant having no point-to-point correspondence with its controlling stimuli. For example, 4 is an intraverbal occasioned by the stimulus 2 + 2 =. Used as both noun and adjective. (25)

James-Lange theory An early theory of emotional behavior in psychology. Common sense says that after hurting somebody, we feel sorry and therefore we cry. This theory changed the sequence such that, we hurt someone, we cry, and, therefore, feel sorry. The emotion always followed a bodily event rather than caused it. (16)

latency of the response The time between the onset of a stimulus and the onset of a response. (4)

Lloyd Morgan's Canon A statement by Lloyd Morgan that higher level explanations should not be used to explain a phenomenon if a lower level explanation could suffice. (25)

mand A verbal operant under the control of specific state conditions such as deprivation or aversive stimulation. (25)

matching to sample A conditional discrimination in which a subject first attends to a stimulus (the standard or sample) then indicates which of a group of stimuli (the comparisons or choices) is identical to the sample. Variations of this task may require the subject to indicate choice stimuli which are not identical to it. The task is a form of conditional discrimination. (13)

maturation The structural development of parts of the body. (24)

medical model of behavior The application to problem behavior of the disease model of medicine, particularly the idea that abnormal behavior is merely a symptom of underlying "mental pathology." (21)

metalinguistics The use of language to understand the nature and structure of language. (25)

micro-kinesics The study of a fractional movements of living organisms. Characterized by first dividing movements into small parts via frame-by-frame photographic analysis and correlating these movements with environmental events that occur at the same time. (25)

minimal brain dysfunction (MBD) A descriptive term indicating that a child behaves differently than his peers on basic academic tasks (e.g., reading, writing) and on tests of "perceptual motor" skill. This behavioral evidence is then employed (fallaciously) to suggest neural pathology or at least neural disorganization. (1)

minimal social situation A situation in which two persons control each other's reinforcers and punishers, and in which communication between subjects is prevented. Typically, the subjects do not know they are working with another person, hence, minimal social. (23)

mixed schedule A sequence of simple schedules in which unconditioned reinforcement occurs after the completion of each schedule. There are no stimuli associated with the individual schedules. (11)

modeling (imitation) The performance of a response by an individual who has seen the same (or a similar) response emitted by another individual. (21)

morpheme The smallest unit utterance an individual can make that has meaning; often is smaller than a word e.g., "ah hah!" Has linguistic meaning independent of context. (25)

multiple baseline design A research design in which several responses of a single subject are individually and successively exposed to an independent variable (e.g., reinforcement). Is frequently used where practical exigencies preclude engaging in a reversal or where in fact a response appears non-reversible. (22)

multiple schedule A sequence of simple schedules in which unconditioned reinforcement occurs after the completion of each schedule. There is a unique stimulus correlated with each schedule. (11)

nativism The school of thought believing that much of man's behavior is innately determined. (25)

negative reinforcement The operation of removing a negative reinforcer dependent on a response. An example is the termination of a shock for a brief period when a lever is pressed. (8)

negative reinforcer A stimulus which upon removal or termination dependent on a response, *increases* the frequency of the response. (8)

observing response A response which produces a discriminative stimulus. For example, when a pigeon steps on a pedal, a red light might illuminate the food key and the red light is associated with an FR 100 schedule.
The pedal response is the observing response. (11)

operant A class of responses under the control of its consequences; the basic datum of psychology for many conditioning psychologists. An operant is defined not by its topography (its physical characteriestics), but by its functionality with respect to the consequences it produces. A stutterer may repeat the first sound of a word, block, clench his jaws, roll his eyes, blink his eyes, have facial tics, and so on. All of these responses have similar consequences — increased attentiveness on the part of the listener — hence, they are all operants in the same response class because they are all functional for the same set of consequences. (6)

operant conditioning Conditioning which occurs when the emission of an operant is followed by the presentation of a stimulus; originally synonymous with conditioning by positive reinforcement. Now, connotes any modification of operant behavior by its consequences. (6)

operant level The rate of an operant prior to any experimental manipulation. May assume a wide range of values and not just a low value as is sometimes supposed. (5)

Or dependency A cooperative dependency in which two or more subjects can work to fulfill a response quota and response requirements for individuals are unspecified. When the quota is satisfied, all subjects receive reinforcement. (23)

ordinate The vertical axis on a figure or graph, also referred to as the Y axis. Some measureable property of behavior (latency, rate of responding, or correct responses) is plotted on this axis. (2)

parapsychology That branch of psychology which studies so called "psychic" phenomena. These phenomena are events which have not been explained scientifically because they have not been objectively measured. Reputable researchers are now using scientific methods in an attempt to prove the existence of psychic pheonomena. (1)

parasympathetic nervous system A branch of the autonomic nervous system, outflow of which is through the cranial and sacral regions of the central nervous system. Antagonistic in function to the sympathetic branch; helps conserve the body's resources. (16)

peak shift A shift in the location of maximum responding in a post-discrimination gradient to a stimulus other than the S^D and away from the S^Δ (15)

phobia A reduced or zero frequency of a specific behavior because of irrational fear o hypothesized consequences of the behavior. (17)

phoneme The basic sounds of a language; the smallest unit utterance of speech which has little or no meaning of its own, but distinguishes one utterance from another, e.g., *r*un; *s*un. (25)

placebo A catch condition in drug research, where an inert pill is given to some subjects. Effects of this condition are compared to a condition in which subjects are administered a real drug. More generally, a catch condition in which subjects are given a sham treatment. (16)

positive acceleration of a response An increase in the rate of responding; that is an increase in number of responses in a given period of time. Also conceptualized as successive decreases in the time between responses. (10)

positive reinforcement The operation of delivering a positive reinforcer. An example is presenting food to a food-deprived subject dependent on a response. (6)

positive reinforcer A stimulus, which when presented dependent on a response, increases the frequency of that response. (6)

post-discrimination gradient (PDG) A generalization gradient obtained after discrimination training (reinforcement and extinction) has taken place. (15)

post-reinforcement pause The time from reinforcement to a subsequent response. Usually occurs on fixed-ratio and fixed-interval schedules. (11)

prediction In psychology, the act of describing events to communicate to others exactly when a given behavior will occur. This will usually entail a description of the rate of the behavior, changes therein, under what stimulus conditions the behavior will occur, and what the limiting conditions are (e.g., subject must be deprived of food; subject must have a certain history of reinforcement; etc). (1)

Premack's rule A rule which states that for any two behaviors, the more probable can be used to reinforce the less probable. (12)

priming Instigation of a response by physical guidance or verbal description. (15)

protection dependency A DRO-dependency inserted at the end of a time period to prevent a subject receiving adventitious reinforcement. Typically used in training a discrimination and inserted at the end of the extinction period. (11)

psychology The scientific study of the behavior of animals, including man. Implies the search for laws relating the behavior of organisms and their environments. (3)

psychological model of behavior change The model of behavior modification in which man's behavior is considered lawful and conditionable, rather than a product of unmeasureable mental forces. (21)

punishment 1. Type I: An operation in which a negative reinforcer is presented dependent on a response. (18)
2. Type II: An operation in which a positive reinforcer is removed dependent on a response. See response cost and time out from positive reinforcement. (19)

rate of responding The number of responses emitted per unit time. One of the main measures of operant behavior. (6)
1. Overall rate: The rate of responding over a long period of time i.e., a session.
2. Local rate: The rate of responding between reinforcements, excluding the post-reinforcement pause. Synonymous with running rate. (11)

receptive language Inferred language based on the fact that an individual's behavior can be systematically controlled by the verbal responses of another. For example, an individual has receptive language if he can carry out (i.e., "understand") a set of instructions. (25)

reciprocal inhibition A neurological phenomenon. When nerve A is stimulated, it contracts muscle A; when nerve B is stimulated, it inhibits the action of nerve A. Thus, when both nerves are stimulated simultaneously, muscle A is inhibited from contracting. (17)

reciprocal schedule A schedule which specifies that x amount of one response be made in order that y amount of a second response can be made and vice versa, e.g., ten lever presses allow a rat to make fifteen revolutions in an activity wheel and fifteen revolutions of the wheel allow it to make ten lever presses. (12)

reification The act of using an adjective as a noun and in so doing, giving existence to an abstraction. (1)

relativity principle of reinforcement The principle which states that any activity can serve either as the reinforcer or as the activity to be reinforced. Both Premack's rule and the response-deprivation hypothesis illustrate the relativity principle. (12)

resistance to extinction 1. The time required for responding in extinction to reach a criterion such as the operant level.
2. The number of responses made in extinction prior to reaching a criterion. (7)

respondent Another name for reflexive behavior. The knee-jerk, pupil contraction and startle response are examples of respondents because they are elicited by specificable classes of stimuli; so called "involuntary" responses. These responses can be classically conditioned. (4)

respondent conditioning The formation of a conditional reflex through the repeated pairing of a neutral stimulus with an unconditional stimulus for a given reflex. Eventually, the neutral stimulus, when presented by itself, will elicit the unconditional response. When this happens, a conditonal reflex has been established. Respondent conditioning is also referred to as classical or Pavlovian conditioning. (4)

respondent stimulus control The probability with which an unconditional or conditional stimulus will elicit an unconditional or conditional response. (13)

response Anything an animal does as it interacts with its environment. Responses are defined by their function, that is, what they are related to; they are also unavoidably characterized by what they look like. (3)

response cost A form of punishment, Type II, in which an undesirable response leads to the loss of a specified amount of a reinforcer such as money, tokens or points. (19)

response-deprivation hypothesis When the opportunity to engage in operant A is restricted and the emission of operant A is dependent on operant B, the necessary and sufficient conditions for reinforcement of operant B exist. (12)

response differentiation The progressive narrowing of a class of responses through differential reinforcement so that operants within the narrowing portion of the class are strengthened by reinforcement and operants outside the class are weakened by extinction. Cf., shaping. (8, 24)

response-shock (R-S) interval The time between a response and a subsequent shock in the nondiscriminated avoidance procedure. Cf., S-S interval. (20)

reversal probe A control condition in which the dependencies are changed in at least one of two ways: a) by removal as in extinction, or b) by reinforcing incompatible behavior as in DRO. (21)

S^D(ess-dee) A discriminative stimulus which sets the occasion on which a response will be reinforced. Labelled S^+ when errorless discimination procedures have been used. (14)

S^Δ (ess-delta) A discriminative stimulus which sets the occasion on which a response will *not* be reinforced. Labelled S^- when errorless discrimination procedures have been used. (14)

satiation A state functionally defined by a cessation of responding due to frequent reinforcement. *Cf.*, deprivation. (21)

schedule An experimenter-arranged dependency between a response or series of responses and a consequence. (10)

schedule control The production of characteristic response rates and patterns by a reinforcement schedule. (13)

second-order schedule A label given to lengthy chain schedules in which a simple schedule is itself characterized as a response unit. For example, an FR10 leads to a brief stimulus, e.g., a token, and 50 of these FR 10's lead to unconditioned reinforcement; written as FR 50 (FR 10), but is actually *chain* FR 10, FR 10, FR 10 . . . and so on. (11)

self-concept A descriptive term classifying behavior emitted by an individual which describes how he views himself. (1)

self-control (self-management)
1. Responses emitted by an individual to change the probability of other responses emitted by the same individual. (1)
  2. The systematic scheduling by an individual of consequences delivered for his own behavior. (22)

semantics The study of meaning in language. (25)

shaping (differential reinforcement of successive approximations) The progressive modification and subsequent shifting of the boundaries of a response class within which responses are reinforced, outside of which they are extinguished. Used when the operant level of a response is very low or when the final response is too complex initially. In shaping, the boundaries of the response class to-be-formed may be shifted radically while in response differentiation, the reinforced response class is pre-existent and simply narrowed. Thus, response differentiation takes place in shaping, but shaping does not take place in response differentiation. Cf., response differentiation. (6)

shock-shock (S-S) interval The time between shocks in a nondiscriminated avoidance procedure when no responses occur in the interval. Cf., R-S interval. (20)

spontaneous recovery In extinction, the recovery of a conditioned response after a brief recess from the experimental situation. (7)

standard stimulus (sample) The first stimulus presented in a matching-to-sample task; the stimulus to be matched. (13)

steady-state behavior A behavior pattern or rate that does not very over several sessions. e.g., lack of deviation of the daily response rate, within limits, from the mean rate of the previous five sessions. (11)

stimulus 1. Energy changes in the environment described in the language of physics (physically defined).
  2. Energy changes in the environment which are related to changes in responses (functionally defined). Often is used synonymously with environment. (3)

stimulus control The general observation that stimuli preceding and following responses control those responses when systematically programed. There are several ways this occurs. See dimensional control, discriminative control, schedule control, and respondent stimulus control. (13)

stimulus generalization The occurrence of a response in the presence of a stimulus which was not present during the conditioning of the response. (15)

stimulus-response chain A series of stimuli and responses conceptualized as a unit. Any response in a chain produces a stimulus which reinforces that response and is discriminative for the next response. (9).

superstitious behavior Behavior which is not operationally related to the production of a consequence. May result from the chance pairings of responses with reinforcement. (5)

sympathetic nervous system A branch of the autonomic nervous system, outflow of which takes place through the thoracic and lumbar regions of the spinal cord; involved in mobilizing the body to meet energy requirements such as in emergency or work situations. (16)

symptom substitution An assumption by those who hold the medical model of abnormal behavior. If only an abnormal behavior (symptom) is treated, another abnormal behavior appears soon after treatment in place of the former. Purportedly, the underlying cause of the first abnormal behavior had not been treated. There is no basis in fact for this assumption. (21)

syntax The ordering of words in a language and their interrelation. Synonymous with grammar. (25)

systematic desensitization A behavior therapy technique. The patient imagines a feared situation while relaxed. This procedure is repeated with a variety of feared stimuli. Eventually, the patient interacts with the feared stimulus without the production of anxiety and without the cessation of the interaction. See counterconditioning. (17)

tact A verbal operant under the control of a particular object or event or property thereof, i.e., under the control of a discriminative stimulus. Readily translates to labelling or naming. Used as both noun and verb. (25)

tandem schedule A sequence of simple schedules in which unconditioned reinforcement occurs after completion of the final schedule. There are no stimuli associated with each schedule. (11)

tantrum cycle A procedure by which parents inadvertently shape tantrums in their child. Both parent and child are reinforced in this interaction — the parent when the child's tantruming stops (negative reinforcement), the child when the parent grants the child's request (positive reinforcement). (8)

threshold of a response That intensity of a stimulus which produces a response 50 percent of the time. The threshold is one measure of the strength of a reflex. (4)

time out (TO) from positive reinforcement A form of punishment, Type II, in which the subject is removed from a positively reinforcing situation for a specified period of time after making an undesirable response. (19)

titrated escape A procedure for placing a subject on an intermittent escape schedule. At first, each response produces a time out from shock of a given duration. The time outs after each response are progressively shortened and eventually eliminated, while the nth response continues to lead to a full time out. (20)

unconditional reflex An innate stimulus-response relationship. Consists of a stimulus (UCS) *and* response (UCR). There may be more than one UCS for a given UCR. (4)

unconditional response (UCR) The response component of an unconditional reflex. (4)

unconditional stimulus (UCS) The stimulus component of an unconditional reflex. Elicits the unconditional response without prior training. (4)

unconditioned reinforcer A stimulus which is reinforcing without having been paired with other stimuli. (9)

unconscious An abstraction from Freudian psychology reified when used as a noun instead of an adjective. One part of the "personality" that supposedly controls behavior. (1)

variable-interval schedule A schedule of reinforcement in which the first response after a variable period of time is reinforced. On a VI 60 seconds, 60 represents a mean which could be based on a quasi-random series of times from thirty to ninety seconds. (10)

variable-ratio schedule A schedule of reinforcement in which the nth response, on the average, is reinforced. On a VR 100, 100 represents a mean which could be based on a quasirandom series of numbers from 50 to 150. (10)

Xanthippe syndrome A class of behaviors exhibited by a mother who scolds and nags in an effort to control others; she rarely uses positive reinforcement. Xanthippe, Socrates' wife, had a reputation as a scold, hence the term. (19)

INDEX

†